Informing Our Practice

Useful Research on Young Children's Development

Eva L. Essa and Melissa M. Burnham, eds.

D1413968

National Association for the Education of Young Children
Washington, DC

National Association
for the Education
of Young Children
1313 L Street NW, Suite 500
Washington, DC 20005-4101
202-232-8777 • 800-424-2460
www.naeyc.org

NAEYC Books

Director, Publications and
Educational Initiatives
Carol Copple

Managing Editor
Bry Pollack

Design and Production
Malini Dominey

Editorial Associate
Melissa Edwards

Editorial Assistant
Elizabeth Wegner

Permissions
Lacy Thompson

Marketing Director
Matt Munroe

Photo credits: *Barbara Bent*, middle cover; *Rich Graessle*, 1; *Jonathan A. Meyers*, top cover; *Marilyn Nolt*, 97; *Ellen B. Senisi*, bottom cover, 31, 141, 189

Informing Our Practice: Useful Research on Young Children's Development

Library of Congress Control Number: 2009924419

ISBN: 978-1-928896-65-4

NAEYC Item #255

Editors

Melissa M. Burnham is an associate professor in the Human Development and Family Studies Department at the University of Nevada, Reno. Her overarching area of research is the examination of children's development in different contexts. Her current work focuses on the impact of progressive educational philosophies on children's development and learning.

Eva L. Essa is foundation professor and chair of the Human Development and Family Studies Department at the University of Nevada, Reno. She is author of several books, and her research interests relate to progressive early education and the impact teachers have on young children's behavior.

Contributing Authors

Arthur J. Baroody received his Ph.D. from Cornell University and is currently a professor of curriculum and instruction, specializing in early childhood and elementary mathematics education, at the University of Illinois at Urbana-Champaign. His research focuses on the teaching and learning of basic counting, number, and arithmetic concepts and skills by young children and children with learning difficulties.

Leann L. Birch, Ph.D., is a distinguished professor of human development and nutritional sciences at the Pennsylvania State University, where she is also director of the Center for Childhood Obesity Research. Her research program is focused on the development of the behavioral controls of food intake among infants, children, and adolescents.

Martha B. Bronson is retired from Boston College, where she was a professor of developmental and educational psychology. She has also been a teacher of young children. Her published works include two books related to early childhood: *Self-Regulation in Early Childhood: Nature and Nurture* and *The Right Stuff for Children Birth to 8: Selecting Play Materials to Support Development*.

Frances A. Campbell is a senior scientist at the Frank Porter Graham Child Development Institute at the University of North Carolina at Chapel Hill. She was the evaluator for the early phases of the Abecedarian longitudinal study and is now the primary investigator of the age-30 follow-up of the sample.

Swetha Chakravarthi is a doctoral student in human development and family studies at the University of North Carolina at Greensboro.

Her research interests include outdoor play and environments for young children, preschool teacher beliefs and practices, and issues related to working with young immigrant children and their families.

Karen E. Diamond is a professor of developmental studies, former editor of *Early Childhood Research Quarterly*, and consulting editor for the *Journal of Early Intervention* and for *Topics in Early Childhood Special Education*. Her research focuses on experiences of children with disabilities and their typically developing peers, as well as language and literacy interventions for teacher professional development in Head Start.

Stacy M. Ellis, Ph.D., is the assistant director for educational development at Baby Gator Child Development and Research Centers at the University of Florida. She is focused on the training and professional development of early childhood educators in the areas of curriculum, developmentally appropriate practice, and social development.

Linda M. Gagen, Ph.D., is an assistant professor of physical education and health teacher preparation at Old Dominion University and the graduate program director for Physical Education Curriculum and Instruction. Her research interests include exploring and enhancing movement experiences for young children.

Kathleen Cranley Gallagher, Ph.D., is an assistant professor in the School of Education at the University of North Carolina at Chapel Hill. Having worked with children and families in early education programs for 15 years, she now focuses her research and teaching on children's social relationships with families, peers, and teachers.

Eugene E. García, Ph.D., serves as professor of education and vice president for education partnerships at Arizona State University. His research addresses early learning in linguistically and culturally diverse populations.

Celia Genishi is professor and chair of the Department of Curriculum and Teaching at Teachers College, Columbia University. A former secondary Spanish and preschool teacher, she teaches courses on early language and literacy and qualitative research methods. She is co-author (with Anne Haas Dyson) of *Children, Language, and Literacy: Diverse Learners in Diverse Times.*

Nancy Getchell, an associate professor at the University of Delaware, examines the development of motor coordination in atypical populations, including children with learning disabilities, developmental coordination disorder, and autism. She studies perception-action coupling in motor skills, with the belief that quantifying developmental coordination differences may allow for earlier detection and intervention in atypical populations.

Penny Hauser-Cram is professor of applied developmental and educational psychology at the Lynch School of Education at Boston College. A former preschool teacher, she now conducts longitudinal studies on children's development. Her research focuses on how the family as well as educational and health systems support optimal development.

Linda L. Hestenes, Ph.D., is an associate professor in the department of Human Development and Family Studies at the University of North Carolina at Greensboro. She teaches in the area of early childhood education and development, and her area of study is indoor and outdoor environments for young children.

Alice Sterling Honig is professor emerita of child development at Syracuse University, a researcher and clinician, and author/editor of two dozen books and 500 articles and chapters. A licensed psychologist in the state of New York, she helps parents with stressful childrearing issues. Annually at Syracuse University, she directs a week-long national workshop on quality infant/toddler caregiving.

Andrea Smith Honig is a doctoral student in early childhood education at Teachers College, Columbia University. A former preschool teacher, her research interests are early literacy development, preschool teaching practices, and the impact of early learning standards on curriculum and teaching.

Susan L. Johnson, Ph.D., is an early childhood nutritionist in the Department of Pediatrics, University of Colorado at Denver. Her research focuses on factors that influence the development of children's food intake and eating patterns. She conducts research that centers on how child-feeding practices impact children's food preferences, their energy intake patterns, and their weight outcome.

Kristen M. Kemple, Ph.D., is a professor of early childhood studies at the University of Florida. She is a founding member of the Unified Early Childhood Proteach Program, a five-year teacher education program designed to prepare teachers to work with diverse children in inclusive programs.

Janet Kuebli is a developmental psychologist at Saint Louis University, where she teaches undergraduate and graduate child development courses as well as a graduate seminar on the Teaching of Psychology. Her research interests include children's emotion-related understanding, socialization of safety understanding and behavior, parenting cognitions, and parent-child interactions related to schooling, math, and science.

Accalia R. Kusto holds a master's degree in developmental psychology from Saint Louis University with a minor in research methods and a graduate certificate in women's studies. Her research interests include the socialization of emotion regulation, with a focus on how family practices and child characteristics are related to emotion understanding.

Linlin Li, Ph.D., is an evaluator and researcher for Hatchuel Tabernik & Associates. Her research and evaluation focuses on the education and development of children and their families.

Xia Li is a doctoral student at the University of Illinois at Urbana-Champaign. Her research focuses on the development of toddlers' nonverbal and verbal number abilities, and mathematics instruction in early childhood education.

Rebecca A. Marcon is a developmental psychologist and professor at the University of North Florida where she is director of the Center for Applied Research in Child and Adolescent Development. Her main research interest is early intervention for children at-risk for school failure and social difficulties.

Hermine H. Marshall, Ph.D., is professor emerita at San Francisco State University, where she was coordinator of the Early Childhood and Elementary Master's Degree programs in the College of Education. She has conducted research on self-concept and self-evaluation as well as on classroom learning processes. Her research publications have appeared in many journals.

Kelley Mayer is an assistant professor of early childhood education in the Department of Teacher Education at the College of Charleston. Her research focuses on associations between teacher-child relationship quality and children's writing. Before becoming a professor, Kelley spent five years teaching kindergarten in public schools.

Darcy B. Mitchell, Ph.D., is the project director and senior research associate for the Early Intervention Collaborative Study at Boston College. Her research focuses on how children with developmental disabilities and their families influence the development and well-being of one another.

Lynn Okagaki is professor emerita of child development and family studies at Purdue University. Her research focuses on academic achievement as influenced by culture and family values. She served as the first deputy director for science at the Institute of Education Sciences in the U.S. Department of Education and currently is Commissioner for Education Research.

Patrick M. O'Leary is a Ph.D. candidate in the Department of Child Development and Family Studies at Purdue University. He is a former early childhood teacher with research interests in how preschool teachers promote children's oral language development.

Greg Payne, PED, is a professor in the Department of Kinesiology and special assistant to the dean in the College of Applied Sciences and Arts at San Jose State University. His academic interests include aging, physical activity, and children's physical activity, obesity, sports, and fitness. He is lead author of *Human Motor Development: A Lifespan Approach.*

Douglas R. Powell is a distinguished professor in the Department of Child Development and Family Studies at Purdue University. His research focuses on strategies to strengthen the contributions of families and early childhood programs to children's well-being.

Patricia G. Ramsey is professor of psychology and education at Mount Holyoke College. She is a former early childhood teacher and received her doctorate from University of Massachusetts at Amherst. She has studied the development of children's attitudes about race and class and has written several articles and books on this subject.

Karen B. Taylor has been a research associate at the Frank Porter Graham Child Development Institute at the University of North Carolina since 1992. She has worked on several research and evaluation projects involving state and federally funded programs for young children and their families.

Alison K. Ventura is a postdoctoral fellow at the Monell Chemical Senses Center. Her research is focused on how experiences during infant feeding and the introduction of solid foods contribute to children's preferences, eating behaviors, and dietary intake patterns. She received her doctorate from the Department of Human Development and Family Studies at the Pennsylvania State University.

Emmy E. Werner is a developmental psychologist and a research professor in human development at the University of California at Davis. She was the principal investigator of the Kauai Longitudinal Study and has published a dozen books and numerous articles on resilient children who successfully overcame major adversities in their lives.

Contents

About This Book

In this age of accountability, we early childhood professionals often find ourselves having to justify the practices we use with the young children in our care. A vague response to parents, administrators/directors, funders, or state agencies about the importance of considering young children's development in designing programs and activities simply doesn't satisfy questions about the value of developmentally appropriate strategies. When we can cite research related to our practices, we are standing on firmer ground. This anthology of research reviews is intended to provide an arsenal of research-based evidence related to important developmental domains in early childhood.

How this book came to be

Our goal in developing this volume was to bring outstanding research reviews together into one easily accessible book that early childhood students and practitioners could use to better understand development, and so answer for themselves and for others the question of why we do what we do with young children. A firm understanding of child development and its implications for daily practice is a cornerstone of effectively implementing developmentally appropriate practices in classrooms.

The National Association for the Education of Young Children has long demonstrated a commitment to helping practitioners access and understand relevant research findings. *Young Children*, NAEYC's bimonthly journal, has regularly included a "Research in Review" section for the past several decades. The reviews provide a channel through which classroom teachers and caregivers can access research findings and researchers can explain their topic of expertise and make specific suggestions for how the findings can be made visible in practice with children. In particular, we extend thanks to the editors who helped bring into being the original reviews that were updated for this volume: Laura Berk, Elizabeth Brady, Martha Bronson, Cary Buzzelli, Ellen Frede, Celia Genishi, Alice Honig, Susan Kontos, Rebecca Marcon, Mary Benson McMullen, Douglas Powell, Aisha Ray, Dianne Rothenberg, Sharon Ryan, Carol Seefeldt, Eva Marie Shivers, Steven Silvern, Janis Strasser, and Diane Horm Wingerd.

This book is a selective compilation of "Research in Review" articles whose focus was *child development* and important contextual factors that influence development. Thus, this volume helps close an important gap, as no other such compilation casts such a wide net over the many aspects of children's development *with* an applied focus. We collected these reviews because many research articles focus only on one particular aspect of one developmental domain and thus are not easily understood within the whole picture of early childhood practice.

In fact, it was our frustration over the absence of an applied research volume on development that compelled us to pursue this project. In teaching early childhood development courses, we found ourselves relying on *Young Children*'s "Research in

Review" articles to help our students gain an understanding of child development research and its relevance to practice. Many of the articles, however, were becoming rather dated. This led us to ask authors on particularly valuable topics to revise their original articles with attention to more recent studies, themes that had changed substantially since original publication, and the like.

This book's purpose and scope

We have designed this book to be useful for several purposes. First, it can inform early childhood professionals on research and theory related to development as well as practices that support optimal development. This is important not only for the sake of enhancing their knowledge (which we would argue is important in its own right!), but also for providing them with strong responses to the perennial question, "Why do you do that?" With a firm understanding of the research that supports developmentally appropriate practice, early childhood professionals are armed to respond well.

Second, this book can be a textbook or a supplemental text in college-level early childhood education and applied child development courses. Textbooks that focus exclusively on development within the early childhood age range and that include strong links between research and practice are virtually nonexistent.

This book will also be a useful resource for anyone interested in the current state of knowledge regarding early child development and its relationship to the classroom. For example, administrators of early childhood programs could summarize findings from this volume for parents and others to whom they are accountable. Parents could use the book to learn

firsthand about child development and its relation to what happens in their child's program.

And finally, the volume would make an outstanding reference book for resource and referral staff, as well as for agencies involved in supporting quality in early childhood education in their states.

The chapters in this volume are organized around five central themes: social development, emotional development, cognitive and language development, physical development, and influencing factors on development. Each group of chapters is introduced with a brief overview of the reviews included in it.

Each chapter has been thoroughly updated by its original author(s) to reflect current research in that particular topic area. Further, the reviews retain their original intention of describing the relevant literature *and* helping early childhood professionals see how this knowledge can impact daily classroom practices—a strong feature of the "Research in Review" series.

And finally . . .

Cumulatively, the chapters provide an overview of how research on individual domains of child development is linked to practice in early child care and education settings. They also invite readers to be part of the cycle of inquiry in which practice leads to research that then informs future practice. In effect, teachers and caregivers are researchers themselves as they work directly with young children, and what they do both informs and is informed by the early childhood knowledge base. This book thus highlights the essential association between a thorough understanding of child development and the implementation of developmentally appropriate practice in early childhood settings.

Part I

Social Development

Introduction

The process of *social development* refers to children's growing competency in interactions with others. While humans are born with an innate desire to engage in social relationships, the skills involved in becoming competent social partners must be learned. Group care settings provide challenges to this growing competence as well as opportunities for young children to learn and practice essential social skills.

One of the most important roles early childhood professionals play is that of facilitating the development of children's social skills with peers and other adults. Thus, a thorough understanding of social competence and its related skills is essential for those invested in young children. Equally important to recognize is that children are developing the foundation of self-identity during the early childhood years. Early childhood professionals can facilitate a healthy development of self by being actively involved in establishing an accepting and inclusive environment for young children.

This section, containing three chapters, contributes important insight into the development of social competence in young children. The first and third chapters relate to children's budding relationships: one with peers and one with adults. The second chapter examines children's growing awareness of, understanding of, and feelings about race and class differences.

Kristen Kemple and Stacy Ellis' chapter, **"Peer-Related Social Competence in Early Childhood: Supporting Interaction and Relationships,"** is an update of Dr. Kemple's 1991 research review, "Preschool Children's Peer Acceptance and Social Interaction." This chapter was substantially revised to reflect the growth in our understanding of how to measure social competence effectively and how best to facilitate the development of social competence in young children. The original article focused on correlates and predictors of peer acceptance and, from the literature on these, extrapolated suggestions for practitioners. Since then, however, considerably more research has been done about factors that promote social competence in young children. Thus, the revision focuses on peer-related social competence and on evidence-based practices that support competence development in children's peer interactions.

The second chapter in this section is an update of Patricia Ramsey's 1995 article **"Growing Up with the Contradictions of Race and Class,"** which addresses questions of how much young children notice and understand racial and socioeconomic class differences, how they feel about these differences, how differences affect their relationships with others, and how teachers can help children value diversity and challenge inequities. The contexts of exposure and experience, including the pervasive influence of the media, are considered as these shape children's increasingly more complex views of such differences. The author has interwoven examples of recent events (e.g., the destruction of the Twin Towers on 9/11 and continuing negative attitudes toward Muslims) into the implications for teachers. This chapter reminds early childhood professionals that they can be active in promoting children's self-identity and awareness of the differences of others. In addition, early childhood professionals can facilitate a climate of acceptance and fairness through democratic classroom practices.

A recent research review from *Young Children* provides a perspective on adult-child relationships, with a chapter by Kathleen Cranley Gallagher and Kelley Mayer, **"Enhancing Development and Learning Through Teacher-Child Relationships."** Because it was published in 2008, the article was only lightly revised. The authors provide a review of the research on relationships between young children and their teachers, offering research-based strategies that teachers can use to develop and maintain high-quality relations with children. They make the link between the importance of secure, high-quality adult-child relationships in early childhood and the development of social, emotional, cognitive, and language skills. The authors go on to consider the research and relevant strategies for teachers to build high-quality relationships with young children of different age groups. The chapter highlights the importance of recognizing the role of relationships with adults in early childhood settings. While secure and nurturing relationships are the foundation of developmentally appropriate care for infants and toddlers, they are no less important for older children.

The chapters in this first section will provide early childhood professionals a snapshot of topics related to social development. Gaining a deeper understanding of children's social development will help practitioners meet children's needs as they interact with each other and with adults in ongoing relationships.

Peer-Related Social Competence in Early Childhood: Supporting Interaction and Relationships

1

Kristen M. Kemple and Stacy M. Ellis

Social competence refers to the personal knowledge and skills children develop to deal with the many choices, challenges, and opportunities they face in life (Leffert, Benson, & Roehlkepartan 1997). Social competence has been described as the "ability to achieve personal goals in social interaction while simultaneously maintaining positive relationships with others over time and across situations" (Rubin & Rose-Krasnor 1992, 285). A full description of social competence involves a broad range of values, knowledge, and concepts about self and others. Social competence can be conceived as consisting of six domains in which a child develops to reach his or her full potential as a socially competent individual: positive self-identity, interpersonal skills, self-regulation, planning and decision-making skills, cultural competence, and social values (Kostelnik et al. 2002).

This chapter focuses on a limited portion of the whole of social competence. Specifically, this chapter explores research-based strategies for encouraging peer interaction and for supporting the development of interpersonal skills and knowledge that lead to successful peer interaction and relationships in the early childhood years. These competencies include initiating interaction, responding appropriately to the initiations of others, communicating ideas and feelings, expressing affection, taking the perspective of another, reading social cues, resolving conflicts peacefully, and giving and receiving emotional support (Leffert, Benson, & Roehlkepartan 1997).

Important to young children's development and well-being

The early childhood literature has traditionally stressed the central importance of children's ability to engage in social interaction with peers (Odom & McLean 1996; Bredekamp & Copple 1997). The ability of young children to manage their emotions and behaviors and make meaningful friendships is an important contributor to the quality of later relationships and adjustment (Ladd & Troop-Gordon 2003; Zins et al. 2004). A large body of research supports the importance of competent interaction to children's general social competence and acceptance by peers. Research suggests that the development of social skills, positive peer relationships, and social acceptance all contribute to children's long-term development in unique and important ways (Hartup & Moore 1991; Ladd 1999; Zins et al. 2004).

The ability to interact effectively with peers is important not only to social development, but to cognitive development and school success, as well. Current research suggests that young children who are more socially competent (i.e., skilled in self-regulation, perspective taking, emotional expression, cooperation, sharing, and problem solving) and engage regularly in meaningful friendships are more likely to make an easier transition to school and to achieve academic success (Birch & Ladd 1996; Ladd & Colemen 1997; Raver & Zigler 1997).

The extent to which kindergartners make new friends and are accepted by their classmates predicts cooperative participation in classroom activities and self-directed completion of learning tasks (Ladd, Kochenderfer, & Coleman 1997; Ladd, Birch, & Buhs 1999). Friendship, a special form of mutual dyadic liking and affiliation, predicts young children's adjustment to school (Ladd, Kochenderfer, & Coleman 1997) and can provide an important context for the refinement of some social competencies. For example, preschoolers give and receive twice as much reinforcement (e.g., greetings, praise, and compliance) and are more emotionally expressive with children they identify as friends (Hartup 1999; Berk 2002). Furthermore, although friends get into more conflicts than do other peers, they are more likely to peacefully work out their differences (Hartup & Laursen 1991).

Strategies to support peer interactions

Children are, of course, not born with the knowledge or skills that enable them to build friendly relationships and engage in effective interactions; mastering these re-quires time, growth, and a variety of social experiences. Proficiency can be facilitated by the support and teaching of a well-informed, skilled adult. The early childhood years are often pinpointed as a crucial time for nurturing the development of positive peer skills and relationships (Katz & Mc-Clellan 1997). The ability to establish and maintain these relationships is integral to the development of social competence and marks a critical developmental milestone for preschool children (Guralnick 1993).

Early childhood teachers are uniquely positioned to support the growth of young children's peer-related social competence: Their work obviously places them in the context of the early childhood peer group for extended periods of time. The classroom teacher is the adult who knows and observes children most intimately within the peer setting and should be an adult who is familiar with evidence-based practices to support children's growing ability to interact competently with their age-mates.

A knowledgeable, skilled, and observant teacher can select strategies of support and intervention to match the needs of individual children and the demands of particular situations. It has been suggested that teachers begin by trying "class-wide" environmental arrangement strategies first, and then move to more individualized and higher-intensity strategies as needed (Brown & Conroy 1997; Brown, Odom, & Conroy 2001).

Environmental arrangements

In any early childhood education program, teachers and children interact within an environmental context. The way in which a teacher creates that context—through arranging the physical space, influencing the structure of social groups, teaching and supporting classroom routines and cooperative experiences, and constructing a secure emotional climate—can impact the quality and/or frequency of peer interactions. Arranging the physical classroom environment to support peer interactions, social skills, and cooperation may seem simple or insignificant, yet sometimes such subtle interventions can be very powerful.

Research suggests that physical environment and classroom climate are involved in the successful development of social competence in young children and that the teacher's role as guide is also invaluable (Sainato & Carta 1992; Kemple 2004). When the environment is arranged to support social goals, quality interactions between adults and children and among peers can be facilitated.

Environmental arrangements are generally considered to be the most natural interventions to support peer interactions, as they require the least alteration of ongoing classroom activity and are generally implemented on a class-wide (rather than individualized) basis. Though there has not been much recent research on the impact of the physical classroom arrangement, many older studies have demonstrated how arrangement of physical space and provision of materials can affect children's social behavior in the classroom (for reviews, see Sainato & Carta 1992; Trawick-Smith 1992).

Simply providing structured space and materials that invite social pretend play may be considered a basic first step toward promoting interaction among peers. A thoughtfully equipped block center and a dramatic play (or "housekeeping") area provide important contexts for social play (Trawick-Smith 1992; Wasserman 2000; Kemple, Duncan, & Strangis 2002). Teachers can also encourage social interaction by arranging the classroom into interest areas that accommodate small groups. The smaller clusters of children that result from such an arrangement can provide more manageable and inviting opportunities for peer play and successful interaction.

Spatial density, ratio of children to adults, amount of materials/toys, and time scheduling are additional components of the environment that teachers may consider. High child:adult ratios have been associated with punitive, disruptive, and less supportive interventions by teachers (Kemple, David, & Hysmith 1997). Too many children in a small space can increase the rate of aggressive behavior, while too few children in a large space can contribute to limited social contact (Smith & Connolly 1980; Driscoll & Carter 2004).

Making plenty of developmentally appropriate materials available to the children can help decrease conflicts, hitting, and fighting over possessions (Brown, Fox, & Brady 1987). A useful guide is to provide enough toys and materials so that each separate play space in a classroom provides four or five possible activities per child (Prescott 1984).

> Arranging the classroom to support peer interactions may seem simple or insignificant, yet sometimes such subtle interventions can be very powerful.

The amount of time children are allowed to play and interact together is also an important environmental component to consider. The longer children have to play and engage with one another, the more complex their interactions tend to be (Christie & Wardle 1992). When children have to change activities too frequently, they may not be able to complete tasks or collaborate effectively (Gareau & Kennedy 1991). Research suggests that, as a general rule, teachers should provide a minimum of 30 minutes of free choice or play time at one specific setting (Christie & Wardle 1992). Of course, not all children are developmentally ready to handle that amount of time, so observant teachers often adjust the structuring of time according to their individual children.

There are numerous ways to organize an early childhood environment to encourage more frequent and satisfying peer interactions. When environmental arrangement is not enough, teachers are encouraged to try naturalistic strategies as the next step.

Naturalistic interventions

With the basic foundation of an age-appropriate classroom context in place, teachers can use planned and spontaneous interventions to further support children's developing social competence. Interventions that can be easily embedded in ongoing classroom routines and activities, and that require minimum adult effort and time, are more likely to be considered feasible by teachers and therefore be implemented consistently (Odom, McConnell, & Chandler 1993). On-the-spot support, group affection activities, effective praise, and PALS centers (Chandler 1998) are a few examples of naturalistic interventions.

On-the-spot support. Social skills are learned and practiced primarily through natural interactive processes (i.e., through the give and take of peer play and work). Intervention offered in the natural context provides young children the opportunity to interact about something meaningful to them while in the presence of a supportive adult; an attentive adult can suggest ways to apply appropriate social strategies to the specific context. Supportive teaching that occurs within the natural context of preschool activities and routines has been referred to as "on-the-spot and just-in-time" intervention (Katz & McClellan 1997).

The teacher's role in such in vivo mediation of interaction involves acting as an interpreter (Hazen, Black, & Fleming-Johnson 1984). For example, a child who rejects playmates' ideas without providing explanations or alternatives could be guided

> To help children implement problem-solving skills in the context of real and meaningful conflict situations, teachers can give guidance.

to do so by the teacher. In such situations, a teacher may say, "Sally, I don't think Kara understands why you don't want to play dress-up. Can you tell her why?" or "Can you tell her what you could both do together instead of playing dress-up?"

Similarly, a child who appears to have difficulty reading and interpreting others' emotional cues might be guided through such suggestions as, "Look at Jared's face. Do you think he likes it when you shove him that way?" (Kemple & Hartle 1997). Incidental teaching is a planful, targeted form of on-the-spot teaching, in which the teacher identifies particular social competence goals for an individual child and then identifies specific natural settings and times of day in which to support and teach those goals (Conroy & Brown 2002).

Another type of on-the-spot teaching is the process of scaffolding children's ability to resolve interpersonal conflicts. To help children implement problem-solving skills in the context of real and meaningful conflict situations, teachers can give guidance, encouraging each child involved to voice his or her perspective, generate potential solutions, and jointly decide upon and implement a mutually acceptable solution. The process of mediating young children's conflicts has been described in Chen (2003), Dinwiddie (1994), and Carlsson-Paige and Levin (1992).

Group affection activities. In group affection activities, intervention is embedded in the natural context of typical group-time activities. McEvoy, Twardosz, and Bishop (1990) described group affection activities as typical preschool games, songs, and experiences that have been modified to include teacher prompts for varying types of affectionate responses.

For example, the traditional preschool song "If You're Happy and You Know It, Clap Your Hands" can be modified to "If You're Happy and Your Know It, Hug a Friend" or "Smile at a Friend" or "Give Your Neighbor a Handshake."

Group affection activities are easy to implement and can help children make connections with peers with whom they may not ordinarily choose to interact (McEvoy, Odom, & McConnell 1992). This strategy is meant to be used in a highly intentional and purposeful manner. Teachers introduce the purpose of the activity (e.g., "We are going to practice some friendly ways to say hello"), reinforce children's appropriate behavior (e.g., "Jason gave friendly, gentle handshakes to two friends.... Good job, Jason"), and recap the activity (e.g., "It's important to use friendly ways to say hello. That lets children know you want to be friends").

PALS centers. A PALS center is a play activity center that is available during free choice time. In creating a PALS center, the teacher arranges four factors in order to promote peer interactions: (1) peer selection is done by the teacher so that children with social needs are paired with peers who have greater social competence; (2) the adult provides prompts and reinforcements for social behavior as necessary; (3) the adult equips the center with materials that promote social play, and materials are limited in variety and number; and (4) the teacher provides an initial structure by describing child roles and social goals. For example:

> Jessica, a shy and withdrawn 4-year-old, is having trouble initiating play with her peers. Her teacher, Ms. Polland, decides to set up a PALS center to help her interact with some of the other kids in the class in a nonthreatening setting. Ms. Polland chooses two well-liked and socially skilled peers to participate in an organized and structured collage art project with Jessica (art is her favorite activity).

> After introductions and a review of the activity goals and time limit, Ms. Polland steps back to observe the interactions. When needed, she interjects comments, prompts, and suggestions. After the allotted time, the children are dismissed.

> That afternoon, Ms. Polland notices that Jessica is hanging around the dramatic play center where the two girls involved in the PALS center are playing—one step closer than she had previously been.

The PALS center is a freely chosen center activity, lasting about 5 to 15 minutes and involving two or three children at a time. Teachers equip the center with limited materials that invite interaction. This might include providing simple games, materials for a collaborative collage, or a simple cooperative learning project. The teacher introduces the activity, describes or demonstrates how to use the materials if needed, describes the social activity goals of the center, and then asks the children to play together. Studies demonstrate that children show an increased frequency in peer interactions when playing in a PALS center (Chandler & Dahlquist 2002; for a more detailed description of PALS center possibilities, see Chandler 1998).

Higher-intensity strategies

For some children with serious social competence needs, environmental arrangements and naturalistic interventions may provide important but insufficient supports. Such children might be those at risk for challenging behaviors due to environmental and biological factors and children with disabilities that put them at particular social disadvantage or contribute to deficits in social knowledge, social behavior, or communication skills.

Higher-intensity strategies are typically individualized, systematic programs of intervention. Such interventions are based on careful and detailed observation of individual children's behavior. These interventions target precisely defined social behaviors and include adult-mediated approaches, in which an adult typically provides prompts and systematic reinforcement for prescribed social behaviors, and peer-mediated approaches, in which an adult trains a socially competent peer to initiate and/or to provide social reinforcement for desired social behaviors performed by a "target" child.

Such interventions require some specialized knowledge and should be carried out in collaboration with a colleague who is knowledgeable and experienced in working with children with very difficult behavior or children who have disabilities that severely impact their social competence (for further information, see Kohler & Strain 1999; Chandler & Dahlquist 2002; Conroy & Brown 2002).

Conclusion

A large research literature supports the importance of young children's peer-related social competence, and a myriad of strategies to support the growth of peer-related social competence in the early childhood classroom have been described in the literature. In addition to those mentioned in this chapter, teachers can choose from strategies including cooperative learning activities, guided discussion, children's literature dealing with social and emotional topics, and social skills training programs such as I Can Problem-Solve (Shure 1992), Play Time/Social Time (Odom & Mc-Connell 1993), Second Step (Committee for Children 2002), and the Buddy Skills Training Program (English et al. 1997), to name just a few. For useful discussion of several such programs, see Joseph and Strain (2003).

Teachers who are informed and skilled in using a variety of strategies can use their knowledge of those strategies, their knowledge of the individual children they teach, and their knowledge of impor-

tant social-emotional goals as they make decisions about approaches to use. For children who are experiencing significant problems in peer-related social competence (including children with disabilities that make their development of relationships and peer-related skills particularly challenging), professional collaboration is important. Teachers can work together with other early childhood professionals (e.g., a behavioral specialist, a speech pathologist, a special educator) to select appropriate strategies.

Addressing the social competence needs of all young children is an important component of preparing them for success in school and in life.

Updated from the Research in Review article in the July 1991 issue of *Young Children*.

Kristen M. Kemple is a professor at the University of Florida. **Stacy M. Ellis** is the assistant director at a child research center at the University of Florida.

References

Berk, L. 2002. *Child Development*. 6th ed. Boston: Allyn & Bacon.

Birch, S., & G. Ladd. 1996. Interpersonal relationships in the school environment and children's early school adjustment: The role of teachers and peers. In *Social motivation: Understanding children's school adjustment*, eds. K. Wentzel & J. Juvonen. New York: Cambridge University Press.

Bredekamp, S., & C. Copple, eds. 1997. *Developmentally appropriate practice in early childhood programs*. Washington, DC: NAEYC.

Brown, W., & M. Conroy. 1997. Promoting and supporting peer interactions in inclusive classrooms: Effective strategies for early childhood educators. In *Inclusion of preschool children with developmental delays in early childhood programs*, eds. W. Brown & M. Conroy, 79–108. Little Rock, AR: Southern Early Childhood Association.

Brown, W., J. Fox, & M. Brady. 1987. The effects of spatial density on the socially directed behavior of three and four-year-old children during freeplay: An investigation of setting factors. *Education and Treatment of Children* 10: 247–58.

Brown, W., S. Odom, & M. Conroy. 2001. An intervention hierarchy for promoting preschool children's peer interactions in naturalistic environments. *Topics in Early Childhood Special Education* 21 (3): 162–75.

Carlsson-Paige, N., & D. Levin. 1992. Making peace in violent times: A constructivist approach to conflict resolution. *Young Children* 48 (1): 4–12.

Chandler, L. 1998. Promoting positive interaction between preschool-age children during free-play: The PALS center. *Young Exceptional Children* 1 (3): 14–19.

Chandler, L., & C. Dahlquist. 2002. *The PALS center: Strategies to promote peer social interaction.* Poster presented at the Applied Behavior Analysis and Behavior Analysis Society of Illinois Conference, Chicago, IL.

Chen, D.W. 2003. Preventing violence by promoting the development of competent conflict resolution skills: Exploring roles and responsibilities. *Early Childhood Education Journal* 30 (4): 203–08.

Christie, J., & F. Wardle. 1992. How much time is needed for play? *Young Children* 47 (2): 28–32.

Committee for Children. 2002. Second Step: A violence prevention curriculum—Preschool/kindergarten. Seattle, WA: Committee for Children.

Conroy, M., & W. Brown. 2002. Preschool children: Putting research into practice. In *Promoting social communication: Children with developmental disabilities from birth to adolescence*, eds. H. Goldstein, L. Kacmarek, & K. English. Baltimore: Paul H. Brookes.

Dinwiddie, S. 1994. The saga of Sally, Sammy, and the red pen: Facilitating children's social problem-solving. *Young Children* 49 (5): 13–19.

Driscoll, C., & M. Carter. 2004. Spatial density as a setting event for the social interaction of preschool children. *International Journal of Disability, Development & Education* 51 (1): 7–37.

English, K., H. Goldstein, K. Shafer, & L. Kacmarek. 1997. Promoting interactions among preschoolers with and without disabilities: Effects of a buddy skills training program. *Exceptional Children* 63: 229–43.

Gareau, M., & C. Kennedy. 1991. Structure time and space to promote pursuit of learning in the primary grades. *Young Children* 46 (4): 46–51.

Guralnick, M. 1993. Developmentally appropriate practice in the assessment and intervention of children's peer relations. *Topics in Early Childhood Education* 13: 344–71.

Hartup, W. 1999. Peer experience and its developmental significance. In *Developmental psychology: Achievements and prospects*, ed. M. Bennett, 106–25. Philadelphia: Psychology Press.

Hartup, W., & B. Laursen. 1991. Relationships and developmental contexts. In *Context and development*, eds. R. Cohen & A. Seigel, 253–79. Hillsdale, NJ: Lawrence Erlbaum.

Hartup, W., & S. Moore. 1991. Early peer relations: Developmental significance and prognostic implications. *Early Childhood Research Quarterly* 5: 1–7.

Hazen, N., B. Black, & F. Fleming-Johnson. 1984. Social acceptance: Strategies children use and how teachers can help children learn them. *Young Children* 39 (6): 26–36.

Joseph, G.E., & P.S. Strain. 2003. Comprehensive evidence-based social-emotional curricula for young children: An analysis of efficacious adoption potential. *Topics in Early Childhood Special Education* 23 (2): 65–76.

Katz, L., & D. McClellan. 1997. *Fostering children's social competence: The teacher's role.* Washington, DC: NAEYC.

Kemple, K. 2004. *Let's be friends: Peer competence and social interaction in early childhood programs.* New York: Teachers College Press.

Kemple, K., G. David, & C. Hysmith. 1997. Teacher's interventions in young children's peer interactions. *Journal of Research in Childhood Education* 12 (1): 34–47.

Kemple, K., T. Duncan, & D. Strangis. 2002. Supporting young children's peer competence in an era of inclusion. *Childhood Education* 79 (1): 40–48.

Kemple, K., & L. Hartle. 1997. Getting along: How teachers can support children's peer relationships. *Annual editions in early childhood education*, 4th ed., 130–37. Guildford, CT: Dushkin/McGraw-Hill.

Kohler, F., & P. Strain. 1999. Maximizing peer-mediated resources in integrated preschool classrooms. *Topics in Early Childhood Special Education* 19 (2): 92–102.

Kostelnik, M., A. Whiren, A. Soderman, L. Stein, & K. Gregory. 2002. *Guiding children's social development: Theory to practice.* Albany, NY: Delmar.

Ladd, G. 1999. Peer relationships and social competence during early and middle childhood. *Annual Review of Psychology* 50: 333–59.

Ladd, G., S. Birch, & E. Buhs. 1999. Children's social and scholastic lives in kindergarten: Related spheres of influence? *Child Development* 70: 1373–400.

Ladd, G., & C. Coleman. 1997. Children's classroom peer relationships and early school attitudes: Concurrent and longitudinal associations. *Early Education and Development* 8 (1): 51–66.

Ladd, G., B. Kochenderfer, & C. Coleman. 1997. Classroom peer acceptance, friendship, and victimization: Distinct relational systems that contribute uniquely to children's school adjustment. *Child Development* 68: 1181–97.

Ladd, G., & W. Troop-Gordon. 2003. The role of chronic peer difficulties in the development of children's psychological adjustment problems. *Child Development* 74 (5): 1344–67.

Leffert, N., P. Benson, & J. Roehlkepartan. 1997. *Starting out right: Developmental assets for children.* Minneapolis, MN: Search Institute.

McEvoy, M., S. Odom, & S. McConnell. 1992. Peer social competence interventions for young children with disabilities. In *Social competence of young children with disabilities: Issues and strategies for intervention*, eds. S. Odom, S. McConnell, & M. McEvoy, 113–33. Baltimore: Paul H. Brookes.

McEvoy, M., S. Twardosz, & N. Bishop. 1990. Affection activities: Procedures for encouraging young children with handicaps to interact with their peers. *Education and Treatment of Children* 13: 159–67.

Odom, S., & S. McConnell. 1993. *Play time/social time: Organizing your classroom to build interaction skills.* Tucson, AZ: Communications Skill Builders.

Odom, S., S. McConnell, & L. Chandler. 1993. Acceptability and feasibility of classroom-based social interaction interventions for young children with disabilities. *Exceptional Children* 60: 226–36.

Odom, S.L., & M.E. McLean. 1996. *Early intervention/early childhood education: Recommended practices.* Austin, TX: PRO-Ed.

Prescott, J. 1984. The physical setting in day care. In *Making day care better*, ed. J. Greenman. New York: Teachers College Press.

Raver, C., & E. Zigler. 1997. Social competence: An untapped dimension in evaluating Head Start's success. *Early Childhood Research Quarterly* 12: 363–85.

Rubin, K., & L. Rose-Krasnor. 1992. Interpersonal problem-solving. In *Handbook of social development*, eds. V. Van Hasselt & M. Hersen, 283–324. New York: Plenum.

Sainato, D., & J. Carta. 1992. Classroom influences on the development of social competence in young children with disabilities. In *Social competence of young children with disabilities: Issues and strategies for intervention*, eds. S. Odom, S. McConnell, & M. McEvoy, 93–109. Baltimore: Paul H. Brookes.

Shure, M. 1992. *I can problem-solve: An interpersonal cognitive problem solving program.* Champaign, IL: Research Press.

Smith, P., & K. Connolly. 1980. *The ecology of preschool behavior.* Cambridge: Cambridge University Press.

Trawick-Smith, J. 1992. How the classroom environment affects play and development: A review of research. *Dimensions of Early Childhood* 20 (2): 27–30.

Wasserman, S. 2000. *Serious players in the primary classroom*, 2d ed. New York: Teachers College Press.

Zins, J.E., R.P. Weissberg, M.C. Wang, & H.J. Walberg. 2004. *Building academic success on social and emotional learning: What does the research say?* New York: Teachers College Press.

2 Growing Up with the Contradictions of Race and Class

Patricia G. Ramsey

As American society becomes more ethnically diverse and more economically polarized, teachers face the challenge of how to present and explore issues of diversity and inequality in meaningful and hopeful ways with young children. Different classrooms and communities pose varying challenges. In a classroom with children from a number of social class and ethnic groups, fostering connections between children who may speak a range of languages and have different home experiences and play and conversational styles is a priority. In contrast, teachers working with relatively homogeneous groups of middle-class, white children need to prepare them to live in a diverse world that may seem very distant to them.

Over the past few decades, researchers have studied the development of children's awareness and feelings related to race and class which have been sources of some of the most profound divisions in our society. Although many gaps in this knowledge base remain, some findings can be applied to teaching practices and curriculum. This review will address some of the questions that teachers trying to transform their teaching and their curriculum often ask themselves:

- How much do children notice race and class differences?
- How does their understanding of race and class change during the early childhood years?
- How do children feel about racial and class differences?
- How do these differences affect relationships between children in a program?
- How can we prepare children to value diversity and to challenge the divisiveness and inequities that often accompany racial and class differences?

Children's awareness of and feelings about race

Race in this review refers to groups of people who share visible physical attributes that traditionally are defined as "racial," such as hair color/texture, skin color, or facial features. Although race is often viewed as a biological distinction, in reality there is more genetic variation within racial groups than between them (Quintana 1998). Thus, race is a socially constructed label that is defined by social, political, and economic forces (Omi & Winant 2002); moreover, it often is applied in inconsistent and biased ways (Smedley 1993). The contradictions of race have become even more apparent with increasing numbers of interracial births, transracial adoptions, and immigrants with mixed racial heritage (Root 1996). Despite these ambiguities and the biological insignificance of race, discrimination based on it continues to profoundly affect a person's status and prospects in American society (Ogbu 1991).

Teachers often ask whether young children notice racial differences. The answer is an emphatic *yes*. Contrary to popular beliefs (and possibly hopes), young children are *not* "color-blind." Infants notice racial cues, and by the age of 3 or 4 most children have a rudimentary concept of race (Katz 2003) and can accurately apply socially conventional labels of "black" and "white" to pictures, dolls, and people.

The salience of race in children's perceptions varies. Katz (2003) found that black and white preschoolers used racial cues 63 percent of the time to sort pictures (as opposed to using gender 16 percent of the time); but McGraw, Durm, and Durnam (1989) found that children from both groups categorized others according to sex more readily than by race. How prominently race figures in children's perceptions of themselves and others depends, in part, on whether their own racial group has majority or minority status in their local community and on the extent and quality of their own contacts with other racial group members (Rotheram & Phinney 1987; Ramsey & Myers 1990; Ramsey 1991a).

During their elementary school years, children develop more complex racial views as they begin to associate social

> Preschoolers are often inconsistent when asked whom they look like, and they frequently make distinctions based on attributes such as hairstyle or clothing.

information, such as the differential status of various groups, with the physical attributes characteristic of the groups (Katz 1976). As this shift occurs, children see race less rigidly in terms of purely physical differences and begin to grasp the social meaning of racial terms (Alejandro-Wright 1985). Children who have difficulty forming flexible and multifaceted categories in general acquire rigid stereotypes more readily and are more resistant to changing them (Bigler & Liben 1993).

Children begin to develop their own racial identity during the preschool and elementary school years. Preschoolers are often inconsistent when asked whom they look like, and they frequently make distinctions based on nonracial attributes such as hairstyle or clothing. As they get older, children consistently identify themselves with a racial group.

The development of racial identity may be affected by current attitudes in one's own group as well as in society at large. Studies done in the 1940s and 1950s suggested that African-American children had somewhat ambivalent racial identities, but more recent studies show that African-American children develop a clear and unambiguous black reference group orientation (e.g., Cross 1985; Branch & Newcombe 1986; Cross 1991). In a series of Canadian studies, black elementary school children expressed more in-group pride and more consistent racial identities than did their white peers (Aboud & Doyle 1993; Aboud & Amato 2001).

In the last decade, authors have been focusing on white children's identities and the extent to which these embody attitudes of racial privilege and superiority (e.g., Derman-Sparks & Ramsey 2005; 2006). In an observational study in a multiracial preschool, Van Ausdale and Feagin (2001), for example, recorded numerous instances in which white children claimed privileges based on their race.

Given that young children notice race and are beginning to identify themselves according to racial group, the next obvious question is, How do they feel about different-race people in general and different-race classmates in particular?

Some studies have shown that young children in multiracial classrooms tend to choose their friends on the basis of sex (preferring same-sex classmates) and that there is little evidence of same-race preference during the preschool years (Jarrett & Quay 1983) or elementary grades (Singleton & Asher 1977). However, other studies have found evidence of racial bias in preschool children's actual and hypothetical friendship choices (Finkelstein & Haskins 1983; Ramsey & Myers 1990).

According to some researchers, children's same-race preferences become more consistent and elaborated during the elementary years (Goodman 1952; Porter 1971; Katz 1976; Schofield 1981; Asher, Singleton, & Taylor 1982; Milner 1983; Schofield 1989). This trend, however, is potentially offset by children's increasing cognitive capacities to differentiate and understand the perspectives of other individuals and groups (Aboud 1988; Garcia Coll & Garcia 1995; Aboud & Amato 2001).

Whether or not children become more or less same-race biased may depend largely on their social environment and the values that they are learning. For example, children in monoracial schools tend to develop more cross-race aversion than those in multiracial schools do (Kistner et al. 1993; Rotenberg & Cerda 1994; Holmes 1995; McGlothlin & Killen 2005; 2006).

Family and community attitudes may also play a role. Although some studies have found little connection between

parents' and children's expressed racial attitudes (see, e.g., Aboud & Doyle 1996), Katz (2003) observed that parents' subtle—and often unconscious—behaviors and attitudes (e.g., *not* mentioning race, spending more time talking about pictures of same-race individuals) were related to their children's level of bias.

During the elementary school years, racial divisions often intensify as children absorb more of the prevailing social attitudes, and racial divisions become more firmly established (Katz 1976; Aboud, Mendelson, & Purdy 2003). However, Howes and Wu (1990) found that in a very diverse setting, third-graders played more with different-race peers than did the kindergartners, suggesting that increasing racial cleavage with age is not inevitable. Some interventions, such as racially integrated cooperative learning teams, seem to have a positive effect on interracial friendships (Slavin 1980; Rosenfield & Stephen 1981; Johnson & Johnson 2000) and may help to counteract the tendency to divide by race.

Research spanning several decades shows that from preschool to adolescence, white children consistently show stronger same-race biases and preferences than do their African-American classmates (Fox & Jordan 1973; Stabler, Zeig, & Rembold 1976; Rosenfield & Stephan 1981; Newman, Liss, & Sherman 1983; Ramsey & Myers 1990). Using data from a longitudinal study, Katz (2003) reported that black children expressed a slight preference for same-race hypothetical playmates at age 30 months, and 32 percent did by age 36 months; among white children, however, 86 percent made same-race playmate choices by age 36 months.

These preferences were also reflected in the children's actual playmate choices in their classrooms, as seen in observational studies in which black children more often seek out different-race peers than white children do (Hallinan & Teixeira

1987; Howes & Wu 1990; Ramsey & Myers 1990; Katz 2003). The fact that white children show stronger same-race bias is not surprising, because they are immersed in a world of media images and power structures that overtly and covertly convey messages of white superiority. Moreover, many white children live in racially isolated communities, so that people of color are a distant "other."

Children's awareness of and feelings about class

American society's deep disparities in wealth and resources profoundly affect all aspects of children's lives and development (for specific studies of these effects, see Huston 1991; the 1994 *Child Development* Special Issue on Children and Poverty; Gottfried et al. 2003). Moreover, economic inequities have been increasing over the past three decades. For example, between 1979 and 1997, the after-tax income of the poorest 20 percent of Americans *declined* from $10,900 to $10,800, while the incomes of the top 1 percent *rose* from $263,700 to $677,900 (Lott 2002).

Because the concepts of *economics* and *class* are developmentally difficult for young children to grasp (Harrah & Friedman 1990), most studies of children's understanding of class have focused on older elementary school children and adolescents. The research that has been done with young children has explored three areas: (1) children's awareness and understanding of class differences; (2) their feelings about people in different class groups; and (3) their ideas about whether or not it is "fair" that some people have more money than others.

Many indicators of class distinctions, such as education and occupational prestige, are too abstract for young children to see, but they can readily observe more concrete manifestations of class. Preschoolers are able to sort "rich" people from "poor"

people based on their clothing, homes, and possessions (Ramsey 1991b). Preschoolers' ideas about wealth and poverty, however, are quite rudimentary; and they tend to associate being rich with gold, crowns, and treasures. Likewise, early-elementary school children are likely to describe and explain poverty and wealth in observable and concrete terms, such as number of possessions and types of homes (Leahy 1983).

Young children also are becoming concerned about possessions and possession-related rules (Dawe 1934; Newman 1978; Ramsey 1987) and are learning that ownership is a source of power and control (Furby 1980). In the American media-saturated and consumer-oriented society, children are exposed to a lot of information about available goods and the role of money in acquiring them, and they are beginning to grasp the advantages of having a lot of money. Young children also begin to absorb prevailing attitudes about the desirability of wealth and to assume that rich people are happier and more likeable than poor people (Leahy 1981; Naimark 1983; Ramsey 1991b).

Finally, in their day-to-day lives, young children are beginning to develop a sense of fairness and to notice inequality, especially if they are personally at a disadvantage (Damon 1980), for example, in disputes over playdough or turns on the trikes or swings. At the same time, young children begin to see that economic disparities are not just. They often comment that "it is not fair" (Ramsey 1991b) and that rich people should share with poor people (Furby 1979). Elementary school children frequently argue that everyone should get equal amounts of money and that people with more should share with those who have less (Furby 1979; Leahy 1983). However, as they approach adolescence, children begin to justify inequalities and say that poor people get what they deserve (Leahy 1990), even though adolescents are developmentally capable of understanding the role that social and economic structures play in perpetuating inequality (Leahy 1983). For many children in American society, the ideals of democratic equality give way to the rewards of economic competitiveness and individualism as they grow up and are socialized into the economic system (Chafel 1997).

Conclusions and implications for teaching practice

Collectively, these findings suggest that during the early childhood years, children begin grappling with concepts of race and class, as well as with the intersections and contradictions of the two in American society. Although race and class are treated separately in this chapter and in most research, they are connected—in reality and in the images and other messages that children get. Disproportionately more children of color live below the poverty line—for example, 34.1 percent of African-American and 29.7 percent of Hispanic-American children, versus 9.8 percent of non-Hispanic white children (Children's Defense Fund 2004). The wrenching photographs of low-income African-American families stranded by the New Orleans flood following the Hurricane Katrina were a vivid example of the intersection of race and class.

From these experiences, young children are learning to associate power and privilege with white people, and poverty and subordinate status with people of color. They are learning to value "fairness" and recognize inequality; but at the same time, they are beginning to accept racist ideologies and rationalize the unequal distribution of resources in society.

Returning to the question posed at the beginning of this chapter, then: How can teachers prepare children to value diversity and to challenge the divisiveness and inequities that often accompany

Young children are learning to value "fairness" and recognize inequality.

racial and class differences? Teachers and schools play a crucial role in the course of children's attitude development; all aspects of practice are potentially affected. Although the following discussion focuses on what individual teachers can do, let it be said first that authentically grappling with these issues requires school-wide and system-wide commitments to transform perspectives and practices.

As teachers, we need to understand for ourselves the dynamics of race and class and how attitudes about them play out in particular communities and families. Teacher preparation programs should include courses in sociology and economics to provide background information and field experiences. School staff can collaborate with parents and local agencies to learn about the local community, including the history and current status of relationships among its particular racial, cultural, class, and religious groups. By knowing the local situation, teachers can anticipate what attitudes children may be absorbing at home and in their communities and what issues their families may raise.

As teachers working with young children, we must constantly examine our own attitudes, backgrounds, and perspectives and monitor how those influence our assumptions about society and about the individual children and families in their program (Ramsey 2004). In particular, white, middle-class teachers need to be alert to how their position of privilege in American society might be limiting their awareness and understanding of the social stratification and discrimination imposed on other groups (Sleeter 1991; Derman-Sparks & Ramsey 2006), and they must struggle to push beyond these limits.

At the classroom level, teachers can assess each child's knowledge and feelings about issues related to race and class.

A book, a picture, or an event—in the classroom or in the community—can often stimulate these discussions. In particular, teachers should try to identify children who are feeling marginalized or who are developing rigid stereotypes about particular groups. Teachers can learn about families' experiences and views related to race and class by having conversations with parents. With this information, teachers can plan and implement classroom activities and partner with parents more effectively.

Teachers can address issues of race and class along two dimensions: planned curriculum (including routines) and spontaneous conversations. We can develop activities with books, pictures, music, art, and so on, that affirm children's own racial and class groups, support children's sense of solidarity with all people, and contradict stereotypes. Stretching and challenging children's ideas about the world are especially crucial in classrooms that are homogeneous in terms of class and race.

In more diverse classrooms, teachers may focus on the groups that are represented and ways to support the connections among children from different groups and between families and the school. Cooperative activities can foster children's interpersonal and intergroup relationships and begin to challenge society's pervasive (and often divisive) emphasis on individualism and competition. Teachers can also plan activities that help children think about what is and isn't "fair" in the classroom, in children's local communities, and in American society (Derman-Sparks & the ABC Task Force 1989; Pelo & Davidson 2000).

Children's questions—and therefore, many of teachers' ongoing conversations with them—often reflect the contradictions and injustices in today's society. Teachers do not need to explain all these contradictions and injustices to children. Rather, they can puzzle along with children, providing appropriate information, as they try to understand specific events. For example, after the 9/11 attack and the resulting anti-Muslim sentiment, many teachers introduced positive images and stories about Muslim people in order to counteract the negative images in the media and any tendency children might have to form negative stereotypes.

Sometimes holidays give rise to these discussions:

> When he was 5 years old, my older son indignantly asked me why we celebrated Christopher Columbus if he (as we had taught him) was mean to the natives he encountered? Why didn't we celebrate Native Americans Day instead?

Teachers can help children think about such questions in ways children can understand. The effect of local strikes or layoffs on families, reductions in social services such as food stamps, a stereotyped book, or exclusionary play during recess are examples of the many "teachable moments" when children may be open to challenging unfairness and bias.

In both planned and spontaneous activities and conversations, we need to provide children with hopeful and empowering experiences and images so that they are not overwhelmed and discouraged by the unfairness and bias they see around them. Writing class letters to government officials and newspaper editors about local problems or to publishers about stereotyped books and toys, for example, lets children experience the positive energy and power of collaborative action. Children can also get involved by collecting food for a soup kitchen or raising money to provide scholarships for extracurricular activities so that all children can participate regardless of their economic circumstances.

However, teachers need to be sure that such projects are not one-time "charity" efforts to "help the less fortunate." To counteract the tendency to either pity or blame people who are poor, the projects rather should help children understand society's structural inequities. Ideally, projects should last for several months and include forming personal and collaborative relationships among the children, their families, and members of the group they are working with.

Reading biographical stories about people who have taken risks and acted to make a difference—whether the action was delivering a speech, refusing to give up a seat on the bus, leading slaves to freedom, overcoming poverty, or joining a team in the face of strong opposition—can support children in feeling empowered to take actions of their own. Such accounts can stimulate conversations about being strong and courageous in ways that children can understand. These stories also can provide a compelling antidote to the images of power and strength through violence or the supernatural that dominate the television and toy market. Teachers and parents who themselves participate in movements for social change and justice also provide authentic and encouraging models for children (Sleeter 1991).

To make these changes in our hearts and minds and in our teaching practice, we all need support and time. As we teach children to see and challenge the contradictions and injustices of our world, we need to work closely with colleagues and communities to expand our own understanding and to reflect on our work with children's and families. In particular, we must stay attuned to how our children's understanding of and feelings about race and class issues are evolving, and use their questions, concerns, and insights to support them in becoming strong, critical, caring adults.

Updated from the Research in Review article in the September 1995 issue of *Young Children*.

Patricia G. Ramsey is a professor at Mount Holyoke College.

References

Aboud, F.E. 1988. *Children and prejudice*. New York: Blackwell Publishers.

Aboud, F.E., & M. Amato. 2001. Developmental and socialization influences on intergroup bias. In *Blackwell handbook of social psychology: Intergroup processes*, eds. R. Brown & S.L. Gaerther, 65–85. Oxford, England: Blackwell Publishers.

Aboud, F.E., & A.B. Doyle. 1993. The early development of ethnic identity and attitudes. In *Ethnic identity, vol. 1: Formation and transmission among Hispanics and other minorities*, eds. M.E. Bernal & G.P. Knight, 46–59. Albany, NY: SUNY Press.

Aboud, F.E., & A.B. Doyle. 1996. Does talk of race foster prejudice or tolerance in children? *Canadian Journal of Behavioural Science* 28: 162–70.

Aboud, F.E., M.J. Mendelson, & K.T. Purdy. 2003. Cross-race relations and friendship quality. *International Journal of Behavioral Development* 27 (2): 165–73.

Alejandro-Wright, M.N. 1985. The child's conception of racial classification: A socio-cognitive development model. In *Beginnings: The social and affective development of black children*, eds. M.B. Spencer, G.K. Brookins, & W.R. Allen, 185–200. Hillsdale, NJ: Lawrence Erlbaum.

Asher, S.R., L.C. Singleton, & A.J. Taylor. 1982. *Acceptance versus friendship: A longitudinal study of racial integration*. Paper presented at the annual meeting of the American Educational Research Association, New York, NY.

Bigler, R.S., & L.S. Liben. 1993. A cognitive-developmental approach to racial stereotyping and reconstructive memory in Euro-American children. *Child Development* 64: 1507–18.

Branch, C.W., & N. Newcombe. 1986. Racial attitude development among young black children as a function of parental attitudes: A longitudinal and cross-sectional study. *Child Development* 57: 712–21.

Chafel, J.A. 1997. Children's views of poverty: A review of research and implications for teaching. *The Educational Forum* 61: 360–71.

Child Development Special Issue on Children and Poverty. 1994. *Child Development* 65: 275–715.

Children's Defense Fund. 2004. *2003 Facts on Child Poverty in America*. Online: cdf.childrensdefense.org/site/PageServer?pagename=familyincome_childpoverty_basicfacts.

Cross, W.E. 1985. Black identity: Rediscovering the distinction between personal identity and reference group orientation. In *Beginnings: The social and affective development of black children*, eds. M.B. Spencer, G.K. Brookins, & W.R. Allen, 155–71. Hillsdale, NJ: Lawrence Erlbaum.

Cross, W.E. 1991. *Shades of black*. Philadelphia, PA: Temple University Press.

Damon, W. 1980. Patterns of change in children's social reasoning: A two-year longitudinal study. *Child Development* 51: 1010–17.

Dawe, H.C. 1934. An analysis of two hundred quarrels of preschool children. *Child Development* 5: 139–57.

Derman-Sparks, L., & the ABC Task Force. 1989. *Anti-bias curriculum: Tools for empowering young children*. Washington, DC: NAEYC.

Derman-Sparks, L., & P.G. Ramsey. 2005. What if all the children in my class are white?: Anti-bias/multicultural education with white children. *Young Children* 60 (6): 20–27.

Derman-Sparks, L., & P.G. Ramsey. 2006. *What if all the kids are white? Anti-bias multicultural education with young children and families*. New York: Teachers College Press.

Finkelstein, N.W., & R. Haskins. 1983. Kindergarten children prefer same-color peers. *Child Development* 54: 502–08.

Fox, D.J., & V.B. Jordan. 1973. Racial preferences and identification of black, American Chinese, and white children. *Genetic Psychology Monographs* 88: 229–86.

Furby, L. 1979. Inequalities in personal possessions: Explanations for and judgments about unequal distribution. *Human Development* 22: 180–202.

Furby, L. 1980. The origins and early development of possessive behavior. *Political Psychology* 2 (1): 30–40.

García Coll, C.T., & H.A. Vázquez García. 1995. Developmental processes and their influence on interethnic and interracial relations. In *Toward a common destiny: Improving race and ethnic relations in America*, eds. W.B. Hawley & A. Jackson, 103–30. San Francisco: Jossey-Bass.

Goodman, M.E. 1952. *Race awareness in young children*. Cambridge, MA: Addison-Wesley.

Gottfried, A.W., A.E. Gottfried, K. Bathurst, D.W. Guerin, M.M. Parramore. 2003. Socioeconomic status in children's development and family environment: Infancy through adolescence. In *Socioeconomic status, parenting, and child development*, ed. M. Bornstein, 189–207. Mahwah, NJ: Lawrence Erlbaum.

Hallinan, M.T., & R.A. Teixeira. 1987. Opportunities and constraints: Black-white differences in the formation of interracial friendships. *Child Development* 58: 1358–71.

Harrah, J., & M. Friedman. 1990. Economic socialization in children in a Midwestern American community. *Journal of Economic Psychology* 11: 495–513.

Holmes, R. 1995. *How young children perceive race*. New York: Sage Publications.

Howes, C., & F. Wu. 1990. Peer interactions and friendships in an ethnically diverse school setting. *Child Development* 61: 537–41.

Huston, A.C., ed. 1991. *Children in poverty: Child development and public policy*. New York: Cambridge University Press.

Jarrett, O., & L. Quay. 1983. *Cross-racial acceptance and best friend choice in racially balanced kindergarten and first-grade classrooms*. Paper presented at the biennial meeting of the Society for Research in Child Development, April 21–24, Detroit, MI.

Johnson, D.W., & R.T. Johnson. 2000. The three C's of reducing prejudice and discrimination. In *Reducing prejudice and discrimination*, ed. S. Okamp, 239–68. Mahwah, NJ: Lawrence Erlbaum.

Katz, P.A. 1976. The acquisition of racial attitudes in children. In *Towards the elimination of racism*, ed. R.P. Katz, 125–54. New York: Pergamon.

Katz, P.A. 2003. Racists or tolerant multiculturalists? How do they begin? *American Psychologist* 58 (11): 897–909.

Kistner, J., A. Metzler, D. Gatlin, & S. Risi. 1993. Classroom racial proportions and children's peer relations: Race and gender effects. *Journal of Educational Psychology* 85 (3): 446–52.

Leahy, R. 1981. The development of the concept of social inequality. I. Descriptions and comparisons of rich and poor people. *Child Development* 52: 523–32.

Leahy, R. 1983. The development of the conception of social class. In *The child's construction of inequality*, ed. R. Leahy, 79–107. New York: Academic.

Leahy, R. 1990. The development of concepts of economics and social inequality. *New Directions for Child Development* 46: 107–20.

Lott, B. 2002. Cognitive and behavioral distancing from the poor. *American Psychologist* 57 (2): 100–10.

McGlothlin, H., & M. Killen. 2005. Children's perceptions of intergroup and intragroup similarity and the role of social experience. *Applied Developmental Psychology* 26: 680–98.

McGlothlin, H., & M. Killen. 2006. Intergroup attitudes of European American children attending ethnically homogeneous schools. *Child Development* 77: 1375–86.

McGraw, K.O., M.W. Durm, & M.R. Durnam. 1989. The relative salience of sex, race, age, and glasses in children's social perception. *Journal of Genetic Psychology* 150 (3): 251–67.

Milner, D. 1983. *Children and race*. Beverly Hills, CA: Sage Publications.

Naimark, H. 1983. *Children's understanding of social class differences*. Paper presented at the biennial meeting of the Society for Research in Child Development, April 21–24, Detroit, MI.

Newman, D. 1978. Ownership and permission among nursery school children. In *Studies in social and cognitive development, vol. 1*, eds. J. Glick & K.A. Clarke-Stewart, 213–49. New York: Gardner.

Newman, M.A., M.B. Liss, & F. Sherman. 1983. Ethnic awareness in children: Not a unitary concept. *The Journal of Genetic Psychology* 143 (1): 103–12.

Ogbu, J.U. 1991. Immigrant and involuntary minorities in comparative perspective. In *Minority status and schooling: A comparative study of immigrant and involuntary minorities*, eds. M.A. Gibson & J.U. Ogbu, 3–33. New York: Garland.

Omi, M., & H. Winant. 2002. Racial formation. In *Race critical theories: Text and context*, eds. P. Essed & D. Goldberg, 123–45. Oxford: Blackwell.

Pelo, A., & F. Davidson. 2000. *That's not fair: A teacher's guide to activism with young children*. St. Paul, MN: Redleaf Press.

Porter, J.D.R. 1971. *Black child, white child: The development of racial attitudes*. Cambridge, MA: Harvard University Press.

Quintana, S.M. 1998. Children's developmental understanding of ethnicity and race. *Applied and Preventive Psychology* 7: 27–45.

Ramsey, P.G. 1987. Possession episodes in young children's social interactions. *Journal of Genetic Psychology* 148 (3): 315–25.

Ramsey, P.G. 1991a. Salience of race in young children growing up in an all white community. *Journal of Educational Psychology* 83: 28–34.

Ramsey, P.G. 1991b. Young children's awareness and understanding of social class differences. *Journal of Genetic Psychology* 152 (1): 71–82.

Ramsey, P.G. 2004. *Teaching and learning in a diverse world: Multicultural education of young children*. 3d ed. New York: Teachers College Press.

Ramsey, P.G., & L.C. Myers. 1990. Young children's responses to racial differences: Relations among cognitive, affective, and behavioral dimensions. *Journal of Applied Developmental Psychology* 11: 49–67.

Root, M.P.P., ed. 1996. *The multiracial experience: Racial borders as the new frontier*. Thousand Oaks, CA: Sage Publications.

Rosenfield, D., & W.G. Stephan. 1981. Intergroup relations among children. In *Developmental social psychology*, eds. S.S. Brehm, S.M. Kassin, & F.X. Gibbons, 271–97. New York: Oxford University Press.

Rotenberg, K.J., & C. Cerda. 1994. Racially based trust expectancies of Native American and Caucasian children. *The Journal of Social Psychology* 134 (5): 621–31.

Rotheram, M.J., & J. Phinney. 1987. Introduction: Definitions and perspectives in the study of children's ethnic socialization. In *Children's ethnic socialization: Pluralism and development*, eds. J. Phinney & M.J. Rotheram, 10–28. Beverly Hills, CA: Sage Publications.

Schofield, J.W. 1981. Complementary and conflicting identities: Images and interaction in an interracial school. In *The development of children's friendships*, eds. S.R. Asher & J.M. Gottman, 53–90. New York: Cambridge University Press.

Schofield, J.W. 1989. *Black and white in school: Trust, tension, or tolerance*. New York: Teachers College Press.

Singleton, L.C., & S.R. Asher. 1977. Peer preferences and social interaction among third-grade children in an integrated school district. *Journal of Educational Psychology* 69: 330–36.

Slavin, R.E. 1980. Cooperative learning. *Review of Educational Research* 50: 315–42.

Sleeter, C.E. 1991. *Keepers of the American dream: A study of staff development and multicultural education*. Washington, DC: Falmer.

Smedley, A. 1993. *Race in North America*. Boulder, CO: Westview.

Stabler, J.R., J.A. Zeig, & A.B. Rembold. 1976. Children's evaluation of the colors black and white and their interracial play behavior. *Child Study Journal* 6 (4): 191–97.

Van Ausdale, D., & J.R. Feagin. 2001. *The first R: How children learn race and racism*. Lanham, MD: Rowman & Littlefield.

3 Enhancing Development and Learning Through Teacher-Child Relationships

Kathleen Cranley Gallagher and Kelley Mayer

From across the room, Miss Jilane notices that Miguel has lost his toy to another toddler, and he is beginning to lean forward. She has seen Miguel in these frustrating situations before. Calling his name gently, Jilane prevents him from biting his classmate. "Miguel, please help me with snack, I need a great snack helper. When we're done we can play with that toy."

Tamara, the teacher, is sitting on a beanbag chair with Nick, reading a book about cars. They stop the story to talk about their own cars, with Tamara sharing how she likes her truck, and Nick explaining how his minivan has lots of room. They talk about what car Nick might get when he's "big," and what features it might have. They agree it will have to be one that "is safe and goes fast."

Adam, the teacher, is leaning over a set of connecting blocks with first-grader, Krysta. Tears are welling in Krysta's eyes, reflecting the frustration she feels with solving this math problem. Adam reassures Krysta that math can be hard work, and proceeds to "think out loud" with her about how to solve the problem, regrouping the connecting blocks. "You don't have to do math alone, Krysta, it often helps to do it with another person. We can figure this out together."

Some researchers believe that children form ideas about relationships from their early experiences with parents and apply these ideas to other relationships (Sroufe 2000). Others believe that children learn from teachers' modeling, and they imitate teachers' social behavior (Baumrind 1979). It is likely that children use both of these strategies and more to learn how to be in a relationship—one of the most important "skills" children ever learn. While many teachers acknowledge the importance of their role in helping children learn early academic and social skills, they sometimes underestimate the value their personal relationship with a child has on that child's healthy development and learning. As the previous vignettes illustrate, effective teachers use their attunement to and knowledge of every child to scaffold each child's individual development and learning.

This chapter reviews research on relationships between young children and their teachers, with the goal of offering research-proven strategies that teachers can use to develop and sustain high-quality relationships with children ages birth to 8. Quality and influence of teacher-child relationships for infants and toddlers, preschoolers, kindergartners, and primary school children are considered, with ideas for how teachers may reflect on and enhance relationships within their daily classroom routines.

Early relationships and development

High-quality relationships during early childhood support a child's developing social, emotional, and cognitive skills (Goosens & van IJzendoorn 1990; Howes, Galinsky, & Kontos 1998). Children who have secure relationships with their primary caregivers have better language skills (Sroufe 2000), more harmonious peer relationships (Howes, Hamilton, & Matheson 1994; Howes, Matheson, & Hamilton 1994), and fewer behavior problems (Rimm-Kaufman et al. 2002).

In high-quality teacher-child relationships, teachers respond to children's needs appropriately and in a timely manner. Teachers are gentle, and they take frequent opportunities to interact with children face-to-face. When teachers develop high-quality relationships with young children, they support children's problem solving, allowing children to experience success without too much or too little assistance (Copple & Bredekamp 2009).

Teachers in high-quality relationships with young children also support children's learning by assessing children's instructional needs and offering each child support at his or her level. For example, when helping a particular young child comprehend a difficult story, the teacher may introduce key vocabulary words *before* the reading, which helps scaffold the child's understanding of the story and prevents the child from becoming overwhelmed by the complexity of the language in the text. The teachers in the vignettes at the start of this chapter were providing this kind of child-specific support—a delicate dance in which learning

emerges in the context of the teacher-child relationship.

Relationships between teachers and children do not develop in isolation, however. They develop ecologically (Bronfenbrenner & Morris 1998), influenced by many factors such as child and teacher characteristics, interactive processes, and context over time. Teachers certainly set the tone for the relationships, but some children have a behavior style, or temperament, that is challenging (Sturm 2004) and may make relationship building more difficult. Research suggests that children who respond to their environment with intense negative emotion, are highly fearful, or are very resistant to outside guidance are more likely to have relationships with teachers that are less close and higher in conflict (Birch & Ladd 1998).

Children with disabilities, especially language-based disabilities that make communicating their needs more difficult, sometimes have greater difficulty building relationships (Mahoney & Perales 2003). Culture and ethnicity also influence relationships, and some teachers report more conflict in their relationships with children from ethnic minority groups (Gallagher, Kainz et al. 2008) and closer relationships with children who share their culture. Additionally, some teachers report less closeness and more conflict in their relationships with boys than with girls (Birch & Ladd 1998; Gallagher et al. 2006).

To foster a child's development and keep informed about the child's needs and potentials, it is important for teachers to know each child and family well and to "establish positive, personal relationships with each child and each child's family to better understand that child's individual needs, interests and abilities and that family's goals, values, expectations and childrearing practices. Teachers talk with each child and family…and use what they learn to adapt their actions and planning" (Copple & Bredekamp 2009, 18). Children have different needs, and their needs change as they grow and develop. As their needs change, their relationships with teachers change, as well.

For example, in a study examining the stability of teacher-child relationships over the early childhood years (Howes & Hamilton 1992), most children had secure attachment relationships with their child care teacher. When children experienced frequent teacher turnover before their second birthday, they showed less stable attachment relationships with their subsequent teachers. However, older toddlers' (30+ months) relationships with teachers were less affected by teacher turnover. Howes and Hamilton speculated that preschoolers had established expectations that teachers were either stable caregivers in their lives, or they weren't. The implications are that early consistent care has a long-term effect on children's understanding of relationships.

It is important to consider teacher-child relationships across development and schooling, paying particular attention to how the relationship functions to sustain and enhance development at each age. Knowledge of the particular needs of children at each developmental stage will help teachers understand how best to support children in their development and learning. The following sections highlight features of teacher-child relationships for different developmental periods, as well as some ways that teachers and programs can enhance these relationships.

Teachers' relationships with infants and toddlers

In infancy, social interaction forms the basis for the developing brain, supporting development of emotion regulation and attention (Shonkoff & Phillips 2000). Social relationships also teach infants and toddlers what they can expect from interacting with people. By crying, cooing, and

> Social relationships teach infants and toddlers what they can expect from interacting with people.

smiling, infants express their needs and draw adult attention. Adults anticipate, sense, and interpret the infants' behavior and then respond in a timely and appropriate manner. Through positive affect, body language, and tone of voice, adults communicate warmth, positive regard, and safety. The infants, sensing comfort, safety, and security in the presence of the adult, explore their environment and attempt new challenges.

Bowlby (1969) believed that children form cognitive schemas of their interactions with adults and use these schemas to form ideas about self and relationships. For example, infants whose caregiver responds sensitively to their needs learn to expect that their needs will be met and that future interactions with adults will be positive. In these positive interactions, infants come to think that they are "worthy" of these interactions and relationships. In contrast, infants whose needs are not met responsively (or are met inconsistently) learn that they cannot rely on others to care for them. These infants may become detached or aggressive in their relationships (Sroufe 2000).

Before children are 6 months old, it may be difficult to tell the quality of the teacher-child relationship by looking at them. But soon after children begin to creep or crawl, evidence of their relationship with a caregiver is reflected in several behaviors. For instance, the secure infant stays close to a trusted caregiver, watching newcomers with a healthy suspicion. Observational methods of examining qualities of teacher-infant relationships have been important in describing how sensitive and responsive teachers behave and influence children's development (Goosens & van IJzendoorn 1990; Howes & Smith 1995; Howes, Gallinsky, & Kontos 1998).

A sensitive teacher responds to children's cues and comforts distressed children (Howes & Smith 1995; Howes, Gallinsky, & Kontos 1998). The teacher provides multiple opportunities for creative play, engages toddlers in prolonged conversations, and frequently joins in children's play to encourage their successful cognitive development. When children misbehave, the sensitive teacher redirects and gently reminds children of expectations (Howes & Smith 1995; Howes, Gallinsky, & Kontos 1998). The teacher asserts expectations for children's respectful social behavior, while affirming affection for them.

When teachers behave in a sensitive, responsive manner, the child seeks closeness and contact with them (Goosens & van IJzendoorn 1990), shares with them the excitement and discovery in his or her play, and responds to teachers' suggestions and directions readily (Howes & Smith 1995; Howes, Gallinsky, & Kontos 1998). Children who have close relationships with their teacher also have better relationships with other children (Howes, Hamilton, & Matheson 1994; Howes, Matheson, & Hamilton 1994; Howes & Phillipsen 1998). In one study, toddlers who demonstrated a secure relationship with their teacher were less aggressive with peers at 4 years old and more sociable and skilled in imaginative peer play.

Implications for infant/toddler teachers and programs

In consideration of children's developing attachment system, a key role of programs serving infants and toddlers is to support the development of caring, responsive relationships (Copple & Bredekamp 2009). To that end, programs serving infants and toddlers must take care to maintain the lowest child:teacher ratios possible. However, low ratios alone are not sufficient in creating an environment supporting intimacy between teachers and young children (Lally, Torres, & Phelps 1994).

Program environments should be touchable and comfortable. Spaces for infants and toddlers should be inviting and should contain interesting objects and textures to explore, as well as interesting and attractive visual stimuli. The lighting should be soft, and there should be plenty of soft, comfortable seating or floor space where caregivers and children can interact with one another comfortably (Lally, Torres, & Phelps 1994). To provide for infants' and toddlers' need for continuity of care, each child should have one primary caregiver who remains the child's caregiver for as long as possible.

As in all teaching, but particularly with infants and toddlers, teachers need to attend to the individual needs of children in the context of a group (Lally, Torres, & Phelps 1994). In order to respond to infants' and toddlers' individual needs, teachers must be attuned to each child's cues and be keen observers of child behavior. It is essential that programs provide the support teachers need to spend time observing and interpreting their children's behavior. For example, low child:teacher ratios help teachers to provide one-on-one attention, and sufficient allocation of teacher preparation time helps teachers plan for individual children's needs.

Finally, each child lives in a unique family culture that a teacher must understand to develop a quality relationship with the child. Therefore, programs should support teachers' relationships with children's families by setting aside time for communication, conferencing, and home visits.

Teachers' relationships with preschoolers

As children enter preschool, they are typically ready for more complex relationships. Their language, motor, and cognitive abilities allow them to more easily initiate interactions and respond to other people. Preschoolers' readiness for new and more complex relationships is apparent in their engagement in diverse activities and increased interest in the people and world around them.

Interactions with teachers and children are essential to the quality of their relationship and to children's learning and development (Kontos & Wilcox-Herzog 1997a/b). When exploring interactions between teachers and children, researchers observed key teacher behaviors that enhanced relationships with children (Rimm-Kaufman et al. 2002) and supported social and academic competence (Kontos & Wilcox-Herzog 1997a).

Teachers who had high-quality relationships with children helped them to focus their attention and interpret their emotions (Howes & Hamilton 1992). Sensitive and responsive teachers assessed children's learning styles and used that knowledge to meet children's instructional and social needs (Hamre & Pianta 2005). The highest-quality relationships between teachers and children were characterized by closeness (warmth and open communication) and low conflict (hostility and opposition) (Pianta, Hamre, & Stuhlman 2003).

Research has emphasized the importance of intentional, responsive teaching for children's learning in the context of play (Kontos &Wilcox-Herzog 1997a; Lobman 2006). Reflecting a complex set of practices, responsive teaching involves assessing children's individual needs, contextual needs, and cognitive and social competencies and responding in a timely and appropriate manner. Because different children require varying levels and qualities of teacher involvement, responsive teaching is a delicate—but not impossible—dance.

Lobman (2006) elaborated the complex processes of responsive teaching through the lens of theatrical improvisation. Using this lens in a case study, one teacher participated in preschool children's play, leading and responding to innovation, and eventu-

> Preschoolers with close teacher relationships had better school achievement, better social skills, and fewer behavior problems throughout elementary school.

ally leading to more complex, collaborative play. Lobman demonstrated that even subtle language differences within the realm of responsive teaching modified the trajectory of children's engagement with the teacher, peers, objects, and ideas. Collectively, this evidence suggests that what teachers do and say matters highly in children's development and learning.

Close relationships with teachers had remarkable benefits for children. Children who developed close relationships with their teacher explored the classroom environment (Coplan & Prakash 2003) and demonstrated more complex play (Howes, Matheson, & Hamilton 1994) than their peers with less-close relationships with the teacher. Preschoolers with secure relationships with their teacher were sought out more by their playmates (Howes, Matheson, & Hamilton 1994). Finally, preschoolers with close teacher relationships had better school achievement, better social skills, and fewer behavior problems in first grade and throughout elementary school (Hamre & Pianta 2001; Pianta & Stuhlman 2004).

Implications for preschool teachers and programs

Practice that is developmentally appropriate optimizes opportunities and strategies for developing close, positive teacher-child relationships (Copple & Bredekamp 2009). Children should begin the school day with a feeling of warmth and comfort as they transition from their parents' care to their teacher's. Teachers focused on relationships with children take time to recognize children and personally greet children and their families each morning and again at their departure. Acknowledging children's presence and welcoming them involves modeling very basic principles of respect and commitment to relationships.

Teachers can build positive relationships with children by spending time with them in individual and small-group settings. Teachers may improve their relationship with children by engaging in one-on-one activities, such as shared story reading (Gallagher et al. 2006; Gallagher, Sylvester et al. 2008). Story reading with individual children can stimulate conversations about topics that are meaningful to individual children, such as their families, after-school experiences, and pets. Becoming familiar with children's lives and interests helps a teacher better meet their needs, while also modeling for them how to get to know and care about another person. Teachers should also feel comfortable sharing things that are personally important to them. Likewise, children enjoy knowing about their teachers' lives outside of school, and they develop empathy as they come to understand all the different roles people can have in life (e.g., not just "my teacher" but also Sean's mother, a jogger, Mr. Harrison's wife, etc.).

When children experience conflict in their relationships with others, teachers who value relationships understand that the process of learning social skills is challenging and takes time and practice. Teachers can use their own positive relationship with a child to foster that learning; for example, by providing a suitable outlet to express negative feelings. For some children, it might be through conversations. For others writing and drawing to express anger or sadness can help some children reflect and regain control (Mayer 2007).

Teachers' relationships with primary school children

In the primary classroom, teachers usually become responsible for more children, while at the same time having to respond to demands to focus on academics and state standards (Barnett et al. 2005). Despite the greater responsibility to expose children to effective instruction in all content areas, teachers must continue to provide caring environments, in which children feel emotionally supported and valued, if children are going to benefit academically and socially from schooling (Hamre & Pianta 2001; Davis 2003; Pianta, Hamre, & Stuhlman 2003; Klem & Connell 2004; Koomen, van Leeuwen, & van der Leij 2004; La Paro, Rimm-Kaufman, & Pianta 2006).

Furthermore, emerging evidence suggests that teachers' provision of support is even more important for children who are vulnerable to school failure (Henricsson & Rydell 2004; Hamre & Pianta 2005; Hughes, Gleason, & Zhang 2005; Picklo 2005; Hughes & Kwok 2007). High-stakes standards, larger class sizes, and decreased time for informal, relaxed engagement in the primary grades make it much more difficult for teachers to build strong relationships with children.

Research has demonstrated that classroom climate, specifically teachers' emotional and instructional support, is associated with their relationships with children in the primary grades (Hamre & Pianta 2005). Teachers providing high levels of emotional support tended to be aware of the child's needs and interests, to engage in conversations, to exhibit positive affect toward the child, and to maintain high, yet attainable, expectations for student behavior. Highly supportive teachers spent considerable time and effort on literacy instruction, gave children evaluative feedback, encouraged child responsibility, and were conversational (not just didactic) in their instruction (Hamre & Pianta 2005).

In addition to teacher support in the classroom, relationships between teachers and individual children are associated with children's academic growth, social competence, and engagement in the primary grades. When kindergarten teachers' relationships with children were high in conflict, first grade teachers reported more behavior problems and poorer social competence (Stuhlman & Pianta 2002). Subsequently, these children's relationships with their first-grade teachers were associated with their social skills *and* academic achievement in first grade.

Children in close teacher-child relationships participated more in classroom activities (Ladd, Birch, & Buhs 1999), exhibited better work habits (Hamre & Pianta 2001; Baker 2006) and liked school more (Birch & Ladd 1997). Children with high-conflict teacher relationships reported liking school less (Birch & Ladd 1997) and had poorer academic achievement (Hughes, Gleason, & Zhang 2005; Hughes & Kwok 2007).

Quality of the teacher-child relationship also influenced children's relationships with peers in the primary grades. When teachers reported less closeness and more conflict in their relationships with second-graders, these children exhibited more aggression with their classroom peers. When teachers reported closer, lower-conflict relationships with second-graders, the children were more prosocial with classroom peers (Howes 2000).

Implications for primary school teachers and programs

How teachers deliver instruction is important for determining children's success in learning as well as their comfort and security when interacting with the teacher. Primary grade teachers need time for individual instruction with students (Ostrosky & Jung 2003). During this time the teacher can observe and interact with each child while engaged in a learning activity. This helps teachers better assess children's needs. It also gives children opportunities to ask questions and express ideas in a safe space.

As with preschoolers, teachers can build positive relationships with children through interactive storybook reading (Gallagher et al. 2006). Teachers read aloud to children and encourage children's involvement in the story by engaging them in extended conversations about the text and making personal connections (Neuman, Copple, & Bredekamp 2000). These proven comprehension strategies help children process story information and allow teachers opportunities to become familiar with children's personal experiences.

Individual conferences between teachers and children provide opportunities for children to receive both emotional and instructional feedback from teachers. Inviting the involvement of the child's family in the conference can help the teacher build a relationship with the child as well as the child's family. Children can participate in their conferences also, assessing their achievements and setting goals. This enables the children to feel care and support from the multiple adults responsible for their education and to own their own progress.

Teachers can find opportunities to get to know children by having lunch with them or taking time to talk with them on the playground. Primary grade teachers can also get to know children better through participation in after-school activities and events. Attending these events allows teachers to see children immersed in their interactions with family members and peers, helping teachers to learn more about what is important to these children.

Conclusion

Research confirms that "young children benefit from opportunities to develop ongoing, trusting relationships with adults outside the family and with other children. Notably, positive teacher-child relationships promote children's learning and achievement, as well as social competence and emotional development" (Copple & Bredekamp 2009, 13). To appropriately address children's needs, teachers and programs must put children's relationships at the forefront of planning and implementation of interactions and activities.

Putting relationships at the forefront involves recognizing the child, becoming familiar with the child and family, respecting the child's individuality, and committing to the ongoing process of being in the relationship (Gallagher & Mayer 2006). The beauty of working with young children is that while teachers practice building relationships, they also model relationship-building practices.

The privileges of caring for and educating children are not separate. Teachers do both each day, building relationships with children and supporting their development and learning.

[In my role] as a child care director, prospective parents would often ask, "Is your program a daycare or a preschool?" My response was always, "We are both. We cannot care for children without educating them, and we cannot educate children without caring for them." We do both by building relationships.

Updated from the Research in Review article in the November 2008 issue of *Young Children*.

Kathleen Cranley Gallagher is an assistant professor at the University of North Carolina at Chapel Hill. **Kelley Mayer** is an assistant professor at the College of Charleston.

References

Baker, J. 2006. Contributions of teacher-child relationships to positive school adjustment during elementary school. *Journal of School Psychology* 44 (3): 211–29.

Barnett, W.S., J.T. Hustedt, K.B. Robin, & K.L. Schulman. 2005. 2005 state preschool yearbook. In *The state of preschool*. New Brunswick, NJ: National Institute for Early Education Research.

Baumrind, D. 1979. *The development of instrumental competence through socialization.* Paper presented at the Minnesota Symposia on Child Psychology, Minneapolis, MN.

Birch, S.H., & G. Ladd. 1997. The teacher-child relationship and children's early school adjustment. *Journal of School Psychology* 35 (1): 61–79.

Birch, S.H., & G.W. Ladd. 1998. Children's interpersonal behaviors and the teacher-child relationship. *Developmental Psychology* 34 (5): 934–46.

Bowlby, J. 1969. *Attachment and loss, vol. 1: Attachment.* New York: Basic.

Bronfenbrenner, U., & P. Morris. 1998. The ecology of developmental processes. In *Theoretical models of human development*, ed. R.M. Lerner. New York: John Wiley & Sons.

Coplan, R.J., & K. Prakash. 2003. Spending time with teacher: Characteristics of preschoolers who frequently elicity versus initiate interactions with teachers. *Early Childhood Research Quarterly* 18: 143–58.

Copple, C., & S. Bredekamp, eds. 2009. *Developmentally appropriate practice in early childhood programs serving children from birth through age 8.* 3d ed. Washington, DC: NAEYC.

Davis, H.A. 2003. Conceptualizing the role and influence of student-teacher relationships on children's social and cognitive development. *Educational Psychologist* 38 (4): 207–34.

Gallagher, K.C., K. Kainz, K.L. Mayer, & L. Vernon-Feagans. (2008). Development of student-teacher relationships in early education. Unpublished manuscript.

Gallagher, K.C., & K.L. Mayer. 2006. Teacher-child relationships at the forefront of effective practice. *Young Children* 61 (6): 44–49.

Gallagher, K.C., K.L. Mayer, P.R. Sylvester, M.P. Bundy, & P. Fedora. 2006. *Teacher-child relationships and developing literacy and social-emotional skills in pre-kindergarten.* Paper presented at the annual meeting of the American Educational Research Association, San Francisco, CA.

Gallagher, K.C., P.R. Sylvester, K.L. Mayer, & M.P. Bundy. (2008). Storytime in pre-kindergarten: Teacher-child story reading and associations with temperament, development, and teacher-child relationship. Unpublished manuscript.

Goosens, F.A., & M.H. van IJzendoorn. 1990. Quality of infants' attachments to professional caregivers. Relationship to infant-parent attachment and day-care characteristics. *Child Development* 61: 832–37.

Hamre, B.K., & R.C. Pianta. 2001. Early teacher-child relationships and the trajectory of children's school outcomes through eighth grade. *Child Development* 72 (2): 625-638.

Hamre, B.K., & R.C. Pianta. 2005. Can instructional and emotional support in the first-grade classroom make a difference for children at risk for school failure? *Child Development* 76 (5): 949–67.

Henricsson, L., & A.M. Rydell. 2004. Elementary school children with behavior problems: Teacher-child relations and self-perception. A prospective study. *Merrill-Palmer Quarterly* 50 (2): 111–38.

Howes, C. 2000. Social-emotional classroom climate in child care, child-teacher relationships and children's second grade peer relations. *Social Development* 9 (2): 191–204.

Howes, C., E. Galinsky, & S. Kontos. 1998. Child care caregiver sensitivity and attachment. *Social Development* 7 (1): 25–36.

Howes, C., & C.E. Hamilton. 1992. Children's relationships with child care teachers: Stability and concordance with parental attachments. *Child Development* 63: 867–78.

Howes, C., C.E. Hamilton, & C.C. Matheson. 1994. Children's relationships with peers: Differential associations with aspects of the teacher-child relationship. *Child Development* 65: 253–63.

Howes, C., C.C. Matheson, & C.E. Hamilton. 1994. Maternal, teacher, and child care history correlates of children's relationships with peers. *Child Development* 65: 264–73.

Howes, C., & L. Phillipsen. 1998. Continuity in children's relations with peers. *Social Development* 7 (3): 340–49.

Howes, C., & E.W. Smith. 1995. Children and their child care caregivers: Profiles of relationships. *Social Development* 4 (1): 44–61.

Hughes, J., K.A. Gleason, & D. Zhang. 2005. Relationship influences on teachers' perceptions of academic competence in academically at-risk minority and majority first grade students. *Journal of School Psychology* 43 (4): 303–20.

Hughes, J., & O. Kwok. 2007. Influence of student-teacher and parent-teacher relationships on lower achieving readers' engagement and achievement in the primary grades. *Journal of Educational Psychology* 99 (1): 39–51.

Klem, A.M., & J.P. Connell. 2004. Relationships matter: Linking teacher support to student engagement and achievement. *Journal of School Health* 74 (7): 262–73.

Kontos, S., & A. Wilcox-Herzog. 1997a. Influences of children's competence in early childhood classrooms. *Early Childhood Research Quarterly* 12 (3): 247–62.

Kontos, S., & A. Wilcox-Herzog. 1997b. Teachers' interactions with children: Why are they so important? *Young Children* 52 (2): 4–12.

Koomen, H., M. van Leeuwen, & A. van der Leij. 2004. Does well-being contribute to performance? Emotional security, teacher support and learning behaviour in kindergarten. *Infant and Child Development* 13: 253–75.

La Paro, K.M., S.E. Rimm-Kaufman, & R.C. Pianta. 2006. Kindergarten to 1st grade: Classroom characteristics and the stability and change of children's classroom experiences. *Journal of Research in Childhood Education* 21 (2): 189–202.

Ladd, G., S. Birch, & E.S. Buhs. 1999. Children's social and scholastic lives in kindergarten: Related spheres of influence? *Child Development* 70 (6): 1373–400.

Lally, J.R., Y.L. Torres, & P.C. Phelps. 1994. Caring for infants and toddlers in groups: Necessary considerations for emotional, social, and cognitive development. *Zero to Three* 14 (5): 1–8.

Lobman, C.L. 2006. Improvisation: An analytic tool for examining teacher-child interactions in the early childhood classroom. *Early Childhood Research Quarterly* 21 (4): 455–70.

Mahoney, G., & F. Perales. 2003. Using relationship-focused intervention to enhance the social-emotional functioning of young children with autism spectrum disorders. *Topics in Early Childhood Special Education* 23 (2): 77–89.

Mayer, K.L. 2007. Research in Review: Emerging knowledge on emergent writing. *Young Children* 62 (1): 34–40.

Neuman, S.B., C. Copple, & S. Bredekamp. 2000. *Learning to read and write: Developmentally appropriate practices for young children.* Washington, DC: NAEYC.

Ostrosky, M.M., & E.Y. Jung. 2003. Building positive teacher-child relationships. In *What works briefs.* Champaign, IL: Center on the Social and Emotional Foundations for Early Learning.

Pianta, R.C., B.K. Hamre, & M.W. Stuhlman. 2003. Relationships between teachers and children. In *Comprehensive handbook of psychology,* eds. W.M. Reynolds & G.E. Miller. New York: John Wiley & Sons.

Pianta, R.C., & M.W. Stuhlman. 2004. Teacher-child relationships and children's success in the first years of school. *School Psychology Review* 33 (3): 444–58.

Picklo, D.M. 2005. Behaviourally at-risk African American students: The importance of student-teacher relationships for school outcomes. *Dissertation Abstracts, International Section A: Humanities and Social Sciences, ProQuest Information and Learning.*

Rimm-Kaufman, S.E., D.M. Early, M.J. Cox, G. Saluja, R.C. Pianta, & C. Payne. 2002. Early behavioral attributes and teachers' sensitivity as predictors of competent behavior in the kindergarten classroom. *Applied Developmental Psychology* 23: 451–70.

Shonkoff, J.P., & D.A. Phillips, eds. 2000. *From neurons to neighborhoods: The science of early childhood development.* Washington, DC: National Academies Press.

Sroufe, A.L. 2000. Early relationships and the development of children. *Infant Mental Health Journal* 21 (1–2): 67–74.

Stuhlman, M.W., & R.C. Pianta. 2002. Teachers' narratives about their relationships with children: Associations with behavior in classrooms. *School Psychology Review* 31 (2): 148–63.

Sturm, L. 2004. Temperament in early childhood: A primer for the perplexed. *Zero to Three*: 4–11.

Part II

Emotional Development

Introduction

The process of *emotional development* refers to the changes that take place in young children's expression and perception of emotions, in their communication of emotions, and in their ability to regulate their own emotions. Each of these facets of emotional development is essential for the young child to mature, and also important for his or her successful integration into the social group of the classroom. Indeed, emotion regulation and social competence are closely tied.

Five chapters have been selected to provide a cumulative picture of emotional development in young children. Early childhood professionals have daily opportunities to support effective emotional growth in young children; thus, an understanding of the ways in which young children develop in the emotional domain is essential. The last two chapters of this section focus on sources of stress in children's lives, the coping strategies they typically employ, and elements that contribute to resilience in early childhood.

Janet Kuebli and Accalia Kusto provide an updated version of Dr. Kuebli's 1994 article, **"Young Children's Understanding of Everyday Emotions."** The chapter has shifted in focus from the link between young children's understanding of emotion and their language skills to the connection between emotion understanding and social competence. While discussion of the relevance of language development and vocabulary learning related to expressing emotions is still present, a new section, citing recent studies and examples, provides insight into the link between emotional and social understanding. This chapter draws another connection between the research on understanding of emotions and the recent work in the neuroscience of emotional development. A more condensed discussion of relevant theories has been counterbalanced by expanded consideration of culture, siblings, peers, and gender. The chapter aims to provide a firm grounding in the relevance of emotional development to successful peer interactions and highlights the importance of emotional development in preparing children for school.

The second chapter in this section, **"Recognizing and Supporting the Development of Self-Regulation in Young Children,"** is Martha Bronson's update of her 2000 research review. In the nine years since the original publication of this review, interest in the development of self-regulation has increased dramatically, and the literature on the topic has expanded rapidly. Dr. Bronson includes new material on Lev Vygotsky's view that sociodramatic play makes an important contribution in supporting the development of self-regulation. The relevance of sociodramatic play is further emphasized in the suggestions for caregivers and teachers as they support the development of preschool and kindergarten children's self-regulation. This chapter provides early childhood professionals with a nice overview of the development of emotion regulation and how early childhood professionals can support children's growing ability to regulate their emotions.

Over the past few decades, considerably more attention has been paid to the important influence of culture on children's development. Thus, Hermine Marshall's update of her 1989 research review, **"The Development of Self-Concept,"** includes a reconceptualization of the topic by viewing it through *cultural lenses*. The chapter provides updates on the research about how cultural differences affect our views of self-concept, as well as factors that impact children's development of self-concept. The chapter ends with practical suggestions for early childhood educators to help them integrate cultural awareness into their teaching practices.

In 1986, Alice Honig's two-part research review, "Stress and Coping in Children," was published in *Young Children*. In the following 23 years, a considerable amount of new research has been conducted, which is reflected in Dr. Honig's combined and updated, **"Stress and Young Children."** The author provides a thorough review of potential risk factors for stress, taking into consideration changes in society as well as national and world events that have added new sources of stress for children. Recent research related to attachment problems, a range of neurological and physical problems, child gender, and difficult child temperament provides insight into child variables that can be potential stressors. The chapter highlights many sources of stress in children's lives as well as effective techniques that early childhood professionals can apply to help children cope with difficult, stress-producing circumstances in their lives.

The final chapter in this section is an update of Emmy Werner's 1984 research review, **"Resilient Children."** The version published in this volume, by Dr. Werner and Eva Essa, takes into consideration the wealth of new research that has been conducted since, including recent outcomes from longitudinal studies that were discussed in the earlier article. This particular chapter responds well to the previous chapter by Dr. Honig; the authors provide in-depth insight into factors that protect and buffer children who face a host of risks. Specifically relevant to early childhood professionals is the finding that poor developmental outcomes are not inevitable for children exposed to a range of severe adversities. The authors of this chapter conclude with specific strategies for those working with vulnerable populations of young children to enhance children's resilience, thus improving their outcomes.

These chapters will provide early childhood professionals with an overview of topics related to emotional development. Knowledge of emotional development will lead to a deeper understanding of children's emotional lives, thus improving early childhood professionals' ability to appropriately respond to children's growing capacity to express both ordinary and more intense emotions.

4 Young Children's Understanding of Everyday Emotions

Janet Kuebli and Accalia R. Kusto

What young children understand about emotion states and behaviors is of importance to early childhood educators who must deal with children's feelings daily. Children, like adults, experience many emotions in the course of each day. Strong emotions arising from their own experiences may be very confusing for children. Making sense of other people's emotional reactions may also challenge children. The need to support young children's emotion understanding is especially clear when they encounter traumatic life events, such as parents divorcing or someone in the family becoming very sick or dying.

Children also benefit from help in understanding everyday emotions. Teachers and parents, for example, suggest to children how they can cope with distress, fear, or shyness on the first day of school or explain how feeling sad and happy at the same time is normal when a friend moves away. Sometimes adults urge children to talk about their anger or sadness as a way of handling minor daily conflicts or setbacks. By helping children to understand emotions, parents and teachers hope to help them channel their feelings in posi-

tive ways and to prepare them to deal with similar experiences in the future.

As children mature, adults also expect them to master their emotions to some extent. Learning how to express some feelings and mask others is a common, everyday lesson in children's lives. Parents may teach children to mask a sad feeling with a smile when an excited friend goes off to summer camp. Hochschild (1983) called this learning how to do "emotion work."

Getting along with others often means learning to manage feelings in a socially acceptable fashion. Children who get mad because they have to wait their turn or who laugh at a tearful child who has fallen and skinned a knee are often reminded to think about how others feel. A child who overexuberantly boasts about winning may be urged to remember how it feels to lose. The ability to regulate and manage emotions is a key component of social competence and often is a sign that a child is ready for new challenges (Denham, Bassett, & Wyatt 2007).

Researchers over the last couple of decades have shown keen interest in the nature of children's understanding of emotion, especially as it relates to social-cognitive development. Much of this work has concerned school-age children. Results from these studies suggest, not surprisingly, that emotion understanding becomes more complex and sophisticated during the elementary school years. In a review of the literature, Denham and Kochanoff (2002) noted that at these ages, children understand and can enact social guidelines for emotion expression and use cognitive strategies for regulating their emotions.

School-age children also can appreciate that they can experience more than one emotion at a time, even emotions of opposing valences (e.g., happy and sad), and they can understand complex emotions such as those that involve self-evaluations (e.g., pride, guilt, shame). Moreover, they can take into greater account the situations that cause emotional reactions (Brody & Harrison 1987; Camras & Allison 1989; Lagattuta, Wellman, & Flavell 1997; Lagattuta & Wellman 2001).

Research also has begun to yield information about what preschool-age children know about emotions and how this early understanding develops. At the heart of the studies with young children are two related issues. The first issue concerns identifying links between early developments in emotion understanding and social competence. The second issue centers on how preschoolers' emotion understanding is socialized in the course of children's interactions with others. One major conclusion derived from these studies is that conversations about feelings are an important context for learning about emotions and how to manage them.

This chapter begins with a brief review of the general nature of emotional experience. The focus shifts to studies describing children's early emotion understanding, followed by research on how emotions are discussed by young children with others. The studies described here, while not exhaustive of the work in this area, provide a selective overview of what

is known about how emotion understanding develops in young children. Finally, suggestions are offered for ways that teachers can use these findings to facilitate children's understanding of their own and others' feelings.

Emotional experience

According to Lewis (Lewis & Michalson 1983; Lewis 1992), emotional behavior consists of multiple components. One of these components, *emotional experience*, refers to how people interpret and evaluate their emotions. Other components include (1) emotion states and (2) their expression, either verbal or nonverbal (e.g., changes in facial expressions, physical posture, or movement).

The componential model of emotion proposes that emotional experiences, states, and expressions do not always correspond to each other, nor do they necessarily develop in sync. Sometimes people are unaware of their emotions or simply unable to name the particular feelings they are having. At other times, someone might intentionally express one emotion while experiencing a different feeling or might recognize what the feeling is but lack insight into the reasons for it.

Among these various emotion components, emotional experience is considered the most cognitive (Lewis & Saarni 1985) because it relies on basic mental processes of attention, perception, and memory. That is, unless a person can pay attention to and recall his or her emotions, that person cannot begin to understand them. Further, emotional experience consists of cognitive judgments and insights about emotion states and expressions. Emotional experience, in effect, depends on a person being able to "introspect," or reflect upon himself or herself (Lewis 1992). Cognitive processes bring emotions into consciousness and provide the basis for emotional experiences.

Researchers hypothesize that having a self-concept is a fundamental developmental prerequisite for emotional experience; that is, children need a sense of an "I" who owns and knows her own emotion states and expressions in order to experience them. Even prior to forming a self-concept, however, children acquire several important cognitive skills related to self-understanding that may also underlie their capacity for emotional experience.

Collectively these skills are known as *self-referential behaviors*. They are first evident between 15 and 24 months of age and include acquiring: (1) an awareness of oneself as separate from others, (2) knowledge that objects independent of oneself have a permanent existence, (3) a sense of oneself as a causal agent, and (4) the ability to visually recognize oneself (Bertenthal & Fischer 1978; Lewis & Brooks-Gunn 1979; Sroufe 1979; Kagan 1981; Harter 1983; Lewis et al. 1989).

Awareness of self forms the foundation for the child's initial self-concept, enabling children to make themselves objects of thought. Thereafter, emotional experience probably develops gradually, most likely in concert with changes in children's self-concepts, thus explaining why children have emotions and express them before they are able to reflect upon and understand those feelings (Michalson & Lewis 1985; Lewis 1992). Nonetheless, emotions become integral to children's developing sense of who they are, and emotions help them to interact successfully with the world around them.

Young children's emotion understanding

Emotion theorists suspect that learning to talk is a second critical factor in the development of emotional knowledge and experience. At the beginning, simply acquiring word labels for emotions is important for children's developing understanding of emotions (see Table). Parents start referring

> In order to experience emotions, children need a sense of an "I" who owns and knows her own emotion states and expressions.

to emotions in conversations with their children almost from birth. Emotion talk enables parents and others to draw children's attention to emotional expressions.

However, children's emotional self-understanding may start with being able to name emotion states and behaviors (for a review of research on how children learn to talk about emotions, see Bretherton et al. 1986). By 36 months, children use emotion words to refer to both self and others, and in reference to events in the present, past, and future (Bretherton & Beeghly 1982). This finding suggests that children's early emotion understanding of themselves and of others may be closely related rather than developing separately.

Studies investigating emotion understanding and theory of mind demonstrate how the development of emotion understanding is linked to social understanding. *Theory of mind* refers to children's recognition of mental states (i.e., beliefs, desires, and intentions) in themselves and in others and knowledge of how these states influence behavior (Olson, Astington, & Harris 1988; Wellman, Cross, & Watson 2001). In other words, possessing a theory of mind corresponds to having a psychological understanding of others.

In an early study about children's first words, mothers reported that their children used more emotion words (e.g., *sad, scary, happy*) than mental-state terms (e.g., *knowing, remembering, dreaming*) (Bretherton & Beeghly 1982). Notably, children also talked about causes for emotions more often than for other kinds of internal states (i.e., mental, physiological, or perceptual). For instance, children's talk included more about what causes sadness than what causes memory or physical pain.

Some Characteristics of Young Children's Emotion Language and Understanding

Approximate age of child	Description
Birth to 18 months	Display emotions and respond to emotions in others at preverbal stage
	Use emotion cues of others to guide own responses to new or ambiguous situations
	Do not produce or comprehend emotion terms with a few exceptions
18 to 20 months	Use first emotion words in vocabulary (e.g., cry, happy)
	Begin to discuss emotions spontaneously in conversations with others
	Experience self-conscious emotions (e.g., pride, guilt)
2 to 3 years	Increase emotion vocabulary most rapidly
	Correctly label simple emotions in self and others, and talk about past, present, and future emotions
	Talk about the causes and consequences of some emotions and identify emotions associated with certain situations
	Use emotion language in pretend play
4 to 5 years	Show increased capacity to verbally reflect on emotions and to consider more complex relations between emotions and situations
	Understand that the same event may call forth different feelings in different people and that feelings sometimes persist long after the events that caused them
	Demonstrate growing awareness about controlling and managing emotions in accord with social standards
6 to 11 years	Exhibit conceptual advances in their understanding of complex emotions (e.g., pride and shame) and of mixed or multiple emotions
	Show marked improvements in the ability to suppress or conceal negative emotional reactions and in the use of self-initiated strategies for redirecting feelings
	Take into fuller account the events leading to emotional reactions

Additional links between emotion and mental-state understanding are demonstrated in several studies examining young children's ability to predict and explain emotional reactions of story characters. Lagattuta (Lagattuta, Wellman, & Flavell 1997; Lagattuta & Wellman 2001) presented children with stories about a character who is reminded of a past experience (e.g., losing a dog) by an external cue (e.g., seeing a dog that looks like the lost pet). In these studies, children as young as 3 years of age demonstrated an understanding that another person's mental state can lead to certain emotional reactions (e.g., sadness) for *that* person but not necessarily for other people (e.g., not everyone would be saddened by seeing the dog). Notably, all children performed better when explaining negative emotions (rather than positive ones), regardless of the amount or type of details in the story.

To further explore how emotional situations might facilitate children's understanding of others, Lagattuta and Wellman (2002) analyzed everyday parent-child discussions about positive versus negative emotions. Findings supported the researchers' initial hypotheses: Parent-child conversations about past negative emotions involved higher frequency of talk about emotion causes and links to mental states, and thus were more complex, than did conversations about positive emotions.

As children got older, frequency of discussions about causal explanations and links to mental states increased. In general, these findings underscore the importance of emotion understanding as a special context for the development of children's psychological understanding of themselves and others.

Denham and Zoller (1991) were particularly interested in what preschoolers think about the causes of various emotions. They showed children puppets with happy, sad, fearful, or angry faces and then asked them to think of what would make the puppets "feel that way." Results indicated that the children more often associated happiness with nonsocial causes (e.g., playing or going somewhere, without reference to being with others) than with social ones. By contrast, the reasons children gave for sadness and anger were mostly social in nature. Children said that being hurt or left by others caused sadness, whereas their reasons for anger included being punished, fighting, or not liking someone else. Again, negative emotions seemed to enhance children's social awareness.

Overall, young children's understanding of the causes of emotion approaches the understanding of adults around the age of 4 (Denham & Kochanoff 2002). Some preschoolers also recognize that a single event sometimes triggers different feelings in different people (Gove & Keating 1979; Lagattuta, Wellman, & Flavell 1997; Denham & Kochanoff 2002).

The complexity of this understanding increases throughout the preschool years, with older children being more likely to cite personality, external, or abstract factors as causes for emotions (Lagattuta, Wellman, & Flavell 1997; Lagattuta & Wellman 2001; Denham & Kochanoff 2002). What preschoolers can tell adults about the causes of emotions reflects, therefore, what they understand about the thoughts and feelings of others.

Competence

Emotion understanding additionally predicts aspects of children's socially competent behavior (Saarni 1999; Izard et al. 2001; Denham & Kochanoff 2002; Denham, Bassett, & Wyatt 2007; Denham et al. 2007). Prosocial behavior and empathy are good indicators of a socially competent child, although sometimes teacher or peer nominations are used to measure this outcome. Denham and colleagues (2002) assessed 3- to 5-year-olds' understanding of emotion expressions and guidelines for expression by asking children to:

1. label and assign facial expressions to puppets in certain situations;

2. report how a story character felt in situations of mixed emotions; and

3. explain how a story character would both feel and look in situations in which expressing their emotion was socially inappropriate (e.g., receiving a disappointing gift).

One year later, children who had demonstrated emotional competence across the three tasks now displayed more prosocial emotions and were better at inhibiting aggression; children who had shown deficits in emotion understanding were more likely now to display anger and aggression, both as observed in the classroom and as rated by teachers.

Emotion understanding in preschoolers ages 3 to 5 attending Head Start programs were the focus of another study (Miller et al. 2006). In interviews, children's emotion knowledge was assessed in terms of their ability to label emotion expressions, understand emotion situations, and read others' feelings. In addition, teachers' ratings provided measures of children's emotion regulation and social adjustment at school.

Of interest here, children with more emotion knowledge were perceived by teachers to have more positive emotion regulation abilities, such as showing empathy for others. However, emotion knowledge did not predict teachers' ratings of children's dysregulation of emotion, such as poor anger management. These results suggest that emotional competence is multifaceted, and its links with children's emotion understanding are complex and not yet fully understood.

Given the important role emotion knowledge plays in social functioning, researchers also work to understand how emotion understanding develops. What they find is that through interactions with others, children learn about emotions.

Socialization of emotion understanding

Recent advances in technology have led to the study of the role of brain and neural processes, as well as genetic factors, in emotion regulation development (Goldsmith & Davidson 2004). However, even within this emerging literature, researchers emphasize the impact that everyday situations can have on emotions and that finding the best way to study neural processes in such situations is a challenge for the up-and-coming field of affective neuroscience (Campos, Frankel, & Camras 2004).

Research focused on identifying experiences in children's lives that influence the particular forms of emotion understanding plays an important role in what teachers know about children's emotion knowledge. A key assumption is that children's insights into their own emotions are socially shaped in important ways (e.g., Lutz 1985; Gordon 1989). Whereas research on emotional aspects of social competence has concentrated on older children, studies examining how emotions are socialized have been conducted with younger children (Denham, Bassett, & Wyatt 2007).

The goal of *emotion socialization* is to redirect or change children's spontaneously expressed emotions so that they conform more closely to social rules or conventions. Sometimes this means substituting one feeling for a different one, as when someone cheers for a friend who has just won first place despite her own loss or looks on the bright side of things that worry or sadden him.

How does socialization occur?

Saarni (1985; Saarni & Crowley 1990) first outlined general processes by which emotions may be socialized. Saarni highlighted adult behaviors as the starting point for emotion socialization, although Eisenberg, Cumberland, and Spinrad (1998) later cautioned that child characteristics and the adult-child relationship itself not be overlooked. For example, impulsive children may be more likely to express any emotion they feel, thereby eliciting more socialization behaviors from their parents. Unfortunately, socialization research has been slow to rise to Eisenberg's challenge. Consequently, most of what is known about how emotions are socialized still focuses on what adults do.

According to Saarni, *direct socialization* refers to occasions when adults chide or praise children's immediately prior emotional behaviors. In this case, an adult's behavior contingently reinforces the child's expression of emotions, providing explicit information about the way certain emotions are valued by others. Didactic teaching is another form of direct socialization often used with children to convey social conventions for expressing emotions. A parent may, for example, instruct that "girls don't brag" about their successes or that "boys don't cry" about their failures.

Second, emotions are socialized indirectly. A classic example is when a child imitates the emotional reactions of another person, such as when one child's fearful reluctance to try something new is copied by another child who was unafraid only moments before. There are times when uncontrolled laughter seizes a group of children one by one or sadness sweeps through a classroom. These examples demonstrate how one person's emotional reactions are "catching."

Adults also provide ready models, of course, for children's emotional reactions. Research shows that infants will use social referencing; that is, they will scan a caregiver's face in search of cues for the appropriate emotional response when faced with a situation in which they do not know how to react (e.g., Feinman & Lewis 1983).

The family's emotional climate can also impact children's emotion understanding, because children learn about emotion expression by observing how emotions are handled at home. In one study, children from families who tended

> Infants will scan a caregiver's face in search of cues for the appropriate emotional response when they do not know how to react.

to communicate emotions nonverbally (i.e., through facial expressions and body language) more frequently than other families were less skilled at displaying posed emotional expressions (e.g., making a convincing sad face when asked) and at judging certain aspects of affective communication (Halberstadt 1986); these differences persisted as children got older, suggesting that children learn about emotions from their family environment.

Another example of indirect socialization through the family climate can be seen in studies of preschoolers' awareness of parental discord. Children who experienced marital discord in their families avoided playing with other children (i.e., avoided having fun) and had difficulty regulating emotions such as anger (Gottman & Katz 1989). Similar problems are evident in young children who have witnessed conflict and violence in their communities (Hughes 1988; Shahinfar, Fox, & Leavitt 2000). The message from studies such as these is that preschoolers learn about emotion states, expressions, and events by watching and being exposed to the emotional behaviors of others.

A third channel for emotion socialization involves expectancy communication. Saarni and Crowley (1990) identified *emotion expectancies* as beliefs about how emotions should be felt and expressed that adults convey to children in anticipation of children's experiences with emotionally charged events. Saarni and Crowley likened the process to hypnosis, in which adults plant "suggestions" in children's minds about how to respond in certain situations.

An example of emotion expectancies are *display rules*, defined as social or cultural guidelines for the appropriate management of emotional responses in a situation (Ekman & Friesen 1969; Saarni 1979; Gnepp & Hess 1986). A common display rule in the United States is that people should show gratitude even when receiving a disappointing gift. Before gifts are opened at a child's birthday party, parents may have conversations with their child about appropriate emotional expressions. Other display rules may call for neutralizing a felt emotion by showing a "poker face." If children subsequently encounter similar situations, they may use this information to guide their own emotional responses. In this way, children remember and act at later times on information previously acquired about emotions.

So, when adults tell, for example, about how they felt afraid (or excited) their first time on a Ferris wheel ride or sleeping away from home, these verbal suggestions may be internalized as expectancies on which the child subsequently relies. By such means, Saarni and Crowley (1990) contended, strategies for managing emotions initiated "outside" the child are imported into children's own private, emotional lives.

Influence of language on emotional socialization

Most perspectives on emotion socialization emphasize the importance of language, particularly everyday social speech. Seeds of this modern theoretical stance can be found in classic writings by Cooley (1902), Mead (1956), and Vygotsky (1978), and it has been supported by research. Denham and colleagues (2007) concluded that children's emotion knowledge and regulation are enhanced in contexts in which adults discuss and elaborate on children's emotion experiences.

Some researchers speculate that talking about emotions provides children with "reflective distance" from their feeling states (Stern 1985; Bretherton et al. 1986; Dunn, Brown, & Beardsall 1991; Laible

& Song 2006). Discussing emotions may distance children from the rush and immediacy of emotions and permit them to interpret and evaluate their feelings and reflect upon causes and consequences.

Emotion discourse may further allow adults and children to work out socially acceptable meanings of feeling states. Especially significant may be how adults interpret and attribute meaning to children's own emotional behavior. Talking about the past with young children appears to be an especially rich context for fostering emotion understanding. Laible and Song (2006) found that emotion talk during mother-child conversations about past emotion-related events in preschoolers' lives exceeded the amount of emotion talk during joint book reading.

Emotion socialization through talk is also evident during other everyday family interactions. Garner (2006) conducted two-hour home visits with African-American preschoolers and their mothers. Close attention was paid to maternal emotion socialization behaviors during cleanup after a snack. Of particular interest were instances when mothers comforted their children or when mothers expressed, mentioned, or explained emotions to their children. Two weeks later, children were again observed at their preschools during interactions with their peers.

Garner found that children of mothers who engaged in more emotion conversation behaviors at home were better emotionally regulated at school. Parent-child conversations about feelings appear to promote children's enhanced understanding of others, which, "in turn, shapes our selves, our social interactions, and our cultural identities" (Lagattuta & Wellman 2002, 578).

Indeed, children begin as preschoolers to formulate emotion concepts specific to their own culture or subculture (Lutz 1983; Lutz & White 1986; Miller & Sperry 1987). Emotion concepts are embedded in broader cultural knowledge about situations and social relationships. How children come to understand emotions depends on the particular cultural vocabulary and meaning systems available to children for talking about emotions (Levy 1984; Lutz & White 1986; Gordon 1989) and on existing social norms for ways emotions should be felt and expressed. Thus, group differences in children's emotion understanding, both between and within cultures, are to be expected.

Both psychologists and anthropologists have studied how emotions are variously viewed and talked about in different cultures. A growing number of cross-cultural studies have suggested that how adults approach childrearing is related to their cultural knowledge and beliefs about emotions (Lutz & White 1986; Miller & Sperry 1987; Markus & Kitayama 1991). For example, Americans and Chinese identify different types of causes for pride (Stipek, Weiner, & Li 1989), and Japanese culture emphasizes shame more than other groups do (Lewis 1992).

Emotions that are downplayed or left undefined in some cultures are central to how other cultures make sense of experiences. A Pacific Island group called the Ifaluk does not talk about "emotions"; instead they have words related to their "insides" that often refer to experiences unfamiliar to English-speaking groups (Lutz 1982). Children growing up in a rural Peruvian village that values inhibition of emotions understand causal connection between beliefs and emotions later (around 8 years old) than British children typically do (around 5–6 years old) (Tenenbaum et al. 2004).

Even when parents do discuss emotions with their children, depending on cultural values, they may intend these conversations to serve different functions. Reminiscing is intended in Euro-American families to encourage children to develop emotion regulation skills and an indepen-

> **Emotions that are downplayed or left undefined in some cultures are central to how other cultures make sense of experiences.**

dent self, while talking about past experiences in Chinese families serves to help children form emotional bonds with others and to internalize moral lessons (Wang & Fivush 2005).

In one classic study (Miller & Sperry 1987), researchers interviewed three working-class mothers of 2½-year-old daughters and observed how the mothers socialized anger and aggression. Notably, the mothers led lives in which violence and aggression were all too commonplace; they typically discussed these events in their daughters' presence but usually while talking to other family members or friends.

One child's own stories about anger and aggression were closely patterned after her mother's recollections. These mothers also sometimes intentionally provoked their daughters' anger by teasing or trading insults with them. They explained their actions as a way of teaching their daughters how to stand up for themselves.

Influence of family on emotional socialization

The focus in most studies on emotion socialization has been on children and their mothers. However, some studies have considered how siblings, peers, and fathers contribute to emotion socialization of young children. One study (Dunn, Bretherton, & Munn 1987) observed family interactions at home, first when younger siblings were 18 months old and again later, when they were 24 months old. Researchers found that family references to emotion states and to their causes and consequences increased from the first visit to the second. Moreover, the more frequently that mothers and older siblings had referred to feeling states at the

18-month home visit, the more often the younger sibling talked about emotions at the 24-month visit.

In other research, Dunn and Kendrick (1982) found that 2- and 3-year-olds whose mothers commented more often about what the children's new baby sibling might be feeling, the more likely were the older children to have friendly interactions with that younger sibling one year later. However, Dunn and her associates also examined sibling conflicts as contexts for emotion socialization. Between the ages of 14 and 36 months, younger siblings' ability to tease and upset their older siblings increased significantly (Dunn & Munn 1985; Dunn, Brown, & Beardsall 1991). This finding demonstrates how young children are learning to anticipate and influence others' feelings. Finally, 3-year-olds from families with more emotion talk showed at age 6 a better understanding of others' emotions (Dunn, Brown, & Beardsall 1991). These results further support the claim that family emotion talk provides an important context for learning about feelings.

In a study of child-peer interactions, children who talked more about emotions with their friends interacted in a more cooperative manner than did children who shared less emotion talk (Brown, Donelan-McCall, & Dunn 1996). A later study found that friendship quality was affected both by the child's emotion knowledge and also by the emotion knowledge of the friend (Dunn & Cutting 1999). One specific finding was that a child's conflict resolution skills were related to the emotions expressed within the child-peer dyad (Dunn & Herrera 1997; Dunn & Cutting 1999).

One possible source of individual differences in children's emotion understanding is gender. Especially intriguing in this regard are reports of differences in how mothers talk about emotions with daughters and with sons. In the study by Dunn, Bretherton, and Munn (1987), for example, references to emotions were more frequent in mother-daughter than mother-son conversations at both 18 and 24 months; by 24 months, girls also talked about feeling states more often than boys did.

Gender differences were also reported by Fivush (1989; 1991) in studies where mothers talked with children about specific events in their child's past. In one study with 30- to 35-month-olds, Fivush (1989) found that mothers attributed more talk about sadness to daughters and more talk about anger to sons. Mother-daughter pairs also focused more on feelings, whereas mother-son pairs were more apt to discuss causes and consequences for emotions.

In related research, adult women were more likely than men to say they were emotional, to value the expression of emotions, and to report experiencing a variety of emotions (Allen & Hamsher 1974; Allen & Haccoun 1976; Balswick & Avertt 1977; Fitzpatrick & Indvik 1982). Yet there is some evidence that fathers, like mothers, may also talk differently about past emotions with daughters than with sons. When mothers and fathers individually talked about past events with 3- to 4-year-olds, they each talked about a greater number and variety of emotions with daughters than they did with sons; sadness was again more often a topic in conversations with girls (Kuebli & Fivush 1992; Fivush et al. 2000).

More recently, Wang and Fivush (2005) found that Chinese mothers attributed more negative than positive emotions to their daughters but not to their sons. However, talk about emotion resolutions and explanations did not differ by child gender. These results suggest that girls' and boys' emotional lives may be socialized in somewhat different ways.

While some studies like these find gender-related patterns in emotion socialization, others have not. Indeed, current investigations of mother-child emotion-related conversations are less apt to focus primarily on gender in investigations. Emotion researchers' attention has turned lately to investigations of child characteristics other than gender, such as temperament, that may predict individual differences in emotion regulation (e.g., Blair et al. 2004) and that also may yield new insights about variation in young children's developing emotion understanding.

Applications for early childhood educators

Emotion understanding is but one aspect of emotional and social competence. Certainly, studies examining the practices of teachers as emotion socializing agents have not kept pace with research on emotion socialization in families. However, some studies suggest that preschool curriculums focused on emotion and social skills, as implemented by the teacher, improve the classroom emotional climate and result in more social-emotionally competent children (Domitrovich, Cortes, & Greenberg 2007; Raver et al. 2008). Fantuzzo and colleagues (2007) concluded that social and emotional competence constitutes a "constellation of skills [that] strongly relates to school readiness and future school success" (46).

For educators and parents, it is certainly not earthshaking to find that children learn about emotions from them; but emotions are sometimes so "close to the skin" and fleeting that it is easy for feelings to slip out of one's conscious awareness. As teachers and parents become conscious of the roles they play in children's emotion socialization, they are empowered to provide children with better opportunities in their daily lives for understanding themselves and others.

Teachers have some unique occasions for structuring children's activities in ways that can encourage children to talk about their own and others' emotions. Making this type of learning a priority will help prepare preschoolers for the emotional and

> Making learning a priority will help prepare preschoolers for the emotional and social demands of kindergarten.

social demands of kindergarten and establish a long-term foundation for successfully interacting with their world. Consider the following recommendations for meeting this objective.

1. Evaluate whether the emotional climate of the classroom itself is conducive to expressing emotions

In other words, teachers need to legitimate children's feelings in order for children to feel it is acceptable to talk about and reflect upon their emotions. Leavitt and Power (1989) contend that adults give meaning to children's emotions when they recognize and respond to children's feelings.

Essentially, this means entering into authentic emotional relationships with children and regarding them as "emotional associates" (Leavitt & Power 1989, 37) who are capable of interpreting and understanding their own and others' emotions. Children's emotional expressiveness and receptivity to emotion socialization will be enhanced if this is a warm relationship and the classroom climate is positive (Denham et al. 2007; Domitrovich, Cortes, & Greenberg 2007; Raver et al. 2008).

2. Pay attention to the physical environments in which children may learn about feelings

Play centers no doubt vary in the opportunities they afford for emotional engagement and reflection. Family living or dramatic play areas, for example, may encourage children to act out social interactions into which emotions figure. Well-stocked play centers can also provide suggestions to children's imaginations for reworking earlier emotional altercations or experiences. Similarly, puppets and dolls are excellent vehicles for emotion play.

Research suggests that greater emotional self-awareness is evident in children who engage in pretend play with more-experienced play partners (Galyer & Evans 2001). Introduce themes and ask questions that prompt children to vicariously explore the causes and consequences of emotions. Therefore, either from the sidelines or as players, adults can observe how individual children play out emotion scripts dramatically.

3. Use the arts center as another valuable context for emotion conversation

Encourage children to make pictures that tell about past personal events in their lives. This idea, borrowed from therapists who work with disturbed children, adapts well for children whose "troubles" are within the typical range of life experiences. Children might be encouraged to "draw about the time when..." they were upset with another child, afraid of something new, and so forth. Engaging children in conversations about their pictures, either as they are drawing or afterward, can give children chances to reflect upon their emotions.

Children can also dictate the stories and feelings that go with their pictures. Older children may want to construct longer picture stories, several pages in length. Sometimes, children will enjoy "reading" back their picture stories to someone else, either during group times or on their own to other children and teachers.

4. Make available stories written for children as a resource for talking about emotions

Books can be selected that show other children being emotional and dealing with their feelings. Children and teachers can discuss the causes and consequences of story characters' emotions and then link the emotions with children's own experiences. Certainly other media (e.g., TV, movies, plays, children's magazines) provide similar options.

5. Use tape recorders and video equipment

Children can make audio or video recordings of each other telling stories in which they recreate emotions. Subsequent sharing of these recordings can serve as a springboard for later discussion about the choices children have in responding to their own or others' emotions. Audiovisual projects can also be sources of collaborative production and pride. A teacher shows children that she values their emotions if she puts the emotion work they do in projects of this sort on display for others to see and share. Invite an audience of parents or other classes, or put children's story tapes or CDs on loan for other children's listening.

6. Deal with children's quarrels and disputes in a context that helps children develop their understanding of emotions

Research suggests that negative emotions may be somewhat better than positive emotions as opportunities for children to acquire emotion knowledge. Fighting children learn more about anger and aggression if teachers do more than simply separate them. Allow each child to "tell what happened" from his or her perspective without interruption by the other participant(s). Teachers can convey back what the child says, asking for any corrections or clarifications, before calling on the other child to tell his or her part in the altercation. All children should be urged to examine their personal contributions to the conflict. Teachers can also ask children to talk about how the events made them feel and how they think the other child feels, along with what they each could do differently next time.

In this way teachers can help children to manage their feelings rather than simply to suppress or deny them. In fact, using these opportunities didactically, as moments of clarification or sharing of feelings rather than as times for preaching or correction, is associated with more prosocial expressivity by children (Denham et al. 2007). Leavitt and Power (1989) claim that by being didactic, teachers enhance children's ability to develop authentic emotion understandings and relationships.

Conclusion

The research base on young children's emotion understanding and socialization continues to grow. Based on what is known so far, however, parents and teachers can expect that children will show individual differences in the kinds of emotion understandings they possess. Differences will be apparent among children of different ages and even in the rate at which age-mates gain new insights into emotions; moreover, children's family backgrounds and histories are likely to translate into different ways of conceptualizing and using emotions.

Cross-cultural evidence on emotion understanding should make teachers particularly sensitive to multicultural variation in the ways emotions figure in children's lives. Despite the differences, however, research also suggests that the basic processes by which children learn about emotions are similar, although more needs to be learned about the nature of these mechanisms.

What is, perhaps, fundamentally important is realizing that a great deal of what young children understand about feelings is learned in the informal curriculum provided by their social interactions with others. Emotions frequently are at the heart of these interactions, and children may greatly benefit socially when caring adults direct their attention to talking about these experiences.

Updated from the Research in Review article in the March 1994 issue of *Young Children*.

Janet Kuebli is a psychologist at Saint Louis University. **Accalia R. Kusto** is a doctoral student at Saint Louis University.

References

Allen, J.G., & D.M. Haccoun. 1976. Sex differences in emotionality: A multidimensional approach. *Human Relations* 29: 711–22.

Allen, J.G., & J.H. Hamsher. 1974. The development and validation of a test of emotional styles. *Journal of Consulting and Clinical Psychology* 42: 663–68.

Balswick, H., & C.P. Avertt. 1977. Differences in expressiveness: Gender, interpersonal orientation, and perceived parental expressiveness as contributing factors. *Journal of Marriage and the Family* 39: 121–27.

Bertenthal, B.I., & K.W. Fischer. 1978. Development of self-recognition in the infant. *Developmental Psychology* 14: 44–50.

Blair, K.A., S.A. Denham, A. Kochanoff, & B. Whipple. 2004. Playing it cool: Temperament, emotion regulation, and social behavior in preschoolers. *Journal of School Psychology* 42: 419–43.

Bretherton, I., & M. Beeghly. 1982. Talking about internal states: The acquisition of an explicit theory of mind. *Developmental Psychology* 18: 906–21.

Bretherton, I., J. Fritz, C. Zahn-Waxler, & D. Ridgeway. 1986. Learning to talk about emotions: A functionalist perspective. *Child Development* 57: 529–48.

Brody, L.R., & R.H. Harrison. 1987. Development changes in children's abilities to match and label emotionally laden situations. *Motivation and Emotion* 11: 347–65.

Brown, J.R., N. Donelan-McCall, & J. Dunn. 1996. Why talk about mental states? The significance of children's conversations with friends, siblings, and mothers. *Child Development* 67: 836–49.

Campos, J.J., C.B. Frankel, & L. Camras. 2004. On the nature of emotion regulation. *Child Development* 75: 377–94.

Camras, L.A., & K. Allison. 1989. Children's and adults' beliefs about emotion elicitation. *Motivation and Emotion* 13: 53–70.

Cooley, C.H. 1902. *Human nature and the social order*. New York: Scribner's.

Denham, S.A., H.H. Bassett, & T. Wyatt. 2007. The socialization of emotional competence. In *Handbook of socialization: Theory and research*, eds. J.E. Grusec & P.D. Hastings, 614–37. New York: Guilford.

Denham, S.A., S. Caverly, M. Schmidt, K. Blair, E. DeMulder, S. Caal, et al. 2002. Preschool understanding of emotions: Contributions to classroom anger and aggression. *Journal of Child Psychology and Psychiatry* 43: 901–16.

Denham, S.A., & A. Kochanoff. 2002. "Why is she crying?" Children's understanding of emotion from preschool to preadolescence. In *The wisdom in feeling: Psychological processes in emotional intelligence*, eds. L.F. Barrett & P. Salovey, 239–70. New York: Guilford.

Denham, S., R. Pasnak, R. Saracina, H. Bassett, & M.K. Gadzichowski. 2007. *Measuring emotion processes during early childhood: Methods and meanings*. Symposium conducted at the biennial meeting of the Society for Research in Child Development, March, Boston, MA.

Denham, S.A., & D. Zoller. 1991. "When my hamster died, I cried": Preschoolers' attributions of the causes of emotions. *Journal of Genetic Psychology* 152: 371–73.

Domitrovich, C.E., R.C. Cortes, & M.T. Greenberg. 2007. Improving young children's social and emotional competence: A randomized trial of the preschool "PATHS" curriculum. *Journal of Primary Prevention* 28: 67–91.

Dunn, J., I. Bretherton, & P. Munn. 1987. Conversations about feeling states between mothers and their young children. *Developmental Psychology* 23: 132–39.

Dunn, J., J.R. Brown, & L.A. Beardsall. 1991. Family talk about emotions, and children's later understanding of others' emotions. *Developmental Psychology* 27: 448–55.

Dunn, J., & A.L. Cutting. 1999. Understanding others and individual differences in friendship interactions in young children. *Social Development* 8: 201–19.

Dunn, J., & C. Herrera. 1997. Conflict resolution with friends, siblings, and mothers: A developmental perspective. *Aggressive Behavior* 23: 343–57.

Dunn, J., & C. Kendrick. 1982. *Siblings: Love, envy and understanding*. Cambridge, MA: Harvard University Press.

Dunn, J., & P. Munn. 1985. Becoming a family member: Family conflict and the development of social understanding in the second year. *Child Development* 54: 878–87.

Eisenberg, N., A. Cumberland, & T.L. Spinrad. 1998. Parental socialization of emotion. *Psychological Inquiry* 9: 241–73.

Ekman, P., & W.V. Friesen. 1969. The repertoire of nonverbal behavior: Categories, origins, usage, and coding. *Semiotica* 1: 49–98.

Fantuzzo, J., R. Bulotsky-Shearer, P.A. McDermott, C. McWayne, D. Frye, & S. Perlman. 2007. Investigation of dimensions of social-emotional classroom behavior and school readiness for low-income urban preschool children. *School Psychology Review* 36 (1): 44–62.

Feinman, S., & M. Lewis. 1983. Social referencing at ten months: A second-order effect on infants' responses to strangers. *Child Development* 54: 878–87.

Fitzpatrick, M.A., & J. Indvik. 1982. The instrumental and expressive domains of marital communication. *Human Communications Research* 8: 195–213.

Fivush, R. 1989. Exploring sex differences in the emotional content of mother-child conversations about the past. *Sex Roles* 20: 675–91.

Fivush, R. 1991. Gender and emotion in mother-child conversations about the past. *Journal of Narrative and Life History* 1: 325–41.

Fivush, R., M.A. Brotman, J.P. Buckner, & S.H. Goodman. 2000. Gender differences in parent-child emotion narratives. *Sex Roles* 42: 233–53.

Galyer, K.T., & I.M. Evans. 2001. Pretend play and the development of emotion regulation in preschool children. *Early Child Development and Care* 166: 93–108.

Garner, P.W. 2006. Prediction of prosocial and emotional competence from maternal behavior in African American preschoolers. *Cultural Diversity and Ethnic Minority Psychology* 12 (2): 179–98.

Gnepp, J., & D.L.R. Hess. 1986. Children's understanding of verbal and facial display rules. *Developmental Psychology* 22 (1): 103–08.

Goldsmith, H.H., & R.J. Davidson. 2004. Disambiguating the components of emotion regulation. *Child Development* 75: 361–65.

Gordon, S.L. 1989. The socialization of children's emotions: Emotional competence, culture, and exposure. In *Children's understanding of emotion*, eds. C. Saarni & P.L. Harris, 319–49. New York: Cambridge University Press.

Gottman, J.M., & L.G. Katz. 1989. Effects of marital discord on young children's peer interaction and health. *Developmental Psychology* 25: 373–81.

Gove, F.L., & D.P. Keating. 1979. Empathic role-taking precursors. *Developmental Psychology* 15: 594–600.

Halberstadt, A.G. 1986. Family socialization of emotional expression and nonverbal communication styles and skills. *Journal of Personality and Social Psychology* 51 (4): 827–36.

Harter, S. 1983. Developmental perspectives on the self-system. In *Handbook of child psychology, vol 4: Socialization, personality, and social development*, ed. E.M. Hetherington, 275–385. New York: John Wiley & Sons.

Hochschild, A.R. 1983. *The managed heart: Commercialization of human feelings*. Berkeley, CA: University of California Press.

Hughes, H.M. 1988. Psychological and behavioral correlates of family violence in child witnesses and victims. *American Journal of Orthopsychiatry* 58: 77–90.

Izard, C., S. Fine, D. Schultz, A. Mostow, B. Ackerman, & E. Youngstrom. 2001. Emotion knowledge as a predictor of social behavior and academic competence in children at risk. *Psychological Science* 12 (1): 18–23.

Kagan, J. (1981). *The second year: The emergence of self-awareness*. Cambridge, MA: Harvard University Press.

Kuebli, J., & R. Fivush. 1992. Gender differences in parent-child conversations about past emotions. *Sex Roles* 27: 683–98.

Lagattuta, K.H., & H.M. Wellman. 2001. Thinking about the past: Knowledge about links between prior experience, thinking, and emotion. *Child Development* 72: 82–102.

Lagattuta, K.H., & H.M. Wellman. 2002. Differences in early parent-child conversations about negative versus positive emotions: Implications for the development of psychological understanding. *Developmental Psychology* 38: 564–80.

Lagattuta, K.H., H.M. Wellman, & J.H. Flavell. 1997. Preschoolers' understanding of the link between thinking and feeling: Cognitive cuing and emotional change. *Child Development* 68: 1081–104.

Laible, D., & J. Song. 2006. Constructing emotional and relational understanding: The role of affect and mother-child discourse. *Merrill-Palmer Quarterly* 52 (1): 44–69.

Leavitt, R.L., & M.B. Power. 1989. Emotional socialization in the postmodern era: Children in day care. *Social Psychology Quarterly* 52: 35–43.

Levy, R.I. 1984. Emotion, knowing, and culture. In *Culture theory: Essays on mind, self, and emotion*, eds. R.A. Shweder & R.A. LeVine, 214–37. Cambridge, MA: Cambridge University Press.

Lewis, M. 1992. *Shame: The exposed self.* New York: Free Press.

Lewis, M., & J. Brooks-Gunn. 1979. *Social cognition and acquisition of self.* New York: Plenum.

Lewis, M., & L. Michalson. 1983. *Children's emotions and moods.* New York: Plenum.

Lewis, M., & C. Saarni. 1985. Culture and emotions. In *The socialization of emotions*, eds. M. Lewis & C. Saarni, 1–17. New York: Plenum.

Lewis, M., M.W. Sullivan, C. Stanger, & M. Weiss. 1989. Self-development and self-conscious emotions. *Child Development* 60: 146–56.

Lutz, C. 1982. The domain of emotion words on Ifaluk. *American Ethnologist* 9: 113–28.

Lutz, C. 1983. Parental goals, ethnopsychology, and the development of emotional meaning. *Ethos* 11: 246–62.

Lutz, C. 1985. Cultural patterns and individual differences in the child's emotional meaning system. In *The socialization of emotions*, eds. M. Lewis & C. Saarni, 37–55. New York: Plenum.

Lutz, C., & G.M. White. 1986. The anthropology of emotions. *Annual Review of Anthropology* 15: 405–36.

Markus, H.R., & S. Kitayama. 1991. Culture and the self: Implications for cognition, emotion, and motivation. *Psychological Review* 98: 224–53.

Mead, G.H. 1956. *On social psychology: Selected papers.* Chicago, IL: University of Chicago Press.

Michalson, L., & M. Lewis. 1985. What do children know about emotions and when do they know it? In *The socialization of emotions*, eds. M. Lewis & C. Saarni, 117–39. New York: Plenum.

Miller, A.L., S.E. Fine, K.K. Gouley, R. Seifer, S. Dickstein, & A. Shields. 2006. Showing and telling about emotions: Interrelations between facets of emotional competence and association with classroom adjustment in Head Start preschoolers. *Cognition and Emotion* 20 (8): 1170–92.

Miller, P., & L.L. Sperry. 1987. The socialization of anger and aggression. *Merrill-Palmer Quarterly* 33: 1–31.

Olson, D.R., J.W. Astington, & P.L. Harris. 1988. Introduction. In *Developing theories of mind*, eds. J.W. Astington, P.L. Harris, & D.R. Olson, 1–18. New York: Cambridge University Press.

Raver, C.C., S.M. Jones, C.P. Li-Grining, M. Metzger, K.M. Champion, & L. Sardin. 2008. Improving preschool classroom processes: Preliminary findings from a randomized trial implemented in Head Start settings. *Early Childhood Research Quarterly* 23: 10–26.

Saarni, C. 1979. Children's understanding of display rules for expressive behavior. *Developmental Psychology* 15 (4): 424–29.

Saarni, C. 1985. Indirect processes in affect socialization. In *The socialization of emotions*, eds. M. Lewis & C. Saarni, 187–209. New York: Plenum.

Saarni, C. 1999. *The development of emotional competence.* New York: Guilford.

Saarni, C., & M. Crowley. 1990. The development of emotion regulation: Effects on emotional state and expression. In *Emotions and the family: For better or for worse*, ed. E.A. Blechman, 53–73. Hillsdale, NJ: Lawrence Erlbaum.

Shahinfar, A., N.A. Fox, & L.A. Leavitt. 2000. Preschool children's exposure to violence: Relation of behavior problems to parent and child reports. *American Journal of Orthopsychiatry* 70: 115–25.

Sroufe, L.A. 1979. Socioemotional development. In *Handbook of infant development*, ed. J.D. Osofsky, 462–516. New York: John Wiley & Sons.

Stern, D. 1985. *The interpersonal world of the infant.* New York: Basic.

Stipek, D., B. Weiner, & K. Li. 1989. Testing some attribution-emotion relations in the People's Republic of China. *Journal of Personality and Social Psychology* 56: 109–16.

Tenenbaum, H.R., P. Visscher, F. Pons, & P.L. Harris. 2004. Emotional understanding in Quechua children from an agro-pastoralist village. *International Journal of Behavioral Development* 28: 471–78.

Vygotsky, L.S. 1978. *Mind in society: The development of higher psychological processes.* Cambridge, MA: Harvard University Press.

Wang, Q., & R. Fivush. 2005. Mother-child conversations of emotionally salient events: Exploring the functions of emotional reminiscing in European-American and Chinese families. *Social Development* 14: 473–95.

Wellman, H.M., D. Cross, & J. Watson. 2001. Meta-analysis of theory-of-mind development: The truth about false belief. *Child Development* 72: 655–84.

5 Recognizing and Supporting the Development of Self-Regulation in Young Children

Martha B. Bronson

Distressing headlines and teachers' own experiences in homes and classrooms point to the need for children to develop self-control, self-direction, and positive strategies for coping with life situations. Teachers want to help children develop these skills—to help them learn to control their emotions, interact with others in positive ways, avoid inappropriate or aggressive actions, and become self-directed learners. Each of these abilities has been investigated as a form of what is termed *self-regulation*.

There has been a striking increase in both public and academic interest in self-regulation in recent years (Barkley 1997; Bronson 2000; Shonkoff & Phillips 2000; Baumeister & Vohs 2004; Gross 2007).

In order to support the development of self-regulatory skills, teachers need to understand how the skills develop and how psychological theory and research suggest that social and physical environment can help.

Research suggests that the capacity to develop self-regulatory functions is present from birth (Barkley 1997), is somewhat affected by innate factors such as tempera-

ment (Rothbart, Ellis, & Posner 2004), and is highly influenced by the environment (Grolnick & Farkas 2002; Calkins & Hill 2007). It is related to both social competence (Eisenberg & Fabes 1992) and success in school (Zimmerman & Schunk 1989; McClelland, Acock, & Morrison 2006). There is also evidence that early self-control is related to self-control in later childhood (Eisenberg et al. 1996; 1997) and throughout life (Sroufe, Carlson, & Schulman 1993).

During the early childhood years, there is a great increase in self-regulation. This increase is a "central and significant" developmental hallmark of this period (Flavell 1977) and a "cornerstone" of early development that cuts across all domains of behavior (Gillespie & Seibel 2006). During these years, the child makes tremendous progress toward regulating emotional responses (Eisenberg & Fabes 1992; Fox 1994; Eisenberg et al. 2004) and is increasingly able to comply with external requests (Kopp 1982; 1989), control behavior in familiar settings (Luria 1961; Mischel & Mischel 1983), control attention (Holtz & Lehman 1995; Barkley 1997; Rueda, Posner, & Rothbart 2004; 2005), and engage in self-directed thinking and problem solving (Brown & Deloache 1978; Deloache & Brown 1987; Friedman, Scholnick, & Cocking 1987; Hudson & Fivush 1991; Rueda, Posner, & Rothbart 2005).

A classic summary by Kopp (1982) described the developmental progression—from control of arousal and sensory motor functions in the early months of life, to a beginning ability to comply with external suggestions at the end of the first year, to emergence of internal impulse control in the second year. Kopp notes that increasingly sophisticated forms of self-regulation develop from age 3 or 4 onward. With maturation and appropriate experiences, the child becomes increasingly capable of deliberate action, planning ahead, and conscious control.

Self-regulation is described in a number of different ways. The terms *impulse control* and *self-control* (Logue 1995; Barkley 1997) are usually used to describe the ability to inhibit inappropriate responses, delay engagement in an activity, or wait for rewards. Terms such as *self-direction* and *independence* (Ryan, Deci, & Grolnick 2006) are used to describe the ability to control and manage ongoing activities.

Self-regulated learning and problem solving require higher-level regulatory skills such as planning, using strategies, monitoring progress, correcting errors, and persisting until the (social or cognitive) goal is reached successfully. These higher-level abilities are often called *executive skills* by researchers interested in cognitive control functions in the brain (Barkley 1997).

Perspectives on the development of self-regulation

In addition to differences in terminology and emphasis, a variety of theoretical explanations for the origins and growth of self-regulation have contributed to early childhood professionals' understanding of regulatory development. This section gives a brief overview of the major theoretical perspectives on how children develop the capacity for self-regulation, as well as how theorists and researchers suggest the social and physical environment can nurture it. A final section discusses applications for caregivers and teachers.

The psychoanalytic perspective

In the psychoanalytic tradition, the development of self-regulation has been related to the development of a strong ego (Block & Block 1980). Freud (1920; 1923) defined *ego* as that part of the mind that channels basic drives into goals and behaviors acceptable to society, thus keeping internal control over behavior. More recently, psychologists in the psychoanalytic tradition view the ego as more active and autonomous and suggest other ego goals such as competence, control, and positive relationships with others (White 1960; Rogers 1963; White 1963; May 1969).

From the psychoanalytic perspective, self-regulation increases as the child develops ego strength. The ego is strengthened when the child is successful in coping with the social and physical world around her and feels competent and accepted by others. The development of a strong ego has been related to warm and responsive relationships with caregivers (Sroufe 1995) and support for autonomous and effective interactions with the social and physical environment (White 1960; Ryan, Deci, & Grolnick 2006).

The behavioral perspective

Behavioral theorists focus on the power of the environment to shape behavior. They stress aspects of self-control that are learned through reward and punishment (Skinner 1938; 1974) and link the growth of emotional and behavioral control to learned strategies for controlling impulses (Logue 1995). Self-control is described as the ability to choose larger but more de-

> The child internalizes the instructions given by others and begins to give himself audible directions.

layed rewards and is contrasted with impulsiveness, which is choosing smaller but more immediate rewards. Effective control also includes being able to use behavior strategies to obtain rewards.

From the perspective of behavioral theory, a child needs to learn to: (1) assess the relative value of different rewards ("If I take Jake's truck, he won't play with me anymore"); (2) choose appropriate goals (for the setting and the child's own level of skill); (3) give himself previously learned instructions ("I have to wait till it's my turn," "I have to put the toys away"), or successfully follow instructions provided by others; and (4) monitor his own actions (noticing when he is doing something successfully and when he has made a mistake).

Behavioral psychologists also suggest teaching children to reward themselves in the short term, with statements to themselves about their progress and competence (e.g., "I am listening to the teacher," "I am waiting in line quietly"), for behaviors that will ultimately be rewarded or that will keep them from being punished in the external environment (Mischel & Mischel 1983; Meichenbaum 1984; Mischel, Shoda, & Rodriguez 1989; Baldwin & Baldwin 1998).

The social learning perspective

Social learning theorists focus on children's ability to learn through observation as well as through the rewards and punishments they experience (Bandura 1977; 1997). They note that children learn through observation, even when that learning is not demonstrated in behavior (Bandura, Ross, & Ross 1963). For instance, a child may learn what not to do from observing a behavior that has negative outcomes (e.g., seeing another child fall when running down too steep a slope) or is punished (e.g., seeing a child removed from the block area when he knocks down another's structure).

However, the ability to imitate comes before the ability to learn from the consequences of observed behaviors. Toddlers and young preschoolers may see another child fall off a high wall and still may climb the same wall themselves. They may imitate observed hitting behaviors although they have witnessed negative consequences for hitting.

Social learning theorists (i.e., Bandura 1997) argue that self-evaluation is more powerful than external rewards and punishments in supporting self-regulation. They propose that the ability to observe and evaluate one's own behavior provides both motivation to engage in independent activities and guidance in carrying them out. Children gradually develop performance standards for self-evaluation from their own experiences of receiving rewards and punishments and from observing others.

These standards are being developed during the early childhood years and become the basis for self-regulated learning and behavior (Zimmerman 1995; Zimmerman, Bonner, & Kovach 1996; Bandura 1997). As the standards become clearer and more internalized during the primary school years, children may begin to reward themselves (with feelings of self-efficacy) for meeting the standards or punish themselves (with feelings of self-contempt) for failing to meet them.

From the social learning theory perspective, the development of self-regulation depends on having good models, on being rewarded for appropriate behavior or seeing others rewarded for it, and, ultimately, on internalizing appropriate performance standards. If a child has inappropriate or inaccurate expectations about the outcomes of behavior in a particular environment, she may not direct behavior adaptively in that setting. If a child's internalized standards are too high for his age and skills, self-reward will be unlikely because he will rarely be able to meet the standards. If internalized standards are too low, they will be reached too easily, and the child may not make independent efforts that match her potential.

Cognitive-developmental perspectives

Cognitive-developmental theorists such as Piaget (1952; 1954) and Vygotsky (1962; 1978) suggested that young children construct their understanding of the world and the ability to act effectively in it. Both theorists assumed that children have an innate interest in controlling themselves and aspects of the environment, and both assumed that the ability to exercise control effectively develops in interaction with the environment. While Piaget focused more on the child's individual efforts to construct a model of the world that was predictive enough for effective action, Vygotsky emphasized the role played by the social environment in assisting that construction.

Both Piaget and Vygotsky associated the development of control over emotions and behavior with overall cognitive development. Piaget (1952; Piaget & Inhelder 1969) proposed that self-regulatory mechanisms, in the form of assimilation and accommodation, are innate to the child's mental functioning and that development proceeds in stages as the child progressively reorganizes her understanding of objects, the physical world, and the perspectives of others. Piaget considered that, as higher levels of understanding of the social and physical world are reached, the child is able to regulate behavior and thought more effectively in these areas.

Vygotsky (1962; 1978) emphasized social supports for development and, particularly, the role of language in developing internal control of action and thought. Vygotsky considered language the primary means for developing both understanding and self-regulation. The child internalizes the instructions given by others and begins to give himself audible directions (e.g., "The green ones go there," "That piece doesn't fit"). Later, at age 6 or 7, this private speech becomes inaudible as the child learns to think the directions without speaking (Berk 1992; 1994). From this perspective the child can be helped to learn to direct his own activities by providing verbal directions he can use later in independent thinking and problem solving.

Vygotsky (1977) also underlined the importance of sociodramatic play in supporting the development of self-regulation. In play, children can practice both regulating and being regulated by others. The roles and rules of dramatic play help children control their activities in a more advanced way by providing supports ("scaffolds") for internal control. High levels of sociodramatic play are related to self-regulatory behavior (Elias & Berk 2002; Berk, Mann, & Ogan 2006).

Information processing perspective

Information processing theorists focus on the mental processes that support thinking, decision making, and problem solving, using the computer as a metaphor for cognitive functioning (Sternberg 1984). They relate the development of self-regulation to the development of executive processes that control thinking and action, and suggest that what develops in children is the ability to engage in more organized, efficient, and effective cognitive processing. From this perspective, children develop by actively organizing information in their minds and by making use of feedback from the environment to modify these organizations or the way information is handled (i.e., "processed") as they think.

With maturation and experience children are better able to take in (i.e., "encode") information from the environments, organize it, and retrieve it more effectively from memory (Case 1985). They develop more complex strategies for mentally manipulating information and making decisions (Siegler & Jenkins 1989), and they learn to monitor their ongoing activities, modifying the strategies they are using if necessary (Sternberg 1984).

Toward the end of the early childhood period, children begin to be aware of and able to control their own thinking processes (Brown 1978). Support for the development of self-regulated thinking and problem solving can be provided by suggesting useful strategies and making children aware of strategies they are already using (Brown & Campione 1981).

How caregivers and teachers can support the development of self-regulation

Supporting and nurturing the development of self-regulation in young children requires an integrated approach that considers the whole child and the developmental level of each child. Young children cannot separate their feelings, actions, and thoughts as older children and adults learn to do. Caregivers need to consider the physical, emotional, social, and cognitive aspects of control required in a given situation. In addition, the requirements for supporting self-regulation change somewhat with age.

Infants

Infants need to discover their capacity for understanding and influencing the activities of objects and other people. They need enough predictability in their environments that they can begin to connect events and anticipate what will come next (Barkley 1997). When infants can anticipate events, they learn to expect order in the world and begin to look for it.

Through their interactions with caregivers and the cycles and changes in their environments, infants begin to regulate their own arousal (waking and sleeping cycles) and their emotional responses to internal and external stimulation (Kopp 1982). In order to support development, caregivers can arrange routines and events in the environment so that the infant can discover regularities. These regularities help the child learn when it is time to be awake and alert for interesting things and when it is time to sleep. They help her learn to recognize the signals that mean food or comfort or stimulation is coming and then regulate her emotions and arousal accordingly.

Infants also discover their own ability to affect or control the environment in interaction with people and objects. When caregivers are responsive to infants' signals, infants learn that they are capable of influencing others. When infants can create interesting effects by their own actions, they learn that they can have an impact on their environment and that their explorations will be interesting and rewarding (Sroufe 1995). Infants are rewarded by evidence of their own effectiveness and show their pleasure by smiles and persistent efforts to increase this effectiveness. They begin to expect to be successful in interaction with people and objects, and their confidence and motivation for competence in these areas grow.

Toddlers

Toddlers love to exercise their developing skills and are very interested in independent action. There is a strong push for autonomy during these years, but toddlers also use imitation as a means of acquiring new behaviors. Caregivers can model appropriate behavior sequences that toddlers can carry out independently (Crockenberg, Jackson, & Langrock 1996). Toddlers are able to engage in more active exploration than infants and are beginning to use simple self-regulated routines or strategies when they are interacting with people or objects (Jennings 1993). Caregivers can provide materials that support these play activities and allow appropriate choices that help children learn how to choose.

Toddlers are beginning to be able to carry out simple requests and may get upset if they violate known rules (especially if a caregiver is present). To support developing impulse control, caregivers can use responsive guidance techniques that emphasize individual control over behavior, provide simple cause and effect reasoning for desired behaviors, use suggestions rather than commands, and use language to assist self-control (Sroufe 1995).

Language is developing quickly during this period, and toddlers are using it to label their own actions as well as aspects of the social and physical world around them. Language also helps the children remember routines and rules and provides categories for organizing information (Berk 1992). Caregivers can use it to highlight important aspects of the environment, including cause and effect and other connected sequences or routines.

Preschool and kindergarten children

Preschool and kindergarten children are increasingly capable of voluntary control of their emotions, their interactions with others, and their problem-solving activities. They can focus attention for longer periods, follow more complex directions, and comply with rules more reliably. They are increasingly able to interact cooperatively with peers and engage in sociodramatic play.

Caregivers can support growing self-regulation by giving children age- and skill-appropriate responsibilities, allowing choices among appropriate social and cognitive activities, supporting the growth of complex dramatic play with roles and rules, and encouraging independent learning and problem solving (Berk, Mann, & Ogan 2006). Teaching strategies that help children feel competent and give them the tools to carry out tasks independently are also important.

During these years, children are also internalizing the values and the standards of behavior and achievement of those around them (Sroufe 1995). To assist internalization of positive and appropriate standards, caregivers can model positive behaviors, minimize exposure to violent or antisocial models, expect and encourage independent and responsible effort, and use guidance strategies that provide reasons for rules and help children understand the consequences of their actions (Zahn-Waxler et al. 1992; Katz & McClellan 1997).

School-age children

School-age children have more advanced self-regulatory skills and are becoming more consciously aware of their ability to control their actions and thoughts (Berk 1992). Support for self-regulation in learning tasks can now include providing more complex strategies for problem solving, such as decoding strategies for reading (Zimmerman, Bonner, & Kovach 1996). Teachers can also help children become consciously aware of when and how to use specific strategies.

School-age children's growing awareness makes them more vulnerable to external events and judgments that threaten their feelings of competence and control. They are beginning to compare themselves with others and to use internal standards for judging their behavior and achievements (Zimmerman, Bonner, & Kovach 1996). The challenges posed by formal schooling can lower the child's perceived control and willingness to try if there is an over-emphasis on competition or external

> School-age children's growing awareness makes them more vulnerable to external events that threaten their feelings of competence and control.

standards that he cannot reach. Teachers can support self-regulated learning by allowing individual choices among appropriately challenging alternatives and providing assistance in ways that support the child's independent effort and perceived control over the outcome (Barkley 1997).

School-age children are also more interested in and affected by influences outside the family and school environments than younger children are. Peer judgments and standards are becoming more important. A history of positive, trusting, and mutually respectful relations with adults; guidance strategies that promote mutual respect and problem solving; and continuing positive expectations for responsible behavior help children direct their behavior appropriately and resist negative influences (Berk & Winsler 1995; Katz & McClellan 1997).

Conclusion

Children learn self-regulatory skills in a responsive social and material environment that provides opportunities for effective action, and is predictable enough to allow children to recognize the effects of their efforts. They develop internal control of emotions and behavior in a warm and trustworthy environment where responsible action is modeled, approved, and expected and where guidance strategies involve clarifying the effects of actions and a problem-solving approach to difficulties or disagreements. Opportunities to make meaningful choices and assistance in developing strategies for carrying out independent social and learning activities also support the growth of self-regulation in young children.

Updated from the Research in Review article in the March 2000 issue of *Young Children.*

Martha B. Bronson is a retired professor and a former teacher of young children.

References

Baldwin, J.D., & J.I. Baldwin. 1998. *Behavior principles in everyday life.* Upper Saddle River, NJ: Prentice-Hall.

Bandura, A. 1977. *Social learning theory.* Englewood Cliffs, NJ: Prentice Hall.

Bandura, A. 1997. *Self-efficacy: The exercise of control.* New York: W.H. Freeman.

Bandura, A., D. Ross, & S.A. Ross. 1963. Imitation of film-mediated aggressive models. *Journal of Abnormal and Social Psychology* 66: 3–11.

Barkley, R.A. 1997. *ADHD and the nature of self-control.* New York: Guilford.

Baumeister, R.F., & K.D.Vohs, eds. 2004. *Handbook of self-regulation: Research, theory, and applications.* New York: Guilford.

Berk, L.E. 1992. Children's private speech: An overview of theory and the status of research. In *Private speech: From social interaction to self-regulation,* eds. R.M. Diaz & L.E. Berk, 17–53. Mahwah, NJ: Lawrence Erlbaum

Berk, L.E. 1994. Why children talk to themselves. *Scientific American* 271 (November): 78–83.

Berk, L.E., T.D. Mann, & A.T. Ogan. 2006. Make believe play: Wellspring for development of self-regulation. In *Play = learning: How play motivates and enhances children's cognitive and social-emotional growth,* eds. D.G. Singer, R.M. Golinkoff, & K. Hirsh-Pasek, 77–100. New York: Oxford University Press.

Berk, L.E., & A. Winsler. 1995. *Scaffolding children's learning: Vygotsky and early childhood education.* Washington, DC: NAEYC.

Block, J.H., & J. Block. 1980. The role of ego-control and ego-resilience in the organization of behavior. In *Minnesota Symposia on Child Psychology, vol. 13: Development of cognition, affect, and social relations,* ed. W.A. Collins, 39–101. Minneapolis, MN: University of Minnesota Press.

Bronson, M.B. 2000. *Self-regulation in early childhood: Nature and nurture.* New York: Guilford.

Brown, A.L. 1978. Knowing when, where, and how to remember: A problem in metacognition. In *Advances in instructional psychology, vol. 1,* ed. R. Glaser. Hillsdale, NJ: Lawrence Erlbaum.

Brown, A.L., & J. Campione. 1981. Inducing flexible thinking: A problem of access. In *Intelligence and learning,* eds. M. Friedman, J. Das, & N. O'connor, 515–529. New York: Plenum.

Brown, A.L., & J.S. Deloache. 1978. Skills, plans, and self-regulation. In *Children's thinking: What develops?,* ed. R.S. Siegler, 3–35. Hillsdale, NJ: Lawrence Erlbaum.

Calkins, S.D., & A. Hill. 2007. Caregiver influences on emerging emotion regulation: Biological and environmental transactions in early development. In *Handbook of emotion regulation,* ed. J.J. Gross, 229–48. New York: Guilford.

Case, R. 1985. *Intellectual development: Birth to adulthood*. Orlando, FL: Academic Press.

Crockenberg, S., S. Jackson, & A.M. Langrock. 1996. Autonomy and goal attainment: Parenting, gender and children's social competence. In *New directions for child development, no. 73: Children's autonomy, social competence, and interactions with adults and other children: Exploring connections and consequences*, ed. M. Killen. San Francisco: Jossey-Bass.

Deloache, J.S., & A.L. Brown. 1987. The early emergence of planning skills in children. In *Making sense: The child's construction of the world*, eds. J. Bruner & H. Haste, 108–30. London: Methuen.

Eisenberg, N., & R.A. Fabes. 1992. Emotion, regulation, and the development of social competence. In *Review of personality and social psychology, vol. 14: Emotion and social behavior*, ed. M.S. Clark, 119–50. Newbury Park, CA: Sage Publications.

Eisenberg, N., R.A. Fabes, I.K. Guthrie, B.C. Murphy, P. Maszk, R. Holmgren, & K. Suh. 1996. The relations of regulation and emotionality to problem behavior in elementary school children. *Development and Psychopathology* 8: 141-162.

Eisenberg, N., R.A. Fabes, S.A. Shepard, B.C. Murphy, I.K. Guthrie, S. Jones, J. Friedman, R. Poulin, & P. Maszk. 1997. Contemporaneous and longitudinal prediction of children's social functioning from regulation and emotionality. *Child Development* 68: 642–64.

Eisenberg, N., C.L. Smith, A. Sadovsky, & T. Spinrad. 2004. Effortful control: Relations with emotion regulation, adjustment, and socialization in childhood. In *Handbook of self-regulation: Research, theory, and application*, eds. R.F. Baumeister & K.D. Vohs, 259–82. New York: Guilford.

Elias, C.L., & L.E. Berk. 2002. Self-regulation in young children: Is there a role for socciodramatic play? *Early Childhood Research Quarterly* 17 (2): 216–38.

Flavell, J.H. 1977. *Cognitive development*. Englewood Cliffs, NJ: Prentice-Hall.

Fox, N.A. 1994. *The development of emotion regulation: Biological and behavioral considerations*. Monographs of the Society for Research in Child Development, vol. 59, nos. 2–3, serial no. 240. Chicago: University of Chicago Press.

Freud, S. 1920. *General introduction to psychoanalysis*. New York: Washington Square Press.

Freud, S. 1923. *The ego and the id*. London: Hogarth Press.

Friedman, S.L., E.K. Scholnick, & R.R. Cocking. 1987. Reflections on reflections: What planning is and how it develops. In *Blueprints for thinking: The role of planning in cognitive development*, eds. S.L. Friedman, E.K. Scholnick, & R.R. Cocking, 515–34. Cambridge, England: Cambridge University Press.

Gillespie, L.G., & N. Seibel. 2006. Self-regulation: A cornerstone of early childhood development. *Young Children* 61 (4): 34–39.

Grolnick, W.S., & M. Farkas. 2002. Parenting and the development of children's self-regulation. In *Handbook of parenting, vol 5: Practical issues in parenting*, 2d ed., ed. M.H. Bornstein, 89–110. Mahwah, NJ: Lawrence Erlbaum.

Gross, J.J. 2007. *Handbook of emotion regulation*. New York: Guilford.

Holtz, B.A., & E.B. Lehman. 1995. Development of children's knowledge and use of strategies for self-control in a resistance-to-distraction task. *Merrill-Palmer Quarterly* 41: 361–80.

Hudson, J.A., & R. Fivush. 1991. Planning in the preschool years: The emergence of plans from general event knowledge. *Cognitive Development* 6: 393–415.

Jennings, K.D. 1993. Mastery motivation and the formation of self-concept from infancy through early childhood. In *Mastery motivation in early childhood: Development, measurement and social processes*, ed. D.J. Messer. London: Routledge.

Katz, L.G., & D.E. McClellan. 1997. *Fostering children's social competence: The teacher's role*. Washington, DC: NAEYC.

Kopp, C.B. 1982. Antecedent of self-regulation: A developmental perspective. *Developmental Psychology* 18: 199–214.

Kopp, C.B. 1989. Regulation of distress and negative emotions: A developmental view. *Developmental Psychology* 25: 343–54.

Logue, A.W. 1995. *Self-control*. Englewood Cliffs, NJ: Prentice-Hall.

Luria, A.R. 1961. *The role of speech in the regulation of normal and abnormal behavior*. London: Pergamon.

May, R. 1969. *Love and will*. New York: Norton.

McClelland, M.M., A.C. Acock, & F.S. Morrison. 2006. The impact of kindergarten learning-related skills on academic trajectories at the end of elementary school. *Early Childhood Research Quarterly* 21: 471–90.

Meichenbaum, D. 1984. Teaching thinking: A cognitive behavioral perspective. In *Thinking and learning skills, vol. 2*, eds. J. Sigal, S. Chipman, & R. Glaser. Hillsdale, NJ: Lawrence Erlbaum.

Mischel, H.N., & W. Mischel. 1983. Development of children's knowledge of self-control strategies. *Child Development* 54: 603–19.

Mischel, W., Y. Shoda, & M.L. Rodriguez. 1989. Delay of gratification in children. *Science* 244: 933–38.

Piaget, J. 1952. *The origins of intelligence in children*. New York: International Universities Press.

Piaget, J. 1954. *The construction of reality in the child*. New York: Basic Books.

Piaget, J., & B. Inhelder. 1969. *The psychology of the child*. New York: Basic Books.

Rogers, C.R. 1963. Actualizing tendency in relation to motives and to consciousness. In *Nebraska Symposium on Motivation*, ed. M.R. Jones. Lincoln, NE: University of Nebraska Press.

Rothbart, M.K., L.K. Ellis, & M.I. Posner. 2004. Temperament and self-regulation. In *Handbook of self-regulation: Research, theory and applications*, eds. R.F. Baumeister & K.D. Vohs, 357–70. New York: Guilford.

Rueda, M.R., M.I. Posner, & M.K. Rothbart. 2004. Attentional control and self-regulation. In *Handbook of self regulation: Research, theory, and applications*, eds. R.F. Baumeister, & K.D. Vohs, 283–300. New York: Guilford.

Rueda, M.R., M.I. Posner, & M.K. Rothbart. 2005. The development of attention: Contributions to the emergence of self-regulation. *Developmental Neuropsychology* 28: 573–94.

Ryan, R.M., E.L. Deci, & W.S. Grolnick. 2006. The significance of autonomy and autonomy support in psychological development and psychopathology. In *Developmental psychopathology, vol. 1: Theory and method*, 2d ed., eds. D.C. Ciccetti, & D.J. Cohen, 795–849. Hoboken, NJ: John Wiley & Sons.

Shonkoff, J.P., & D.A. Phillips, eds. 2000. *From neurons to neighborhoods: The science of early childhood development*. Washington, DC: National Academies Press.

Siegler, R.S., & E. Jenkins. 1989. *How children discover new strategies*. New York: Lawrence Erlbaum.

Skinner, B.F. 1938. *The behavior of organisms: An experimental analysis*. Englewood Cliffs, NJ: Prentice-Hall.

Skinner, B.F. 1974. *About behaviorism*. New York: Knopf.

Sroufe, L.A. 1995. *Emotional development: The organization of emotional life in the early years*. Cambridge: Cambridge University Press.

Sroufe, L.A., E. Carlson, & S. Schulman. 1993. Individuals in relationships: Development from infancy through adolescence. In *Studying lives through time: Personality and development*, eds. D.C. Funder, R.D. Parke, C. Tomlinson-Keasey, & K. Widaman, 315–42. Washington, DC: American Psychological Association.

Sternberg, R.J. 1984. Mechanisms of cognitive development: A componential approach. In *Mechanisms of cognitive development*, ed. R.J. Sternberg, 163–86. New York: Freeman.

Vygotsky, L.S. 1962. *Thought and language*. Cambridge, MA: MIT Press.

Vygotsky, L.S. 1977. Play and its role in the mental development of the child. In *Soviet developmental psychology*, ed. M. Cold. White Plains, NY: M.E. Sharp.

Vygotsky, L.S. 1978. *Mind in society: The development of higher psychological processes*. Cambridge, MA: Harvard University Press.

White, R.W. 1960. Competence and the psychosexual stages of development. In *Nebraska Symposium on Motivation, vol. 8*, ed. M.R. Jones, 97–141. Lincoln, NE: University of Nebraska Press.

White, R.W. 1963. *Ego and reality in psychoanalytic theory: A proposal regarding independent ego energies*. New York: Independent Universities Press.

Zahn-Waxler, C., M. Radke-Yarrow, E. Wagner, & M. Chapman. 1992. Development of concern for others. *Developmental Psychology* 28: 126–36.

Zimmerman, B.J. 1995. Self-efficacy and educational development. In *Self-efficacy in changing societies*, ed. A. Bandura, 202–32. New York: Cambridge University Press.

Zimmerman, B.J., S. Bonner, & R. Kovach. 1996. *Developing self-regulated learners: Beyond achievement to self-efficacy*. Washington, DC: American Psychological Association.

Zimmerman, B.J., & D. Schunk. 1989. *Self-regulated learning and academic achievement: Theory, research, and practice*. New York: Springer-Verlag.

6 | The Development of Self-Concept

Hermine H. Marshall

A dults generally assume that when children try new things with enthusiasm and approach peers and adults with confidence, they have a positive view of themselves. Conversely, when children are hesitant, adults assume that their self-view is less positive. These assumptions are supported by a study showing that preschool and kindergarten teachers described children as having high self-esteem if they displayed "confidence, curiosity, initiative, and independence," whereas teachers believed that children who lacked these characteristics had low self-esteem (Harter 2006, 515).

Self-concept and factors that affect its development are important areas of concern for early childhood educators because research indicates that young children who have a positive view of themselves are more able to cope with the demands and stresses of school (Verschueren, Buyk, & Marcoen 2001). Moreover, low self-concept is related to poor mental health, poor academic achievement, and delinquency (e.g., Harter 1983).

Self-concept defined

Self-concept refers to the perceptions, feelings, and attitudes that a person has about himself or herself. This term and *self-image* are often used interchangeably to designate a global conception of self. Global self-concept is made up of many dimensions, among them aspects such as physical characteristics, psychological traits, and gender and ethnic identity.

One dimension especially important to development and learning is *self-esteem* (or *self-worth*), which refers specifically to one's self-evaluations—that is, a person's judgments about her own worthiness. Another is *perceived competence*, which reflects one's beliefs about the ability to succeed at particular tasks. According to White (1959), feelings of competence result from being able to act effectively and master one's environment. When a person's capacities extend to new heights, one feels competent.

Cultural lenses

A caveat is in order before proceeding: Teachers can't forget that everyone views the world through cultural lenses. That is, a person's perceptions, actions, and interactions always derive meaning from his or her cultural context. Different cultures value and encourage different traits and behaviors. Thus, the definition of a *positive* self-concept, and what particular behaviors are evidence of it, will vary culturally.

In Western cultures, striving toward independence and individuality and asserting oneself are seen as important accomplishments (Markus & Kitayama 1991). As a consequence, Westerners perceive children who are outgoing and who eagerly explore new situations as demonstrating competence and having a positive self-concept, especially compared with children who do not appear to seek out and actively participate in these situations.

In contrast, Eastern cultures and many African, Latin American, and southern European cultures place greater emphasis on maintaining harmonious, interdependent relationships (Garcia Coll 1990; Markus & Kitayama 1991; see also Greenfield 1994 and Marshall 2001). In cultures influenced by Confucian and Taoist philosophies, self-restraint and control of emotional expressiveness are considered indications of social maturity (Chen et al. 1998); asserting oneself may be seen as a sign of immaturity (Markus & Kitayama 1991).

For example, in Chinese culture, children who are shy, reticent, and quiet are likely to be considered competent and well-behaved by parents and teachers (Chen et al. 1998; Rubin 1998). In contrast, North American teachers might see these same children as inhibited and lacking in self-confidence, whereas in reality, they have a positive view of themselves and of their social relationships. Similarly, in some cultures, such as traditional Navajo cultures, children are expected to observe before attempting new things (Bacon & Carter 1991). For these children, too, teachers should not mistake their standing back and observing rather than exploring as an indication of low self-esteem.

> Teachers need to have expansive views of what is important to self-concept, beyond the typical Western notions.

Teachers need to have expansive views of what is considered important to self-concept, beyond the typical Western notions of autonomy, self-assertion, self-enhancement, and uniqueness to also include characteristics such as empathy, sensitivity to others, modesty, cooperation, and caring. How children see themselves in relationship to others is also part of self-concept.

Furthermore, teachers cannot always depend on children's self-descriptions to assess self-concept. In contrast to the positiveness of how most young white American children describe themselves, young Chinese children describe themselves in more neutral tones (Wang 2004). These differences in self-descriptions need to be recognized as a function of culture rather than accurate as measurements of a child's self-view.

Conversely, teachers must be careful not to assume that just because children or families are from a particular ethnic or racial group that they necessarily share a common cultural experience. There are differences within cultures and between families.

Differences in how families raise their children and in the way they learn to interpret behavior can be a factor of their country of origin, how long they have been in the United States, how acculturated to mainstream America they have become, their educational background, and their social status (Delgado-Gaitan 1994; Killen 1997; McLloyd 1999). For example, although mainland Chinese parents value interdependence and cohesion and may devalue development of individuality within the family, many Taiwanese and immigrant Chinese parents seem to encourage independence so that children will be able to succeed in the larger society (Lin & Fu 1990). Likewise, as some Mexican immigrant families become acculturated, they are more likely to sanction their children's independent thinking related to school topics (Delgado-Gaitan 1994).

Some children and families are also influenced by multiple cultures. It is therefore important to be sensitive to the beliefs and attitudes of each child and family and to how that family's beliefs, attitudes, and values may affect behavior, regardless of their child's apparent ethnic or cultural context.

Differentiation and components of self-concept

In mainstream American culture, self-esteem and feelings of competence are related to acquiring a sense of personal control (Harter 1983). As children perceive themselves gaining competence in a gradually widening sphere, they begin to see themselves as causal agents and are able to feel that they have greater ability to control or interact well with more of their environment. In other cultures, personal control may not be so important for self-esteem.

Beginning in about second grade, children's self-concepts become increasingly differentiated into multiple domains (Measelle et al. 1998). Perceptions of competence in the social skills domain become differentiated from perceptions of competence in cognitive and physical domains (Harter & Pike 1984). Self-perceptions about interactions with peers become separated from those about interactions with parents and teachers. Cognitive (or "academic") self-concept gradually further differentiates into math and verbal areas (Marsh 1984).

Furthermore, the importance of each of these domains differs for individual children and families and among cultures. A low self-evaluation in one domain, such as athletic ability, may have little effect

on that child if the physical domain is not considered important in the child's particular family or culture. On the other hand, in families or cultures where athletic skills are important—or where skills that underpin academic ability are highly valued, for another example—low self-esteem in that personally or culturally relevant area can have increasingly devastating effects as children move through school (Harter 1986). In addition, self-esteem may be affected by possessing culturally valued traits, such as helpfulness or honesty.

Gender and racial identity

Gender and racial identity are components of self-concept that are also influenced by culture. Parents' and other caregivers' labeling of a child's gender reflects culturally important gender differences and highlights gender roles and expectations. For example, in Western cultures, girls have traditionally been expected to be well-behaved and acquiescent; boys are supposed to be strong and assertive. Behaviors consistent with these expectations are rewarded and integrated into views of self.

The issue of racial (or ethnic) identity and self-concept may be a difficult topic for teachers as well as parents and children because of the legacy of racism in America. It is also complicated by the common notion that a person's racial identity can be assumed from their physical characteristics (Morrison & Bordere 2001). However, especially for children of dual or multiple ethnicities, special care needs to be taken to ascertain how families view themselves and how they are choosing to raise their children.

One strategy is for teachers to schedule an early conference with the family and ask. For many parents, a positive solution is to teach their children to accept both or all of their ethnic and cultural backgrounds (Morrison & Rodgers 1996). Nevertheless, parents and educators need to understand that the concept of multiple classification is difficult for children younger than age 7 or 8. For younger children, a person can, for example, be *either* black or white but not both simultaneously. With further cognitive development, however, children become capable of understanding classification in multiple categories.

Self-concept measurement

Again a note of caution at the outset: Much of the research on self-concept in children has been conducted within mainstream Anglo culture, and items on those self-esteem scales reflect the values of that culture. Consequently, the childrearing and educational factors that have been found to be correlated with these indexes of self-esteem are relative to that culture particularly.

Other measurement problems have hampered researchers' progress in understanding the development of self-concept, as well. For example, investigators sometimes use different definitions and examine different dimensions of self-concept. This makes it difficult to compare and synthesize results from different studies (Shavelson, Hubner, & Stanton 1976).

Problems in measuring self-concept in early childhood have further hindered researchers. For example, the influence of momentary events on young children's self-esteem, such as a temporarily frustrating experience, often causes indicators of self-concept to vary over time and appear "unstable." Children's ability to see their own characteristics as stable over time develops gradually. Furthermore, young children often have difficulty understanding and verbalizing abstract ideas and internal processes such as self-concept. Measurement items appropriate for older elementary school children, such as "I'm pretty sure of myself," may be meaningless and difficult for preschoolers to understand.

A more concrete method of assessing self-esteem uses pictures of children succeeding or having difficulty with tasks (Harter & Pike 1984). Another less abstract but labor-intensive method uses hand puppets to playfully ask children as young as age 4½ questions to which the children respond as if they were the hand puppet (Cassidy 1988; Measelle et al 1998; Verscheuren, Buyk, & Marcoen 2001). It is important to note that the results from these two methods are not necessarily consistent with each other (Measelle et al. 1998).

Influences on the development of self-concept

Possible genetic influences

Recent genetic research, especially in twin studies, has suggested the possibility that self-esteem has genetic roots. But the link between genes and self-esteem is more likely to be indirect than direct. That is, if children have inherited, for example, intellectual ability, athletic ability, or an attractive appearance, and/or if they have inherited a sociable temperament, they are likely to enjoy the basis for high self-esteem. Then, if they are rewarded for these inherited traits by significant others, high self-esteem is likely to ensue. That is, these *positive traits* may be inherited rather than high self-esteem itself (Harter 2006).

Appearance and body image

Adult reaction to a child's physical appearance begins when the child is still an infant (Harter 1998). Adults, and later the child's peers, continue to react positively to what are regarded as culturally valued physical traits. Interestingly, it is *perceived* physical appearance, rather than actual physical appearance, that is most closely related to global self-worth at all ages (Harter 1998; Verschueren, Buyk, & Marcoen 2001). Since physical appearance is difficult to change, a possible key to promoting positive self-feelings may be to influence children's *perceptions* of their own appearance.

There is some beginning evidence that girls as young as age 6, particularly those exposed to media images of ultra slim models, may desire a thinner body (Dohnt & Tiggemann 2006). Whether this desire translates into dissatisfaction with their body image and affects self-esteem has not yet been explored. Although most young girls are generally satisfied with the way they look and this satisfaction is related to their self-esteem, caregivers and teachers should be aware of the possible influence of the media.

Responsiveness of caregivers

Self-concept develops largely within a social context. The interpersonal environment that caregivers provide has important influences on the development of self-concept. The quality, consistency, and timing of adults' responses to infants can carry messages about trust, caring, and the value of the infant. Caregiver responsiveness can also convey information about the developing child's capacity to become competent and to control her or his environment (see Honig 1984).

When caregivers respond positively and consistently to infants' cues, infants can come to learn that they are of value and that they can influence their social environment (Harter 1983; 2006). This can contribute to beginning feelings of self-worth, personal control, and competence. On the other hand, when care is less optimal, infants and young children can feel unlovable or unworthy and may not develop the skills that underlie the development of competence. Their self-views are likely to be negative.

Parental attitudes and childrearing practices

Sears (1970) found that parents who were warm and accepting when their children were young (age 5) had children with high

The impact of parental approval does not diminish through adolescence despite an increased influence of peer approval.

self-esteem when remeasured at age 12. A child whose parents are sensitive to the child's needs and who support the child's efforts at mastery are likely to see him or herself as lovable, worthy, and competent (Harter 1998).

Parents who use an "authoritative"— as opposed to an authoritarian or permissive—childrearing pattern (see Honig 1984) are also more likely to have children with high self-esteem. Authoritative parents make reasonable demands that are accepted by children, but they do not impose unreasonable restrictions, and they allow their children some choice and control (Maccoby & Martin 1983).

For young children, parental approval is obviously related to self-esteem—more so than peer approval is. The impact of parental approval does not diminish through adolescence despite an increased influence of peer approval (Harter 1998).

Education in effective parenting, where parents learn to be more accepting of their children's feelings and behavior, leads to higher self-concepts in kindergarten and second-grade children (Summerlin & Ward 1978). Such studies point to the importance of efforts to help parents understand and implement practices that enhance self-esteem.

Peers

Peer relationships affect children's self-perceptions. For example, children who are neglected by their peers have a poorer self-concept than those who are not neglected. Children who have a positive self-concept have more friends, although it is unclear whether having friends influences self-concept or whether having a positive self-concept affects the number of friends (Vandell & Hembree 1994).

However, there may be gender differences in the role that peer acceptance plays in influencing self-perceptions of competence. One study found that 4-year-old girls who initiated interactions with others successfully—and thus seemed to be accepted by their peers—perceived themselves as more competent in the cognitive domain when they were 7 than those who did not interact as well with their peers. In contrast, 4-year-old boys who spent more time in solitary play rather than interacting with others did see themselves as competent in the cognitive domain when they were 7. It may be that at age 4, these nonsocial behaviors reflect boys' engagement with other cognitively stimulating activities that influenced their cognitive competence. Unfortunately, perceptions of *social* competence were not measured in this study. Although this study supported the importance of peer interactions for the development of positive views of competence, at least for girls, it may have been limited in that it was conducted in a laboratory setting with groups of unfamiliar same-sex peers rather than in a natural setting with familiar peers (Nelson, Rubin, & Fox 2005).

Although this study supports the importance of peer interactions for the development of positive self-views of competence, it may be limited in that it was conducted in a laboratory setting with groups of unfamiliar same-sex peers rather than in a natural setting with familiar peers. In general, however, research supports the importance of peer acceptance for the development of positive views of self and suggests a role for educators in supporting the development of social skills for children who appear withdrawn—remembering, however, that reticence may be a culturally learned characteristic.

Physical environment

During the infants and toddlers years, a number of aspects of the physical environment can influence the development of children's conceptions of their physical self and of themselves as separate and different from others. Mirrors and similar light-reflecting surfaces, for example, provide opportunities for very young children to learn not only about their physical characteristics but also about themselves as independent agents who can make things happen. When infants can see both themselves and their mirror image moving at the same time, they can learn about the effects of their own actions and their ability to control their world (Lewis & Brooks-Gunn 1979).

Other aspects of the environment may influence the development of self-concept at other ages, too. For example, if developmentally appropriate materials (those that provide both challenge and success) are made easily accessible to young children for exploration in an encouraging environment, children are likely to acquire feelings of competence and confidence in approaching new materials (see Copple & Bredekamp 2009).

Cognitive development

Preschool and kindergarten. The level of children's cognitive development influences self-concept development. Preschool children can often use multiple categories to describe themselves, but these categories are not yet very stable or consistent. For example, we may hear a preschooler say both, "I am a boy" and "I will be a mommy when I grow up." Preschoolers' self-descriptions are also constrained by the particular events they are experiencing. A girl may say, "I'm strong. I can lift this rock," but not be bothered if she cannot lift a heavy chair.

In making self-judgments that can appear to reflect their self-esteem, preschoolers' attention is often focused on the value of a specific act. A child who says, "I am a good boy" may mean "I did something good," such as share his toys. Preschoolers also appear to view themselves—as well as others—as either all good or all bad. They do not believe they can be both at the same time. The self-evaluation may shift to the opposite pole as the child shifts attention to other actions or events (Selman 1980).

Self-descriptions of preschool children often seem overly positive. In fact, the socializing environment may reinforce this positivity in part by the use of praise general ("Good boy!"). Moreover, at this age, children are not skilled at comparing themselves with others, nor are they generally able to distinguish their actual abilities from their wishes to be competent. These characteristics should be interpreted not as bragging but as a function of normal development. Furthermore, these positive self-views may have the advantage of serving as emotional buffers (Harter 2006).

Preschoolers see the self in both physical and action terms (Damon & Hart 1982). When asked what an observer could "write about you," 3- to 5-year-old children most frequently described themselves in terms of physical actions, such as "I can ride a bike" or "I can help set the table" (Keller, Ford, & Meacham 1978).

Kindergartners, too, describe themselves largely in terms of activities such as play (Damon & Hart 1982). Young children seem to see themselves as "good at doing things" or not—without making the distinction between physical and academic competence that older children do (Harter & Pike 1984). Nevertheless, about 5 percent of the responses of the youngest children in the Keller study referred to psychological aspects, such as their likes and dislikes.

Primary grades. Primary grade children begin to acquire more mature thinking skills, such as the ability to organize logically and classify hierarchically, and can extend these abilities to their thinking about the self. By age 7 or 8, their ability to hold two dimensions in mind simultaneously allows them to make comparisons

Young children seem to see themselves as "good at doing things" or not.

between themselves and their peers concerning their abilities (Ruble et al. 1980). By third grade, children still frequently describe themselves in terms of activities, but they add comparison with others in their self-descriptive statements, such as "I can ride a bike better than my little brother" (Damon & Hart 1982). They are also able to think inductively and may conclude that "I'm not very smart because I'm in the low group in reading and math."

Primary grade children also develop new perspective-taking skills that allow them to imagine what other people are thinking, especially what others are thinking about *them*. Children of this age begin to be more influenced by their perceptions of what significant adults think of them. As they develop further, what peers think of them becomes increasingly important.

Classroom environments

Classroom structure and teachers' control orientations can influence children's self-concept, as well (Marshall & Weinstein 1984). This is exemplified in studies comparing the effects of "unidimensional" versus "multidimensional" classrooms (Rosenholtz & Rosenholtz 1981). In unidimensional classrooms, teachers emphasize a narrow range of students' abilities (e.g., valuing reading ability to the neglect of artistic ability), group students according to ability, assign similar tasks, and publicly evaluate performance. In such classrooms, comparing oneself with others can become salient.

Where social comparison is obvious, even 4- and –5-year-olds compare themselves with others (Butler 1998) and may see themselves as less competent. Yet, where children believe in the effectiveness of effort (Nicholls 1978), social comparison may not have a negative effect on self-concept.

In contrast, in multidimensional classrooms, teachers emphasize multiple dimensions of ability (e.g., artistic and problem-solving skills as well as reading skills), have students work on a variety of different tasks at the same time using different materials, and evaluate students more privately. Although preschools typically are more similar to multidimensional classrooms, many kindergartens and "academic" preschools are under pressure to become more unidimensional.

In settings that emphasized academics with characteristics similar to unidimensional classrooms, kindergartners' perceptions of their ability were lower than those of kindergartners in more multidimensional classrooms—although the two groups were learning the same skills (Stipek & Daniels 1988). Teachers need to be aware, therefore, that pressures to prepare children for academics and to include and evaluate more school-like tasks in the curriculum may have detrimental effects on children's self-concept of their ability.

Whether teachers support children's autonomy or tend to control children through external means also affects children's perceptions of competence and self-esteem. Children in classrooms that supported autonomy had higher perceptions of their own cognitive competence, self-worth, and mastery motivation than those in classrooms where teachers retained control (Ryan, Connell, & Deci 1985). Because this study was conducted with older children, it is unknown what age this effect might begin. Nevertheless, it is clear that providing opportunities for children to strive toward independence and develop a sense of personal control is likely to have a positive effect on most children's perceptions of competence and self-esteem, especially within mainstream American culture.

Expectations

Teachers' and parents' expectations can influence children's self-esteem both directly, through opportunities adults provide for children to learn and become competent, and indirectly, through more subtle cues that children eventually come to perceive. If an adult believes that certain children can learn or do more than others can, the adult might furnish additional materials for these children. In this way, adults provide some children opportunities to become competent in more areas, and thus they directly influence the children's perceived competence and self-esteem. The converse would be true where adult expectations are low.

In addition, teachers' and parents' expectations influence self-concept in more subtle ways, as children gradually become more adept at "reading" environmental cues. Young children are not very accurate in judging adults' expectations for them. They generally hold higher expectations for themselves than their teachers hold for them (Weinstein et al. 1987). The discrepancy between young children's expectations and those of their teachers can be due to children's relatively undeveloped ability to take the perspectives of others.

Young children may also have less need to focus on what their teachers expect of them, because most preschool and kindergarten classrooms do not emphasize evaluation. However, even at the kindergarten level, if teachers make their evaluations of children salient by, for instance, pointing out whose work is best, children's self-evaluations can show some consistency with those of the teacher (Stipek & Daniels 1988). Consequently, kindergarten and primary teachers need to be aware of the subtle ways that their expectations are being conveyed to children and thus influence children's self-esteem.

Use of praise

Many people believe that praise is important to enhancing self-esteem. However, research indicates that the effect of praise is not simple. In fact, praising children for traits that underlie performance, such as ability (e.g., "You're so smart"), can be detrimental. For example, because ability is generally misperceived as fixed and immutable, when children who in the past have been praised for their ability cannot perform a task, they may think they are incapable of succeeding and consequently may feel dumb or bad, and their self-esteem may plummet.

On the other hand, praising their effort or the strategies they use (e.g., "You really listened carefully") does not appear to undermine self-esteem because children can exert greater effort or learn new strategies (Kamins & Dweck 1999). Yet just telling children to "try harder" without giving them new strategies to use may cause them to give up if they think they are already trying as hard as they can. Again, this may lead to lowered self-views (see also Katz 1993).

Implications and applications: Ways to influence self-concept

Because most of the studies reported in this review use correlational methods that do not indicate cause and effect, interpretations must be made cautiously. Nevertheless, many of the findings do suggest steps likely to enhance children's self-concept.

Help children feel they are of value

Listen attentively to what children say. Ask for their suggestions. Solicit and respect their ideas.

Help children identify their own positive and prosocial behavior. When children display cooperation, helpfulness, and other prosocial behavior, give children the words to describe themselves with these terms. For example, "You are being very helpful." They may then come to see themselves in a positive manner and act accordingly. This is a positive use of the self-fulfilling prophecy.

Affirm the ethnic and cultural identity of every child, including children of dual or multiple ethnicities. Find ways of highlighting the value of diversity in general and the cultures represented by the children in your group in particular. Read books that include children of different cultures. Invite adults of various ethnic groups to share their expertise with the children. Display pictures of women, men, and children of different ethnic groups succeeding in a variety of tasks.

Help children feel they are competent

Provide experiences for children where they can succeed. Some children need to have a series of tasks that can be accomplished initially with little effort but that gradually increase in difficulty. Try to relate the task to something that children already recognize they can do.

Provide new challenges and comment on positive attempts. Some children appear to need a lot of encouragement and verbal reinforcement. Encouragement and statements of confidence in the child's ability to succeed may be necessary at first. However, the effects of general verbal praise and persuasion may be short-lived (Hitz & Driscoll 1988). Children will be more likely to benefit by seeing for themselves that they can, in fact, succeed.

Allow children to carry out and complete tasks by themselves. Because self-concept reflects perceived competence, allowing children to do for themselves whatever they can is important—even when some struggle is necessary to accomplish their task. Avoid the temptation, for example, to button children's coats or put lids on the paints to save time. Help them do it themselves. Doing things for them can convey to children the message that they are not competent.

Teach children strategies to accomplish tasks. Help children attribute their successes to effort and to their use of specific strategies. "I can't" sometimes means "I don't know how." Rather than encouragement, children sometimes need specific instruction in particular strategies to carry out a task. Break these strategies down into smaller steps.

Avoid comparison between children; avoid competition. The self-concepts of many children suffer when comparisons between children are made. Comparison and competition point not only to winners but also to those who have not come out on top. Support each child's accomplishments independently and encourage them improving on their personal best.

Help children feel they have some control

Provide opportunities for choice, initiative, and autonomy. Provide opportunities for children to accomplish a variety of tasks at a variety of levels. Give young children simple choices: for example, which task to do first or which of two colors to use. Let children choose which song to sing or game to play next.

Help children learn to evaluate their own accomplishments. Children need to learn to evaluate their own performance so that they will not become dependent on adults for feelings of self-worth. Ask them what their favorite part of their picture or story is, or ask them to look at how their letters compare with those they did last month, so they can see their progress for themselves.

Help children learn interpersonal skills

Help children learn skills to enter interactions with others. Give children the words they need to express their desires and feelings. Help them learn how to enter play and how to resolve conflicts. Knowledge of how to interact appropriately with peers is likely to enhance peer acceptance and liking. Being accepted and liked, in turn, is related to children's social self-concept.

Become aware of your own expectations for children

Be open to perceiving new information about children and looking at them in new ways. Young children are surprising. All of a sudden, they seem to show new skills. Reappraise your expectations frequently. Let children know you have confidence in their ability to learn new skills.

Monitor whether your expectations differ for girls and boys or for children of different racial and ethnic groups. Having different expectations for girls and boys can convey cues to children about areas where it is and isn't "appropriate" to become competent. If teachers support only boys in playing with blocks, for example, they deprive girls of an opportunity to develop positive attitudes and competence at certain skills related to success in mathematics and certain types of problem solving. Implement activities in all areas so that both boys and girls and children from all cultures can and do explore them.

Updated from the Research in Review article in the July 1989 issue of *Young Children*.

Hermine H. Marshall is professor emerita at San Francisco State University.

References

Bacon, J., & H.L. Carter. 1991. Culture and mathematics learning: A review of the literature. *Journal of Research and Development in Education* 25: 1–9.

Butler, R. 1998. Age trends in the use of social and temporal comparison for self-evaluation: Examination of a novel development hypothesis. *Child Development* 69 (4): 1054–73.

Cassidy, J. 1988. Child-mother attachment and the self in six-year-olds. *Child Development* 59 (1): 121–34.

Chen, X., P.D. Hastings, K.H. Rubin, J. Chen, G. Cen, & S. Stewart. 1998. Child-rearing attitudes and behavioral inhibition in Chinese and Canadian toddlers. *Developmental Psychology* 34: 677–86.

Copple, C., & S. Bredekamp, eds. 2009. *Developmentally appropriate practice in early childhood programs serving children from birth through age 8.* 3d ed. Washington, DC: NAEYC.

Damon, W., & D. Hart. 1982. The development of self-understanding from infancy through adolescence. *Child Development* 53: 841–64.

Delgado-Gaitan, C. 1994. Socializing young children in Mexican-American families: An intergenerational perspective. In *Cross-cultural roots of minority child development,* eds. P.M. Greenfield & R.R. Hocking, 55–86. Hillsdale, NJ: Lawrence Erlbaum.

Dohnt, H.K., & M. Tiggemann. 2006. Body image concerns in young girls: The role of peers and media prior to adolescence. *Journal of Youth and Adolescence* 35 (2): 141–51.

Garcia Coll, C. 1990. Developmental outcome of minority infants: A process-oriented look into our beginnings. *Child Development* 61: 270–89.

Greenfield, P.M. 1994. Independence and interdependence as developmental scripts: Implications for theory, research, and practice. In *Cross-cultural roots of minority child development,* eds. P.M. Greenfield & R.R. Hocking. Hillsdale, NJ: Lawrence Erlbaum.

Harter, S. 1983. Developmental perspectives on the self-system. In *Handbook of child psychology, vol. 4: Socialization, personality and social development,* 4th ed., ed. E.M. Hetherington, 275–386. New York: John Wiley & Sons.

Harter, S. 1986. Processes underlying the construction, maintenance, and enhancement of the self-concept in children. In *Psychological perspectives of the self1, vol. 3,* eds. J. Suls & A. Greenwald, 137–81. Hillsdale, NJ: Lawrence Erlbaum.

Harter, S. 1998. The development of self-representations. In *Handbook of child psychology, vol. 3: Social, emotional and personality development,* 5th ed., ed. N. Eisenberg, 553–617. New York: John Wiley & Sons.

Harter, S. 2006. The self. In *Handbook of child psychology, vol. 3: Social, emotional and personality development,* 6th ed., ed. N. Eisenberg, 505–70. New York: John Wiley & Sons.

Harter, S., & R. Pike. 1984. The pictorial scale of perceived competence and social acceptance for young children. *Child Development* 55: 1969–82.

Hitz, R., & A. Driscoll. 1988. Praise or encouragement? New insights into praise: Implications for early childhood teachers. *Young Children* 43 (5): 6–13.

Honig, A. 1984. Research in review: Risk factors in infants and young children. *Young Children* 39 (4): 60–73.

Kamins, M.L., & C.S. Dweck. 1999. Person versus process praise and criticism: Implications for contingent self-worth and coping. *Developmental Psychology* 35 (3): 835–47.

Katz, L.G. 1993. Are we confusing self-esteem and narcissism? *Young Children* 49 (1): 2–3.

Keller, A., L. Ford, & J. Meacham. 1978. Dimensions of self-concept in preschool children. *Developmental Psychology* 14: 483–89.

Killen, M. 1997. Commentary—Culture, self and development: Are cultural templates useful or stereotypic? *Developmental Review* 17: 239–49.

Lewis, M., & J. Brooks-Gunn. 1979. *Social cognition and the acquisition of self.* New York: Plenum.

Lin, C.C., & V.R. Fu. 1990. A comparison of child-rearing practices among Chinese, immigrant Chinese, and Caucasian-American parents. *Child Development* 61: 429–33.

Maccoby, E., & J. Martin. 1983. Socialization in the context of the family: Parent-child interaction. In *Handbook of child psychology, vol. 4: Socialization, personality, and social development,* 4th ed., ed. E.M. Hetherington, 1–102. New York: John Wiley & Sons.

Markus, H.R., & S. Kitayama. 1991. Culture and the self: Implications for cognition, emotion, and motivation. *Psychological Review* 98 (2): 224–53.

Marsh, H. 1984. Relations among dimensions of self-attributions, dimensions of self-concept and academic achievement. *Journal of Educational Psychology* 76: 1291–308.

Marshall, H.H. 2001. Cultural influences on the development of self-concept: Updating our thinking. *Young Children* 56 (6): 19–25.

Marshall, H.H., & R.S. Weinstein. 1984. Classroom factors affecting students' self-evaluations. *Review of Educational Research* 54: 301–25.

McLloyd, V. 1999. Cultural influences in a multicultural society: Conceptual and methodological issues. In *Cultural processes in child development: The Minnesota Symposia on Child Psychology, vol. 29,* ed. A.S. Masten, 123–26. Mahwah, NJ: Lawrence Erlbaum.

Measelle, J.R., J.C. Ablow, P.A. Cowan, & C.P. Cowan. 1998. Assessing young children's views of their academic, social and emotional lives: An evaluation of the self-perception scales of the Berkeley Puppet Interview. *Child Development* 69 (6): 1556–76.

Morrison, J.W., & T. Bordere. 2001. Supporting biracial children's identity development. *Childhood Education* 77 (3): 134–38.

Morrison, J.W., & L.S. Rodgers. 1996. Being responsive to the needs of children from dual heritage backgrounds. *Young Children* 52 (1): 29–33.

Nelson, L.J., K.R. Rubin, & N.A. Fox. 2005. Social withdrawal, observed peer acceptance, and the development of self-perceptions in children ages 4 to 7 years. *Early Childhood Research Quarterly* 20 (2): 185–200.

Nicholls, J.G. 1978. The development of the concepts of effort and ability, perceptions of academic attainment and the understanding that difficult tasks require more ability. *Child Development* 49 951–59.

Rosenholtz, S.J., & S.H. Rosenholtz. 1981. Class-room organization and the perception of ability. *Sociology of Education* 54: 132–40.

Rubin, K.H. 1998. Social and emotional development from a cultural perspective. *Developmental Psychology* 34: 611–15.

Ruble, D., A. Boggiano, N. Feldman, & J. H. Loebl. 1980. Developmental analysis of the role of social comparison in self-evaluation. *Developmental Psychology* 16: 105–15.

Ryan, R., J. Connell, & E. Deci. 1985. A motivational analysis of self-determination and self-regulation in education. In *Research on motivation in education, vol. 2: The classroom milieu,* eds. C. Ames & R. Ames, 13–52. New York: Academic.

Sears, R. 1970. Relation of early socialization experiences to self-concepts and gender role in middle childhood. *Child Development* 41: 267–89.

Selman, R. 1980. *The growth of interpersonal understanding.* New York: Academic.

Shavelson, R., J. Hubner, & G. Stanton. 1976. Self-concept: Validation of construct interpretations. *Review of Educational Research* 46: 407–42.

Stipek, D., & D. Daniels. 1988. Declining perceptions of competence: A consequence of changes in the child or in the educational environment. *Journal of Educational Psychology* 80: 352–56.

Summerlin, M.L., & G.R. Ward. 1978. The effect of parental participation in a parent group on a child's self-concept. *Psychological Reports* 100: 227–32.

Vandell, D.L., & S.E. Hembree. 1994. Peer social status and friendship: Independent contribuors to children's social and academic adjustment. *Merrill-Palmer Quarterly* 40 (4): 461–71.

Verscheuren, K., P. Buyk, & A. Marcoen. 2001. Self-representations and socioemotional competence in young children: A 3-year longitudinal study. *Developmental Psychology* 31 (1): 126–34.

Wang, Q. 2004. The emergence of cultural self-constructs: Autobiographical memory and self-descriptions in European American and Chinese children. *Developmental Psychology* 40 (1): 3–15.

Weinstein, R.S., H.H. Marshall, L. Sharp, & M. Botkin. 1987. Pygmalion and the student: Age and classroom differences in children's awareness of teacher expectations. *Child Development* 58: 1079–93.

White, R. 1959. Motivation reconsidered: The concept of competence. *Psychological Review* 66: 297–333.

7 Stress and Young Children

Alice Sterling Honig

It's a truism that stress is a fact of life. Children's stress can easily be recognized as they learn to use utensils rather than fingers, ask for a toy rather than snatch it from a peer, and remember to say "thank you" to grandparents bearing gifts. Still, such socialization milestones will prove more stressful for some children than for others. So what is *stress*?

"Stress is a nonspecific response of the body to any demand that exceeds that particular person's ability to cope" (Honig 1986a, 51). Selye, the father of stress research, specified that when a stressed person perceives a stimulus event as being severe enough, then it produces disequilibrium in the homeostatic system (1982). Different persons respond in different ways to restore homeostasis, or balance, physiologically and emotionally. The circumstances that provoke stress responses vary a great deal for different children, and their responses also differ markedly. Risk factors for stress in some children might pose a positive challenge or seem more manageable for a resilient youngster. A child whose family moves frequently mourns the loss of neighborhood play-

mates and is angry and noncompliant with parents. Yet another child is excited about the possibilities of exploring and adventuring in the new neighborhood.

Some children will respond to stress based on how much control they *feel* they have over the situation. Some children are more likely to respond with strong negative emotions. Others, more secure and more sure of their skills, respond by trying to problem solve rather than dissolve into tears or terror.

Stress can have *short term* or *more lasting effects*. Stress from a single bout of illness may be debilitating and worrisome, but again, the results may be short-lived. Children do differ in resilience and resourcefulness. A child whose parents are neglectful may seek out a nurturing neighbor or aunt to provide the cherishing attentiveness that permits a child to thrive. However, some one-time events may create stress that is overwhelmingly traumatic, as when children in Darfur watch a mother raped and killed, or a child's father has been maimed or killed in the Iraq war. The effects of such horrific stress may last a lifetime for a child, regardless of temperament or resourcefulness. In today's world, *economic and societal stresses*, as when parents become unemployed and face home foreclosure, urgently impact children's lives. In 2006 in the United States:

- 8 million children did not have health insurance,
- more than 3 million children were reported abused or neglected, and
- 13 million children lived in poverty (Every Child Matters Education Fund 2009).

Some stressors have *severe long term effects*, as when a child undergoes frequent chemotherapy for cancer, is regularly beaten by a caregiver, suffers severe burns in a fire, or is badly hurt in a traffic accident.

Some stresses are *direct*, as when a child is bullied and menaced by classmates or a child with cancer undergoes a painful bone marrow transplant. Some stresses are *indirect*, resulting from parental or neighborhood events. A parent, afraid of gang activity and violence outside, keeps her high-energy young child cooped up in a small apartment. Crabby and demanding, that child shows he is feeling stressed by acting cranky and unhappy because he cannot romp and run and play outdoors.

Multiple stresses do not just add up. Rather, they have multiplicative effects. Rutter's (1983) research in England revealed far more severe and long-lasting psychiatric effects when children have experienced four or more stresses all together—such as poverty, single-parent family, parental drug abuse, and low maternal education. Other family stresses include parent unemployment, poor maternal health, food insecurity, large family size (more than four children at home), receipt of welfare, and teenage parenting.

Research on sources of stress for children gives insights into many different *sources* of and evidence for child stress. An interesting measure of child stress is absenteeism from school. According to the Early

> **Multiple stresses do not just add up. Rather, they have multiplicative effects.**

Childhood Longitudinal Study (Walston & West 2004), when there were three or more long-term family stressors, kindergartners tended to have higher absenteeism than did peers from families with fewer stressors. Examining these data, Romero and Lee (2008) emphasize the importance of assessing a wide variety of stress risk factors and signs. Across ethnic groups, *cumulative exposure* to risk best predicted stresses that resulted in chronic absenteeism in early schooling.

Potential risk factors for stress

There are many potential contributors to children's stress.

Attachment problems

Across many cultures, infants are likely to be securely attached when their mothers provide nurturing care. Nurturing caregivers observe individual child distress signals that reflect baby's need for nursing, soothing, intimate social interaction, cuddling, or a fresh diaper. When such needs are promptly and effectively responded to, then children grow up to become *securely attached*. They act more friendly with peers; they settle fusses more peaceably. They are more likely to try hard to solve a problem, more likely to cooperate with adult suggestions, and less likely to give up and have a temper tantrum when faced with challenges (Honig 1986b; Sroufe & Fleeson 1986; Honig 2002).

When their distress signals are not noticed or appropriately responded to, children develop a range of insecure attachment behaviors with caregivers. Parent stress affects *how* a child responds to stress, and, if severe and prolonged, it can potentially lead to neurological brain change (Gunnar & Quevedo 2007) as well as to insecure attachment. Some children's insecure attachments are *anxious/ambivalent*. These children have not been able to count on consistent, harmonious attentiveness during the first years of life.

Some infants and toddlers eventually cease signaling distress; after many frustrating attempts to gain adult comfort when they feel stressed, they have learned that they are rarely likely to get their needs met. These *avoidantly attached* babies look more "mature" on entry to child care, since they may not act upset when left in the care of others. However, a few years later, their bullying behaviors and their impulsive angers when thwarted reveal the avoidant attachment (Ainsworth 1973). The direct impact of insecure attachment between infant and parent—a stressor that negatively impacts a variety of child behaviors and interpersonal interactions over time—has been verified in a wide range of cultures (van IJzendoorn & de Wolff 1997).

Neurological and physical problems

Despite nurturing care, autism, epilepsy, hydrocephalus, and other chronic neurological problems present formidable stresses that may result in lifelong frustrations and problems in school and socialization. Neurological problems can be genetic, arise in utero, or be a result of birth traumas and prematurity. Some neurological disorders stem from maternal drug use during pregnancy. For example, children whose mothers were alcoholics during pregnancy are born with facial abnormalities, lower cognitive abilities, and behavioral difficulties. Babies who are heroin-addicted in the womb show marked stress responses to drug withdrawal—strong bodily tremors after birth, difficulties with sleep, difficulties with being soothed, and more.

Swaddling and low-key soothing techniques sometimes help when caring for babies burdened with such stresses. Cerebral palsy and spasticity conditions require interdisciplinary cooperation among parents and specialists. Specialists' interventions that assist children (e.g., physiotherapy, specific feeding techniques, orthopedic leg splints) often reduce parental stress, as well (Odom et al. 2003).

ADD (Attention Deficit Disorder) and ADHD (Attention Deficit and Hyperactivity Disorder), more and more frequently diagnosed in children, are associated with increased activity levels, high distractibility, and lack of ability to focus attentively and persevere to accomplish school tasks. Such stresses cause classroom disruptions and teacher disapproval, which may take the form of blaming parents for a child's inappropriate classroom behaviors. In some cases, pediatricians prescribe medication, used just for school hours, that supports a child's ability to stay in seat and to focus during class time. Improved classroom behaviors and more successful school achievements relieve the stress on both parents and children.

Sensory integration deficits increase misery and stress. Some children cannot bear the touch of certain clothing, even a tag on a T-shirt. Some have auditory sensitivities. Other children have trouble processing auditory requests, especially if adult speech is too rapid (Roley, Blanche, & Schaaf 2001). Seasoned clinicians vividly describe the difficulties some children have in managing to organize responses to the world (Greenspan & Weider 1998). Their work provides supportive suggestions for therapists, parents, and teachers to gain insights and ideas to increase these children's comfort and competence.

Hearing or visual loss and language difficulties contribute to stress when peers avoid befriending a child because of them. Children struggle with speech and/or literacy when they have dysarthria (abnormal tongue protrusion and misarticulation arising from difficulty controlling speech musculature), apraxia (articulation errors, repetitions, and sound reversals in expressive speech), and dyslexia (troubles with reading). Such stresses seriously increase child frustrations and feelings of anguish when they are unable to communicate with peers or unable to do academic work with ease (Harris 1990).

Maternal employment during the first year of life

Researchers have assessed the potential stress arising from timing of maternal entry into employment and daily differences in *duration* of time infants spend in nonmaternal care. Reports suggest that toddlers with employed mothers express more anger and aggression toward adults and peers and are less cooperative with caregivers, and some infants tend to exhibit more insecure attachments (Crockenberg & Litman 1991). Teachers reported that preschoolers whose mothers were employed full time during the children's first year of life had somewhat higher aggression levels and also increased abstraction ability (Park & Honig 1991). NICHD longitudinal research (1998) at a variety of sites across the United States found that during the first 15 months of life, infants in poor-quality care or in nonmaternal care more than 10 hours a week were only more likely to be insecurely attached if their mothers were less sensitive in responding to them (Owen 2002). British longitudinal studies of extensive, full-time child care in infancy and early childhood showed that home environment factors were more significant than center quality (Deater-Deckard & Scarr 1996).

Maternal behavior prior to return to work may affect child stress afterward. A Canadian study of stressed infants reported that mothers' health status and anxieties *prior* to choosing infant/toddler care had significant effects. Children of stressed mothers showed more anxious/withdrawn and aggressive/destructive behaviors six months after mother's return to employment (McKim, Stuart, &

O'Connor 1996). In comparing groups of 10- to 12-month-old infants with insecure avoidant attachment who were either in part-time or full-time care, Belsky (1991) observed them as they were reunited with their mothers after being briefly left alone with an unfamiliar adult. Those infants with extensive experience in nonparental care whimpered, fussed, and cried more than did the other babies, and they played with toys less.

It is possible that the stresses of full-time, nonmaternal care are greater when infants have insecure attachments to mothers. The findings of these studies provide a powerful rationale for educators to include supports for families as integral components of care provision. Ahnert and Lamb (2003) suggested that maladaptive behavior of children who spend many hours in child care may reflect lack of parental ability to *buffer* the levels of stress that the child experiences in nonmaternal care. Thus, infant stress may result from *indirect effects* of lengthy maternal employment.

Effects of maternal employment may also depend on *time of data collection*. When infants were followed up at 20 months in a study of infant-father attachment, but not at 12 months, a higher proportion of insecure attachment was found between fathers and sons, but not between fathers and daughters, in dual- compared with single-earner families (Chase-Lansdale & Owen 1987). In the Wisconsin Maternity Leave and Health project, fathers with unemployed wives expressed greater positive affect, sensitivity, and responsiveness and had higher levels of involvement when their infants were 4 and 12 months old. When moms worked fewer than 25 hours per week, there was no association between paternal parenting quality and involvement.

However, fathers whose wives worked more than 25 hours per week were *required* to provide more infant care. When the babies were 4 months old, these fathers showed lower levels of positive affect and more stress (especially with babies who had difficult temperaments). Thus, maternal employment does not have simple, direct effects on the developing father-child relationships (Grych & Clark 1999). Many factors, including the father's feelings of increasing competence and pleasure at caregiving, marital quality, and infant temperament *all* need to be considered when seeking to understand and reduce potential stress in the lives of infants and young children in dual career families.

Repetti and Wood (1997) interviewed employed mothers and videotaped reunion activities with their children at pickup time at the end of the work day. After a day where they had experienced high stress from co-workers and supervisors, moms described themselves as acting more withdrawn from their preschoolers. When videotaped during reunion play sessions at the end of the day, highly work-stressed moms tended to give their children fewer signs of approval. They acted less caring and loving, but not more impatient with their preschoolers. Employed mothers seemed to *protect* their preschoolers from the adult high-stress experiences by emotional withdrawal and less social interaction rather than display irritability.

Child gender

Gender must be considered as a possible stressor. Although the negative effects of poor-quality child care on child behavior were greater for children of employed mothers, boys (but not girls) of employed mothers were rated as more defiant than children with non-employed mothers (Crockenberg & Litman 1991). This gender effect was found even though mothers who worked longer hours were more responsive to their children at dinner time and in a laboratory setting.

Third-grade boys who had experienced extensive nonmaternal care during the first two years of life showed more

> Head Start boys with close teacher-child relationships had higher behavioral competence and lower aggression.

negative behaviors with parents, teachers, and peers (Vandell & Corasaniti 1990). In a study of middle-class group care in Israel, boys but not girls showed more stress and social difficulties when there were fewer caregivers per group (Bornstein et al. 2006). Head Start boys (but not girls) with close teacher-child relationships had higher behavioral competence and lower aggression (Ewing & Taylor 2009).

Difficult child temperament

Children's temperament behaviors cluster into three major styles. Some infants are *easy*. They nurse well, have predictable rhythms for sleeping and feeding, respond happily to adult handling and soothing, respond less intensely when distressed, are able to self-soothe, and recover fairly easily from upsets. Children referred to as *slow to warm up* or *inhibited* withdraw from new experiences, such as new foods or caregivers, and they take a long time to adjust after feeling stressed.

In a French child care research project, when responsive caregivers were attentive to the children early in play sessions, their stress levels were even lower than for children at home. During a later free play session without adult support, most of the children's cortisol levels remained stable, rather than decreasing as they did for at-home children. But, significantly, one third of the children whose mothers had stated that their children particularly needed adult attentive supports, showed an increase in cortisol levels, a reflection of increased stress (Legendre 1998). Most children love free play. But teachers will want to note those children who need more supportive adult interactions during the free play situations that other children anticipate with pleasure.

A third temperament group has been called *difficult* or *feisty*. These babies have irregular bodily schedules for feeding, sleeping, and voiding. They respond with intense emotions when stressed and have difficulties in self-regulation or being soothed. Some are distractible and unable to persevere at frustrating tasks. Their high activity levels present challenges that stress caregivers and may make teacher-child interactions problematic. High-risk, predominantly Mexican-American mothers who perceived they had low "power" (as measured by a Family Stress Checklist) acted with higher stress toward infants and toddlers who had a highly active, more anger-prone temperament (Matorell & Bugental 2006). The mothers used more harsh control practices, such as spanking; they blamed their hard-to-manage toddlers more and felt angry. However, the mothers with lower "perceived control over failure" scores did not act harshly toward infants who had "easy" temperaments.

The researchers speculated that mothers of temperamentally difficult babies perceived apparent unresponsiveness and noncompliance not as a temperament trait, but as a way for the children to show that they were more powerful than their moms, and that perhaps the mothers were reacting with fear-oriented defensive aggression. Child stress reactivity (measured by cortisol level) and parents' own perception of "powerlessness" interacted to produce negative stressful outcomes for children. On a hopeful note, the researchers described their earlier work in a cognitively-based home visitation program, which had enhanced parent empowerment and was able to "lead parents away from feelings of powerlessness and/or blame of children and toward mastery over the challenges associated with parenting a difficult infant" (Matorell & Bugental 2006, 646).

Cortisol, the primary stress hormone and the measure of stress in much of the research, is measured by a saliva swab

> Child stress and parents' own perception of "powerlessness" interacted to produce negative stressful outcomes for children.

from a child's cheek. Stress attributed to group care has been asserted to activate a child's hypothalamic pituitary-adrenal axis (HPA) and cause overproduction of stress hormones (Brandtjen 2001). Lower cortisol levels have been reported for children cared for at home rather than in group care. Other research has found more subtle effects. Nachmias and colleagues (1996) reported elevated cortisol levels only when mothers interfered with their 18-month-old toddler's coping efforts in play with a clown toy *and* the toddlers had both an inhibited, shy temperament and also an insecure attachment relationship with the mother.

Gender and temperament interact to increase children's stress. In Switzerland, 5-year-old children's HPA system activity varied by child gender (Hatzinger et al. 2007). Girls showed a significantly higher hormonal release during stress than boys. Yet, when challenged by stress, the kindergarten boys' (but not the girls') increased HPA systems were significantly associated with hyperactivity, impulsivity, and emotional problems. The researchers alert us to the fact that observed neurobiological changes under stress are gender specific already by age 5! Teachers need to be aware that stress seems to have more worrisome behavioral consequences for young boys than young girls. Long-term follow-up gender studies of response to stress are urgently needed.

In the Netherlands, low-income mothers of highly irritable infants (1–6 months) provided less physical contact, and were less responsive to positive signals (van den Boom & Hoeksma 1994). Mothers with "easy" infants showed an initial higher level of visual and physical involvement and were more responsive to positive infant signals. The researchers concluded that care and level of involvement provided for nonirritable infants was high from the start, and that *harmonious interactions* enabled nonirritable infants to develop skills to regulate distress on their own. Infant temperament in combination with adult care patterns may lead over time to more worrisome predictions for irritable infants.

Mothers with postpartum depression are more likely to rate their babies as temperamentally difficult (Whiffen 1990). Yet earlier research reported that when mothers of irritable infants were initially highly engaged with their babies and also had spousal support, there was no difference in rates of secure attachment when irritable infants were compared with nonirritable babies at 1 year (Crockenberg 1981).

Researchers suggest a *differential susceptibility hypothesis*: Children possibly differ in the degree to which parenting interactions affect their stress and adjustment. In an analysis of data from the National Institute of Child Health and Human Development Study of Early Child Care:

> Temperament moderated associations between maternal parenting styles during early childhood and children's first-grade academic competence, social skills, and relationships with teachers and peers. Relations between parenting and first-grade outcomes were stronger for difficult than for less difficult infants. Infants with difficult temperaments had better adjustment than less difficult infants when parenting quality was high and poorer adjustment when parenting quality was lower. (Stright, Gallagher, & Kelley 2008, 186)

Problematic parenting behaviors and interactions

Some parental behaviors increase child stress. More than 95 percent of parents of toddlers in national studies report spanking their toddlers. Parents in 10 child care centers in Chicago who reported child behavior problems also reported that they themselves had more stress, lower self-efficacy, and used coercive, irritable, and inconsistent discipline strategies with their toddlers (Gross & Fogg 1999).

Some parents use harsh physical punishment routinely, while others spank minimally and rarely. Frequent corporal punishment has been linked to child behavior problems such as physical violence. The more corporal punishment a child experiences, the more stressed the child and worse the child's behavior (Straus 2001). Even five years after the researchers recorded parental corporal punishment patterns, the more corporally punished children fought more in school, and teachers reported higher levels of antisocial behaviors, such as cheating, bullying others, disobedience at school, and trouble getting along with teachers. Programs can help by providing safe, high-quality care for their children, in addition to facilitating better parent education. Thus, children's participation in Head Start has been related to an increase in parental reports of less domestic violence and a marked decrease in spanking children (Magnuson & Waldfogel 2005).

Maternal depression negatively affects even newborns. Babies show dysregulation of behavior possibly deriving from prenatal chemical imbalance. Field (2000) reported that the disorganizing influence of depressed mothers' interactions after birth led to long-lasting stresses for children. In a multiethnic sample of high-risk Early Head Start families, over one third of the variance in child aggression by 43 months was accounted for by parent depression, stress, and bickering (Malik et al. 2007).

Parenting interaction styles exacerbate or mitigate child stress. A stressed child might, for example, be feeling resentment that the parents consider a sibling "prettier" or "smarter." An older child might express anger and act jealous of attention given to younger sibling, or vice versa—and then the child's aggressive and hurtful actions toward the sibling lead to parental angry punishment that may increase the jealous child's stress. When maternal life stresses, attachment style, and preschool behavior problems were investigated together, children who had internalizing and externalizing behavior problems had also experienced significantly higher levels of dyadic stress with mothers (Call 1999).

Children respond with subtle and indirect effects such as imitating inappropriate parenting behaviors in aggressive or sexualized play with other children. *Goodness of fit* between child and adult matters. Adult emotional characteristics impact children. When parent-child relationships are characterized by mutually enjoyed, shared activities and cooperation, then children show increased positive mood and prosocial interactions with peers (Rutter 1979; Kochanska 2002). When parents had low levels of pessimism, then their children were more likely to be engaged in positive social and dramatic play and conversations with peers. These results were even more evident for children rated low in emotional affect by parents (Jones & Lagace-Sequin 2006).

Childhood family trauma

The greatest stress for children is caused by loss of a parent through death or abandonment. Bowlby, the father of attachment theory, believed that the effects of such loss and bereavement on children are among the most severe and long lasting (1958).

Violent or neglectful parenting also causes severe stress. PTSD (Post-Traumatic Stress Disorder) is the most common psychiatric diagnosis for children (Perry 1994). Insensitive, intrusive, or abusive care stimulates increases in cortisol. Suffering from violence in childhood proves overwhelmingly traumatic for children.

Perry (2002), a child psychiatrist specializing in child abuse/neglect, noted that *freeze, flight, or fight* characterize the stress responses of these children.

Perry's long clinical experience confirms that stresses from abuse/neglect have devastating and long-lasting, stressful impacts on brain development as well as behavior. These stress symptoms cluster and include: oppositional defiant disorder; phobias; separation anxiety disorder; frequent and sudden behavioral regressions; aggressions against self and others; bodily loss of regulation for eating, sleeping, and self-care; frequent somatic complaints; seeming lack of awareness of danger; self-hatred and self-blame; and chronic feelings of incompetence (Kirmayer, Lemelson, & Barad 2007).

Work with families can ameliorate these worrisome prognoses (Perry, Kaufmann, & Knitzer 2007; Lieberman & Van Horn 2008). In a follow-up study 15 years after program babies' birth, Olds and colleagues (1997) reported that unmarried, low-income women who were visited by nurses during pregnancy and infancy (in comparison with not-visited control mothers) "were significantly less likely to be identified as perpetrators of child abuse and neglect" (637). Notable also is their review of New York State records revealing that the home-visited mothers in comparison with controls had much lower levels of arrest. Thus, home visitation was instrumental in decreasing the distress children would otherwise be likely to suffer if their parents were incarcerated.

Effects of parent stress on children. Low-income African-American mothers (of school age children) who reported experiencing violent physical and verbal partner abuse also reported high levels of stress, as measured by the Abidin Parenting Stress Index (Owen, Thompson, & Kaslow 2006). Child stress was reported by these mothers using the 113-item CBCL (Child Behavior Checklist) (Achenbach & Edelbrock 1991).

> When parent-child relationships are characterized by mutually enjoyed, shared activities, then children show increased positive mood.

Dysfunctional parent interactions were highly associated with difficult child behaviors. Thus, Achenbach and Edelbrock (1991) concluded that the effect of high levels of parental interpersonal violence on child stress was mediated "through mothers' experience of parenting stress" (509). That is, the marital stress mothers experience is transmitted to children via the mothers' feelings and actions with their children, which increases children's stress. Mothers who reported their 3-year-olds as oppositional, defiant, and hyperactive also tended to report more high-intensity couple conflict with more maternal verbal aggression and higher levels of family stressors than did mothers of non-problem children (Goldstein et al. 2007). *Clusters of family stressors* adversely affect very young children.

Internalizing as well as externalizing behaviors are markers of high child stress (Mash & Barkley 1996). Internalizing is characterized by social withdrawal, social anxiety, shyness, or behavioral inhibition. Externalizing behaviors include oppositionality, aggression, lack of impulse control, and disruptive conduct. In an Australian study of 2-year-old children, predictors of early childhood *internalizing* difficulties were identified as overprotective/overinvolved parenting, low parental warmth and engagement, and high parental anxiety/depression (Bayer, Sanson, & Hemphill 2006).

Almost a half century ago, Baumrind (1967) identified three major parenting styles. Both *permissive* and *authoritarian* parenting lead to more problematic child behaviors. Battered mothers in homeless shelters endorsed higher levels of permissive parenting than control mothers from the same community. Among these mothers, parental hostility particularly exacerbated children's internalizing and externalizing behavior problems. In contrast, *authoritative* parenting promotes child adjustment in the face of domestic violence (Rossman & Robbie 2005). Authoritative parents show warmth and active interest in their children, have high standards for child behavior, and set clear rules and reasons for rules; teachers rate these children as well adjusted in class (Baumrind 1967).

Parenting stress decreases maternal ability to offer warmth and empathic responding. Also, Head Start mothers who felt less competent said that they experienced more parenting stress (Singh 2003). How can parental stress be reduced? Wolfe and Hirsch (2003) report that allowing parents to share experiences, to reflect on their childhood experiences, and to develop supportive relationships with other parents in the group effectively reduced parenting stress in low-income parents of color.

Divorce and custody battles between parents thrust children into painful conditions that can have long-lasting stress effects. Some schools have programs where trained social workers meet in the school with groups of children who can freely talk about their painful, worried, and angry experiences and feelings about their parents' divorce and share their feelings in the group.

School and classroom stresses

Stress is easy to diagnose if a hungry baby wakes from a nap in nursery and yowls loudly for a feeding. A few years later, signs of stress may be subtler. A preschooler persistently cannot settle into sleep; he lies alert and tense on his cot in child care. Or a kindergarten child grimaces with fear of being slapped as the adult stretches out her arm to stroke her hair. The alert teacher recognizes stressed responses and consults with the center director about reaching out to the family. A teacher notices that one child bites his fingernails until they bleed. A family child care provider notices that other kids always designate a particular child to play the role of "baby" and never let him play any other role in their dramatic play. Unrecognized child stresses can have far reaching effects.

Children in school suffer stress when they appear "different" to classmates. Perhaps their speech is impaired. Playmates who cannot understand them avoid them. Some children are obese and slower in sport activities. Obese children as young as 3 years old are more likely to be characterized by peers as "mean, stupid, ugly, and sloppy" (Christoffersen 2007, A-4).

In gym class, an obese 5-year-old could only hang from the bars a few seconds before falling down on the mat. Other preschoolers could hold on much longer. The children all laughed loudly at his failure as he forlornly returned to sit among his classmates with tears silently running down his face.

Identifying sources of stress and finding creative ways to intervene to ameliorate stress may not be easy. High-quality care makes a crucial difference in child stress levels. Children attending high-quality programs in Perth, Australia showed a decline in cortisol across the child care day (Sims et al. 2006). In contrast, children attending low-quality child care showed a cortisol increase across the day. Child care quality plays a vital role in reducing child stress!

Bullying is an endemic stress for many children in school. There are books and games available to help teachers learn to recognize different types of bullying and to engage classmates in solving social situation scenarios so that children can be included and feel safe and befriended. Teachers inspire children to think more empathically and flexibly about others' motives. Children then become aware of different reasons for what seems like provocative peer behavior. Then a child will be less likely to "beat up" a peer who

bumped into him accidentally while just galloping past to get to a tricycle on the playground. Teachers can actively engage children to consider and employ anger management techniques (Honig 2004; Orpinas & Horne 2006; Honig 2008).

Physical and social attributes of child care settings also influence child stress. Cross-cultural research has pinpointed the sources of child stress in care settings. In U.S. centers, the most common sources of stress found for 2-, 3-, and 4-year-olds involve struggles over toys or freedom of locomotion and situations when a child is the victim of peer aggression (Fleury 1998). Researchers in France found that cortisol increased among toddlers when there was large group size and less available play area per child in the centers, and among infants in care who were less than 6 months old (Legendre 2003).

Child stress increases with too many changes in care venues and personnel. In the Netherlands, children enrolled in fewer different care arrangements showed less internalizing behavior and more well being in child care. When caregivers were familiar, trusted, and available and when staff turnover rate was lower, then positive caregiving behavior was higher (de Schipper, van IJzendoorn, & Tavecchio 2004).

Catastrophes

War, rape, hurricanes, tsunamis, and terrorist attacks cause immense pain and suffering for adults as well as children. In Holman's national study of over 2500 adults, roughly one in five adults cited severe stress symptoms just after the terrorist attacks of 9/11. Stress symptoms included "constant rumination about the events, emotional detachment, and loss of concentration…these superstressed individuals—most of whom saw the attacks on television—displayed a 53 percent increase in new cases of heart and blood vessel disorders over the next 3 years" (Bower 2008, 61).

After the terrorist attacks of 9/11, many child care providers reported that children obsessively carried out play scenarios bombing block towers with toy airplanes. Eleven-year-old children and their middle-class mothers were interviewed after those attacks. Hock and colleagues (2004) reported that children who vocalized anger seemed less frightened and worried. Perhaps expressions of anger warded off feelings of anxiety and fear. Strikingly, mothers were more likely to underreport, overlook, or misinterpret children's emotional stress reactions to this traumatic event. The children reported that they had experienced more intense emotions than their moms reported. Preexisting traits for both child and mother also predicted stress. Almost one third of the variance in self-reported fearful feelings was accounted for when children had high anxiety symptoms and mothers had heightened feelings of separation anxiety. Silverman and LaGreca (2002) observed:

> In all likelihood, parents who are having adjustment difficulties are less able to provide needed support and comfort to their children following disaster, which may adversely affect children's adjustment. Importantly, if children feel that adults are in control, it may prevent the children's symptoms from escalating. (29)

Stress reducers

Helping children feel safe and cherished is the first line of defense against stress. It's important to hone noticing skills. Observant teachers are alert to potentially worrisome neurobiological organization patterns. One child may have sensory threshold difficulties. Another reacts with intense body reactions and wild emotionality to a mild stress. Some infants find it difficult to develop harmonious patterns of feeding and sleeping. Others cannot organize sustained play behaviors alone or with peers; they wander across a room and carelessly swipe materials from tables. Some have troubles developing reciprocal social interactions with teachers or other children.

Teachers who are alert noticers become more effective "stress-busters" (Honig 2009). They tune into child discomforts; worried, sad looks; physical shrinking away from gentle adult touches; compulsive self-stimulation; sudden physical lashing out when criticized or angry; intense, emotional, frustrated meltdowns when a toy doesn't work as planned; inability to play peacefully with others; and tense shoulders, among other signs of stress. Empathy in combination with self-confidence has been shown to moderate adverse effects of high child stress (Walker & Cheng 2007).

Physical caresses, intimate turn-taking in talk, prompt responses to children's distress signals (such as hunger, pain, and need for cuddling), and intimate engagements with infants and toddlers promote secure attachment with adult caregivers (Honig 2002).

Tune into signals of social distress when a lonesome child is unable to engage purposefully or with pleasure with classroom materials and peers. Teachers boost sociability and group entry skills of shy children as they model words and ways that allow a child that coveted place in the play group (Honig & Thompson 1994).

Comforting separation rituals decrease child stress. Infants 6 to 18 months, whose mothers left them each day at a nursery, cried less when the separation was not prolonged in the morning, when caregivers consoled them empathically after mom left, and when the mother and baby evolved ritual patterns in morning good-byes and in greetings at the end of the day. In the morning, a caregiver most frequently held the child facing the mother, saying "good-bye, mommy" and waving good-bye either with or for the child. The mother's rituals consisted of kissing, patting, and embracing the child before leaving. These rituals evolved over months. Initially, children cried more if the staff urged the mother to leave quickly, but later in the year, the rituals served to decrease initial crying at separation by 85 percent (Klein, Kraft, & Shohet 2008).

Create an alternative, safe, intimate world in family child care, centers, or schools for children in chaotic life situations. Teachers and other child care providers are particularly crucial agents in keeping stress levels low and in helping to decrease stress levels when children are exposed to multiple stressors in their daily living environments. In the classic 40-year longitudinal study of children born at risk in 1955 on the island of Kauai, Werner (1993) specified the factors that promoted resiliency as well as stress. All the children had been born into poverty to low-education mothers. Almost half had suffered birth complications, and their families suffered discord, divorce, alcoholism, desertion, and mental illness. Despite these early stresses, about one third of the children grew into competent and caring adults. Infants who had experienced severe birth complications had lower IQ scores as toddlers (by as much as 37 points) when living in unstable family situations compared with stable families.

Over the next decades, the resilient children showed more resourcefulness at gaining other people's positive attentiveness and at solving their problems. The social environments of the resilient children also provided protective buffers. These included: small family size and several years of spacing between births, a child with an ongoing and continual relationship with a caring adult (including a grandparent or neighbor), low levels of family conflict, and the availability of remedial and counseling help. Notable in these findings is the powerful effect of consistent adult nurturing and effective supports for early literacy.

Intervention programs specifically designed to provide sustained support for at-risk families show impressive reductions of risk for later stresses in children's lives. When trained and caring home visitors provided information and nurturing and also modeled positive interactions with low-income, single, high school dropout, teen moms, then several years later, rates of conviction for child abuse/neglect were significantly lower for the home-visited families in comparison with stressed, at-risk mothers who did not receive the home visits (Honig & Morin 2001). More remarkably, when the home visitors began their work *prior* to the birth of the babies, those families were significantly less likely to have convictions of child abuse/neglect years later, even if the mothers dropped out of program without completing the full 18–24 months. Early intervention was crucial in decreasing stress and protecting young children from abuse/neglect.

Reflectivity is powerful in affecting the quality of child-caregiver relationships. Brophy-Herb and Honig (1997) studied mother-infant relations of teen mothers randomly assigned either to the control group or to home visitation over several months. Despite the weekly delivery of information and supports, whether teen mothers had expressed *reflectivity* proved most influential in how positive the young mothers were with their infants several months after home visitation had ended. Those teen mothers who reflected on how they had been parented and expressed strong wishes that their children not experience some of the harsh or inappropriate parenting they themselves had experienced in childhood had the most nurturing relationships with their infants, regardless of whether or not they had participated in several months of home visitation.

In Holland, low-income mothers with highly irritable infants were randomly assigned to intervention or to the control group. The home-visited mothers learned how to become good observers of their babies' stress and how to soothe and comfort their babies. At 1 year, intervention infants were far more likely to be securely attached to their mothers compared with control infants (van den Boom 1994). Home visitation supports for parents can serve as an impressive bulwark to counteract family stress due to difficult infant temperament (Honig 2002).

Comforting touch and comfort "lovies" ease infant stress. Soothing pats help bring up a gas bubble that was causing acute distress to a baby. Back rubs at naptime help toddlers sink into sleep. Sucking objects such as pacifiers and knobby, chewy tubes soothe teething babies and those stressed by worrisome, unfamiliar situations like a new child care setting. A child's beloved blanket, familiar and warm, soothes troubles and relaxes a stressed young one. Any "lovey" will do, as long as the child has endowed it with the *meaning* of familiarity and comfort.

Familiar lullabies and songs soothe children (Honig 2005). Songs also invigorate and give pleasure to children and ease them into group participation. In the 3-year-old classroom, one little fellow restlessly wriggled on his cot at naptime. The teacher softly sang the verses of "Hush little baby." He raised his head and smiled radiantly. "My Mama sings that!" he exclaimed and was then easily able to snuggle down for his nap.

Artwork can release child tensions. Provide materials such as playdough or clay for molding a ferocious dragon (representing the child's worries) that the child can safely squash back into a lump of clay while releasing some tense feelings. Physical freedom to romp, create body movements, and dance to music, as well as group exercises and rhythmic stretches and bends—all allow release of bodily tensions. Pretend play with props and materials that allow even angry symbolic acts, such as acting out fights between fantasy figures or animals, helps children master their fears and aggravations. Trained adults use these therapeutic techniques in safe spaces to help children interpret and recover from traumatic experiences (Haight et al. 2006; McCarthy 2007).

High-quality preschool programs help prevent the stress of later school failure.

Bibliotherapy is an important teacher technique to introduce children to other ways of thinking about their worry and figuring out how to cope with personal stresses. Books abound with themes that support children's particular sorrows, such as a parent's abandonment of the family or rejection by a former playmate who now chooses another friend to play with exclusively. Roberts and Crawford (2008) offer bibliotherapy resources for children experiencing family stressors.

High-quality preschool programs help prevent the stress of later school failure. The Abecedarian project in North Carolina provided intensive enrichment for infants of low-education, low-income, single mothers. Infants were randomly assigned to the program or control group. All the babies received free nutrition and pediatric care. By 3 years old, the program children were achieving scores of 98 on the Stanford-Binet intelligence test (where the normative mean is 100). Even those babies born biologically more at-risk due to low PI (Ponderal Index; low PI means longer, skinnier babies) scored 96. In contrast, the control preschoolers who had not been in the enrichment program had a mean IQ score of 84.7, and the low PI control children had a worrisome mean score of 70.6. Thus, years before these children would be going to kindergarten, high-quality child care made an impressive difference in decreasing the risks for later school failure, a major stressor for children (Ramey & Ramey 2007). Positive results persisted into early adulthood: Almost 70 percent of those who received the preschool treatment were either enrolled in higher education or worked skilled jobs, compared to 40 percent of the control youth.

Children who had attended high-quality early childhood education programs in Chicago were later less likely to be held back a grade or to drop out of high school and less likely to be arrested (Reynolds et al. 2001). Children who had attended the Syracuse Family Development Research Program for five years from early infancy were significantly less likely in adolescence to be convicted of juvenile delinquency and more likely to receive positive ratings from their parents and teachers (Lally, Mangione, & Honig 1988).

Stability in child care arrangements decreases stress. In centers in the Netherlands, measures of daily stability were created that carefully described staffing patterns, grouping, quality of care, daily maternal stress about the child's adjustment to care, and other program features. Children who experience fewer changes in their care arrangements during their childhoods showed less internalizing behavior and more well-being in their care settings, particularly when trusted caregivers were more available (de Schipper, van IJzendoorn, & Tavecchio 2004).

Remediation programs boost children's ability to avoid the stresses of school failure and grade repetition. Intensive summer programs in reading and writing for low-income Baltimore kindergarten children (who attended at least 75 percent of the time) boosted scores so that the children outperformed 81 percent of their peers who did not participate (Borman et al. 2004).

Community-wide efforts are needed. Resource and referral agencies that provide parents with information about child care facilities need to provide more guidelines to strengthen family positive interactions as well as choices for care providers.

Coaching caregivers and parents to relax when stressed so that their young children do not pick up on high parental anxiety is important. In a Swiss study of stress in pediatric practice, the researchers observe that talking with parents about "coping-promoting" behaviors "has both a direct impact on children's stress, as the parent becomes an efficient supportive agent for the child in the situation, and an indirect impact, as it lowers the parent's anxiety so that she is less likely to induce fear in her child" (Favez & Reicherts 2008, 53–54). Neither child gender nor social class was associated with stress. What *was* important to lower stress? Those children whose mothers gave them a brief, clear explanation of what was going to happen before they went to the pediatrician's office acted more self-regulated while getting their shots. They were less likely to cry and show resistant behaviors and were more easily comforted. The researchers comment, "What seems of great importance here is that the child is not taken by surprise and *can anticipate the [stressful] event and therefore make use of his own coping skills*" (61).

When emergencies occur, an additional challenge for early childhood educators in decreasing child stress may lie not only in directly mitigating child stressors. Staff may want to plan ways to reduce their own caregiver stresses in case of potential catastrophes (e.g., floods, hurricanes, fires) in order to ensure less child distress. Program goals should be expanded to include methods of reassuring parents in these situations. During a period of heavy artillery shelling attack in Israel, when caregivers had to lead preschoolers into bunkers under the school, the teachers were better able to help the children once telephone communications were set up so that they could both establish communication with the mothers of the children and also check up on the safety of their own children (Milgram 1982). The caregivers then could better handle their own anxiety and develop teaching strategies to increase child security, such as fostering group discussions and drawing and encouraging children to decorate with their own artwork the bomb shelters in which the children had to sleep during bombardments.

Conclusion

Stress will be a part of life for children and adults. However, the quality of care that teachers and parents provide can prevent acute stress and ease current stressors for children. Harmonious classrooms and intimate, caring, and personalized interactions attuned to the uniqueness of each child mitigate stresses the child experiences in other settings. Care providers serve a unique life-reinforcing role as "stress-busters" in the early childhood settings in which they serve.

Updated from the Research in Review article in the May and July 1986 issues of *Young Children*.

Alice Sterling Honig is professor emerita at Syracuse University.

References

Achenbach, T.M., & C.S. Edelbrock. 1991. *Manual for the child behavior checklists/4-18 and 1991 profile*. Burlington, VT: Department of Psychiatry, University of Vermont.

Ahnert, L., & M. Lamb. 2003. Shared care: Establishing a balance between home and child care settings. *Child Development* 74 (4): 1044–49.

Ainsworth, M.D.S. 1973. The development of infant-mother attachment. In *Review of child development research, vol. 3: Child development and social policy*, eds. B.M.Caldwell & H.M. Ricciuti. Chicago: University of Chicago Press.

Baumrind, D. 1967. Child care practices anteceding three patterns of preschool behavior. *Genetic Psychology Monographs* 75: 43–88.

Bayer, J.K., A.V. Sanson, & S.A. Hemphill. 2006. Parent influences on early childhood internalizing difficulties. *Journal of Applied Developmental Psychology* 27 (6): 542–59.

Belsky, J. 1991. Are insecure-avoidant infants with extensive day-care experience less stressed by and more independent in the Strange Situation? *Child Development* 62 (3): 567–71.

Borman, G.D., L.T. Overman, R. Fairchild, M. Boulay, J. Kaplan. 2004. Can a multiyear summer program prevent the accumulation of summer learning losses? In *Summer learning: Research, policies, and programs*, eds. G.D. Borman, M. Boulay, 233–53. Mahwah, NJ: Lawrence Erlbaum.

Bornstein , M., C. Hahn, N.F. Gist, & O.M. Haynes. 2006. Long-term cumulative effects of childcare on children's mental development and socioemotional adjustment in a non-risk sample: The moderating effects of gender. *Early Child Development and Care* 170 (2): 129–56.

Bower, B. 2008. 9/11 attacks stoked U.S. heart ailments. *Science News* 173 (4): 61.

Bowlby, J. 1958. The nature of the child's tie to its mother. *International Journal of Psychoanalysis* 39: 350–73.

Brandtjen, H. 2001. Short and long term effects on infants and toddlers in full time daycare centers. *Journal of Prenatal & Perinatal Psychology & Health* 15 (4): 239–86.

Brophy-Herb, H.E., & A.S. Honig. 1997. The Mother-Infant Program: Results of a pilot study. *NCAST National News* 13 (4): 3–4, 8–9.

Call, M. 1999. Transgenerational attachment, life stress, and the development of disruptive behavior in preschool children. *Dissertation Abstracts International, Section B: The Sciences and Engineering* 60 (4-B): 1884.

Chase-Lansdale, P.L., & M.T. Owen. 1987. Maternal employment in a family context: effects on infant-mother and infant-father attachments. *Child Development* 58: 1505–12.

Christoffersen, J. 2007, July 13. Study: Overweight children face widespread stigma. *The Post Standard*: A-4.

Crockenberg, S.B. 1981. Infant irritability, mother responsiveness, and social support influence son the security of infant-mother attachment. *Child Development* 52: 857–65.

Crockenberg, S.B., & C. Litman. 1991. Effects of maternal employment on maternal and two-year-old child behavior. *Child Development* 62: 930–53.

Deater-Deckard, K., & S. Scarr. 1996. Child care quality and children's behavioral adjustment: A four-year longitudinal study. *Journal of Child Psychology and Psychiatry* 37 (8): 937–48.

de Schipper, J.C., M.H. van IJzendoorn, & L.W.C. Tavecchio. 2004. Stability in center day care: Relations with children's well-being and problem behavior in day care. *Social Development* 13 (4): 531–50.

Every Child Matters Education Fund. 2009. *Homeland Insecurity*. Online: www.everychildmatters. org/images/stories/pdf/homelandinsecurity3. pdf.

Ewing, A.R., & A.R. Taylor. 2009. The role of child gender and ethnicity in teacher-child relationship quality and children's behavioral adjustment in preschool. *Early Childhood Research Quarterly* 24: 92–105.

Favez, N., & M. Reicherts. 2008. Toddlers' adjustment to the stress of immunization in function of mothers' general and specific coping tendencies. *Early Child Development and Care* 178 (1): 49–64.

Field, T. 2000. Infants of depressed mothers. In *Stress, coping and depression*, eds. L. Sheri, A.M. Hayes, R.I. Field, N. Schniederman, & P.M. McCabe, 3–22. Mahwah, NJ: Lawrence Erlbaum.

Fleury, S.A. 1998. Children's exposure to everyday stressors in day care settings: A descriptive study. *Dissertation Abstracts International: Section B: The Sciences and Engineering* 59 (5-B): 2454.

Goldstein, L.H., E.A. Harvey, J.L. Friedman-Weieneth, C. Pierce, A. Tellert, & J.C. Sippel. 2007. Examining subtypes of behavior problems among 3-year-old children, part II: Investigating differences in parent psychopathology, couple conflict, and other family stressors. *Journal of Abnormal Child Psychology* 35 (1): 111–23.

Greenspan, S., & S. Weider. 1998. *The child with special needs: Encouraging intellectual and emotional growth*. Reading, MA: Perseus Books.

Gross, D., & L. Fogg. 1999. Behavior problems among young children in low-income urban day care centers. *Research in Nursing & Health* 22 (1): 15–25.

Grych, J.H., & R. Clark. 1999. Maternal employment and development of the father-infant relationship in the first year. *Developmental Psychology* 35 (4): 893–903.

Gunnar, M.R., & K. Quevedo. 2007. The neurobiology of stress and development. *Annual Review of Psychology* 58: 145–73.

Haight, W., J. Black, T. Ostler, & K. Sheridan. 2006. In *How play motivates and enhances children's cognitive and social-emotional growth*, eds. D.G. Singer, R.M. Golinkoff, & K. Hirsh-Pasek. New York: Oxford University Press.

Harris, J. 1990. *Early language development. Implications for clinical and educational practice*. London: Routledge.

Hatzinger, M., C. Haselbach, S. Perren, A. von Wyl, K. von Klitzing, & E. Holsboer-Trachsler. 2007. Hypothalamic-pituitary-adrenocortical (HPA) activity in kindergarten children: Importance of gender and associations with behaviors/emotions. *Journal of Psychiatric Research* 41 (10): 861–70.

Hock, E., M. Hart, M.J. Kang, & W.J. Lutz. 2004. Predicting children's reactions to terrorist attacks: The importance of self-reports and preexisting characteristics. *American Journal of Orthopsychiatry* 74 (3): 253–62.

Honig, A.S. 1986a. Research in review: Stress and coping in children, Part I. *Young Children* 41 (4): 50–63.

Honig, A.S. 1986b. Research in review: Stress and coping in children, Part II. *Young Children* 41 (5): 47–59.

Honig, A.S. 2002. *Secure relationships: Nurturing infant/toddler attachment in early care settings*. Washington, DC: NAEYC.

Honig, A.S. 2004. How teachers and caregivers can help young children become more prosocial. In *A blueprint for the promotion of prosocial behavior in early childhood*, eds. E. Chesebrough, P. King, T. Gullotta, & M. Bloom, 51–91. New York: Kluwer.

Honig, A.S. 2005. The language of lullabies. *Young Children* 60 (5): 30–36.

Honig, A.S. 2008. Understanding and working with uncooperative, potentially violent young children. *Early Child Development and Care* 178 (7–8): 665–87.

Honig, A.S. 2009. *Little kids, big worries: Stress-busting tips for early childhood educators*. Baltimore: Paul H. Brookes.

Honig, A.S., & C. Morin. 2001. When should programs for teen parents and babies begin? Longitudinal evaluation of a teen parents and babies program. *Journal of Primary Prevention* 21 (4): 447–54.

Honig, A.S. & A. Thompson. 1994. Helping toddlers with peer group entry skills. *Zero to Three* 14 (5): 15–19.

Jones, S., & D.G. Lagace-Seguin. 2006. I think I can't, I think I can't: Associations between parental pessimism, child affect and children's well being. *Early Child Development and Care* 176 (8): 849–65.

Kirmayer, L.J., R. Lemelson, & M. Barrad, eds. 2007. *Understanding trauma: Integrating biological, clinical and cultural perspectives*. New York: Cambridge University Press.

Klein, P.S., R. Kraft, & C. Shohet. 2008. *Behavior patterns in daily mother-child separation: Possible opportunities for stress reduction*. Ramat-Gan, Israel: Baker Centre, Bar Ilan University.

Kochanska, G. 2002. Mutually responsive orientation between mothers and their young children: A context for the early development of conscience. *Current Directions in Psychological Science* 11: 191–195.

Lally, J.R., P. Mangione, & A.S. Honig. 1988. The Syracuse University Family Development Research Program: Long range impact of an early intervention with low-income children and their families. In *Parent education as early childhood intervention: Emerging directions in theory, research, and practice*, ed. D. Powell, 79–104. Norwood, NJ: Ablex.

Legendre, A. 1998. Adult support and adreno-cortical response of three-year-old children in a novel playgroup context. *Current Psychology of Cognition* 17 (3): 635–65.

Legendre, A. 2003. Environmental features influencing toddler's bioemotional reactions in daycare centers. *Environment and Behavior* 35 (4): 523–49.

Lieberman, A.F., & P. Van Horn. 2008. *Psychotherapy with infants and young children: Repairing the effects of stress and trauma on early attachment.* New York: Guildford.

Magnuson, K.A., & J. Waldfogel. 2005. Preschool child care and parents' use of physical discipline. *Infant and Child Development* 14 (2): 177–98.

Malik, N.M., N.W. Boris, S.S. Heller, B.J. Harden, J. Squires, R. Chazan-Cohen, L.S. Beeber, & K.J. Kaczynski. 2007. Risk for maternal depression and child aggression in Early Head Start families: A test of ecological models. *Infant Mental Health Journal* 28 (2): 171–91.

Mash, E., & R. Barkley, eds. 1996. *Child psychopathology.* New York: Guilford.

Matorell, G.A., & D.B. Bugental. 2006. Maternal variations in stress reactivity: Implications for harsh parenting practices with very young children. *Journal of Family Psychology* 20 (4): 641–47.

McCarthy, D. 2007. *"If you turned into a monster": Transformation through play: A body-centered approach.* London: Jessica Kingsley Publishers.

McKim, M.K., B. Stuart, & D.L. O'Connor. 1996. Infant care: Evaluation of pre-care differences hypotheses. *Early Education and Development* 7 (2): 107–19.

Milgram, N.A. 1982. War related stress in Israeli children and youth. In *Stress, coping and development in children,* eds. N. Garmezy & M. Rutter. New York: McGraw-Hill.

Nachmias, M., M.R. Gunnar, S. Mangelsdorf, R. Hornik-Parritz, & K. Buss. 1996. Behavioral inhibition and stress reactivity: The moderating role of attachment security. *Child Development* 67: 508–22.

NICHD (National Institute of Child Health and Development) Early Child Care Research Network. 1998. Early child care and self-control, compliance, and problem behavior at twenty-four and thirty-six months. *Child Development* 69 (4): 1145–70.

Odom, S.L., M.J. Hanson, J.A. Blackman, & S. Kaul. 2003. *Early intervention practices around the world.* Baltimore: Paul H. Brookes.

Olds, D.L., J. Eckenrode, C.R. Henderson, H. Kitzman, J. Powers, R. Cole, K. Sidora, P. Morris, L.M. Pettitt, & D. Luckey. 1997. Long-term effects of home visitation on maternal life course and child abuse and neglect. Fifteen-year follow-up of a randomized trial. *Journal of the American Medical Association* 278 (8): 637–43.

Orpinas, P., & A.M. Horne. 2006. *Bullying prevention: Creating a positive school climate and developing social competence.* Washington, DC: American Psychological Association.

Owen, M.T. 2002. NICHD study of early child care. In *Parenting and the child's world,* eds. J.G. Borkowski & M. Bristol-Power. Mahwah, NJ: Lawrence Erlbaum.

Owen, A.E., M.P. Thompson, & N.J. Kaslow. 2006. The mediating role of parenting stress in the relation between intimate partner violence and child adjustment. *Journal of Family Psychology* 20 (3): 505–13.

Park, K.J., & A.S. Honig. 1991. Infant child care patterns and later teacher ratings of preschool behaviors. *Early Child Development and Care* 68, 89-96.

Perry, B.D. 1994. Neurobiological sequelae of childhood trauma: Post-traumatic stress disorder in children. In *Catecholamines in post-traumatic stress disorder: Emerging concepts,* ed. M. Murberhg, 253–76. Washington, DC: American Psychiatric Association.

Perry, B.D. 2002. Childhood experience and the expression of genetic potential. What childhood neglect tells us about nature and nurture. *Brain and Mind* 3: 79–100.

Perry, D.F., R.K. Kaufman, & J. Knitzer, eds. 2007. *Social and emotional health in early childhood: Building bridges between services and systems.* Baltimore: Paul H. Brookes.

Ramey, C.T., & S.L. Ramey. 2007. Early learning and school readiness. Can early intervention make a difference? In *Appraising the human developmental sciences. Essays in honor of Merrill-Palmer Quarterly,* ed. G.W. Ladd. Detroit, MI: Wayne State University Press.

Repetti, R.L., & J. Wood. 1997. Effects of daily stress at work on mothers; interactions with preschoolers. *Journal of Family Psychology* 11: 90–108.

Reynolds, A.J., J.A. Temple, D.L. Robertson, & E.A. Mann. 2001. Long-term effects of an early childhood intervention on educational achievement and juvenile arrest. *Journal of the American Medical Association* 285: 2339–46.

Roberts, A.K., & P.A. Crawford. 2008. Literature to help children cope with family stressors. *Young Children* 63 (5): 12–17.

Roley, S., E. Blanche, & R. Schaaf, eds. 2001. *Understanding the nature of sensory integration with diverse populations.* San Antonio, TX: The Psychological Corporation.

Romero, M., & Y.S. Lee. 2008. *The influence of maternal and family risk on chronic absenteeism in early schooling.* Online: www.nccp.org/publications/pub_792.html.

Rossman, J.G., & B.B. Robbie. 2005. Children exposed to interparental violence: Does parenting contribute to functioning over time? *Journal of Emotional Abuse* 5 (1): 1–28.

Rutter, M. 1979. Protective factors in children's responses to stress and disadvantage. *Annals of the Academy of Medicine Singapore* 8 (3): 324–38.

Rutter, M. 1983. Stress, coping, and development: Some issues and questions. In *Stress, coping and development in children*, eds. N. Garmezy & M. Ruttter. New York: McGraw-Hill.

Selye, H. 1982. History and recent status of the stress concept. In *Handbook of stress: Theoretical and clinical aspects*, eds. L. Godlberger & S. Breznitz. New York: Free Press.

Silverman, W.K., & A.M. LaGreca. 2002. Children experiencing disasters; definitions, reactions, and predictors of outcomes. In *Helping children cope with disasters and terrorism*, eds. A.M. LaGreca, W.K. Silverman, E.M. Vernberg, & M.C. Roberts, 11–33. Washington, DC: American Psychological Association.

Sims, M., A. Guilfoyle, T.S. Parry, & M. Sims. 2006. Children's cortisol levels and quality of child-care provision. *Child: Care, Health and Development* 32 (4): 454–66.

Singh, D. 2003. Families of Head Start children: A research connection. *Journal of Instructional Psychology* 30: 77–83.

Sroufe, L.A., & J. Fleeson. 1986. Attachment and the construction of relationships. In *Relationships and development*, eds. W.W. Hartup & Z. Rubin. Hillsdale, NJ: Lawrence Erlbaum.

Straus, M.A. 2001. Social science and public policy: New evidence for the benefits of never spanking. *Society* (September/October): 52–60.

Stright, A.D., K.C. Gallagher, & K. Kelley. 2008. Infant temperament moderates relations between maternal parenting in early childhood and children's adjustments in first grade. *Child Development* 79 (1): 186–200.

van den Boom, D.C. 1994. The influence of temperament and mothering on attachment and exploration: An experimental manipulation of sensitive responsiveness among lower-class mothers with irritable infants. *Child Development* 65: 1457–77.

van den Boom, D.C., & J.B. Hoeksma. 1994. The effect of infant irritability on mother-infant interaction: A growth-curve analysis. *Developmental Psychology* 30 (4): 581–90.

van IJzendoorn, M., & M.S. de Wolff. 1997. In search of the absent father—Meta-analyses of infant-father attachment: A rejoinder to our discussants. *Child Development* 68: 592–94.

Vandell, D. L., & M.A. Corasaniti. 1990. Variations in early child care: Do they predict subsequent social, emotional, and cognitive differences? *Early Childhood Research Quarterly* 5 (4): 555–72.

Walker, L.O., & C. Cheng. 2007. Maternal empathy, self-confidence, and stress as antecedents of preschool children's behavior problems. *Journal for Specialists in Pediatric Nursing* 12 (2): 93–104.

Walston, J.T., & J. West. 2004. *Full-day and half-day kindergarten in the United States: Findings from the Early Childhood Longitudinal Study, Kindergarten class of 1998–99*. NCES 2004–078. Washington, DC: U.S. Department of Education, National Center for Education Statistics.

Werner, E. 1993. Risk, resilience, and recovery: Perspectives from the Kauai Longitudinal Study. *Development and Psychopathology* 5: 503–15.

Whiffen, V.E. 1990. Maternal depressed mood and perceptions of child temperament. *Journal of Genetic Psychology* 151: 329–39.

Wolfe, R., & B. Hirsch. 2003. Outcomes of parent education programs based on re-evaluation counseling. *Journal of Child and Family Studies* 12: 61–76.

8 Resilient Children

Emmy E. Werner and Eva L. Essa

Research has identified numerous risk factors that increase the probability of developmental problems in infants and young children. Among them are biological risks, such as pre- and perinatal complications, congenital defects, and low birth weight, as well as intense stresses in the caregiving environment, such as chronic poverty, family discord, or parental mental illness. Until relatively recently, the literature of children's response to such stress and risks focused "gloomily on the ills of mankind and all that can and does go wrong" (Rutter 1979, 49).

This approach created the impression that a poor developmental outcome is inevitable if a child is exposed to trauma, parental mental illness, alcoholism, or chronic family discord, since it examined only the lives of the "casualties," not the lives of the successful "survivors." During the last three decades, however, the perspective has begun to change.

Longitudinal studies that have followed individuals from infancy to adulthood have consistently shown that even among children exposed to multiple stressors, only a minority develop serious emotional disturbances or persistent behavior problems. These findings challenge early childhood professionals to consider the phenomenon of *resilience*, a dynamic process that leads to positive adaptations, even in a context of adversity (Luthar 2003).

The search for protective factors

Since the mid-1980s, a number of investigators from different disciplines—child development, pediatrics, psychology, psychiatry, and sociology—have published findings from longitudinal studies of infants and preschool children who grew up under adverse conditions. Several of these studies have recently come of age and now provide early childhood professionals with a database that extends over several decades.

There are currently 10 large-scale longitudinal studies of high-risk children of different ethnic groups and from different geographic regions of the United States (Wallerstein & Blakeslee 1989; Radke-Yarrow & Brown 1993; Herrenkohl, Herrenkohl, & Egolf 1994; Werner & Smith

2001; Hetherington & Kelley 2002; Bolger & Patterson 2003; Masten & Powell 2003; Reynolds & Ou 2003; Sameroff, Gutman, & Peck 2003; Yates, Egeland, & Sroufe 2003). These include children who have managed to cope successfully, despite significant adversities such as poverty, parental mental illness, child abuse, parental divorce, and/ or an accumulation of multiple risk factors in their families. In addition, several international longitudinal studies complement the findings of these American studies. However, the Kauai Longitudinal Study (Werner & Smith 1992; 2001) is the only study to date that has examined development from birth to midlife.

In these studies, resilience is conceived as an end product of buffering processes that do not eliminate risks and stress but that allow the individual to deal with them effectively (Rutter 1987). What is measured is appropriate developmental outcomes, including the absence of significant developmental delays or serious learning and behavior problems and the mastery of developmental tasks (Havinghurst 1972) or psychosocial stages (Erikson 1959) that are appropriate for a given age and culture. These include the attainment of a sense of trust, autonomy, and initiative by the time a child reaches age 6. Follow-up studies of at-risk children in adolescence and adulthood indicate that the mastery of these early developmental tasks can serve as a strong and enduring protective buffer in the face of later adversity (Werner & Smith 1992; Egeland, Carison, & Sroufe 1993).

The studies on resilience have focused on children like Michael and Mary, for whom the odds, on paper, did not seem very promising.

Michael, the son of teenage parents, was born prematurely and spent his first three weeks of life in the hospital, separated from his mother. Immediately after his birth, his father was sent with the Army to Southeast Asia for almost two years. By the time Michael was 8, he had three younger siblings and his parents were divorced. His mother left the area and had no further contact with the children.

Mary, born to an overweight, nervous, and erratic mother who had experienced several miscarriages, and a father who was an unskilled farm laborer with only four years of education. Between Mary's fifth and tenth birthdays, her mother had several hospitalizations for repeated bouts with mental illness, after having inflicted both physical and emotional abuse on her daughter.

Both Michael and Mary, by age 18, were individuals with high self-esteem and sound values, caring for others and liked by their peers, successful in school, and looking forward to their adult futures.

There appears to be a common core of protective factors found in numerous studies, transcending ethnic, social class, and geographic boundaries. These derive from three sources: protective factors within the child, protective factors within the family, and protective factors within the community.

Protective factors within the child

Resilient children tend to have an affectionate, "engaging" temperament that elicits positive responses from others (Farber & Egeland 1987; Hetherington 1989; Werner & Smith 1992; 2001). For example, the infants in the Kauai Longitudinal Study were characterized by their caregivers as very active, affectionate, cuddly, good-natured, and easy to deal with (Werner & Smith 1989; 1992). They also have available a caring adult—if not the mother, then a grandmother or an older sibling—which was associated with secure attachment (Farber & Egeland 1987). It seems, therefore, that secure attachment in infancy and generally supportive care for the first two years of life make young children more capable of rebounding from a period of developmental difficulty later in life than children with less supportive histories were (Yates, Egeland, & Sroufe 2003).

Resilient toddlers have a well-developed sense of autonomy and appear to meet both familiar adults and strangers on their own terms. During a potentially stressful situation, such as a series of developmental tests, the examiners in the Kauai Longitudinal Study described these toddlers as more alert, cheerful, responsive, self-confident, and independent than children of the same age and sex who later developed serious learning or behavior problems. They were also more advanced in communication, locomotion, and self-help skills and engaged in more social play than the toddlers who later developed problems (Werner & Smith 1989).

Preschool children who successfully weathered the stresses of parental divorce showed similar characteristics (Wallerstein & Kelley 1980; Hetherington, Stanley-Ragan, & Anderson 1989). Such children related to both peers and teachers without excessive anxiety or need for attention. They were more socially mature than preschoolers who had difficulty coping with the marital breakup and were able to distance themselves from their parents' conflict by establishing routines and order in their lives.

By the time children described as resilient move beyond the early childhood years, a sense of competence and self-efficacy appears to be their general hallmark (Werner 2000). The children in the Kauai Longitudinal Study were not unusually talented or intellectually gifted, but they possessed well-developed problem-solving and communication skills, which they put to good use (Werner & Smith 1989). The same predictors of resilience emerge from diverse studies with different ethnic groups in different geographic and sociopolitical contexts (Bracken & Lamprecht 2003).

Resilient children are described repeatedly as sociable, remarkably independent, demonstrating internal locus of control, assertive, and having a positive

> In high-risk families in which a parent is absent, some of the nurturing comes from alternative caregivers.

self-concept. They are also portrayed as having well-developed impulse control, the ability to concentrate on their schoolwork, high achievement orientation, and a cognitive style that is reflective rather than impulsive (Werner 2000). Such characteristics continue to help these children become productive, well-adjusted adults.

Protective factors within the family

Despite chronic poverty, family discord, or parental mental illness, most resilient children have the opportunity to establish a close bond with at least one caregiver from whom they receive lots of attention during the first year of life. The stress-resistant children in the Kauai study (Werner & Smith 1989), as well as the resilient offspring of psychotic parents studied by Anthony (1987), had enough good nurturing to establish a basic sense of trust.

In high-risk families in which a parent is absent or incapacitated, some of the nurturing often comes from alternative caregivers. Children who succeeded against the odds had the opportunity early on to establish a close bond with at least one competent, emotionally stable person who was sensitive to their needs. Resilient children seemed to be especially adept at "recruiting" such surrogate parents (Werner 2005a). Among family members who play important roles as providers of stable care and positive models of identification, grandparents and older siblings emerge as important stress buffers in the lives of many children (Farber & Egeland 1987; Wallerstein & Blakeslee 1989; Werner & Smith 1989; Radke-Yarrow & Brown 1993; Herrenkohl, Herrenkohl, & Egolf 1994).

The example set by a mother who is gainfully and steadily employed appears to be an especially powerful model of identification for resilient girls reared in poverty, whether they are black (Clark 1983), Chicana (Gandara 1982), or Asian-American (Werner & Smith 1989). Such girls tend to come from households that combine an absence of overprotection, an emphasis on risk-taking and independence, and reliable emotional support from their primary caregiver, whether mother, grandmother, sister, or aunt. Resilient boys, on the other hand, appear to come from households where there is greater structure, parental supervision, more rules, and a male available to serve as a model of identification (Werner 2000).

Assigned chores and the need to take on domestic responsibilities and part-time work to help support the family have proved to be sources of strength and competence for resilient children. On Kauai, many of the high-risk, resilient youths had responsibility for the care of younger siblings. Some managed the household when parents were ill or hospitalized; others worked part-time after school to support their family (Werner & Smith 1989). Such acts of "required helpfulness" (Rachman 1979) were also noted by other researchers as important protective factors for children of psychotic and alcoholic parents, orphans of war, and children who lived during the Great Depression (Moskovitz 1983; Elder, Caspi, & Van Nguyen 1985; Anthony 1987; Johnson et al. 1990).

Resilient children also seem to have been imbued by their families with a sense of coherence (Antonovsky 1979). They manage to believe that life makes sense, that they have some control over their fate, and, in the case of religious families, that God helps those who help themselves (Murphy & Moriarty 1976). This sense of meaning persists among resilient children, even if they are uprooted by wars or scattered as refugees. It enables them to love despite hate and to maintain the ability

to behave compassionately toward other people (Moskovitz 1983).

Protective factors within the community

Resilient children find a great deal of emotional support outside of their immediate family. They tend to be well-liked by their classmates and have at least one, and usually several, close friends and confidants (Werner & Smith 1989). Association with friends and the parents of friends who come from stable families can help resilient children gain a perspective and maintain a constructive distance between themselves and their own households, which may be marred by discord, parental psychopathology, or alcoholism (Anthony 1987; Werner & Smith 1989).

Most studies have noted that resilient children enjoy school, whether preschool or grade school. In many cases, such children make school into a home away from home, a refuge from a disordered household (Werner 2000). Hetherington, Stanley-Ragan and Anderson (1989) found a remarkable similarity in the characteristics of both home and school environments that were associated with greater resilience among children of divorced families. In both settings, a greater degree of adaptive behavior among children was associated with a more responsive and nurturing atmosphere and a more organized and predictable environment, which clearly defined and consistently enforced standards, rules, and responsibilities.

Among the most frequently encountered positive role models (outside of the family circle) in the lives of the children of Kauai was a favorite teacher. For a resilient youngster, a special teacher was not just an instructor for academic skills but also a confidant and positive role model (Werner & Smith 1989). Studies that have explored the role of teachers as protective buffers

> When the stressful life events outweigh the protective factors, even the most resilient child can develop problems.

in the lives of children who grew up in homes marred by poverty, parental mental illness, alcoholism, and domestic strife tend to agree in their findings that teachers or mentors can have a significant positive impact on at-risk children (Wallerstein & Blakeslee 1989; Werner & Smith 1992; Freedman 1993; Radke-Yarrow & Brown 1993).

In their studies of London schools, Rutter and colleagues (1979) found that good experiences in the classroom could mitigate the effects of considerable stress at home. Among the qualities that characterized the more successful schools were the setting of appropriate high standards, effective feedback by the teacher to the students with ample use of praise, the setting of good models of behavior by the teachers, and giving students positions of trust and responsibility. Children who attended such schools developed few, if any, emotional or behavioral problems, despite considerable deprivation and discord at home.

Early childhood programs and a favorite teacher can act as important buffers against adversity in the lives of resilient young children. Moskovitz (1983), in a follow-up study in adulthood of the childhood survivors of concentration camps, noted the pervasive influence of such a nursery school teacher, who provided warmth and caring and who taught them "to behave compassionately."

Participation in extracurricular activities or clubs can be another important informal source of support for resilient children. Many youngsters on Kauai were poor by material standards, but they participated in activities that allowed them to be part of a cooperative enterprise, whether being cheerleader for the home team or raising an animal in the 4-H club.

The shifting balance between vulnerability and resilience

Just as vulnerability is relative, depending on complex interactions among constitutional factors and life's circumstances, resilience is governed by a similar dynamic interaction among protective factors within the individual, his or her family environment, and the larger social context in which he or she lives (Cohler 1987).

Longitudinal studies following children from birth to adulthood have found a shifting balance between stressful life events that heighten children's vulnerability and protective factors that enhance their resilience. This balance changes not only with different stages of the life cycle but also varies with sex and cultural context. Most studies, for example, have shown that boys appear to be more vulnerable than girls when exposed to chronic and intense family discord during childhood, but this trend appears to be reversed by the end of adolescence (Werner 2000).

As long as the balance between stressful life events and protective factors is manageable for children, they can cope. But when the stressful life events outweigh the protective factors, even the most resilient child can develop problems. Those who care for children, whether their own or others, can help restore this balance, either by *decreasing* the child's exposure to intense or chronic life stresses, or by *increasing* the number of protective factors, such as competencies or sources of support.

Links between protective factors and successful adaptation in high-risk children

A few large-scale longitudinal studies have demonstrated the interconnections of protective mechanisms that buffer adversity over time. Data from the Kauai Longitudinal Study at six points in the life cycle illustrate the complexity of the phenomenon of resilience. They show how individual dispositions and outside sources of support and stress are linked together from infancy and early childhood to middle childhood and adolescence, and how these variables in turn predict the quality of adaptation in young adulthood and midlife (Werner & Smith 2001).

The protective processes that fostered resilience manifested themselves early in life. Across a span of several decades, maternal competence in infancy was positively related to the children's adaptation in adulthood. When mothers interacted in a consistently positive way with their infant daughters, these girls were more autonomous at age 2 and more competent at age 10. They also attracted more sources of emotional support in childhood and adolescence and encountered fewer stressful life events than did the daughters whose mothers were less competent caregivers. Boys with more competent mothers were more successful at school at age 10, more resourceful and efficacious at age 18, and utilized more sources of emotional support in adulthood than did the sons of mothers who were less competent caregivers (Werner 2005b).

For both boys and girls, there was a positive association between autonomy at age 2 and scholastic competence at age 10. For both sexes, there was a positive association between the number of sources of emotional support they attracted in childhood, their scholastic competence at age 10, and the quality of adaptation at age 40. Individuals who could count on more sources of emotional support in childhood reported fewer stressful life events at later stages of their lives than those who had little emotional support.

In fact, most of the variance in the quality of adaptation at age 40 was accounted for by earlier predictors of resilience. In particular, most variance was attributed to maternal competence in the child's first two years of life, the number of sources of emotional support available to the child between ages 2 and 10, scholastic competence at age 10, and health status early in life. These findings point to the importance of the first decade of life in laying the foundation for resilience (Werner 2005b).

Conclusion

What then are some of the implications of the findings of longitudinal studies of resilient children? Most of all, they provide a more hopeful perspective than can be derived from reading the literature on problem children, which predominates in clinical psychology, child psychiatry, special education, and social work. Research on resilient children provides a focus on the self-righting tendencies that appear to move some children toward normal development under all but the most persistent adverse circumstances.

Teachers and care providers who care for young children, who work with or on behalf of them, can help tilt the balance from vulnerability to resiliency if they:

- accept children's temperamental idiosyncrasies and allow them some experiences that challenge, but do not overwhelm, children's coping abilities;
- convey to children a sense of responsibility and caring, and, in turn, reward them for helpfulness and cooperation;
- encourage children to develop special interests, hobbies, or activities that can serve as a source of gratification and self-esteem;
- model by setting an example the conviction that life makes sense despite the inevitable adversities that each person encounters; and
- encourage children to reach out beyond their immediate family for support.

Research on resilient children has taught early childhood professionals a lot about the special importance of "surrogate parents" in the lives of children exposed to chronic or intense distress. In addition to beloved relatives or friends, there are other powerful role models who can give emotional support to a vulnerable child. The three most frequently encountered in studies of resilient children are: a favorite teacher, a good neighbor, or a member of the clergy.

There is a special need to strengthen such informal support for those children and their families who appear to be most vulnerable because they lack—either temporarily or permanently—some of the essential social bonds that appear to buffer stress: for example, working mothers with no stable child care for their young children; single, divorced, or teen-age parents; hospitalized and handicapped children in need of special care who are separated from their families for extended periods of time; and migrant or refugee children without permanent roots in a community.

A central component contributing to resilient children's ability to cope effectively appears to be a feeling of confidence or faith that things will work out as well as can be reasonably expected—that the odds *can* be surmounted. The stories of resilient children show that such a faith can develop and be sustained, even under adverse circumstances, if children encounter people who give meaning to their lives and a reason for commitment and caring. Every teacher can impart this gift to a child—in the classroom, on the playground, in the neighborhood, in the family—*if* she or he cares enough.

Updated from the Research in Review article in the November 1984 issue of *Young Children*.
Emmy E. Werner is a professor at the University of California at Davis. **Eva L. Essa** is a professor at the University of Nevada, Reno.

References

Anthony, E.J. 1987. Children at high risk for psychosis growing up. In *The invulnerable child*, eds. E.J. Anthony & B.J. Cohler, 147–84. New York: Guilford.

Antonovsky, A. 1979. *Health, stress, and coping: New perspectives on mental and physical well-being*. San Francisco: Jossey-Bass.

Bolger, K.E., & C. Patterson. 2003. Sequelae of child maltreatment: Vulnerability and resilience. In *Resilience and vulnerability: Adaptation in the context of childhood adversity*, ed. S.S. Luther, 156–81. New York: Cambridge University Press.

Bracken, B.A., & M.S. Lamprecht. 2003. Positive self-concept: An equal opportunity construct. *School Psychology Quarterly* 18: 103–21.

Clark, R.M. 1983. *Family life and school achievement: Why poor black children succeed or fail*. Chicago: University of Chicago Press.

Cohler, B.S. 1987. Adversity, resilience, and the study of lives. In *The invulnerable child*, eds. E.J. Anthony & B.J. Cohler, 363–424. New York: Guilford.

Egeland, B., L. Carison, & L.A. Sroufe. 1993. Resilience as process. Special issue: Milestones in the development of resilience. *Development and Psychopathology* 5: 517–28.

Elder, G.H., A. Caspi, & T. Van Nguyen. 1985. Resourceful and vulnerable children: Family influence in hard times. In *Development in context*, eds. R. Silbereisen & H. Eyferth, 167–86. Berlin: Springer Verlag.

Erikson, E.H. 1959. Identity and the life cycle. *Psychological Issues* 1: 1–171.

Farber, E.A., & B. Egeland. 1987. Invulnerability among abused and neglected children. In *The invulnerable child*, eds. E.J. Anthony & B.J. Cohler, 253–88. New York: Guilford.

Freedman, M. 1993. *The kindness of strangers*. San Francisco: Jossey-Bass.

Gandara, P. 1982. Passing through the eye of the needle: High achieving Chicanas. *Hispanic Journal of Behavioral Sciences* 4 (2): 167–80.

Havinghurst, R.J. 1972. *Developmental tasks and education*. New York: David McKay.

Herrenkohl, F.C., R.C. Herrenkohl, & B. Egolf. 1994. Resilient early school age children from maltreating homes: Outcomes in late adolescence. *American Journal of Orthopsychiatry* 64: 301–09.

Hetherington, E.M. 1989. Coping with family transitions: Winners, losers, and survivors. *Child Development* 60: 1–40.

Hetherington, E.M., & J. Kelley. 2002. *For better or for worse: Divorce reconsidered*. New York: Norton.

Hetherington, E.M., M. Stanley-Ragan, & E.R. Anderson. 1989. Marital transitions: A child's perspective. *American Psychologist* 44: 303–12.

Johnson, H.L., M.B. Glassman, K.B. Fisk, & T.S. Rosen. 1990. Resilient children: Individual differences in developmental outcomes of children born to drug abusers. *Journal of Genetic Psychology* 151: 523–39.

Luthar, S., ed. 2003. *Resilience and vulnerability: Adaptation in the context of childhood adversity*. New York: Cambridge University Press.

Masten, A.S., & J.L. Powell. 2003. A resilience framework for research, policy, and practice. In *Resilience and vulnerability: Adaptation in the context of childhood adversity*, ed. S.S. Luthar, 1–28. New York: Cambridge University Press.

Moskovitz, S. 1983. *Love despite hate: Child survivors of the Holocaust and their adult lives*. New York: Schocken.

Murphy, L., & A. Moriarty. 1976. *Vulnerability, coping and growth from infancy to adolescence*. New Haven, CT: Yale University Press.

Rachman, S. 1979. The concept of required helpfulness. *Behavioral Research and Therapy* 12: 1–16.

Radke-Yarrow, M., & E. Brown. 1993. Resilience and vulnerability in children of multiple-risk families. *Development and Psychopathology* 5: 581–92.

Reynolds, A.J., & S.R. Ou. 2003. Promoting resilience through early childhood intervention. In *Resilience and vulnerability: Adaptation in the context of childhood adversity*, ed. S.S. Luthar, 436–62. New York: Cambridge University Press.

Rutter, M. 1979. Protective factors in children's responses to stress and disadvantage. In *Primary prevention of psychopoathology, vol. 3: Social competence in children*, eds. M.W. Kent & J.E. Rolf. Hanover, NH: University Press of New England.

Rutter, M. 1987. Psychosocial resilience and protective mechanism. *American Journal of Orthopsychiatry* 57: 316–31.

Rutter, M., B. Maughan, P. Mortimore, J. Ouston, & A. Smith. 1979. *Fifteen thousand hours: Secondary schools and their effects on children*. Cambridge, MA: Harvard University Press.

Sameroff, A., L.M. Guttman, & S.C. Peck. 2003. Adaptation among youth facing multiple risks: Prospective research findings. In *Resilience and vulnerability: Adaptation in the context of childhood adversity*, ed. S.S. Luthar, 364–91. New York: Cambridge University Press.

Wallerstein, J.S., & S. Blakeslee. 1989. *Second chances: Men, women, and children a decade after divorce*. New York: Ticknor and Fields.

Wallerstein, J.S., & J.B. Kelley. 1980. *Surviving the breakup: How children and parents cope with divorce*. New York: Basic.

Werner, E.E. 2000. Protective factors and individual resilience. In *Handbook of early childhood intervention*, eds. J.P. Shonkoff & S.J. Meisels, 115–32. New York: Cambridge University Press.

Werner, E.E. 2005a. Resilience and recovery: Findings from the Kauai Longitudinal Study. *Focal Point* 19 (1): 11–14.

Werner, E.E. 2005b. What can we learn about resilience from large-scale longitudinal studies? In *Handbook of resilience in children*, eds. S. Goldstein & R.B. Brooks, 91–105. New York: Springer.

Werner, E.E., & R.S. Smith. 1989. *Vulnerable but invincible: A longitudinal study of resilient children and youth*. New York: Adams, Bannister, Cox.

Werner, E.E., & R.S. Smith. 1992. *Overcoming the odds: High risk children from birth to adulthood*. Ithaca, NY: Cornell University Press.

Werner, E.E., & R.S. Smith. 2001. *Journeys from childhood to midlife: Risk, resilience, and recovery*. Ithaca, NY: Cornell University Press.

Yates, T.M., B. Egeland, & L.A. Sroufe. 2003. Rethinking resilience: A developmental process perspective. In *Resilience and vulnerability: Adaptation in the context of childhood adversities*, ed. S.S. Luthar, 76–103. New York: Cambridge University Press.

Part III

Cognitive and Language Development

Introduction

Cognitive and language development provide the foundation for many other developing competencies. While cognitive development—that is, the development of skills related to mental competence and thought—has always been considered a primary focal point in early childhood settings, interest in cognitive development has become even more concentrated given the recent push toward academic standards. The chapters in this section discuss cognitive development as it relates to school readiness, with a reminder that cognitive skills are important in their own right and are not the sole contributors to later academic success. Two of the chapters in this section focus more specifically on language and literacy development and the integral role that both play in all domains of children's development. The chapters will provide early childhood professionals with research-based evidence for developmentally appropriate facilitation of cognitive, language, and literacy skills in early childhood.

Celia Genishi and Andrea Honig set the stage for this section with an updated version of Dr. Genishi's original 1988 article, **"Children's Language: Learning Words from Experience."** The authors support and endorse the original premise that children make sense of the world through experiences from which they construct understandings or theories. From these concepts or theories comes language to describe the experiences. The revised chapter places more emphasis on diversity in children, acknowledging that older studies focused mostly on white, middle-class participants, whereas the more recent studies discussed by the authors include diversity in ethnicity, culture, economic class, and ability—in particular, there is a strong recent emphasis on children who are English language learners. Finally, Genishi and Honig have added a section on storytelling, noting that this common activity is a natural way for children to organize experiences.

"Emerging Knowledge About Emergent Writing," by Kelley Mayer, provides an overview of the research on the development of writing in young children. This 2007 *Young Children* article notes that far more attention and research have focused on reading than on writing, though the two are intertwined and develop simultaneously. Mayer takes us through the emergence of writing skills during the preschool years, moving from scribbles and drawings to letterlike forms, strings of letters, and words. The author also stresses the importance of an environment that supports writing, through both materials and instruction. The article ends with a helpful list of strategies that promote and support emergent writing in young children, thus making available to early childhood professionals some useful techniques that encourage the development of children's early written communication.

Arthur Baroody and Xia Li provide an updated research review, entitled **"Mathematics Instruction That Makes Sense for 2- to 5-Year-Olds."** The original article, published in 2000 by Dr. Baroody, was called "Does Mathematics Instruction for Three- to Five-Year-Olds Really Make Sense?" The differences in the two titles provide some clues about the changes made in the revised chapter. For one thing, the question posed in the original title is no longer pertinent because an affirmative answer is now commonly accepted. In addition, the authors place far more emphasis on the development of number concepts in 2- and 3-year-olds. The authors note the importance for very young children of visually recognizing and verbally labeling small collections of up to three or so items for many reasons, including learning the purpose and principles of counting collections, constructing arithmetic concepts, and mastering basic arithmetic facts such as "two and two is four." The authors also highlight the growing recognition of the importance of language in constructing children's understanding of number, thus underscoring how different developmental domains are inextricably intertwined. This chapter highlights the mathematical competencies of very young children and

provides methods for early childhood professionals to facilitate the development of these competencies in developmentally appropriate ways.

The final chapter in this section on cognitive and language development deals with the role of motivation in young children's development. Penny Hauser-Cram and Darcy Mitchell provide an updated version of Dr. Hauser-Cram's 1998 research review, "I Think I Can, I Think I Can: Understanding and Encouraging Mastery Motivation in Young Children," newly titled, **"I Think I Can, I Knew I Could: Understanding and Encouraging Mastery Motivation in Young Children."** The authors review additional research on learned helplessness, especially recent research that underscores practices during the preschool years that can prevent such helplessness. In addition, the authors include updated information about how goal-directed behavior becomes more complex during the toddler years and new research about environmental (as opposed to genetic) influences on mastery motivation. Early childhood professionals will find important information on how they can best support young children's development of mastery motivation, an essential skill related to both current and later academic success.

The chapters in this section provide a detailed outline of important developments that occur in the cognitive and language domains. Early childhood professionals will gain insight into these domains as well as find tips on how to appropriately support their development in the early childhood years, which will help them aid children's learning.

9 Children's Language: Learning Words from Experience

Celia Genishi and Andrea Smith Honig

The story of children's language development begins long before they say their first words. Parents and caregivers know well that even young infants communicate with a hearty cry, a facial expression, or a motion. Presented here are a theory and related research that place early communicative development in the context of familiar experiences that occur over time. Children—not adults or repetitious teaching techniques—are the main characters in this part of the language-learning story, which focuses on the development of words.

Because words are always given meaning within a variety of contexts, this chapter also carefully considers the collection of words called *stories*. Throughout the chapter, the centrality of *oral* language in the lives of young children is emphasized, even as curricula in early childhood classrooms focus increasingly on language in *print*, or the emergence of reading and writing.

Learning contexts

How do children come to understand the world around them? According to developmental theorists (Piaget 1937/1954; Vygotsky 1978; Bruner 1983), experience with people and objects is the foundation for developing that understanding. In order to make sense of experience, children construct their own understandings, their own theories about the world—about physical reality, time, language, social relationships, and so on. This constructivist view of children as active thinkers has had a strong influence on many researchers whose primary interest is in how children develop language.

Piaget's (1926/1959) classic studies led to a general belief that young children (under age 8) are *egocentric*; that is, they have difficulty taking another person's point of view. Thus, young children assume that everyone sees what they see and thinks what they think; in speech, they do not adjust what they say to take into account the perspective of the listener.

Some language researchers have presented evidence that supports this idea. Glucksberg and Krauss (1967), for example, found that children were unable to perform a communicative task that required them to take their listener's perspective. When children were asked to describe objects they could see, they did not describe them in enough detail to enable their listeners, who were located on the opposite side of a barrier from the children, to identify the objects. Others, such as Clark (1973), investigated the young child's inability to understand abstract terms related to time and space. Clark found that preschoolers confused relational terms such as *more* and *less* and *before* and *after*, interpreting *less* as if it meant *more* and *after* as if it meant *before*.

On the other hand, a number of researchers have demonstrated that young children are more capable linguistically and cognitively than they sometimes appear to be. Shatz and Gelman (1973), for example, demonstrated that children as young as age 4 could modify their ways of talking for 2-year-olds, making their speech simpler and more direct than when they spoke to adults. In other words, the children could take into account the less developed abilities of the 2-year-olds to ensure communication with them.

Donaldson (1978) and others have been critical of Piagetian tasks that seem to highlight young children's egocentricism—for example, the "mountain" task (Piaget & Inhelder 1948/1956). Young children typically fail at this task when researchers strictly follow Piaget and Inhelder's design. In this design, the experimenter asks the subject to choose which picture of three mountains represents what a doll, placed at a viewpoint different from the subject's, can see. Young children often choose the picture of what they, not the doll, can see.

In contrast, even at age 3½, most of Donaldson's subjects succeeded at a task similar to Piaget's mountains, which required them to hide a doll so a toy policeman could not find it. Because the young children understood hiding, they could take the perspective of the policeman in this situation and hide the doll from him. Thus, they were *not* egocentric when the

task presented was one with which the children could identify, or one that made "human sense."

Children develop understanding of events and then label them

Nelson is another developmental psychologist whose theories about language acquisition are grounded in a Piagetian perspective. Some of Nelson's work (1985; 1986) was an in-depth exploration of how children come to make sense of their earliest contexts. Making sense involves (1) mental representations of action-based experience, (2) the concepts that make up experience, and (3) the language used to refer to experience.

Like other constructivist thinkers, Nelson believed that language learning begins with the *action*, rather than words. Children first act or are acted upon: They cry, move, see; they are held, fed, diapered. According to Nelson (1986), actions are part of *event representations* that are the basis for both language and concepts. Although children are not aware of it, an event such as being fed has a particular goal and a particular structure. A series of actions make up the event: From the child's point of view, the actions might be fussing or crying, being picked up, being placed in a high chair, and so on.

Children's understanding of an event is hazy at first. Initially, the infant has only a temporary "snapshot," or perceptual image, of separate actions as they occur; she does not remember or think about the images. After experiencing the event repeatedly, she develops a "videotape" recording, a mental representation, of the whole experience or event (Griffiths 1986). As her perception, attention, and memory also develop, the child accumulates a collection of videotapes, consisting of wholes and not simply snapshots of single objects, which her mind labels and stores. This typically happens within the first 18 to 24 months of life, once the child understands that the objects and people around her have a permanent existence apart from herself.

In other words, the child gradually constructs a holistic representation of events such as feeding or ball throwing. At the core of the event is action. Concepts, or mental "units" that make up the event representation, also evolve. Through interacting with the ball—acting upon it and understanding how it can be used—the child develops the concept of ball. She knows not only what a ball looks like but also what it does and who might use it. The child sorts out, or differentiates, that concept over time. Also over time, she learns that *ball* is the word associated with that object.

Thus, children's language learning proceeds from action or experience to concept to word, not from word to concept to experience. Children gradually understand more clearly, and later label verbally, the concepts that comprise events. These concepts are always grounded in children's social worlds, and the events are the foundation for the development of thinking.

The first words, those landmarks that adults so eagerly await, are often heard around the time of the child's first birthday and are evidence of this gradual process of development. (The first birthday as a developmental milestone is just a rough approximation.) Many children who are developing a first language say their first words well after that time, and second language learners are especially unpredictable as to when they say their first words in one or both languages. If children are learning a second language in school, first words in the second language may follow the first words in a home language by several years (Genishi, Yung-Chan, & Stires 2000).

Children learn words pertaining to objects or actions having meaning for them

In studying how children acquire event representations and words, Nelson has

> **Children's language learning proceeds from action or experience to concept to word.**

consistently focused on what children do in particular settings. Thus, whereas some studies of children's language and thinking highlight what children *cannot* do as compared with adults, Nelson's work focuses on what they *can* do. Nelson has studied the acquisition of both words and event representations.

Nelson's (1973) year-long study of 18 middle-class children between ages 1 and 2 supported the emphasis on *function*, or how objects are used in children's daily lives. The majority of the first 50 words these children learned were nouns, names of objects they acted upon (e.g., *shoe, sock, juice, key*). The children did not learn words such as *table*, a common object in most homes, possibly because they did not act upon it or manipulate it in any way.

Children, then, didn't simply apply labels to common objects in the environment; they matched labels with actions or experiences over which they had some control. In terms of event representations, children learned first the words that referred to the most meaningful events of their daily lives. The children were not strictly "word learners"; they were also active "meaning makers" (Wells 1986).

Further, the children acquired words at different rates and selected different events and words as the most meaningful ones. Some children seemed to approach language learning as an object-naming task (using many nouns), while others used words that helped them initiate or maintain social events (using greetings or words to influence others' behavior). From the very beginning, then, children's language reflects their individual rate of development, preferences, and uniqueness.

Since 1980, Nelson has shifted focus from early words to the development of event representation. French and Nelson

(1981) studied the way children talk about event representations (sometimes called "scripts"). When children between the ages of 2 years and 11 months and 5½ years were asked about familiar events such as making cookies, going to a restaurant, and celebrating birthdays, most had no difficulty talking about the elements of the events in the correct sequential (temporal) order. (In 700 interviews, there were only 19 instances of incorrect ordering, such as describing blowing out the candles *after* cutting the birthday cake.)

Thus, although Clark (1973) found that children failed to comprehend the difference between *before* and *after* in an experimental situation, French and Nelson's subjects were able to produce these words appropriately when answering questions about familiar events. Their subjects also showed an understanding of other relational terms that reflect temporal and logical relationships, such as *because, so, if, or,* and *but.*

Researchers teaching words

Nelson has provided insights into how children learn words as a by-product of experiences. Other researchers have focused more on words themselves, marveling at children's ability to learn words so effortlessly. Children's strategies for learning words develop well before they enter the primary grades. Carey and Bartlett studied the process of learning new words through a simple procedure (1979).

They presented 3-year-old children with two trays, one blue and one olive, and asked what color each was. The subjects knew "blue," but called the olive one either "green" or "brown." Next the experimenters invented a color name and called the olive tray "chromium." They said to each child, "Hand me the chromium tray. Not the blue one, but the chromium one." A week later they asked the children the colors of the trays. The children could not

remember the word *chromium,* but they did not say it was green or brown. This demonstrates that just one experience with the new color and its verbal label led the children to reorganize their color vocabulary: In their mental dictionaries, where there was previously the word *green* or *brown,* there was now a "space" for a new entry.

These results support the view that, by the age of 3 or 4, young children already have an organizing strategy that leads them to categorize words into categories, such as color words. The unconscious identification of the category, or domain, might be a first step in learning new words, which children can later remember after hearing them many times in real-life contexts. The task may also show that children attend to language presented in an interactive context. Note that the experimenters did not simply show children cards with the two colors on them; they created an "event" in which the children handled trays, familiar objects for preschoolers.

A different kind of event that helps children learn words is the story, according to Watson (1987). In one study about stories and word learning, 5-, 7-, and 10-year-olds heard nonsense words and their definitions embedded within a story. After the storytelling, even the 5-year-olds remembered some of the new "words." In a second study, Watson asked two preschool teachers to teach the word *protozoa* to their classes. One teacher presented the word in a lesson-like format, telling the children the definition of *protozoa* and elaborating on the characteristics of the organisms. The other teacher made up a story about protozoa, involving a fisherman who knew about protozoa. When children were asked to recall the meaning of the new word, those who had heard the story performed notably better than those who had not.

The increasing diversity of early childhood classrooms

One of the criticisms of research on children's language development is that it focused for too long on children who were middle class, as Nelson did, for example. In the last two decades, researchers and educators have turned their attention to the increasing numbers of children whose sociocultural heritages are neither middle class nor European American.

Today's teachers face the challenge of providing comfortable environments and multiple opportunities for increasingly diverse classrooms of children to use and develop language. To illustrate, during the 2003–04 school year, 3.8 million children, or 11 percent of the U.S. public school population, were classified as English language learners (ELLs) (NCES 2006). In addition, the number of children in public schools categorized as having speech or language impairments was put at more than one million in a recent study, with an estimated 7–8 percent of kindergartners classified as such (Simpson & Rice 2004).

Since language is at the center of school learning, consideration of the increasingly diverse language backgrounds and abilities of children entering school is paramount. What, then, should teachers do? An in-depth discussion of English language learners or children with language delays is beyond the scope of this chapter, but other reviews contain more detailed descriptions of teachers' work with English language learners (e.g., Genishi 1989; Fassler 1998; Genishi 2002) as well as perspectives on language intervention and delayed acquisition (e.g., Bloom & Lahey 1978; Gerber 2003).

Children's language experiences at home

Thinking about how to work with children in the classroom requires a consideration and understanding of the types of language experiences children have with their families. While a great number of studies have strengthened respect for children's language learning at home (see, e.g., Heath 1983), some of the more recently influential—and contrasting—work is that of Hart and Risley (1995; 1999).

After observing 42 children in their homes for two and a half years (up to age 3), Hart and Risley concluded that, in essence, children end up like their parents. That is, if their parents talked a lot, then the children talked a lot; and if the parents were less talkative, the children were as well. The children in the study represented families of varying levels of socioeconomic status (i.e., professional, middle class, working class, and families on welfare) in an attempt to compare language experiences in different homes.

However, while Hart and Risley did find, for example, that children from professional families had significantly larger vocabularies and heard more words at home than children from families on welfare, they ultimately concluded that regardless of the socioeconomic status of the families, children whose parents spent more time talking to and with them were more likely to have larger vocabularies and score higher on an IQ test at age 3. Both children and parents played active roles in the children's language development, with the children becoming "increasingly heterogeneous dance partners" (Hart & Risley 1999, 4) as they learned to talk, and with the parents acting not as teachers but as "chaperones" (108) as they guided their children along the pathway of learning to talk.

Placed in a child-centered framework, Hart and Risley's findings and their ways of measuring language growth make it worth noting that IQ tests are often based on knowledge associated with middle-class families, and many children are not reliable test-takers at age 3. In addition, different cultures and social groups value different uses of language; some value children's talkativeness more or less than others (Heath 1983). Thus, vocabulary growth for children who are not middle class is something that is best assessed in center or school settings.

Finally, over the last decade or so, vocabulary—in a sense the child's "word count"—has been linked more and more by educators and policy makers to children's ability to read, rather than to their oral language abilities. This shift has occurred as learning the fundamentals of reading has become a primary goal even in the prekindergarten and kindergarten years (Genishi & Dyson 2009 in press). Teachers should not lose sight of the value of learning words for the sake of expanding vocabulary *in the context of meaningful experiences* as the foundation of children's expressive abilities across the curriculum.

Children's word learning and learning through language in school

As children enter the primary grades, words, often called "vocabulary words," take on a new importance and are less likely to be embedded in story-like events or contexts. Words are now meant to be read and written as well as spoken.

There are few studies of vocabulary instruction itself, but some recent findings are illuminating when compared with what researchers know about pre-schooler's acquisition of word meanings. For example, Juel and colleagues (2003) described research in which kindergarten teachers taught vocabulary words in the context of story reading or read-alouds. Similarly, Beck, McKeown, and Kucan (2002) recommended instructional methods in which words are embedded within teachers' read-alouds.

In both studies, vocabulary learning enhanced reading ability. Thus, these researchers support the premise that words do not exist in isolation from the ideas they represent and that they are best learned in an engaging context like that of stories. (See also Paley 2004 and Neuman & Roskos

> A variety of activities ensures the rich base of experiences through which children learn concepts and language.

2005 for hazards of direct instruction of academic skills in early childhood.)

Developmentally appropriate practices that many early childhood teachers already support are compatible with the findings presented here and often place language—spoken, dramatized, and written—in the foreground (e.g., Paley 1992; Gallas 1994; Copple & Bredekamp 2009). These authors emphasize *children's ways of learning* and an *integration of experiences*: Language learning is not separated from music, science, or dramatic play, nor is it separated from math, social studies, art, or health. A variety of activities ensures the rich base of experiences, the diverse contexts through which children learn concepts, and the language needed to talk and learn about them. Variety also makes it likely that children will find particular activities that suit their unique preferences and abilities, whether they feel most comfortable engaging in creative dramatics or computer activities.

For example, as illustrated in the excerpt below (Siegel & Lukas 2008, 43), two children in a kindergarten class in a school with a large population of ELLs collaborate during the balanced literacy block, merging their knowledge of the life cycle of the frog and details of written language. Jewel and Terrance share a computer as Jewel coaches Terrance in the spelling of *frog*:

Terrance: Jewel, how do you write…?
Jewel: I can show you.
Terrance: That's a…
Jewel: No, it's like—skinny legs and big body. Wait! Wait! Let me type my name! Let me do my name first!

Siegel and Lukas explain that Jewel's "skinny legs and big body" links to the discourse of the classroom for talking about letters: the letter g has been taught as a circle with a long stick and a tail. So in the exchange above, Jewel takes on a teacher role, describing how to draw a frog at the same time that she is about to type her own name and help Terrance to spell *frog*. A minute later she calls out for Terrance the letters of *frog life cycle,* which she reads from the board as he types. He then goes on to type his own name.

A recurring theme in this chapter has been that of events embedded in experience, classroom events—embedding the cycle of frogs' lives, for example—that are very much like stories. The events involve particular living things and the sequenced actions that children experience. Often when teachers, researchers, or children have looked for a way to make something accessible and meaningful, they have created stories. Stories seem to be an irresistible context for learning and making sense of experience. Indeed, stories can be viewed as "one of the most fundamental means of making meaning pervading all aspects of learning" (Wells 1986, 194).

The development of storytelling

Engel (1997, 3) noted that "story telling is perhaps the most powerful way that human beings organize experience" and described the sequential way in which many children develop into storytellers. This theory noted the elements of story in toddlers' play scenarios with toys, which are often accompanied by adult narration (e.g., Dad says, "Oh no, the horse is galloping away" as the child moves a toy horse around on the floor). Increasingly, according to Engel, the child takes on greater responsibility for constructing and telling a story until, by about age 3, she can tell a whole story on her own without the support of an adult.

Again, a milestone expressed as a child's age is always approximate, since a child's ability to tell a story on her own relies not only on advancing language skills but also on an understanding of how stories are organized and what a "good

story" is. There is not, however, a universal definition of *story* or single description of a good storytelling style. Moreover, while all children might develop into storytellers, there is still great variation in the types of stories and the ways in which children structure, create, and tell them, as all of these elements are influenced by both culture and community (Heath 1983; Gallas 1992; Engel 1997; Craig et al. 2001).

Thus, as Genishi and Fassler (1999) noted, "stories are like other culturally derived phenomena: There is nothing inherently 'better' about one style of storytelling over another" (71). The classroom, then, needs to provide a space where all types of stories and styles of storytelling are welcomed and encouraged. These should be viewed as an opportunity for children to develop not only their language skills but also their imaginations and the ability to express themselves and connect with others.

Story making comes naturally to children

Indeed, during observations of children in centers or classrooms where they choose some of their own activities, children are often enacting stories, inventing them in dramatic play, dictating them to a teacher, or writing them on their own. In studies of kindergarten and primary grade children, Dyson (1989; 1993; 1997; 2003) had many opportunities to watch the development of stories as children talk about knowledge that they bring with them into the classroom. For example, in a second-grade classroom, Sammy is reading a ninja story based on the film "The Three Ninjas." His story is the narrative that his friends (named in brackets below) are about to dramatize, and he begins this way (Dyson 1997, 51):

Sammy: (*reading*) "Rocky [Nyem] and TumTum [Radha] and Colt [Seth] went for a summer vacation. When their grandpa came" back (*end of literal reading, abandonment of text*) …

Sammy, a speaker of African American Vernacular English, proceeds to compose the story, as he enables his friends to participate. It's much more entertainingly complex than the short one he had written earlier. He invents two aunties, never before seen in the ninja movies, and creates a scenario where aunties and bad guys share the stage. The good guys prevail, though, and Sammy ends the story (52):

> **Sammy:** Rocky, TumTum, and Colt, they said, "Oh my God. We can't fight all these bad guys." And they all start running. They was running, and the bad guys was running (after) them and the bad guys couldn't catch them. And when they got home, Grandpa came down, and Grandpa did karate on all of 'em. ...

Everyone then sits down, knowing that Grandpa took care of things; it's time for questions and comments for Sammy. The children and their teacher, Kristin, focus on content and action and whether each character had a satisfying role in the story, not on the forms of Sammy's speech. This improvised story illustrates how much space Kristin provides both for the language that children know and elements of popular culture that they verbally play with, always in the company of peers (Dyson 1997).

Stories facilitate second language learning

The focus in this chapter has been on first language learners, but a study by Britsch (1989) showed how stories engender second-language learning, as well. In a Native American Head Start center, community members and Britsch started a program to renew the group's language, Tachi Yokuts, which was spoken by only about 30 people in California's Central Valley when the Tachi as a Second Language Program began. The elders came to the classroom to teach the children, who eventually began to ask for specific words as the lessons became interactive.

As the program evolved, the elders began to tell stories of their personal histories during curriculum planning meetings. Britsch later worked these stories into a unit for the elders and the children on picking fiddlehead (a plant with a curled flowering head that resembles a fiddle) and preparing it for eating. As learning became more lifelike and more related to a retelling of the community's past experiences, the use of Tachi grew and extended beyond the Head Start center into the community. Stories were the bridge between traditional second-language lessons and the lived experiences that underlie all of language learning. (See also Paley 1981; Dyson & Genishi 1994; Paley 1997 for other looks at the intimate relationship between thinking, learning, and stories.)

Are children "taught" words, or do they learn from experience?

Making sense of experience—this is what children do naturally. Thus, though it sounds accurate to say that language learning depends on learning words, the research reviewed here suggests that children learn experiences or events first. From an experience embedded in the social contexts of their daily lives, children gradually understand concepts, with which they associate words. Developmental theories about children and research based on those theories give every reason for teachers to believe that children continue to learn in this experience-based way, even beyond the early childhood years.

The many experiences that children have underlie the sounds of language, both in and out of school. These sounds are not those of structured language lessons. No one is repeating sentences such as "This is my friend." Instead, children create their own meanings for the drawings they design, the stories they invent, and the ideas that grow out of the many experiences they have. Their creations and ideas develop over time.

Although child-oriented classrooms lack drill-like, repetitious language, they do have rhythm and stability that enable children to repeat—or, more accurately, replay—what they are learning in the context of activities that make human sense. A word might be repeated 20 times or more, not in the senseless context of an isolated sentence but in a range of contexts: a poem, a child-created song or drama, a caption for a drawing, a chant, a story that children enact together, a game that a child plays and replays with friends, a conversation with other children or the teacher, and so on.

Should, then, teachers teach words? No, not any more than they "teach" experiences. Teachers might introduce a word such as *sticky* to describe the way something feels, but the child's experience of touching the object is as valuable for language development as the introduction of the word itself is. Children do ask questions about words, usually as a result of some event or experience. The concepts behind those words need to be experienced. Words are learned, not taught, in contexts and activities that teachers have arranged and sustained, usually through talk.

Conclusion

It's often said that there is an unbridgeable gap between education theory and practice. The theory and research reviewed here, however, suggest that in the area of children's language development, the gap is not large. There is a "theory for practice"—one that presents the child as an active thinker and language user.

The kind of practice recommended from the research is not new. Many of the activities mentioned are based on longstanding principles of "language experience" programs, which highlight firsthand experiences and much interaction. What *is* new is the increasing number and diversity of young children under age 8 who are learning or expanding their language(s) in

centers and schools, as well as at home. Although inventing new curricula for children and teachers is not necessary, emphasizing the importance of practices in centers or schools that resemble a child's "real life" is critical. These practices, well supported by recent research, are full of events and experiences that make sense to young children.

Updated from the Research in Review article in the November 1988 issue of *Young Children*.

Celia Genishi is a professor at Teachers College, Columbia University. **Andrea Honig** is a doctoral student at Teachers College, Columbia University.

References

Beck, I.L., M.G. McKeown, & L. Kucan. 2002. *Bringing words to life: Robust vocabulary instruction*. New York: Guilford.

Bloom, L., & M. Lahey. 1978. General considerations of language interventions. In *Language development and language disorders*, eds. L. Bloom & M. Lahey, 553–69. New York: Macmillan.

Britsch, S. 1989. The contribution of the preschool to a Native American community. *Language Arts* 66 (1): 52–57.

Bruner, J. 1983. *Child's talk*. New York: Norton.

Carey, S, & E. Bartlett. 1979. The child as a word learner. In *Linguistic theory and psychological reality*, eds. M. Halle, J. Bresnan, & G. Miller, 264–93. Cambridge, MA: MIT Press.

Clark, E.V. 1973. What's in a word? On the child's acquisition of semantics in his first language. In *Cognitive development and the acquisition of language*, ed. T.E. Moore, 65–110. New York: Academic.

Copple, C., & S. Bredekamp, eds. 2009. *Developmentally appropriate practice in early childhood programs serving children from birth through age 8*. 3d ed. Washington, DC: NAEYC.

Craig, S., K. Hull, A.G. Haggart, & E. Crowder. 2001. Storytelling: Addressing the literacy needs of diverse learners. *Teaching Exceptional Children* 33 (5): 46–51.

Donaldson, M. 1978. *Children's minds*. New York: Norton.

Dyson, A.H. 1989. *Multiple worlds of child writers: Friends learning to write*. New York: Teachers College Press.

Dyson, A.H. 1993. *Social worlds of children learning to write in an urban primary school*. New York: Teachers College Press.

Dyson, A.H. 1997. *Writing superheroes: Contemporary childhood, popular culture, and classroom literacy*. New York: Teachers College Press.

Dyson, A.H. 2003. *The brothers and the sisters learn to write: Popular literacies in childhood and school cultures*. New York: Teachers College Press.

Dyson, A.H., & C. Genishi, eds. 1994. *The need for story: Cultural diversity in classroom and community*. Urbana, IL: National Council of Teachers of English.

Engel, S. 1997. The guy who went up the steep nicken: The emergence of story-telling during the first three years. *Zero to Three* 17 (3): 1–9.

Fassler, R. 1998. Room for talk: Peer support for getting into English in an ESL kindergarten. *Early Childhood Research Quarterly* 13 (3): 379–409.

French, L.A., & K. Nelson. 1981. Temporal knowledge expressed in preschoolers' descriptions of familiar activities. *Papers and Reports on Child Language Development* 20: 61–69.

Gallas, K. 1992. When the children take the chair: A study of sharing time in a primary classroom. *Language Arts* 69 (3): 172–82.

Gallas, K. 1994. *The languages of learning: How children talk, write, draw, dance, and sing their understanding of the world*. New York: Teachers College Press.

Genishi, C. 1989. Observing the second language learner: An example of teachers' learning. *Language Arts* 66 (5): 509–15.

Genishi, C. 2002. Young English language learners: Resourceful in the classroom. *Young Children* 57 (4): 66–72.

Genishi, C., & A.H. Dyson. 2009, in press. *Children, language, and literacy: Diverse learners in diverse times*. New York: Teachers College Press, and Washington, DC: NAEYC.

Genishi, C., & R. Fassler. 1999. Oral language in the early childhood classroom: Building on diverse foundations. In *The early childhood curriculum: Current findings in theory and practice*, ed. C. Seefeldt, 54–79. New York: Teachers College Press.

Genishi, C., D. Yung-Chan, & S. Stires. 2000. Talking their way into print: English language learners in a prekindergarten classroom. In *Beginning reading and writing*, eds. D.S. Strickland & L.M. Morrow, 66–80. New York: Teachers College Press, and Newark, DE: International Reading Association.

Gerber, S. 2003. A developmental perspective on language assessment and intervention for children on the autistic spectrum. *Topics in Language Disorders* 23 (2): 74–94.

Glucksberg, S., & R.M. Krauss. 1967. What do people say after they have learned to talk? Studies of the development of referential communication. *Merrill-Palmer Quarterly* 13: 309–16.

Griffiths, P. 1986. Early vocabulary. In *Language acquisition*, 2d ed., eds. P. Fletcher & M. Garman, 279–306. New York: Cambridge University Press.

Hart, B., & T.R. Risley. 1995. *Meaningful differences in the everyday experiences of young American children*. Baltimore: Paul H. Brookes.

Hart, B., & T.R. Risley. 1999. *The social world of children learning to talk*. Baltimore: Paul H. Brookes.

Heath, S.B. 1983. *Ways with words: Language, life, and work in communities and classrooms*. New York: Cambridge University Press.

Juel, C., G. Biancarosa, D. Coker, & R. Deffes. 2003. Walking with Rosie: A cautionary tale of early reading instruction. *Educational Leadership* 60 (7): 12–18.

NCES (National Center for Education Statistics), U.S. Department of Education. 2006. *Public elementary and secondary students, staff, schools and school districts: School year 2003-04* (NCES 2006–307). Online: nces.ed.gov/pubs2006/2006307.pdf.

Nelson, K. 1973. Structure and strategy in learning to talk. *Monographs of the Society for Research in Child Development* 38, no. 1–2, serial no. 149.

Neslon, K. 1985. *Making sense: The acquisition of shared meaning*. New York: Academic.

Neslon, K. 1986. *Event knowledge: Structure and function in development*. New York: Academic.

Neuman, S.B., & K. Roskos. 2005. Whatever happened to developmentally appropriate practice in early literacy? *Young Children* 60 (4): 22–26.

Paley, V.G. 1981. *Wally's stories*. Cambridge, MA: Harvard University Press.

Paley, V.G. 1992. *You can't say you can't play*. Cambridge, MA: Harvard University Press.

Paley, V.G. 1997. *The girl with the brown crayon*. Cambridge, MA: Harvard University Press.

Paley, V.G. 2004. *A child's work: The importance of fantasy play*. Chicago: University of Chicago Press.

Piaget, J. 1926/1959. *The language of thought of the child*. Translated by M. Gabain & R. Gabain. London: Routledge & Kegan Paul.

Piaget, J. 1937/1954. *The construction of reality in the child*. Translated by M. Cook. New York: Basic.

Piaget, J. & B. Inhelder. 1948/1956. *The child's conception of space*. Translated by F.J. Landon & J.L. Lunder. London: Routledge & Kegan Paul.

Shatz, M., & R. Gelman. 1973. The development of communication skills: Modifications in the speech of young children as a function of listener. *Monographs of the Society for Research in Child Development* 38, no. 5, serial no. 152.

Siegel, M. & S. Lukas. 2008. Room to move: How kindergarteners negotiate literacies and identities in a mandated balanced literacy curriculum. In *Diversities in early childhood education: Rethinking and doing*, eds. C. Genishi & A.L. Goodwin, 29–47. New York: Routledge.

Simpson, J., & M.L. Rice. 2004. *Fact sheet number 11 (FS11)*. National Information Center for Children and Youth with Disabilities. Online: www.nichcy.org/pubs/factshe/fs11txt.htm.

Vygotsky, L.S. 1978. *Mind in society: The development of higher psychological processes*. Cambridge, MA: Harvard University Press.

Watson, R. 1987. Learning words from linguistic expressions: Definition and narrative. *Research in the Teaching of English* 21: 298–317.

Wells, G. 1986. *The meaning makers: Children learning language and using language to learn*. Portsmouth, NH: Heinemann.

10 Emerging Knowledge About Emergent Writing

Kelley Mayer

Policy makers now regard preschool as foundational in helping children become successful readers and writers. State and national standards for early education, being implemented across the country, emphasize early experiences with print as important for children's later literacy development.

Although researchers in education have begun to investigate and understand the importance of early reading activities for preschool children, less research has focused on the importance of young children's early writing experiences. Clay (2001) documents the concern, noting that "most parents and teachers believe that preschool reading experiences are very important but know almost nothing about the value of preschool writing experiences" (13).

To focus on reading alone disregards the importance of children's experiences with writing. Reading and writing skills develop simultaneously and are interconnected. Progress in one fuels development of the other. Thus, when studying what is important in helping children become better readers, teachers should also consider children's beginning understandings of the writing process. Like reading, writing abilities emerge as children interact with people, materials, and print in multiple environments.

This chapter reviews the research on young children's emergent writing and discusses the implications of this research base for teaching preschool children today.

How writing skills develop

Generally, theorists agree that children explore writing by drawing and scribbling. Several studies document that children learn to write before beginning school (Freeman & Sanders 1989; McGee & Purcell-Gates 1997). These studies acknowledge that through this exploration children understand that writing conveys meaning. Frequently, children combine writing and drawing in their early development (Barnhart & Sulzby 1986; Morrow & Sharkey 1993; Bus et al. 2001). Young children do not distinguish between the two mediums but use both to express themselves.

As children begin to notice print in their environments, they try to create products that look like real writing in an attempt to communicate messages. For example, children may include letter-like figures or write in continuous lines from left to right. Eventually they learn to form alphabet letters appropriately and start stringing letters together. The ability to write their first names is generally one of the first writing skills children grasp. Tolchinsky (2006) believes this is due to the self-centeredness of children at this age: Their names are meaningful to them; thus they are motivated to learn to write them.

These attempts to write words may or may not represent actual spellings of the words intended, yet children's writing is purposeful and meaningful. Children use their writing to tell stories or relate personal experiences, often exploring topics that are familiar to them. Once children master the idea that letters represent sounds, they use their knowledge of sounds in their attempts to spell words. As their abilities improve, they are likely to create texts of greater length and conventionality as well as compose complex messages from a variety of genres.

Evidence of writing knowledge

While educators can tie writing development to the chronological age of the child, research findings show that children often move between levels of writing (Barnhart & Sulzby 1986; Fox & Saracho 1990; Burns & Casbergue 1992; Whitehurst & Lonigan 1998; Bus et al. 2001). Writing development generally occurs between the ages of 3 and 5, during the preschool years, and can extend into the years of kindergarten and first grade.

Emergent writing means that children begin to understand that writing is a form of communication and their marks on paper convey a message. Emergent forms of writing include drawing, scribbling from left to right, creating letter-like forms,

or creating random strings of letters, *all* used—sometimes even simultaneously—in the child's attempt to communicate an idea through print.

Children continually explore different forms of writing. Even as they add new forms to their knowledge base, older forms continue to be used, but with less and less frequency (Fox & Saracho 1990; Burns & Casbergue 1992; Greer & Lockman 1998; Bus et al. 2001). This process can be thought of as children's attempts to solve the written language puzzle, with children gradually putting the pieces (in this case, writing skills and writing processes) together to build a complete picture, a coherent written message (Fox & Saracho 1990).

Children display their knowledge of writing in many ways, depending on the communication task. The more complex the task, the more primitive the form of writing used by the child (Barnhart & Sulzby 1986; Fox & Saracho 1990; Strickland & Morrow 1991; Burns & Casbergue 1992; Greer & Lockman 1998; Bus et al. 2001). Yet even when young children are aware of the representative function of letters, they may still produce writing samples characteristic of lower levels of development in order to preserve a message they are trying to convey (Barnhart & Sulzby 1986; Fox & Saracho 1990; Burns & Casbergue 1992).

Hannah, a kindergartner, abandons all knowledge of letter sounds when her teacher asks her to write a letter to her friend Sylvia. Hannah generally writes words well, labeling each with its beginning consonant. This time, however, Hannah is eager to tell Sylvia about her upcoming birthday party.

To represent this message, Hannah writes only the date of the party, with assistance from her teacher, and draws a picture of a birthday cake. Rather than attempting to spell a longer word like *birthday*, she chooses to represent the idea by drawing.

When Hannah's teacher asks her to write additional information about the party, she writes only her name and Sylvia's but does not attempt any other words.

Children continue to produce writing at lower levels of skill development until they have gained sufficient confidence in using more advanced skills (Barnhart & Sulzby 1986; Fox & Saracho 1990; Morrow & Sharkey 1993; Greer & Lockman 1998). Moreover, as Schickedanz and Casbergue (2004) argued, children do not initially distinguish between drawing and writing because both convey meaning.

Learning to write—A social process

Children gain knowledge about how to write through their observations and interactions with more advanced writers (Morrow & Sharkey 1993; Teale 1995; Chapman 1996; McGee & Purcell-Gates 1997; Schickedanz 1999). Before formal schooling, a great deal of learning occurs through a child's interactions with people and things in the home and the larger community environment (Teale 1995; Chapman 1996; McGee & Purcell-Gates 1997; Schickedanz 1999).

In these environments, learning to write is an interactive process, with children writing in active and constructive ways (Chapman 1996; Schickedanz 1999). Helping parents construct grocery lists or write letters or e-mails to distant family members are examples. Children also learn a great deal about print when families point out and discuss signs and other environmental print in their neighborhoods, such as signs for a popular restaurant, a store, or a gas station (Neuman & Roskos 1993).

Writing with peers

In addition to their family, children learn from their peers. Having opportunities to explore writing through interactions with peers is important for children in preschool. In studies of children's writing development, Dyson (1997; 2003) illustrates how children learn about writing by constructing texts with one another and expressing their ideas in other unbounded ways.

Through various opportunities to write with other children and interact with them about topics of interest (e.g., famous sports figures, cartoon characters), children play around with conceptions of themselves as authors. These informal writing experiences help children understand the responsibility of a writer to an audience of readers, as they work with others to co-construct the written word or clarify intended messages (Dyson 1997; 2003).

Children's interactions with one another help them explore and understand the process and purposes of writing (Morrow & Sharkey 1993; Teale 1995; Schickedanz 1999). When writing with one another, children discuss choices they make in the message content. Far less often do teachers or families observe children talking about the mechanics of writing or composition strategies. For example, in *The Brothers and Sisters Learn to Write*, Dyson (2003) describes an interaction between two first-grade girls, in which they work together to compose a scary story.

As first-grader Vanessa writes, she consistently seeks spelling help from Denise, as spelling is one of Denise's strengths. However, when trying to come up with a title for the story, Denise seeks the help of Vanessa:

Vanessa: What's the title going to be?
Denise: "One Boy and Two Girls."
Vanessa: That's not good.
Denise: What should it be then? "The Man and Two Women."
Vanessa: That's not good either.
Denise offers several other suggestions, which Vanessa rejects, until...
Denise: I know what it should be called: "The Vampire."

Vanessa: Ah, whatever you want. (*resigned*) Wait! It should be, "Be Careful What You Wish For."

Denise seems to like this suggestion.

Denise: And a girl could say, "I wish I was a vampire." And she could turn into a vampire.

(Dyson 2003, 161)

Denise and Vanessa worked together, calling on each other's strengths to aid their attempts at writing a scary story. From the interaction, both girls benefited from being able to discuss the choices they made while writing.

Writing with teacher support

Children benefit from working not only with peers but also with teachers. Writing with a teacher's support enables children to receive immediate feedback and helps them understand how the writing process works. With supportive teachers, children make greater progress in learning to write. Teachers described as supportive answer student questions thoughtfully, acknowledge writing strengths, scaffold children's writing activities, and encourage writing with verbal affirmations (Saracho 1990; Strickland & Morrow 1991; Burns & Casbergue 1992; Chapman 1996; Whitehurst & Lonigan 1998).

Several studies emphasize the importance of teacher modeling in children's acquisition of writing skills. Modeling is an interactive process in which a child constructs understanding with support from a more advanced writer, such as the teacher. Through interaction, children better understand the purposes as well as the mechanics of writing (Teale 1995; Yaden & Tardibuono 2004). When modeling writing skills, teachers explicitly state each step they take in constructing a text. For example, a teacher may begin by saying,

I want to write a letter to my friend Mya today. She lives far away, so we write letters to tell each other about what is happening in our lives. I want to tell her about my recent vacation in this letter.

I will start my letter by writing, "Dear Mya." Then I usually ask her how she is doing, and then I will write, "I just got back from a great trip." Next, I need to think about the most important or exciting things that happened on the trip that I want to tell her about.

This teacher modeled the process that writers use when they construct a text. She began by stating the purpose for writing and then described her plan for the content of the letter. The teacher took time to explain common structures used in letter writing, like the formal greeting.

Opportunities to witness authors in the act of constructing a text allow children to begin understanding the composing process. Over time, children can internalize the thinking process needed and use it when constructing texts independently. In interacting with teachers, children also can discuss the use of punctuation, spacing, and spelling, among other things.

Environments for writing

Children's writing develops further when the learning environment supports early attempts to write. Such an environment includes attentiveness to the classroom setting and materials as well as the instruction provided. Giving children free access to writing materials and print supports their writing development (Tangel & Blachman 1992; Yaden & Tardibuono 2004).

Printed labels on common classroom objects, where they actively serve a useful function in children's environment, need to be visually accessible for children learning to write (Neuman, Copple, & Bredekamp 2000). Teachers should place labels at children's eye level and print letters fairly large. Children often begin to explore writing by copying the words for familiar things (Saracho 1990; Schickedanz 1999; Clay 2001), such as classmates' names or names of favorite toys. Not only do labels need to be accessible to children, but teachers should continuously refer to these words to stimulate children's awareness of print in their environment (West & Egley 1998). Teachers should label only items that are commonly referred to in everyday activity or written about, for a functional purpose in the classroom such as a sign that reads "Please wash your *hands*" posted on the bathroom door, or "Take one *cup* of *pretzels*" at the snack table.

Labels should always use appropriate capitalization, beginning words with capital letters only when needed, such as in a child's name. Also children should see print in a variety of script (or font) styles to expose them to the variety of ways words and letters can be written in their environments. For example, children need to see a lowercase A written as both **a** and **ɑ**.

When children are writing, teachers may want to refer them to places in the room where words are commonly found. For example, teachers can steer children to words in books or in poems or songs on posters hung on the walls. Teachers can use alphabet blocks, magnet letters, or ABC charts to help children with sound/letter matching or letter formation.

Children need a generous amount of time to write using a variety of writing materials, not just pencils (Aram & Biron 2004; Yaden & Tardibuono 2004). Having opportunities to write with different materials helps motivate children to write and builds fine motor skills (Greer & Lockman 1998). These opportunities are particularly important for children with disabilities. Alternative writing tools that help build the fine motor control needed for writing include pencils with grips, carpenter pencils, pyramid pencils, or crayons. Computers, software programs, and other assistive technology devices are also becoming more readily available to teachers of children with special needs.

Motor control is needed in writing; children learn how to adapt their writing movements when using different implements or writing on varied surfaces. Some

children may need help controlling the paper, so taping it to the surface or using a clipboard can be beneficial. The angle of the writing surface is also a consideration. If children write better when the paper is at an angle rather than flat on a table, affix it to the outside of a large three-ring binder to give the needed support.

Before introducing these tools to children, it is important for teachers to model their appropriate use, discussing with the children how each tool aids their writing (Morrow 2005). A variety of materials encourages creativity, as children can explore and discover new uses. Classrooms with writing centers stocked with multiple materials for children to write with and write on foster a high level of writing development.

> **A supportive environment is one in which children feel empowered to write for real reasons.**

Effective early childhood teachers help children feel free in their writing (Strickland & Morrow 1991). They interact with children engaged in play in classroom activity centers and introduce the idea of using writing as a part of children's play. For example, when children are acting out a hospital scenario, the teacher can encourage them to write prescriptions for one another or record patients' medical problems on a chart.

A supportive environment is one in which children feel empowered to write for real reasons. When engaged in center play where writing materials are readily available, children will be able to brainstorm authentic ways to use the materials to aid their play (Burns & Casbergue 1992; Chapman 1996; McGee & Purcell-Gates 1997). Examples include writing menus at a restaurant center, creating road maps at the block center, or recording observations of the results of experiments conducted at the science center. Children may even enjoy having writing materials available during outdoor play for labeling sandbox creations, drawing treasure maps, or establishing and recording the rules for a new outdoor game (Giles & Wellhousen 2005).

Supporting children's emergent writing

In this synthesis of research on emergent writing are several important implications for preschool teachers.

1. Developmental awareness. Children's writing development is not linear in progression, nor is the progression the same for all children. It is important for teachers to be aware of each child's developmental strengths and needs. Teachers can encourage young children to concentrate more intently on their message than on letter formation or spelling. Children should have plenty of opportunities to choose their own writing topics. These opportunities not only increase children's motivation to write but also serve as effective ways to support children's cultural understandings of literacy.

By encouraging children to write in comfortable ways, teachers are more likely to enhance their development and reduce the chance of hindering learning progress by requiring them to write in an unfamiliar style or genre. By not honoring children's early conceptions of writing expressed in their initial explorations, teachers risk being culturally inappropriate. Children who write in an imaginative, playful style may need help later if they have difficulty writing for more informative purposes.

2. Supportive instruction. Teachers can observe children and provide instruction tailored to address individual interests and needs. When children choose their own topics, they are not overwhelmed by having to both think of something to write about and remember to use appropriate mechanics or accurate spelling.

Once children feel confident with the mechanics of writing, they will begin to demonstrate this knowledge when writing and will benefit from additional support in their use of writing skills. Understanding when children are ready for instruction that focuses on mechanics requires a teacher to do a great deal of "child watching." Observe children in the act of writing. This is the best way to identify developmental needs and to be ready to meet them at the appropriate level.

3. Opportunities to write. Give children plenty of opportunities to write without having to conform to adult standards. Journal writing, for example, is not just for kindergartners; with encouragement, preschoolers can write in journals on a daily basis and choose their own topics. Children are motivated to write in journals that have special meaning, like diaries of activities carried out at home or scientific logs in which children observe and record changes in plant growth. Some may enjoy writing in the traditional, black-and-white composition notebooks or creating their own journals by stapling together blank pieces of white paper along with a construction paper cover with their name. Children can personalize their journal covers by decorating as they choose.

4. Models for writing. Research shows that children learn new skills by observing others engaged in meaningful writing activities (Fox & Saracho 1990; Saracho 1990; Burns & Casbergue 1992; Chapman 1996). Thus, structuring time in the day for children to interact with peers on writing projects is vital. Moreover, exposing children to advanced writers modeling both the mechanics of and purposes for writing furthers their skill development.

Parents, teachers, and older students can serve as writing models for younger children. For example, teachers can engage the whole class (or a small group) in writing a story about a recent field trip or special class event. Using large paper on

> Opportunities to teach writing occur naturally as children ask questions when engaged in writing activities.

an easel allows children to see their teacher model letter formation, directionality, spacing, and text placement, among other things. A parent volunteer might model writing by helping the class handwrite—or use a computer to create—thank-you notes to school staff or a newsletter on class events to be shared with families.

5. Motivating environments and resources. Classrooms encourage appropriate writing development through their physical arrangement and the types of materials and activities available to the children. Young children enjoy and benefit from practice writing with pencils, pens, markers, crayons, chalk, and paint. Provide these materials in a variety of sizes to fit young hands appropriately so children can explore how to use them and grow in skill and creativity.

Children can write on a variety of surfaces and planes other than flat paper, such as chalk boards, dry-erase boards, painting easels, and the playground blacktop. Different surfaces require different amounts of hand strength and positioning. Having choices not only helps increase children's motivation to write but also provides challenges that help build the fine motor skills needed for letter formation. Encouraging children to experiment with writing in more tactile ways, such as in sand, shaving foam, confetti, or salt, stimulates creativity and makes writing fun.

Many young children best demonstrate their learning success through other forms, such as kinesthetic activity, and teachers should be sure to give children these opportunities. Children could, for example, practice letter formation using movements involving their whole arm to write letters in the air or lie down on the ground to create letter shapes together using their entire bodies.

6. Locations for writing. Preschool teachers will want to make materials for writing available throughout the classroom and outdoors to encourage children to write at different times and as a part of varied activities. The teacher can suggest how children can integrate the use of writing materials in various centers as a part of their play. This writing for child-centered, meaningful purposes serves as one way to encourage the development of writing skills.

For example, children can use writing materials in the block center to create road maps, street signs, or blueprints. Teachers can invite children to write about a structure they have created, adding the steps they took to build it. Children might make a sign asking others to leave their building standing. Displaying this writing in the block center encourages other future builders to refer to it and to write additional ideas.

At the reading center, children can use writing materials to express what they enjoyed in the stories or to write letters to friends about a good book they have read. The teacher's goal is tailoring writing instruction to meet children's needs in developmentally appropriate ways, rather than strictly following a direct skills approach. Opportunities to teach writing occur naturally as children ask questions when engaged in writing activities. For example, when asked about a particular spelling, the teacher can refer the child to a resource in the room where the word can be found (like a book or ABC chart) or help the child identify the beginning sound in the word.

Conclusion

Writing develops differently for each child. Understanding this, teachers can use their knowledge to provide learning experiences that meet children's individual needs and engage their individual interests. Giving children opportunities to learn about writing through interactions with peers and teachers are foundational to children's early conceptions of writing. When these opportunities are abundant in preschool classrooms, children enter kindergarten with a strong literacy base and the potential for experiencing school success. Children leave preschool with a feeling of empowerment, seeing themselves as budding readers *and* writers.

Updated from the Research in Review article in the January 2007 issue of *Young Children*.

Kelley Mayer is an assistant professor at the College of Charleston.

References

Aram, D., & S. Biron. 2004. Joint storybook reading and joint writing interventions among low SES preschoolers: Differential contributions to early literacy. *Early Childhood Research Quarterly* 19 (4): 588–610.

Barnhart, J., & E. Sulzby. 1986. How Johnny can write: Kindergarten children's uses of emergent writing systems. Paper presented at the Annual Meeting of the American Educational Research Association in Chicago.

Burns, M.S., & R. Casbergue. 1992. Parent-child interaction in a letter-writing context. *Journal of Reading Behavior* 24 (3): 289–312.

Bus, A., A. Both-de Vries, M. de Jong, E. Sulzby, W. de Jong, & E. de Jong. 2001. Conceptualizations underlying emergent readers' story writing. CIERA Report No. 2-015. Ann Arbor, MI: Center for the Improvement of Early Reading Achievement. Online: www.ciera.org/library/reports/inquiry-2/2-015/2-015.pdf.

Chapman, M. 1996. More than spelling: Widening the lens on emergent writing. *Reading Horizons* 36: 317–39.

Clay, M. 2001. *Change over time in children's literacy development*. Portsmouth, NH: Heinemann.

Dyson, A.H. 1997. *Writing superheroes: Contemporary childhood, popular culture, and classroom literacy*. New York: Teachers College Press.

Dyson, A.H. 2003. *The brothers and sisters learn to write: Popular literacies in childhood and school cultures*. New York: Teachers College Press.

Fox, B., & O. Saracho. 1990. Emergent writing: Young children solving the written language puzzle. *Early Child Development & Care* 56: 81–90.

Freeman, E., & T. Sanders. 1989. Kindergarten children's emerging concepts of writing functions in the community. *Early Childhood Research Quarterly* 4: 331–38.

Giles, R.M., & K. Wellhousen. 2005. Reading, writing, and running: Literacy learning on the playground. *The Reading Teacher* 59 (3): 283–85.

Greer, T., & J. Lockman. 1998. Using writing instruments: Invariances in young children and adults. *Child Development* 69 (4): 888–902.

McGee, L., & V. Purcell-Gates. 1997. So what's going on in research on emergent literacy? *Reading Research Quarterly* 32 (3): 310–18.

Morrow, L.M. 2005. *Literacy development in the early years: Helping children read and write*. Boston: Pearson.

Morrow, L.M., & E. Sharkey. 1993. Motivating independent reading and writing in the primary grades through social cooperative literacy experiences. *The Reading Teacher* 47 (2): 162–65.

Neuman, S.B., C. Copple, & S. Bredekamp. 2000. *Learning to read and write: Developmentally appropriate practices for young children*. Washington, DC: NAEYC.

Neuman, S., & K. Roskos. 1993. Access to print for children in poverty: Differential effects of adult mediation and literacy-enriched play settings on environmental and functional print tasks. *American Educational Research Journal* 30 (1): 95–122.

Saracho, O. 1990. Developmental sequences in three-year-old children's writing. *Early Childhood Development* 56: 1–10.

Schickedanz, J. 1999. *Much more than the ABCs: The early stages of reading and writing*. Washington, DC: NAEYC.

Schickedanz, J., & M. Casbergue. 2004. *Writing in preschool: Learning to orchestrate meaning and marks*. Newark, DE: International Reading Association.

Strickland, D., & L.M. Morrow. 1991. Fostering independent learning. *The Reading Teacher* 44 (9): 694–97.

Tangel, D.M., & B. Blachman. 1992. Effects of phoneme awareness instruction on kindergarten children's invented spelling. *Journal of Reading Behavior* 24 (2): 233–58.

Teale, W.H. 1995. Young children and reading: Trends across the twentieth century. *Journal of Education* 177 (3): 95–128.

Tolchinsky, L. 2006. The emergence of writing. In *Handbook of research on writing*, eds. C.A. MacArthur & J. Fitzgerald. Portsmouth, NH: Heinemann.

West, L.S., & E.H. Egley. 1998. Children get more than a hamburger: Using labels and logos to enhance literacy. *Dimensions of Early Childhood* 26 (3–4).

Whitehurst, G., & C. Lonigan. 1998. Child development and emergent literacy. *Child Development* 69 (3): 848–72.

Yaden, D., & J. Tardibuono. 2004. The emergent writing development of urban Latino preschoolers: Developmental perspectives and instructional environments for second-language learners. *Reading & Writing Quarterly* 20: 29–61.

11 Mathematics Instruction That Makes Sense for 2- to 5-Year-Olds

Arthur J. Baroody and Xia Li

Over the past three decades, researchers have accumulated a wealth of evidence about the mathematical development of young children. The aim of this chapter is to report on the implications of this research in answering three key questions: Can preschoolers construct abstract number and arithmetic concepts, and what role does language play in such learning? What mathematical concepts and skills should be the focus of preschool instructional effort? How should preschoolers be taught mathematics?

Can preschoolers construct abstract number and arithmetic concepts?

Previously, the conventional wisdom about young children's number and arithmetic competence swung like a pendulum from extremely pessimistic to extremely optimistic. It also underestimated the importance of language in the development of these competencies. Recent research points to a more realistic middle ground—one in which language plays a key role in children's construction of number concepts.

Early extremely pessimistic views

For most of the 20th century, psychologists viewed preschoolers as mathematically incompetent. For example, James (1890, 488) described an infant's perception of the world as a "great, blooming, buzzing confusion."

Behavioral theorists further promoted a pessimistic view of preschoolers' mathematical competence. Thorndike (1922), for example, concluded that young children were so mathematically inept that "little is gained by [doing] arithmetic before grade 2, though there are many arithmetic facts that can [be memorized by rote] in grade 1" (198). According to association theorists, children had to be rewarded (bribed) to learn mathematics; understanding was not central to learning useful mathematical skills; and students needed to be spoon-fed mathematics because they were uninformed and helpless.

The pessimistic view of behaviorists is still felt to this day in certain pedagogies (see Ginsburg, Klein, & Starkey 1998). This view served as the rationale for the "drill" approach (Thorndike 1922) and, years later, shaped the doctrine of "direct instruction" (Bereiter & Englemann 1966). These methods (drill, lecture) remain the most widely used to teach school (formal) mathematics.

For early childhood mathematics education specifically, behavioral theory provided a justification for a "minimalist mathematics curriculum," which is still evident in preschools and kindergartens (Balfanz 1999; see also Ginsburg, Inoue, & Seo 1999; Hunting & Kamii 2002; Copley 2004). That is, behaviorism supported the misconceptions that young children start school with little or no prior mathematical knowledge and that only limited instruction on the first 10 numbers and simple addition and subtraction facts were feasible before first grade (Balfanz 1999).

> By listening, young children detect counting patterns, devise counting rules, and sometimes over-apply these rules.

Behavioral theory had another negative impact on early childhood mathematics education. While some preschool teachers and parents unfortunately adopted lecture and drill, many others—also unfortunately—went to the other extreme. That is, fearing that those methods would stifle preschoolers' creativity and interest in learning, they concluded that mathematics instruction should be postponed altogether until primary school.

Such misconceptions are compounded by the math anxiety experienced by inordinately many early childhood teachers (Ashcraft, Kirk, & Hopko 1998). Survey responses such as "I don't do mathematics" and "Young children shouldn't do mathematics … it's not developmentally appropriate" indicate how uncomfortable many early childhood teachers feel about teaching mathematics (Copley 2004).

Piaget's constructivism. Piaget's (1965) research offered a very different view of mathematical teaching and learning (see, e.g., Kamii 1985). In Piaget's constructivist view, young children have a natural curiosity. That is, they have an inherent desire to find patterns and resolve problems, which is the essence of mathematics. For Piaget, the construction of mathematical understanding was the heart of real development. For example, reflecting on the part-whole relations underlying addition, such as *a whole is the sum of its parts and greater than any single part*, advances mathematical thinking; the memorization of number facts by rote does not.

According to Piaget's view, children actively construct their mathematical knowledge by interacting with their physical and social world. For instance, by listening to their parents, older siblings, and peers, young children detect counting patterns, devise counting rules, and sometimes over-apply these rules—rather than passively absorbing (imitating) the counting-word sequence they hear. A clear indication of this construction process is a child's rule-governed counting errors, such as "fourteen, *fifteen*, sixteen…" or "twenty-eight, twenty-nine, *twenty-ten*" (e.g., Ginsburg 1977; Baroody & Coslick 1998). (It does not seem likely that parents, siblings, or preschool teachers would model *fifteen* or *twenty-ten*.) There is now abundant evidence to support Piaget's views (see Ginsburg, Klein, & Starkey 1998).

Although Piaget's work created interest in preschoolers' informal mathematical knowledge, his views reinforced the "minimalist" approach to early mathematics instruction. In this approach, children before age 7 or so are considered incapable of concrete operational thinking (constructing abstract concepts or logical thinking). Thus, they are thought incapable of a true understanding of number or arithmetic. Piagetians have long argued that teaching number and arithmetic concepts before children reach the concrete operational stage in their thinking does not make sense and that premature instruction is worse than no teaching at all (e.g., Hall 1970; May & Kundert 1997).

Today, early educational efforts often still focus on fostering children's logical reasoning ability (e.g., sorting, classifying, ordering) rather than on number and arithmetic directly (see, e.g., Maffel & Buckley 1980). Some constructivists still argue that a genuine abstract understanding of number does not develop until children are at least 4 years old (Copeland 1979; Kamii 1985; Steffe, Cobb, & von Glasersfeld 1988; Bermejo 1996; Munn 1998).

Extremely optimistic view

In the late 20th century, research indicated that preschoolers can glean a wealth of informal mathematical knowledge from everyday activities (Ginsburg 1977; Gelman & Massey 1987; Pound 1999; Ginsburg et al. 2006).

Nativists even concluded that infants had innate knowledge of number and arithmetic. For example, Wynn (1998) noted, "Findings over the past 20 years have shown infants are sensitive to number" (5). Specifically, Wynn argued that children are born with an ability to recognize and distinguish among *oneness*, *twoness*, and *threeness*; and that they even can reason about or operate on very small numbers (e.g., recognize that one object added to another makes two, and that two objects minus one is one)—all before they develop verbal-based counting competencies.

Indeed, Gelman (e.g., Gelman & Meck 1992) argued that children are innately endowed with counting principles. These principles allow infants to nonverbally count (using nonverbal tags or representations), and toddlers to quickly learn number words and how to use them to count collections.

A language-based middle ground

Research over the last 10 years indicates that early childhood educators should not be overly pessimistic or optimistic

about preschoolers' informal mathematical knowledge. It further indicates that language may play a key role in children's abstraction of number and arithmetic concepts.

The concepts-before-language view. Dewey (1898) and Thorndike (1922) concluded that children's initial training in mathematics should focus on counting. But Russell (1917) set the tone for the rest of the 20th century by denouncing this informal approach and arguing that *initial* mathematical training should focus on developing children's logical thinking about classes.

Subsequently, extremely pessimistic theorists (Piagetians) and extremely optimistic psychologists (nativists) agreed that language development did not play a role, directly or otherwise, in children's initial construction of the concept of number. Piaget (1965), for example, dismissed verbal and object counting as skills learned by rote, skills that had no impact on constructing a number concept. He argued that the construction of a number concept depends on the development and synthesis of the logical thinking abilities necessary for classifying and ordering (e.g., Gibb & Castaneda 1975). More recently, early verbal counting (specifically the numbers from "one" to "twelve" or so in English) was considered merely a singsong (Ginsburg 1977) or a meaningless string of sounds (e.g., Fuson 1988).

Clearly, children's *initial* uses of number words are nonfunctional (Baroody 1987; Mix, Huttenocher, & Levine 2002). However, this perspective has obscured the roles even nonfunctional number words may play in constructing a number concept.

The language-supports-concepts view. Since the turn of the 21st century, some researchers have proposed that learning the first few number words may provide children a vehicle for abstracting a concept of the "intuitive" numbers—one, two, and three (Van de Walle, Carey, & Prevor 2000; Benson & Baroody 2002; Sandhofer & Mix 2003; Spelke 2003a; 2003b; Mix, Sandhofer, & Baroody 2005; Baroody, Lai, & Mix 2006).

By repeatedly hearing the word *two*, for instance, associated with different pairs of items ("two toy planes," "two crayons," "two circles," etc.), children may recognize that the total number of items—not their physical arrangement or appearance—is relevant to the concept called *two*. Initially, children may think that *two* represents any collection containing more than one object. But as other number words are applied to non-examples of *two* (i.e., the words *three, four, five,* and so forth, applied to collections larger than two objects), a child can define the boundaries of the concept exactly and apply the term *two* in a reliably accurate manner.

In brief, number symbols (usually verbal number words, but possibly written numerals too) serve as the catalyst for constructing an abstract concept of number, which includes understanding equivalence based on total (cardinal) values.

Educational implications

Although children may not be born with innate knowledge of number and arithmetic, as nativists contend, concepts of number and arithmetic begin to emerge in toddlers and are more robust than suggested by earlier scholars (e.g., James 1890; Thorndike 1922; Piaget 1965). Two key implications for early childhood educators follow from existing research: (1) number and arithmetic concepts do not come to children naturally, but instead require nurturing, and (2) this nurturing can begin as early as toddlerhood (Copley 1999; Baroody & Benson 2001; Clements, Copple, & Hyson 2002).

For example, toddlers and somewhat older children can engage in:

- one-to-one correspondence activities, such as completing shape or knob puzzles or retrieving a cookie for each of several children;
- classification activities, such as sorting objects into egg cartons by rows;
- equivalence activities, such as determining whether there are the same number of spoons as bowls or whether two people have fair shares of candies;
- ordering or ordinal number activities, such as figuring out whether someone 2 years old or 3 years old is older; and
- addition or subtraction activities, such as determining how old a child will be at his next birthday or how many candies will be left if one piece is eaten.

What mathematical concepts and skills should be the focus of preschool instructional effort?

Summarized below are findings regarding concepts fundamental to number sense and an understanding of school (formal) mathematics. By recognizing what young children know about these foundational concepts and can do with them, teachers can incorporate developmentally appropriate activities to nurture children's mathematical development.

Verbal number recognition

Reliable verbal number recognition builds on an informal concept of number and numerical equivalence and entails consistently recognizing the cardinal value of a small number of items and labeling the collection with the appropriate number word. Such recognition of *two* develops at about age 2½. Recognition of *three* does not develop for another six months or so. As suggested by the language-supports-concepts view, reliably labeling small collections of one, two, or three objects with the appropriate number word is a fundamentally important skill. Indeed, it is the foundation of learning a wide variety of counting, number, and arithmetic concepts and skills.

A basis for counting. Parents and preschool teachers often start mathematics instruction with verbal and object counting (Blevins-Knabe & Musun-Miller 1996; Baroody et al. 2004). However, teaching object counting before children can recognize collections up to three or so can confuse them. When modeling object counting with three items, adults will typically indicate the total (cardinal) value of the collection by saying the last number word with special emphasis: by changing the pitch of their voice ("One, two, *three*"), stretching out the word ("One, two, t-h-r-e-e"), repeating it ("One, two, three; see, three"), or some combination of these behaviors.

However, unless a child can recognize a collection of three, it is highly unlikely she will understand what the adult is doing. If the child can recognize the collection has three objects, the emphasis is more likely to make sense. That is, the child may discover the purpose of the counting procedure modeled by the adult (it is just another way of determining the total number of objects in a collection) and the *cardinality principle* (that the last number word has special significance because it represents that total).

Verbal number recognition of the intuitive numbers can also help preschoolers construct an understanding of other counting principles:

- By observing adults enumerate small, recognizable collections, children may be more likely to abstract the *one-to-one principle*—that each item is labeled with a single number word (otherwise the outcome is different than the cardinal value as determined by verbal number recognition).
- By observing adults enumerate a heterogeneous collection and label it with

the cardinal value that can be seen, children may discover the *abstraction principle*—that different items can be considered a collection for counting purposes.

- By observing adults enumerate small, numerically identifiable collections in different directions or arrangements (or doing so themselves), children may also induce the *order-irrelevance principle*—that the order in which items are counted does not matter as long as the one-to-one principle is observed.

A basis for number. Verbal number recognition can enable a child to directly see that a collection of two is more than one and that three is more than two. This is aided by the ability to see *two* as "one and one more" and *three* as "two and one more." Verbal number recognition, then, can underlie children's recognition that the number words represent larger and larger collections, or ordinal relations (e.g., that a collection of three is not merely different from a collection of two items but is *one more* than two), which leads to children's discovery of the *number-ordering principle*—that a collection that requires more counting words than another collection is greater than the latter.

Verbal number recognition can also enable a child to see (de-compose) collections of two (a whole) as "one and one" (its parts), and likewise to see collections of three as "two and one" or even "one, one, and one" (Rosu & Baroody 2006). As such, it can help children construct an understanding of *part-whole relations* (e.g., that a whole is greater than its parts, that a whole often can be created by using different parts).

> Concepts of number and arithmetic begin to emerge in toddlerhood.

A basis for arithmetic. By recognizing that adding one item to another item makes two, taking away one from two makes one, and adding one to two items makes three and vice versa, children construct fundamental informal concepts of addition and subtraction (i.e., that "adding" items makes a collection larger; "taking away" items makes it smaller). Verbal number recognition of such small number transformations can help children see

- That two is "one and one" and that three is "one and one and one" (the *unit principle*—that any natural number can be composed from a particular number of units).
- That "two and one more" and "one and two more" both make three (the *principle of additive commutativity*).
- That "one take away one," "two take away two," and "three take away three" all leave nothing (*subtractive negation principle*).
- Or that "two and one more, take away one" or "three take way two, add two more" results in the original amount (*inverse principle*—that addition of an amount then subtraction of the same amount, or vice versa, leaves a collection unchanged).

Verbal number recognition can provide a basis for memorizing basic arithmetic facts. Consider the case of Alice (described in Baroody & Rosu 2006). Because verbal number recognition allowed Alice to repeatedly see (de-compose) two as "one and one" and three as "two and one," she appeared to learn the basic combinations that "one and another one makes two" (1+1=2) and "two and another one makes three" (2+1=3).

Verbal recognition of two and three also allowed Alice to de-compose larger collections she could not recognize, and it provided her a basis for meaningfully learning larger sums. At age 30–31 months, Alice could not recognize and label collec-tions larger than three items, so in order to quantify "larger" collections of four and five, she de-composed them into collections she could readily recognize (four is "two and two"; five is "two and two and one"). She then used the known relation "two and two makes four" (learned from her parents) to specify the cardinal value of the collection.

Object counting

Between ages 3½ and 4, children's development of verbal and object-counting skills provides them a more powerful tool for quantifying collections, creating collections, and comparing collections or numbers.

Quantifying collections by one-to-one object counting. Counting a collection (*one-to-one object counting*) enables children to determine the number of items in collections larger than those they can recognize. It also permits them to quantify events over time (e.g., four hand claps). This involves matching counting words one for one with each item in the collection.

Counting is not an uncomplicated skill. To count a collection of objects correctly, a child must simultaneously: (1) generate the correct counting-word sequence; (2) label each object in a set with a single counting word (one-to-one tagging); and (3) keep track of counted and uncounted objects so that each object is tagged only once. The second and third subskills follow from the one-to-one principle discussed earlier. Meaningful (functional) counting also requires children to understand two other principles discussed earlier—cardinality and order-irrelevance. The former principle develops between ages 3 and 4; the latter, about a year later.

Creating collections by counting out collections. Verbal production begins with a request for a number of items (e.g., "Please give me three blocks") followed by the creation of a collection with the specified total (cardinality) from a larger collection. This can be a cognitively challenging task because the child must remember the target number ("three blocks"), create a collection, compare the collection with the stored target number word, and make adjustments if necessary.

Children initially use verbal number recognition to put out the correct number of items. For example, preschoolers might look at a group of blocks, visually isolate three blocks, and put them all out at once; or they might put out blocks one at a time until they recognize that the new collection is *three*. Such putting-out strategies work well for small collections up to about four.

However, to verbally produce larger collections, children must learn to count out collections. This is a relatively complicated task because children must realize that the requested number of items indicates when to stop the counting process (Baroody 1987; Wilkins & Baroody 2000).

Young children often count all the items available (make a *no-stop error*), or they count all the available items and then re-label the last item with the requested number (*end-with-n error*). No-stop errors indicate that a child does not understand the goal or purpose of the verbal production task. The end-with-*n* error can occur because children count out items in a one-to-one fashion but fail to constantly compare this count to the counting-out process (Resnick & Ford 1981).

Comparing collections by using a mental number line. Children initially use perceptual cues (e.g., the longer row equals "more") or verbal number recognition (*three* items is more than *two* items). However, appearances can be misleading, and verbal recognition is limited to smaller collections. Using counting or a counting-based mental representation can enable children to overcome these limitations.

Counting-based comparison skills nevertheless build on verbal number recognition skill. Specifically, by counting and visually comparing small collections, children can recognize the *same number-name principle*—that two collections are equal if they share the same number name, despite differences in the physical appearance of the collection (Baroody & Coslick 1998). Because it is a general (abstract) principle, young children can use it to compare any size collection that they can count.

Similarly, by counting and visually comparing two unequal collections, preschoolers can further discover the *larger-number principle*—that the later a number word appears in the counting sequence, the larger the collection it represents (e.g., *five* represents a larger collection than *four* because *five* follows *four* in the counting sequence). Once children can automatically cite "the number after" another in the counting sequence (e.g., "The number after *four* is *five*"), they can use the larger-number principle to mentally compare two numbers (e.g., "Who is older, someone age 9 or someone age 8?" . . . "The 9-year-old, because *nine* comes after *eight*"). This relatively abstract number skill has many everyday applications and can be used for even huge numbers (1,000,129 is greater than 1,000,128 because the former comes after the latter).

Typically, children can cite "the number after" up to *ten,* and they can use this knowledge and the larger-number principle to mentally compare any two numbers up to *five*. They become able to do this between ages 4½ and 5½—before they enter kindergarten. By the time they leave kindergarten, children typically can use their number-after knowledge to mentally compare any two numbers at least up to *ten*.

Arithmetic

Informal addition and subtraction. An understanding of addition and subtraction is fundamental to success with school mathematics and everyday life. Recent research indicates that children begin constructing an understanding of these arithmetic operations long before starting school. During the preschool years, they develop the ability to solve simple, non-verbal addition or subtraction problems (e.g., Huttenlocher, Jordan, & Levine 1994). Such problems involve showing a child a small collection (one to four items), covering the collection, adding or subtracting an item or items, and then asking the child to indicate how many items there now are in the hidden collection by counting out an appropriate number of disks.

For one item plus another item ("1+1"), for instance, a correct response would involve the child counting out a set of two disks rather than, say, one disk or three disks. In Huttenlocher, Jordan, and Levine's (1994) study, for example, most children who had recently turned 3 years old could correctly solve the problem "1+1" or "2–1" (that is, children could imagine adding one object to another object or subtracting one object from a collection of two objects). Most children who were about to turn 4 years old could solve "1+2," "2+1," "3–1," and "3–2," as well; and at least a quarter of the children could also solve "1+3," "2+2," "3+1," "4+1," "4–1," and "4–3." Thus, by the age of 4, children could mentally add or subtract any small number of items.

How do children so young manage these feats of simple addition and subtraction? They apparently can reason about their mental representations of numbers. For "2+1," for instance, children form a mental representation of the initial number of items in the collection before it is hidden from view, form a mental representation of the added (or subtracted) amount, and then can *imagine* this amount added to (or subtracted from) the original collection to make the latter larger (or smaller). In other words, children understand the most basic concept of addition—that addition is a transformation that makes a collection larger. Similarly, they understand the

> Children understand the most basic concept of addition—that addition is a transformation that makes a collection larger.

most basic concept of subtraction—that it is a transformation that makes a collection smaller.

Later, typically before they receive formal arithmetic instruction in school, children can solve simple addition and subtraction word problems (e.g., Huttenlocher, Jordan, & Levine 1994), including those involving numbers larger than four. How do children manage this? Basically, they decipher the meaning of the story by relating it to their informal understanding of addition as a "make-larger" transformation or their informal understanding of subtraction as a "make-smaller" transformation (e.g., Carpenter, Hiebert, & Moser 1983; Baroody & Coslick 1998). At least initially, children use objects (e.g., blocks, fingers, tallies) to model the meaning (type of transformation) indicated by the word problem. Consider the following problem:

> Rafella helped her mom decorate five cookies before lunch. After lunch, she helped decorate three more cookies. How many cookies did Rafella help decorate altogether?

A young child might model this problem by counting out five blocks to represent the initial amount, counting out three more blocks to represent the added amount, and then counting all the blocks put out to determine the solution.

Research further reveals that children invent increasingly sophisticated counting strategies to determining sums and differences (e.g., Resnick & Ford 1981; Carpenter, Hiebert, & Moser 1983; Baroody & Coslick 1998). At some point, children abandon using objects such as fingers or blocks and instead rely on verbal counting procedures. To solve the problem above, for instance, a child might count up to the number representing the initial amount

("One, two, three, four, five. . .") and then continue the count three more times to represent the amount added (". . . six is one more, seven is two more, and eight is three more—eight cookies altogether").

One shortcut many children spontaneously invent is starting with the number representing the initial amount instead of counting from one: "Five. . . . Six is one more, seven is two more, and eight is three more—eight cookies altogether" (Baroody 1995).

As with their number comparisons, children's informal addition initially is relatively concrete (in the sense that they are working nonverbally with real collections or mental representations of them) and is limited to small collections of four or less. Later, as children master and can apply their counting skills, they extend their ability to engage in informal arithmetic both in terms of more abstract contexts (word problems, and even later, symbolic expressions such as "2+1=?") and more abstract numbers (i.e., numbers greater than four).

Part-whole relations—A basis for understanding missing-addend problems. Children's construction of the *part-whole* concept (i.e., an understanding of how a whole is related to its parts) is an enormously important achievement (e.g., Resnick & Ford 1981). For example, part-whole is considered a conceptual basis for understanding and solving missing-addend word problems such as those below and missing-addend equations such as "?+3=5" and "?−2=7."

> **Problem A.** Angie bought some candies. Her mother bought her three more candies. Now Angie has five candies. How many candies did Angie buy?

> **Problem B.** Blanca had some pennies. She lost two pennies playing. Now she has seven pennies. How many pennies did Blanca have before she started to play?

Young children's inability to solve missing-addend word problems and equations has been taken as evidence that they lack a part-whole concept (e.g., Riley, Greeno, & Heller 1983). Some have interpreted such evidence as support for Piaget's (1965) conjecture that the pace of cognitive development limits what mathematical concepts children can and cannot learn, and they have concluded that instruction on missing addends is too difficult to be introduced in the early primary grades (Kamii 1985).

The results of several recent studies suggest otherwise (e.g., Sophian & Vong 1995). Sophian and McCorgray (1994), for instance, gave 4-, 5-, and 6-year-olds problems like A and B above. The investigator read the problem to the child and acted it out using a stuffed bear and pictures of the items mentioned. When the investigator referenced the initial, unknown amount (e.g., "some candies"), the child was shown a round, covered box. When the investigator referenced adding objects ("three more candies"), the child was shown a picture of the objects, and then the investigator put the picture (of the three candies) in the box, out of sight. (For subtraction, a picture of the objects was removed from the box, shown to the child, and then placed out of sight.) When the result was referenced, the investigator showed the child a picture of the corresponding items (e.g., "five candies" in the case of Problem A).

Although 5- and 6-year-olds typically had great difficulty determining the exact answers of such problems, they at least gave answers that were in the right direction. For Problem A, for instance, children knew that the answer (a part) had to be less than five (the whole). For Problem B, they recognized that the answer (the whole) had to be larger than seven (the larger of the two parts). These results suggest that 5- and 6-year-olds can reason (qualitatively) about missing-addend situations and, thus, do have a basic understanding of part-whole relations.

Equal partitioning—A basis for understanding division and other concepts. Subdividing a collection or other quantities into equal-sized parts (*equal partitioning*) is the conceptual basis for division, measurement, and fractions. Research (e.g., Hiebert & Tonnesen 1978; Davis & Pitkethly 1990) has shown that many children of kindergarten age can, for instance, respond appropriately to fair-sharing situations or problems such as this one:

> Three sisters, Martha, Marta, and Marsha, were given a plate of six cookies by their mom. If the three sisters shared the six cookies fairly, how many cookies would each sister get?

Some children solve this type of problem by using a divvying-up strategy: Count out objects to represent the starting amount ("six"), then deal out one object ("cookie") to each pile; repeat the distribution (to the three sisters) until all the objects have been distributed; and then count the number of objects in a pile to determine the solution (Marta has two cookies in her pile).

In effect, then, even the operation of division can be introduced to children as early as kindergarten.

Educational implications

Recent research indicates that preschoolers do have impressive informal mathematical strengths in a variety of areas. Given this and their natural inclination for numerical reasoning, it does make sense to involve them in mathematical instruction.

A key question is: How can teachers best provide preschoolers with engaging, appropriate, and challenging mathematical activities?

How should preschoolers be taught mathematics?

In this section, a new approach for teaching mathematics will be discussed, followed by some key implications for early childhood mathematics instruction.

The investigative approach

Consistent with constructivist theory and its supporting evidence, the National Council of Teachers of Mathematics (NCTM) (1989; 1991; 2000) has recommended shifting from a traditional instructional approach to an approach that better fosters the *mathematical power* of children. As will be evident below, this approach is consistent with the teaching guidelines outlined in the third edition of *Developmentally Appropriate Practice* (Copple & Bredekamp 2009).

What is mathematical power? Mathematical power has three components. The first is a positive disposition to learn and use mathematics. This includes the confidence to tackle challenging problems. As this confidence is learned, teachers need to foster in children the belief that *everyone* is capable of understanding mathematics and solving mathematical problems.

The second component of mathematical power is understanding mathematics. This includes appreciating how school mathematics relates to everyday life, seeing the connections among mathematical concepts, and linking procedures to their conceptual rationales. In order to promote meaningful learning, then, teachers must help children (1) relate school-taught symbols and procedures to their informal, everyday experiences; (2) consider how different ideas such as addition and subtraction are related (e.g., that adding one can be undone by subtracting one and that "3–2=?" can be thought of as "2+?=3"); and (3) learn the whys as well as the hows of mathematics.

The third part of mathematical power is developing an ability to engage in the processes of mathematical inquiry. This includes making and testing conjectures, finding patterns present in the world (inductive reasoning), problem solving, and logical reasoning (deductive reasoning). An especially important but often overlooked process is communicating about mathematics. To promote children's ability to engage in mathematical inquiry, teachers need to find challenging, developmentally appropriate problems and encourage students to discuss their ideas and their solutions with others, including their peers.

Why is mathematical power important? A positive disposition toward mathematics underlies, for example, the confidence and perseverance necessary to tackle challenging problems and lifelong learning of mathematics. Understanding greatly facilitates the remembering (retention) and applying (transfer) of mathematics skills (e.g., Brownell 1935; Hatano 1988; Hiebert & Carpenter 1992; Rittle-Johnson & Alibali 1999). (Meaningful learning requires less drill and practice than does learning by rote.) Moreover, because children can apply what they understand, students can make connections and learn new material more easily on their own. Problem solving and other inquiry skills fundamental to mathematics are more and more necessary in an increasingly complex world.

How can instruction foster mathematical power? Unfortunately, a traditional instructional approach of drill and lecture robs children of mathematical power (Baroody & Coslick 1998). To better foster mathematical power, NCTM (1989; 1991; 2000) has recommended that instruction be purposeful, meaningful, and inquiry-based—what has been called the "investigative approach" (Baroody & Coslick 1998). In this approach, instruc-

> When children can connect new information or a problem to their existing knowledge, they are far more likely to understand it.

tion begins with a worthwhile task that is interesting, is often complex, and *creates a real need* to learn or practice mathematics. Experiencing mathematics in context is not only more interesting to children but more meaningful—both of which make learning mathematics more likely (Donaldson 1978; Hughes 1986).

In the investigative approach, a teacher helps children build on what they already to know in order to learn new concepts or procedures. When children can connect new information or a problem to their existing knowledge, they are far more likely to understand it. The instruction involves children in making conjectures, solving problems, reasoning inductively and deductively, and communicating their ideas, findings, or conclusions. There is no better way to become proficient at these inquiry skills than to engage in real mathematical inquiries.

Planning activities that are purposeful, meaningful, and inquiry-based is at the heart of good early childhood teaching practices.

Implications for early childhood mathematics instruction

The investigative approach seems particularly well suited for preschool children and their mathematics instruction. Below are some suggestions for making mathematics experiences for young children purposeful, meaningful, and inquiry-based.

Purposeful instruction. Teachers need to find or devise worthwhile tasks that create a real need for young children to learn and practice mathematics; for example, incorporating mathematics into everyday situations, children's questions, games, and children's literature.

Provide numerous opportunities to learn or practice mathematics in everyday preschool activities (see, e.g., Kamii 1985; Baroody & Coslick 1998; Fromboluti & Rinck 1999). For instance, in preparing for snack time, table setters for each table can be asked to count the number of children present that day to determine the number of place settings needed (i.e., counting a collection) and then to put out a carton of milk, paper plate, or the like, at each place (i.e., one-to-one matching).

Such tasks might also involve other skills, such as subtraction (e.g., "My table usually has five, but Clayton is sick today, so we have. . ."). It is important that teachers not assign such tasks to a child who is not developmentally ready (e.g., an atypical 4-year-old who cannot yet verbally count to at least *five* or *six*); they also should leave enough time to help children who *are* developmentally ready but who have not yet learned or mastered a needed skill.

Respond to children's questions, which can provide invaluable teachable moments. For example, if Diane asks, "My birthday is next week, how old will I be? Will I be older than Dionte?" The teacher could respond by announcing, "Class, Diane has some interesting questions she needs help with. If she is 3 years old now, how can she figure out how old she'll be on her next birthday?" Note that the teacher did not simply to give the class the solution ("She will be 4") but challenged children to devise their own informal solutions to the problem ("I know, Miss Lacy, she could count and see what number comes after *three*").

The teacher could then follow up by posing a problem involving both number-after and number-comparison skills: "If Dionte is 5 years old and Diane is 4 years old, how could we figure out who is older?" Answering their own real questions can provide children a powerful incentive to engage in mathematical inquiry and to

explore or practice mathematical content. Furthermore, such conversations about mathematics can provide teachers with a rich source of information about each child's present and emerging understandings of number and arithmetic.

Play games to provide a natural, entertaining, and structured way of exploring or practicing mathematics. Children's play is a natural way of exploring their world and mastering skills for coping with it (Bruner 1986). Math games can be an enjoyable way of raising interesting questions or practicing key mathematical skills. Furthermore, teachers can choose or design math games to raise a particular issue or practice a particular skill (see, e.g., Kamii 1985; Baroody 1989; Baroody & Coslick 1998). For example,

Ari and Bret are beginning to play the game Race Car, Ari rolls a large die, and the side with five dots comes up. He immediately recognizes it as *five* (pattern recognition) and moves his car five spaces down the racetrack (counting out a collection). Bret then rolls the die, and five dots come up again. He counts the dots (verbal counting and counting a collection), then, beginning with the space on which his car is resting, counts five spaces.

"Hey," Bret complains, "I started on the same space as Ari, rolled a five like him, and now I'm behind him. How can that be?"

Through a discussion guided by their teacher, the players figure out what happened: Bret had counted as *one* the space he was on. The teacher asks Bret, "If you roll a one, what does that mean?" Bret answers, "I can move one space." "Can you show me?" asks the teacher. Again Bret starts to count the space he is on as *one*, but this time he realizes that would mean his car would not advance.

To help everyone remember how to count out spaces correctly, the teacher recommends starting their counts with *zero* (using the *whole* number sequence "0, 1, 2, 3,....," rather than the *natural* number sequence "1, 2, 3,...").

In brief, the game provided the children with verbal- and object-counting practice, created a real need for them to discuss and correct a common counting error, and brought about an opportunity for the teacher to introduce the whole number sequence.

Use children's literature as a rich and entertaining source of problems and content learning (see, e.g., Burns 1992; Theissen & Mathias 1992; Whitin & Wilde 1992; Fromboluti & Rinck 1999). Consider, for example, *The Doorbell Rang*, by Pat Hutchins. This story begins with a mother presenting a brother and sister a plate of cookies and instructing them to share (fairly). Before reading on, the teacher could ask how this could be done and how many cookies each child would get. Pairs of children could be given poker chips to model the situation, and the children could then share their strategies with the group. With any luck, at least one pair will suggest using an equal partitioning (divvying-up) strategy. As a follow-up activity, the children could role-play this story and others that involve mathematical concepts.

Meaningful instruction. Teachers should focus on promoting meaningful learning rather than learning by rote.

Foster and build on children's informal mathematical knowledge. In particular, it is important to encourage preschoolers' use of verbal, object, and finger counting to represent, reason about, and operate on numbers. Counting is a powerful tool for extending young children's nonverbal numerical and arithmetical competencies. Teachers should provide abundant opportunities for children to learn and practice counting skills and should praise the use of counting solutions.

Focus on helping children see patterns and relations. Instruction on mastering the verbal-counting sequence, for example, should concentrate on helping preschoolers discover counting patterns (e.g., the teens are largely a repetition of the original *one* through *nine* sequence plus the word

"teen": *sixteen, seventeen,...*) and the exceptions to these patterns (e.g., "Although '*fiveteen*' is a good name for the number after *fourteen*, most people call it '*fifteen*'"). Playing an error-detection game, where a puppet or addled adult character tries to count, and children have to help out by pointing out errors such as "*....nineteen, tenteen*," can be an enjoyable way for them to learn and practice counting rules and their exceptions.

Inquiry-based instruction. By involving children in inquiry-based instruction, teachers can foster children's positive disposition to learn and use mathematics. This includes promoting beliefs such as "I can solve mathematical problems"—for mathematics is, at heart, an attempt to find patterns in order to solve problems. Inquiry-based instruction can also promote meaningful learning when children discover a mathematical relation or listen to their peers' discoveries, for instance. Finally, it can improve inquiry skills, such as the ability to reason about and solve real-world or challenging problems.

Involving children in inquiry-based instruction means that teachers should encourage them to discover and do as much for themselves as possible (Polya 1981). This does not mean that teachers should simply allow children to engage in free play all the time. Learning is more likely to occur if wiser adults or older peers mediate younger children's experiences (Vygotsky 1968; Lave, Murtaugh, & de la Rocha 1984; Bruner 1986; Blevins-Knabe & Musun-Miller 1996; Anderson 1997). Some ways teachers can mediate learning are noted below.

Regularly pose worthwhile tasks (e.g., interesting, thought-provoking questions or problems) and encourage children to answer or solve them themselves. For example,

Her teacher asks Suzie, a kindergartner, what she thinks the largest number is. Suzie quickly answers, "A million." The teacher then asks what the number after a million might be. The girl thinks for a moment and responds, "A million and one." "And what do you supposed the number after a million and one might be?" the teacher counters. Suzie answers quickly, "A million and two. So there is no biggest number."

The teacher's questions, in effect, prompted the child to reflect on her knowledge of numbers, apply her knowledge of counting rules to continue the counting sequence past a million, and then deduce from this experience that the counting sequence in theory could go on forever (construct a concept of infinity).

Prompt reflection rather than provide feedback. When children have difficulty arriving at a solution or arrive at an incorrect solution, teachers should provide hints, ask questions, or otherwise promote children's thinking, rather than simply giving them the correct solution. For example,

Kamie concludes that "five and two more" must be six. Her teacher, instead of telling Kamie she was wrong and that the correct sum is seven, asks, "How much do you think five and one more is?" After Kamie concludes it is six, she sets about recalculating "five and two more."

Apparently, the child realized that both "five and one more" and "five and two more" could not have the same answer. In brief, the teacher's question prompted her to reconsider her first answer.

Encourage peer dialogue. Other children can sometimes explain informal mathematical ideas or strategies to a peer better than an adult can. Furthermore, sharing ideas with other children can help a child clarify his or her own thinking. Indeed, because it can often result in disagreements, and disagreements can prompt reconsideration of ideas, peer-to-peer dialogues can be an invaluable way of advancing young children's mathematical thinking.

Conclusion

Preschoolers are capable of mathematical thinking and knowledge that may be surprising to many adults. Teachers can support and build on this informal mathematical competence by engaging young children in purposeful, meaningful, and inquiry-based instruction. Although using the investigative approach requires teachers to be imaginative, alert, and patient, its reward can be significantly increasing the mathematical power of children.

Updated from the Research in Review article in the July 2000 issue of *Young Children*.

The research described was supported, in part, by a grant from the National Science Foundation (BCS-0111829), the Spencer Foundation (Major Grant 200400033), the National Institutes of Health (1 R01 HD051538-01), and the Institute of Education Science (R305K050082). The opinions expressed in the present manuscript are solely those of the authors and do not necessarily reflect the position, policy, or endorsement of the Spencer Foundation, the National Institutes of Health, or the Institute of Education Science.

Arthur J. Baroody is a professor at the University of Illinois at Urbana-Champaign. **Xia Li** is a doctoral student at the University of Illinois at Urbana-Champaign.

References

Anderson, A. 1997. Families and mathematics: A study of parent-child interactions. *Journal for Research in Mathematics Education* 28: 484–511.

Ashcraft, M.H., E.P. Kirk, & D. Hopko. 1998. On the cognitive consequences of mathematics anxiety. In *The development of mathematical skills*, ed. C. Donlan. Hove, England: Psychology Press.

Balfanz, R. 1999. Why do we teach young children so little mathematics? Some historical considerations. In *Mathematics in the early years*, ed. J.V. Copley, 3–10. Reston, VA: National Council of Teachers of Mathematics, and Washington, DC: NAEYC.

Baroody, A.J. 1987. *Children's mathematical thinking: A developmental framework for preschool, primary, and special education teachers.* New York: Teachers College Press.

Baroody, A.J. 1989. *A guide to teaching mathematics in the primary grades.* Boston: Allyn & Bacon.

Baroody, A.J. 1995. The role of the number-after rule in the invention of computational short cuts. *Cognition and Instruction* 13: 189–219.

Baroody, A.J., & A.P. Benson. 2001. Early number instruction. *Teaching Children Mathematics* 8: 154–58.

Baroody, A.J., M. Cibulsksis, M.L. Lai, & X. Li. 2004. Comments on the use of learning trajectories in curriculum development and research. *Mathematical Thinking and Learning* 6: 227–60.

Baroody, A.J., & R.T. Coslick. 1998. *Fostering children's mathematical power: An investigative approach to K-8 mathematics instruction.* Mahwah, NJ: Lawrence Erlbaum.

Baroody, A.J., M.L. Lai, & K.S. Mix. 2006. The development of young children's number and operation sense and its implications for early childhood education. In *Handbook of research on the education of young children,* eds. B. Spodek & O. Saracho, 187–221. Mahwah, NJ: Lawrence Erlbaum.

Baroody, A.J., & L. Rosu. 2006. *Adaptive expertise with basic addition and subtraction combinations: The number sense view.* Symposium conducted at the annual meeting of the American Educational Research Association, April, San Francisco, CA.

Benson, A.P., & A.J. Baroody. 2002. *The case of Blake: Number-word and number development.* Paper presented at the annual meeting of the American Educational Research Association, April, New Orleans, LA.

Bereiter, C., & S. Engelmann. 1966. *Teaching disadvantaged children in the preschool.* Englewood Cliffs, NJ: Prentice-Hall.

Bermejo, V. 1996. Cardinality development and counting. *Developmental Psychology* 32: 263–68.

Blevins-Knabe, B., & L. Musun-Miller. 1996. Number use at home by children and their parents and its relationship to early mathematical performance. *Early Development and Parenting* 5 (1): 35–45.

Brownell, W.A. 1935. Psychological considerations in the learning and the teaching of arithmetic. In *The teaching of arithmetic,* ed. D.W. Reeve, 1–31. New York: Teachers College, Columbia University.

Bruner, J. 1986. Play, thought and language. *Prospects* 16: 77–83.

Burns, M. 1992. *Math and literature (K–3).* Sausalito, CA: Math Solutions Publication.

Carpenter, T., J. Hiebert, & J. Moser. 1983. Problem structure and first grade children's initial solution processes for simple addition and subtraction problems. *Journal for Research in Mathematics Education* 12: 27–39.

Clements, D.H., C. Copple, & M. Hyson, eds. 2002. Early childhood mathematics: Promoting good beginnings. *A joint position statement of the National Association for the Education of Young Children (NAEYC) and the National Council for Teachers of Mathematics.* Rev. ed. Washington, DC: NAEYC, and Reston, VA: National Council for Teachers of Mathematics.

Copeland, R.W. 1979. *How children learn mathematics.* New York: Macmillan.

Copley, J.V., ed. 1999. *Mathematics in the early years, birth to five.* Reston, VA: National Council of Teachers of Mathematics.

Copley, J.V. 2004. The early childhood collaborative: A professional development model to communicate and implement the standards. In *Engaging young children in mathematics: Standards for early childhood mathematics education,* eds. D.H. Clements, J. Sarama, & A.M. DiBiase, 401–14. Mahwah, NJ: Lawrence Erlbaum.

Copple, C., & S. Bredekamp, eds. 2009. *Developmentally appropriate practice in early childhood programs serving children from birth through age 8.* 3d ed. Washington, DC: NAEYC.

Davis, G. & A. Pitkethly. 1990. Cognitive aspects of sharing. *Journal for Research in Mathematics Education* 21: 145–53.

Dewey, J. 1898. Some remarks on the psychology of number. *Pedagogical Seminary* 5: 416–34.

Donaldson, M. 1978. *Children's minds.* New York: Norton.

Fromboluti, C.S., & N. Rinck. 1999. *Early childhood, where learning begins, mathematics: Mathematical activities for parents and their 2- to 5-year-old children.* Jessup, MD: U.S. Department of Education.

Fuson, K.C. 1988. *Children's counting and concepts of number.* New York: Springer-Verlag.

Gelman, R., & C. Massey. 1987. The cultural unconscious as contributor to supporting environments for cognitive development: Commentary on social processes in early number development. *Monographs of the Society for Research in Child Development* 52, no. 2, serial no. 216.

Gelman, R., & E. Meck. 1992. Early principles aid initial but not later conceptions of number. In *Pathways to number,* eds. J. Bideaud, C. Meljac, & J.P. Fischer, 171–89. Hillsdale, NJ: Lawrence Erlbaum.

Gibb, E.G., & A.M. Castaneda. 1975. Experience for young children. In *Mathematics learning in early childhood,* ed. J.N. Payne, 96–124. Reston, VA: National Council of Teachers of Mathematics.

Ginsburg, H.P. 1977. *Children's arithmetic.* New York: D. Van Nostrand.

Ginsburg, H.P., J. Cannon, J. Eisenband, & S. Pappas. 2006. Mathematical thinking and learning. In *The handbook of early child development,* eds. K. McCartney & D. Phillips. Malden, MA: Blackwell Publishing.

Ginsburg, H.P., N. Inoue, & K.H. Seo. 1999. Young children doing mathematics: Observations of everyday activities. In *Mathematics in the early years,* ed. J.V. Copley, 88–99. Reston, VA: National Council of Teachers of Mathematics.

Ginsburg, H.P., A. Klein, & P. Starkey. 1998. The development of children's mathematical knowledge: Connecting research with practice. In *Handbook of Child Psychology, vol. 4: Child psychology in practice,* 5th ed., eds. I.E. Sigel & K.A. Renninger, 401–76. New York: John Wiley & Sons.

Hall, E. 1970. A conversation with Jean Piaget and Barbel Inhelder. *Psychology Today* 3: 25–26.

Hatano, G. 1988. Social and motivational bases for mathematical understanding. In *Children's mathematics*, eds. G.B. Saxe & M. Gearhart, 55–70. San Francisco: Jossey-Bass.

Hiebert, J., & T.P. Carpenter. 1992. Learning, teaching with understanding. In *Handbook of research on mathematics teaching and learning*, ed. D. Grouws, 65–97. New York: Macmillan.

Hiebert, J., & L.H. Tonnessen. 1978. Development of the fraction concept in two physical contexts: An exploratory investigation. *Journal for Research in Mathematics Education* 9: 374–78.

Hughes, M. 1986. *Children and number*. New York: Blackwell Publishers.

Hunting, R.P., & C.K. Kamii. 2002. Fostering the mathematical thinking of young children, pre-K–2. In *Proceedings of the 26th conference of the International Group for the Psychology of Mathematics Education—North American Chapter*, eds. A.D. Cockburn & E. Nardi, 163–67. Athens, GA.

Hutchins, P. 1986. *The doorbell rang*. New York: Greenwillow Books.

Huttenlocher, J., N.C. Jordan, & S.C. Levine. 1994. A mental model for early arithmetic. *Journal of Experimental Psychology: General* 123: 284–96.

Kamii, C.K. 1985. *Young children reinvent arithmetic: Implication of Piaget's theory*. New York: Teachers College Press.

James, W. 1890. *Principles of psychology*. New York: Holt.

Lave, J., M. Murtaugh, & O. de la Rocha. 1984. The dialectic of arithmetic in grocery shopping. In *Everyday cognition: Its development in social context*, eds. B. Rogoff & J. Lave, 67–94. Cambridge, MA: Harvard University Press.

Maffel, A.C., & P. Buckley. 1980. *Teaching preschool math: Foundations and activities*. New York: Human Sciences Press.

May, D.C., & D.K. Kundert. 1997. School readiness practices and children at-risk: Examining the issues. *Psychology in the Schools* 34 (2): 73–84.

Mix, K.S., J. Huttenlocher, & S.C. Levine. 2002. *Math without words: Quantitative development in infancy and early childhood*. New York: Oxford University Press.

Mix, K.S., C.M. Sandhofer, & A.J. Baroody. 2005. Number words and number concepts: The interplay of verbal and nonverbal processes in early quantitative development. In *Advances in child development and behavior, vol. 33*, ed. R. Kail, 305–46. New York: Academic.

Munn, P. 1998. Number symbols and symbolic function in preschoolers. In *The development of mathematical skills*, ed. C. Donlan, 47–71. Hove, England: Psychology Press.

NCTM (National Council of Teachers of Mathematics). 1989. *Curriculum and evaluation standards for school mathematics*. Reston, VA: Author.

NCTM (National Council of Teachers of Mathematics). 1991. *Professional standards for teaching mathematics*. Reston, VA: Author.

NCTM (National Council of Teachers of Mathematics). 2000. *Principles and standards for school mathematics: Standards 2000*. Reston, VA: Author.

Piaget, J. 1965. *The child's conception of number*. New York: Norton.

Polya, G. 1981. *Mathematical discovery: On understanding, learning, and teaching problem solving*. New York: John Wiley & Sons.

Pound, L. 1999. Supporting mathematical development in the early years. Philadelphia: Open Press.

Resnick, L.B., & W.W. Ford. 1981. *The psychology of mathematics for instruction*. Hillsdale, NJ: Lawrence Erlbaum.

Riley, M.S., J.G. Greeno, & J.I. Heller. 1983. Development of children's problem-solving ability in arithmetic. In *The development of mathematical thinking*, ed. H.P. Ginsburg, 153–200. New York: Academic.

Rittle-Johnson, B., & M.W. Alibali. 1999. Conceptual and procedural knowledge of mathematics: Does one lead to the other? *Journal of Educational Psychology* 91: 175–89.

Rosu, L., & A.J. Baroody. 2006. *The case of Alice: A natural experiment regarding number development*. A symposium presented at the research presession of the annual meeting of the National Council of Teachers of Mathematics, April, St. Louis, MO.

Russell, B. 1917. *Introduction to mathematical philosophy*. London: George, Allen, Unwin.

Sandhofer, C. & K.S. Mix. 2003. *Number language and number concepts: Evidence from a long-range microgenetic study*. Paper presented at the biennial meeting of the Society for Research in Child Development, April, Tampa, FL.

Sophian, C., & P. McCorgray. 1994. Part-whole knowledge and early arithmetic problem-solving. *Cognition and Instruction* 12: 3–33.

Sophian, C., & K.I. Vong. 1995. The parts and wholes of arithmetic story problems: Developing knowledge in the preschool years. *Cognition and Instruction* 13: 469–77.

Spelke, E. 2003a. *What makes humans smart?* Invited address presented at the biennial meeting of the Society for Research in Child Development, April, Tampa, FL.

Spelke, E. 2003b. What makes us smart? Core knowledge and natural language. In *Language in mind*, eds. D. Genter & S. Goldin-Meadow. Cambridge, MA: MIT Press.

Steffe, L.P., P. Cobb, & E. von Glasersfeld. 1988. *Construction of arithmetical meanings and procedures*. New York: Springer-Verlag.

Thiessen, D., & M. Mathias, eds. 1992. *The wonderful world of mathematics*. Reston, VA: National Council of Teachers of Mathematics.

Thorndike, E.L. 1922. *The psychology of arithmetic.* New York: Macmillan.

Van de Walle, G.A., S. Carey, & M. Prevor. 2000. Bases for object individuation in infancy: Evidence from manual search. *Journal of Cognition & Development* 1 (3): 249–80.

Vygotsky, L. 1968. *Thought and language.* Cambridge, MA: MIT Press.

Whitin, D.J., & S. Wilde. 1992. *Read any good math lately: Children's books for mathematical learning, K–6.* Portsmouth, NH: Heinemann.

Wilkins, J.L.M., & A.J. Baroody. 2000. *An additional explanation for production deficiencies.* Paper presented at the annual meeting of the North American Chapter of the International Group for the Psychology of Mathematics Education, October, Tucson, AZ.

Wynn, K. 1998. Numerical competence in infants. In *Development of mathematical skills*, ed. C. Donlan, 1–25. Hove, England: Psychology Press.

Additional reviews

Reviews of research on early childhood mathematics teaching and learning and its instructional implications:

Clements, D.H., & J. Sarama, eds. 2004. *Engaging young children in mathematics: Standards for early childhood mathematics education.* Mahwah, NJ: Lawrence Erlbaum.

Clements, D.H., & J. Sarama. 2007. Early childhood mathematics learning. In *Second handbook of research on mathematics teaching and learning,* Vol. 1, ed. F. Lester, 461–555. Greenwich, CT: Information Age Publishers.

I Think I Can, I Knew I Could: Understanding and Encouraging Mastery Motivation in Young Children

12

Penny Hauser-Cram and Darcy B. Mitchell

Two 4-year-olds, Keisha and Kamilah, are each attempting to put together a complex puzzle. Keisha tries to orient a piece but can't locate the place it belongs; she then chooses another piece, tries to orient it, then re-orients it and persistently searches for its place. Kamilah selects a different piece, tries to orient it and then throws it down, running to join another activity in the classroom.

Why does Keisha persist in trying to complete the puzzle while Kamilah abandons it?

Keisha and Kamilah illustrate how children the same age can display different levels of what is called *mastery motivation*. One child will persist in the face of a challenging task, another will give up. What do early childhood professionals know about mastery motivation? How does it vary by age, caregiving processes, and disability? How can early childhood teachers promote it?

What is mastery motivation?

Mastery motivation is defined as a "psychological force that stimulates an individual to attempt independently, in a focused and persistent manner, to solve a problem or master a skill or task which is at least moderately challenging for him or her" (Morgan, Harmon, & Maslin-Cole 1990, 319). Two key components of this definition include attempts to master a task independent of explicit adult instruction and persistence in attempting to master the task even when solutions aren't immediately obvious. The child who exhibits high levels of mastery motivation will seek out a challenging task and derive pleasure from the outcome of having persevered with it.

Mastery motivation is considered to be universal and intrinsic to every child, as indicated by developmental theorists including Piaget (1952), White (1959), and Hunt (1965), who all maintained that a child is born motivated to explore the world. White contended that children have a need to produce an effect on the environment and that they achieve this through exploration and play coupled with selection, direction, and persistence. White defined the process of engagement in such activities as *effectance* or *competence motivation* and proposed that such engagement helps children acquire a "feeling of efficacy" (1959, 329). Harter (1975) further defined effectance motivation as a "desire to solve cognitively challenging problems for gratification inherent in discovering the solution" (370). Harter emphasized several key components: curiosity, preference for challenge, internal criteria of success, and working for one's satisfaction.

A construct similar to mastery motivation and its relative, effectance motivation, was proposed by Dweck (1986) in studies of school-age children. Based on children's approach to challenging tasks, she described some children as "mastery-oriented" and others as "helpless." The mastery-oriented children tended to persist on difficult tasks, attribute their failures to factors they could control (e.g., effort), have positive expectations for future success even after failure, and display positive or neutral affect while working on challenging tasks.

In contrast, the helpless children tended to give up quickly, attribute failures to events out of their control (e.g., ability), have low expectations for success on future similar challenges, and show negative affect during challenges. Dweck (1986) proposed that some children develop "learned helplessness" because they believe, based on past experiences, that they have little control over the events that affect them.

More recent work indicates that these two dimensions of mastery motivation can be identified in early childhood. Results from several studies indicate that about 40 percent of kindergartners show the helpless pattern in response to achievement-based challenges (Ziegert et al. 2001). This finding indicates that preschool might be a critical time to intervene to prevent the formation of the helpless pattern and promote the development of a mastery-oriented one.

Thus, the preschool years are an important time to help children get on a path of being motivated to master tasks as opposed to feeling helpless in the face of challenge.

How does mastery motivation change during early childhood?

During the first two years of life, children begin to develop a "self-system" (Kelley, Brownell, & Campbell 2000); that is, they begin to select activities to engage in, and they begin to evaluate their own performance. Both selection of activities and self-evaluation are aspects of motivation.

Developmentally, children progress through several shifts in mastery motivation, so that the motivated child behaves differently at different life phases. The motivated infant, younger than 6 months, explores objects through reaching, mouthing, and visual exploration. Around 9 months, however, infants begin to understand rudimentary aspects of cause and effect, and the motivated infant begins to engage in goal-directed activity with unfamiliar tasks (Jennings 1993).

Goal-directed behavior becomes more complex as toddlers gradually learn to seek more distant goals that involve a chain of actions for goal attainment (e.g., filling a bucket with sand to be used in building a castle) (Jennings 2004). At around 18 months, children begin to be able to compare their behavior with a standard (Jennings 1993), and the motivated toddler attempts to approximate the standard. Moreover, toddlers who are highly motivated often show great pride in self-agency, as displayed in enthusiastic comments and hand claps. During the preschool years, motivated children begin to self-select challenging tasks and prefer tasks that "make them think" to those that are easy to accomplish (Stipek 1996).

What affects mastery motivation?

Although motivation is considered to be intrinsic, children show individual differ-

Parents who provide "gentle guidance" may
assist in children's development of mastery.

ences in such motivation over their early
childhood years. The transactions that
occur between children and caregivers
appear to be critical to children's mastery
motivation. Bornstein (1989) delineated
two general modes of interaction between
children and caregivers that have consequences for cognitive development: *social*
and *didactic*. Both appear to be important
in the development of mastery motivation.

In a study of twins who were in kindergarten or first grade, Deater-Deckard
and colleagues (2006) demonstrated that
although task persistence has genetic influences, changes in such persistence could
be explained by differences in maternal
behavior, with more positive changes
occurring when mothers expressed both
warmth and support during interaction
with their child. Maternal affect, especially
attempts to soothe and show empathy
when a child demonstrates distress, also
appears to predict mastery motivation in
preschool-age children with disabilities
who were born preterm (Young & Hauser-
Cram 2006).

In relation to caregivers' didactic
behaviors, studies indicate that parental
interference with children's mastery attempts has deleterious effects on children's
mastery motivation. This has been found
for both typically developing children
(Frodi, Bridges, & Grolnick 1985; Wachs
1987) and for those with developmental
disabilities (Hauser-Cram 1993). Researchers (e.g., Morgan et al. 1991) contend that
parents who are highly directive may
encourage children to be efficient respond-
ers but not efficient initiators. In contrast,
parents who provide "gentle guidance"
may assist in children's development of
mastery.

Kelley, Brownell, and Campbell (2000)
found that mothers who scaffolded their
toddler's efforts in attempting challenging
tasks (e.g., who held the toy so the child
could work on it without it slipping; who
asked questions such as "Where do you
think that piece goes?") had children who
demonstrated greater task persistence in
the preschool years. They speculated that
maternal support through scaffolding
might help children understand that they
are able to do the task.

Mastery motivation in children with disabilities

Research findings are mixed as to whether
children with disabilities, especially those
with cognitive disabilities, show lower levels of mastery motivation. Several studies
now indicate that such toddlers and young
preschoolers show levels of motivation
equal to those of their typically developing peers (Hauser-Cram 1996; Glenn et al.
2001; Gilmore, Cuskelly, & Hayes 2003).
By the end of preschool, however, lower
mastery motivation has been noted for
children with cognitive disabilities, at least
based on parent reports (Nicols, Atkinson,
& Pepler 2003).

In a longitudinal study of children
with developmental disabilities, one study
found that mastery motivation measured
at age 3 predicted growth in cognitive and
daily living skills over a 10-year period
(Hauser-Cram et al. 2001), with greater
growth for children with higher levels of
mastery motivation. This suggests that
preschool, again, could be a critical time of
intervention for children with disabilities,
as it is for typically developing children,
in relation to their trajectories of mastery
motivation.

What can teachers do to promote mastery motivation?

Given the importance of children's preschool years in the divergence of pathways
regarding mastery motivation, what are

specific ways that preschool teachers can support and enhance mastery motivation?

Most research has focused on the relation between teachers' behaviors and children's mastery motivation. But such investigations give clues as to ways to improve children's mastery motivation in the classroom. In addition, some intervention studies have been conducted looking at how to increase the task performance of children with disabilities in the preschool classroom (e.g., Karnes, Johnson, & Beauchamp 2005).

Several important suggestions emerge from such work:

1. **Provide children a choice of activities.** A modest number of choices, rather than no choice or a large number of choices, is optimal in enhancing motivation (Stipek 1996).

2. **Provide children with activities that offer an opportunity to learn** rather than only opportunities to be correct or incorrect. For example, provide problem-solving tasks, games, or other activities in which there are several possible ways to solve the problems posed.

3. **Support children in ways that do not interfere with their autonomy.** Sometimes this requires adults to let children experience dead ends when having difficulty rather than the adults anticipating a way to prevent such outcomes. To avoid children's frustration this may need to be coupled with "gentle support," such as a well-timed suggestion (e.g., "Maybe if you turn that piece around…"), rather than a direct command (e.g., "That piece fits here").

4. **Use puppets as a way to demonstrate productive cognitive strategies** (Karnes, Johnson, & Beauchamp 2005). For example, a puppet can model self-talk in working on a task (e.g., "Maybe if I turn this"), when confronting difficulties (e.g., "Maybe I could try it a different way"), and after success (e.g., "Hooray, I did it!").

What future research is needed on mastery motivation?

Despite the growing amount of research on mastery motivation, together with ways of measuring it through parent and teacher reports and direct observation (Morgan, Harmon, & Maslin-Cole 1990), knowledge about what kinds of interventions might be able to enhance this important behavior is lacking. Given the social organization of classrooms, more information is needed on how children support or undermine each other in mastery motivation, as well as on how classroom structure and routines might relate to mastery motivation. Research on which types of interventions might work best for children with certain attributes or interests is also needed.

Although there are many future avenues to explore in understanding and encouraging mastery motivation in young children, we do know that it is a critical area of development. Given that researchers have found that mastery motivation relates to later academic achievement (Shiner 2000), a more thorough focus on this construct during the early childhood years seems to be imperative.

Updated from the Research in Review article in the July 1998 issue of *Young Children*.

Penny Hauser-Cram is a professor at Boston College. **Darcy B. Mitchell** is the project director and senior research associate of a longitudinal study at Boston College.

References

Bornstein, M.H. 1989. Between caretakers and their young: Two modes of interaction and their consequences for cognitive growth. In *Interaction in human development*, eds. M.H. Bornstein & J.S. Bruner, 197–214. Hillsdale, NJ: Lawrence Erlbaum.

Deater-Deckard, K., S.A. Petrill, L.A. Thompson, & L.S. Dethorne. 2006. A longitudinal behavioral genetic analysis of task persistence. *Developmental Science* 9: 498–504.

Dweck, C.S. 1986. Motivational processes affecting learning. *American Psychologist* 41: 1040–48.

Frodi, A., L. Bridges, & W. Grolnick. 1985. Correlates of mastery-related behavior: A short-term longitudinal study of infants in their second year. *Child Development* 56: 1291–98.

Gilmore, L., M. Cuskelly, & A. Hayes. 2003. A comparative study of mastery motivation in young children with Down's syndrome: Similar outcomes, different processes? *Journal of Intellectual Disability Research* 47: 181–90.

Glenn, S., B. Dayus, C. Cunningham, & M. Horgan. 2001. Mastery motivation in children with Down syndrome. *Down Syndrome Research and Practice* 7: 52–59.

Harter, S. 1975. Developmental differences in the manifestation of mastery motivation on problem-solving tasks. *Child Development* 45: 370–78.

Hauser-Cram, P. 1993. Mastery motivation in 3-year-old children with Down syndrome. In *Mastery motivation in early childhood: Development, measurement and social processes*, ed. D. Messer, 230–50. London: Routledge.

Hauser-Cram, P. 1996. Mastery motivation in toddlers with developmental disabilities. *Child Development* 67: 236–48.

Hauser-Cram, P., M.E. Warfield, J.P. Shonkoff, & M.W. Krauss. 2001. Children with disabilities: A longitudinal study of child development and parent well-being. *Monographs of the Society for Research in Child Development* 66, serial no. 266.

Hunt, J.McV. 1965. Intrinsic motivation and its role in psychological development. In *Nebraska symposium on motivation*, ed. D. Levine, 189–282. Lincoln, NE: University of Nebraska Press.

Jennings, J.D. 1993. Mastery motivation and the formation of self-concept from infancy through childhood. In *Mastery motivation in early childhood: Development, measurement and social processes*, ed. D. Messer, 36–54. London: Routledge.

Jennings, J.D. 2004. Development of goal-directed behaviour and related self-processes in toddlers. *International Journal of Behavioural Development* 28: 319–27.

Karnes, M.B., L.J. Johnson, & K.D.F. Beauchamp. 2005. Reprise: Developing problem solving skills to enhance task persistence of handicapped preschool children. *Journal of Early Intervention* 27: 236–46.

Kelley, S.A., C.A. Brownell, & S.B. Campbell. 2000. Mastery motivation and self-evaluative affect in toddlers: longitudinal relations with maternal behavior. *Child Development* 71: 1061–71.

Morgan, G.A., N.A. Busch-Rossnagel, C.A. Maslin-Cole, & R.J. Harmon. 1991. *Mastery motivation tasks: Manual for 15 to 36 month old children.* Bronx, NY: Fordham University Psychology Department.

Morgan, G.A., R.J. Harmon, & C.A. Maslin-Cole. 1990. Mastery motivation: Definition and measurement. *Early Education and Development* 1: 318–39.

Nicols, A., L. Atkinson, & D. Pepler. 2003. Mastery motivation in young children with Down's syndrome: Relations with cognitive and adaptive competence. *Journal of Intellectual Disability Research* 47: 121–33.

Piaget, J. 1952. *The origins of intelligence in children.* New York: International Universities Press.

Shiner, R.L. 2000. Linking childhood personality with adaptation: Evidence for continuity and change across time into late adolescence. *Journal of Personality and Social Psychology* 78: 310–25.

Stipek, D.J. 1996. Motivation and instruction. In *Handbook of educational psychology*, eds. D.C. Berliner & R.C. Calfee, 85–113. New York: Macmillan Library Reference.

Wachs, T.D. 1987. Specificity of environmental action as manifest in environmental correlates of infant's mastery motivation. *Developmental Psychology* 23: 782–90.

White, R.W. 1959. Motivation reconsidered: The concept of competence. *Psychological Review* 66: 297–333.

Young, J.M., & P. Hauser-Cram. 2006. Mother-child interaction as a predictor of mastery motivation in children with disabilities born preterm. *Journal of Early Intervention* 28: 252–63.

Ziegert, D., J.A. Kistner, R. Castro, & B. Robertson. 2001. Longitudinal study of young children's responses to challenging achievement situations. *Child Development* 72: 609–24.

Part IV

Physical Development

Introduction

Physical development is a vitally important—yet often overlooked—aspect of children's development. Skills related to motor development, physical fitness, and nutrition are essential for young children's growth, both physically and in other domains. Yet due to the rising push on academics in early childhood and the decrease in outdoor, free-play experiences at home, these parts of development are sometimes disregarded. The research reviews in this section include recent and updated studies on select topics related to the physical domain of development and provide important information for early childhood professionals as they attempt to facilitate physical development in programs for young children. And because this domain is so important, we have included a brand new chapter, written especially for this book.

The chapters in this section provide an overview of motor development and nutrition, an explanation of the links between physical development and other domains, and a discussion of the importance of establishing healthy eating habits in the early childhood period. Early childhood professionals will find valuable information on topics relevant to the physical domain and will come away from this section with a firmer understanding of the importance of highlighting and supporting young children's physical development in early childhood programs.

Linda Gagen, Nancy Getchell, and Greg Payne provide an excellent review entitled **"Motor Development in Young Children: Implications and Applications,"** which they wrote expressly for this volume. They focus on motor development, or how movement evolves during early childhood. There is an important distinction between motor and physical development: Whereas motor development is concerned with movement, physical development involves structural changes of the body, such as in height and weight. The authors emphasize how important it is for early childhood professionals to understand motor development, due to its interrelatedness with all domains and as a basis for assessing children's developmental progression. The chapter provides early childhood professionals with detailed explanations of the development of emergent motor skills in early childhood and provides specific strategies for supporting these skills.

Rebecca Marcon's chapter, **"Growing Children: The Physical Side of Development,"** has been updated from her 2003 research review in *Young Children*. In the original article, Dr. Marcon provided important links between physical development and other domains, particularly examining the effect of physical development on cognitive and social development. Both the original article and this revised chapter focus on the importance of nutrition to physical development and (in its interconnected relationship) to all other areas of development. In this update, Marcon provides new information to support the importance of the link between physical and overall development. In the discussion of malnourishment and misnourishment, the author provides recent data showing that an alarmingly high number of American children suffer from food insecurity. The chapter was chosen for inclusion particularly because it helps early childhood professionals see the connections between physical development and development in other domains.

The last article in this section is an updated version of the 1995 research review **"Children's Eating: The Development of Food-Acceptance Patterns,"** by Leann Birch, Susan Johnson, and Jennifer Fisher. The refreshed work, written by Alison Ventura, Susan Johnson, and Leann Birch, includes new insights into the growing prevalence of obesity in young children in the context of food-acceptance patterns. In particular, new research about the development of food-acceptance patterns is cited because of the need to consider such patterns in early obesity prevention efforts. Because early childhood professionals are often heavily involved in children's daily food consumption, a firm understanding of the development of food acceptance and preferences is essential information. Further, due to the increasing prevalence of obesity in young children, information regarding its prevention is equally valuable for professionals working with young children and their families. Early childhood professionals will find particularly relevant the inclusion of a number of practical, evidence-based recommendations that guide them in helping young children develop appropriate dietary patterns.

The chapters in this section will provide early childhood professionals with a firm grounding in research related to physical and motor development, including nutrition. A solid understanding of the importance of nutrition and exercise for young children will help teachers to promote these, thus enhancing children's overall well-being and potential for success in learning.

13 Motor Development in Young Children: Implications and Applications

Linda M. Gagen, Nancy Getchell, and Greg Payne

Understanding all aspects of human development, how human beings grow and change throughout life, is critically important. This applies to the way people develop intellectually, socially, emotionally, physically, and *motorically*—that is, how they move their bodies. The purpose of this chapter is to describe human motor development over the first several years of life, examine why it is important, discuss how it evolves over these initial years, and discuss what implications and applications teachers of young children can gather from an understanding of this phenomenon.

What is motor development?

Movement behavior and movement ability in the early childhood years are in a constant state of flux. For more overt aspects of movement, this change is easily observable. One example is the technique employed by very young children the first few times they attempt to employ a writing implement. The action often involves much of the whole body, and certainly the upper body, as the shoulder, arm, and hand all participate in the scrawling actions. Yet, in just a few years, the movement develops into a more controlled, finer action, where the actions are confined to just the forearm, hand, and fingers.

An even more obvious example is perhaps the most significant motor landmark to parents of young children: walking. Children's initial attempts are characterized by widespread feet, arms held flexed and above the waist, the appearance of walking on the toes, inconsistent stride length and direction, and regular falls. However, like handwriting or drawing, the action changes with time. Within a year or so, the spread of the feet narrows and the arms begin to lower and swing in opposition to the legs, as strides lengthen and become more consistent in both length and direction. The overall body posture becomes more upright.

In short, young children's motor proficiency goes through a dramatic change over time, and this change has major influences on their intellectual, social, emotional, and physical development.

Why is motor development important?

Understanding the motor development of children is important for a number of reasons. First, from an academic perspective, understanding the complexity of all human development can never be achieved until the individual pieces of development are understood—and motor development is one of those pieces.

Human development can be subdivided any number of ways. Perhaps the most frequent is in terms of intellectual, social, emotional, physical (structural changes such as limb length, height, and weight), and motor development. Each of these areas of development affects all other areas. For example, improved motor development can affect how people feel about themselves (i.e., emotional development) and consequently affect their social interactions. Improved intellectual development can let them more clearly understand and improve their performance in new and different movement techniques. More mature motor development can motivate them to be more physically active, and that can positively affect intellectual, social, emotional, and physical development (Okely, Booth, & Patterson 2001).

Understanding motor development is important also because it can be a marker for abnormal development of various kinds. If teachers understand expected sequences and rates of motor development, they can notice when a child is lagging and may need assessment and possibly remediation. Infant reflexes are one of the best examples of a motor development that can flag a possible developmental or medical problem. These unique reflex movements generally appear on a quite predictable schedule. In typical, healthy situations, certain infant reflexes appear upon stimulation at birth. If these reflexes do not appear, are too strong or too weak, or occur in any other abnormal form, it may be an indication that the infant needs medical intervention.

Finally, understanding typical sequences and rates of motor development is especially useful in school or other educational settings. Teachers can observe children's movement behaviors to determine those children who may need special instruction or remediation. Or, in the case of children who exhibit more mature motor patterns, teachers may need to create more challenging instructional opportunities.

Motor development during infancy: Infant reflexes

During the first year of life, and especially over the first few months, an infant's movement repertoire is dominated by *reflexes*—involuntarily motor responses to a stimulus or stimuli in the environment. One of the best known examples of an infant reflex is the *palmar grasp reflex*—that is, a closing of the fingers when the infant's palm is gently stroked. This reflex can usually be observed during the first five or six months of life.

Uniquely, reflexes are involuntary; they are not a result of a conscious, voluntary effort by the person, such as the intentional reaching and grasping that occur when a baby seeks to obtain a nearby toy. For that reason, researchers sometimes describe reflexes as being "subcortical," meaning these movements are processed below the level of the brain's cortex, in the lower brain centers (Malina, Bouchard, & Bar-Or 2004). In short, this is a movement that really seems to happen *to* the infant rather than *by* the infant consciously. In addition to being subcortical, the infant reflexes are "patterned" or "stereotypical," meaning they happen the same way every time the stimulus is applied. Thus, every time the infant's palm is stroked, the hand responds with the same closure of the four fingers.

The subcortical nature of infant reflexes makes them one of the more fascinating forms of movement. While the palmar grasp reflex is a relatively well known and seemingly simple example, many other unusual and more complex reflexes exist. An example is the *stepping reflex* (also known as the *walking* or *placing reflex*), in which pressure applied to the bottoms of the infant's feet initiates an alternating raising and lowering of the legs that resembles an attempt at actual walking. This one can be provoked by holding an infant in an upright (vertical) position, with the bottoms of the feet touching a supporting surface such as the floor or a table top.

The stepping reflex is observable very early in life, sometimes within the first few weeks, and often perseveres for five or six months. Researchers have noted that development of this reflex appears to change over this period of time, as the patterns of the muscle contractions appear to become more cooperative (combining to work together) or reciprocal (trading off, with one replacing the other). This could be an indication of the gradual elimination of the reflex in favor of more voluntary, intentional control by infants over their walking ability (Okamoto, Okamoto, & Andrew 2001).

Many experts believe that the infant reflexes, even though they are subcortical and involuntary, are linked to the development of later voluntary movements. This could simply be a result of the reflexes creating an initial and crude form of "practice" of the action whereby muscle tone is established for later voluntary movement.

Classic research has also led to speculation that this purported link may go well beyond the establishment of muscle tone. Zelazo and colleagues (1993) studied 6-week-old infants by routinely stimulating their stepping reflexes. When compared with a nonstimulated control group, these infants stepped more often on their own, with even small amounts of practice yielding a difference. The researchers speculated that this may occur as a result of positive effects on the infant's balance

> Many experts believe that the infant reflexes are linked to the development of later voluntary movements.

or muscle strength. Or perhaps the routine stimulation of the reflex had beneficial effects on the neural system that facilitated the more frequent stepping patterns of the stimulated children. These findings have implications for childrearing, as infants who receive more practice at early movement forms may exceed the norms for typical development.

These findings, then, have influenced the design of toys for very young infants. When a parent or caregiver seeks to create a nurturing and stimulating environment for infants, that environment might include hanging objects that are easy to grasp or bat, hung in a convenient spot to attract their attention and encourage movement toward the objects. Popular child support seats, swings, and play systems hold infants safely in a position where visibility of and interaction with the people and objects in the environment might be easier to manage.

Small rattles and toys that are lightweight and sized and shaped to match an infant's hand or attach to the infant's wrist may attract the child's interest. These can often be held and perhaps "manipulated" for short periods of time with the palmar grasp or early spontaneous arm movements. However, such movements are still reflexive, not purposeful, and cannot be reproduced by the infant intentionally.

Motor development during late infancy: Voluntary movement

After the first few weeks of life, voluntary movement gradually becomes more common across the infant's first year, although as suggested earlier, many infant reflexes are thought to be linked to later voluntary movements. Some reflexes may even be directly incorporated or adapted into the more complex voluntary movements that are evolving. As a result, over the first year of life, caregivers typically see a gradual, consistently more common reliance by the infant on voluntary movements, as many reflexes begin to disappear.

In healthy, typically developing children, the majority of infant reflexes cannot be evoked after approximately 1 year of age. Across the first year of life, the higher brain centers, such as the cerebral cortex, begin to exert control over children's movements, enabling them to have voluntary control—to move as they choose to move, within limits. Some (e.g., Herschkowitz 2000) believe that the cortex is specifically inhibiting some reflexive movement as voluntary movement becomes dominant during this period.

Like many forms of movement, the voluntary movements of very early childhood appear in a sequential and fairly predictable pattern. For the sake of organization and simplicity, in this chapter the more common movement forms for this time of life will be discussed in terms of three categories: stability, locomotion, and manipulation.

Stability

Stability is the ability to place the body or its parts in a desired position and maintain that position. An example is holding the head upright, one of the very first voluntary movements of infancy. Others include rolling over, sitting up, or even standing up.

At birth, infants have virtually no voluntary control of their head, although one of the first motor milestones—raising the head while *prone* (i.e., lying on the belly)—occurs around 2 to 3 months of age. Like most of the voluntary movements of infancy, the exact time of onset of the movement varies considerably from one child to the next. Given the relatively large size and heavy weight of the head at this time of life, this is a particularly significant achievement.

Head control leads to other important behaviors. For example, once infants can control their head, they can more easily begin to visually scan their surroundings and, ultimately, reach for and grasp objects that they spot. This movement can also be a forerunner to raising their chest off the floor, which can subsequently assist in beginning forms of crawling. Several weeks later, at approximately 5 months of age, infants are able to raise their head when in a *supine* position (i.e., lying on the back) (Payne & Isaacs 2008).

Control of the head is generally followed by improved control of more of the body. By extending the arms against the floor when prone with the head elevated, the chest raises. This is no a minor achievement, as chest elevation is a precursor to more advanced movements such as rolling the body from the prone to the supine position (at 6 months or later) and eventually even crawling.

While front-to-back rolling generally occurs around 8 months of age, infants will often roll from their back to their front as early as 6 months. In its earliest forms, this movement is rigid in appearance, although it gradually becomes a more coordinated and sequential series of movements led by the head turning, followed by the shoulders, trunk, and hips. Some infants can become quite mobile by using a series of connected rolls to reach some object within their environment.

Actually achieving upright posture is another motor landmark of infancy, as it unveils an array of new movement possibilities. Once infants can actually sit, their hands are freed and their body is appropriately positioned for selective use of their arms, hands, and fingers. When still in a prone or supine position, infants had much less facility for reaching and grasping, by virtue of their body position.

Infants can often maintain a sitting position as early as 3 months of age, but limited lumbar and abdominal strength means they will require a handhold. Eventually, the need for a handhold lessens; at approximately 5 months of age, infants can maintain the sitting position without assistance, although they may still exhibit a considerable forward lean. By 7 months of age, the need for the handhold has disappeared and infants can maintain a more upright position, which will often become nearly completely upright by 8 months of age.

The ability to sit up without support ("self-sitting") has major implications for many related movement behaviors. In a relevant study, Rochat (1992) examined the relationship of self-sitting on early hand-eye coordination with infants 5 to 8 months old, half of whom were able to self-sit. The infants were presented a series of displays while in different positions, including seated and prone. Self-sitters made contact with the display 98 percent of the time, as opposed to 89 percent for the non-sitters. In addition, the self-sitters tended to reach more with one hand versus the two-handed reach employed by the non-sitters. Rochat believed that this was evidence of the importance of self-sitting on early hand-eye development.

Sitting is, of course, only an initial step toward the attainment of standing. Like sitting, the ability to stand enables an array of other behaviors, such as walking. The initial attempts at standing generally occur around 9 months of age. Children begin by attempting to pull themselves up alongside a supportive object such as a piece of furniture. Eventually, they can achieve a standing position, assisted by the external support. This position is characterized by a wide "base of support" (the area over which the body is balanced) and arms held in a flexed position above the waist, often called a "high guard position." By 1 year of age, children generally have sufficient balance ability and strength to stand unsupported. Of course, upright locomotion (cruising around furniture, independent walking) is soon to follow.

Locomotion

Locomotion first appears in the prone position. In the months before walking is achieved, this prone locomotion is an important part of infant life. The movement is initially made possible by the improvements in stability as well as children's ability to roll from supine to prone position and to elevate their chest slightly off the floor. Initial attempts at crawling are generally seen around 7 months and evolve in a fairly predictable way; although, like most of the voluntary movements of infancy, the rate at which individual children acquire this skill is highly variable.

At first, infants will move only one limb at a time, creating a relatively deliberate and slow form of locomotion.

Although some confusion exists between the terms, *crawling* is generally considered the less mature form of prone locomotion that precedes *creeping* (Piek 2006). At first, around 7 to 8 months of age, the movement is a "belly crawl" that involves minimal use of infants' legs, as their arms extend to reach out and flex to pull their body forward. Soon thereafter, the legs become gradually more involved, flexing up under their body, often initially causing backward propulsion. Eventually, their legs extend in short abrupt thrusts, sometimes simultaneously rather than alternately, to provide a forward locomotion.

Over the ensuing weeks, their body elevates even more, giving the legs additional room to flex under the body. Ultimately, this leads to *creeping*, where the body is sufficiently elevated for children to be on all fours. At first, infants will move only one limb at a time, creating a relatively deliberate and slow form of locomotion. Eventually that movement form evolves into a simultaneous movement of a leg and an arm.

Most commonly, the locomotion involves the arm on one side of the body with the leg on the opposite side of the body, a "contralateral" creep. Less commonly, some infants will simultaneously move the leg and arm on the same side in opposition to the arm and leg on the opposite side of their body, a "homolateral" creep. Although some infants reach it much earlier, an efficient form of creeping may not occur until 1 year of age. At that time, the movement becomes exceptionally efficient, with increasing ability to creep quickly and even up and over obstacles such as stairs.

Research by Adolph, Vereijken, and Denny (1998) found that the progression of crawling to creeping is somewhat variable from one child to the next, with any of several postures employed, depending upon the child. Some infants even skip the belly crawling described earlier and progress directly to the creep—although infants who belly crawl often achieve a more efficient form of creeping. The researchers also determined that infants who were slightly smaller and more slender started the overall prone locomotion process earlier than heavier babies did (Adolph, Vereijken, & Denny 1998).

Manipulation

Manipulation in the form of reaching and grasping is facilitated by the development of stability and locomotion. As mentioned earlier, sitting or standing enables infants to position themselves to more easily use their hands. And, of course, locomotion provides transportation to and from objects, allowing a wider range of targets for reaching and grasping.

For many parents, their child achieving upright posture and taking the first few independent steps are the major motor

> Reaching and grasping greatly enhances cognitive abilities as a result of increased interaction with the environment.

development landmarks. Interestingly, few families anticipate as eagerly the fascinating sequences of development involving reaching and grasping. These hand and finger movements are integral in the evolving life of infants, as they enable greater exploration of objects in the environment. In addition to the very practical and obvious necessity of reaching and grasping, this skill greatly enhances cognitive abilities as a result of increased interaction with the environment.

This chapter previously described the palmar grasp reflex and how this involuntary movement may be a precursor to later voluntary movement forms such as reaching, grasping, and releasing. According to the classic work of Bower (1977), initial attempts at voluntary reaching and grasping are common around 4 months of age. At that time, the reach and grasp typically occur simultaneously: Children reach out as their hand opens and closes. This gives the appearance of considerable uncertainty as to when the hand should actually open and close during this process. Children's initial attempts at reaching and grasping also are characterized by the use of one arm or one hand.

At this age, children visually determine when and if they want to reach. However, once they start to reach, they normally do not control the accuracy of their reach and grasp visually. Then, once they make contact with the target object, they again control the grasp by watching the interaction of their hand and the object.

By 6 or 7 months of age, several changes emerge in the techniques infants employ to reach and grasp. For example, the use of two hands becomes more common. However, with continued practice and experimentation, the simultaneous reach and grasp of younger reachers evolves into a reach more distinctly followed by the grasp, an advantage over the earlier, more random opening and closing of the hand as the arm extends.

Like younger reachers, children in the second half of infancy initiate their reach after making visual contact with a target object. At that point, a very important difference emerges—older infants now monitor their reach by watching their arm. They will use this visual monitoring to correct their movement errors and, ultimately, become more accurate in their reaching attempts. Moreover, the visual control of the grasp evidenced in younger infants gradually gives way in older infants to a grasp that is monitored more closely by *feeling* the object (i.e., tactile control) once the object is reached (Bower 1977).

Moving to toddlerhood: Development of fundamental motor skills

The abilities developed in late infancy that allow stability, locomotion, and manipulation now translate during toddlerhood into greater opportunities to explore and examine the environment. As toddlers begin to move through and adapt to their surroundings in a functional way, they appear to acquire rudimentary motor skills both quickly and naturally—sometimes seemingly appearing out of nowhere. These skills allow a toddler the motor ability to eat (or discard undesired food), communicate, move to a desired location, or even express emotions such as joy (e.g., by spontaneously skipping) or rage (e.g., by striking or pushing away an unwanted object).

In particular, toddlerhood begins the acquisition of "fundamental" motor skills (FMS), the skills essential to and underlying future physical activity of all kinds. For example, toddlers begin crude, uncoordinated attempts at throwing, catching,

running, rolling, dodging, balancing, and so on.

It would be easy to make the case that motor skills appear or emerge solely as a result of maturation. However, such is not the case. As Clark (2007) so eloquently described:

> The belief that maturation is how motor skills develop puts more emphasis on the biological or hereditary aspects than on environmental factors. But the process by which motor skills develop is more complex. Motor skills change through an interactive process between the individual's biological constraints and the environment. The central nervous system, the muscles, and the skeleton all develop; some changes are prescribed by heredity, but our biological heritage is modulated continuously by our environment and our life experiences. (40)

Why is Clark's point so critical when discussing fundamental motor skills? Because it addresses what appears to be the prevailing opinion among parents and many early childhood educators—that fundamental motor skill acquisition "just happens" as part of early childhood. This assumption is perhaps due to a lack of motor development training in teacher-education curricula, as well as the lack of *structured* movement experiences within preschool programs (although most have an abundance of free play opportunities).

On the contrary, it takes a long time for motor skills to develop to maturity—decades, in some instances. Young children require structured movement experiences as well as direct instruction in order to develop the fundamental skills that are the building blocks of proficient motor performance. And it is this proficiency in the specialized movements necessary for hobbies and sports that makes for a lifetime of regular vigorous, healthful physical activity.

Educational implications and applications in motor development

Although there are several different ways in which fundamental motor skills can be classified, below they will be classified as one of three basic types: locomotor, ballistic, or manipulative. Notice that these abilities are directly related to and emanate from the infant and toddler acquisitions of locomotor and manipulative skills discussed previously, with stability (and balance) becoming an overarching need for most fundamental motor skills young children might perform. This developmental continuum is consistent, but not necessarily identical, from infancy into mid childhood, and the underlying preparation in infancy supports the appearance of such skills whenever children begin to utilize particular movement sequences.

Locomotor skills

Locomotor skills are those in which the body moves from one place to another. In infancy, these skills were somewhat limited and included crawling, creeping, rolling, and cruising or early walking. In fact, by most definitions, infants become toddlers when they expand their repertoire of movements to include more stable walking and begin running.

Closely following in development, as those who work with or study young children know, is an almost limitless number of alternative movements. The locomotor skills receiving the most empirical and pedagogical attention are hopping (taking off from and landing on one foot), jumping (taking off from and landing on both feet), galloping (an unevenly timed, rhythmic run), and skipping.

Walking. Walking is the first locomotor skill to emerge, at approximately 15 months, although there is a wide range in the time at which toddlers take their first steps. Early in the 20th century, two prominent researchers of the time, Bayley

(1935) and Shirley (1931), each observed groups of infants and independently established similar age ranges for the onset of walking as 9–17 months. Recently, the World Health Organization, in its Multi-centre Growth Reference Study (de Onis et al. 2004; WHO 2006; de Onis et al. 2007), reestablished this age range for the onset of walking by observing a total of 816 children from five different countries (Ghana, India, Norway, Oman, United States).

Many researchers have investigated the development of walking, with interest not only in *how* young children walk (Clark, Whitall, & Phillips 1988) but also *why* they begin to walk when they do (Adolph, Vereijken, & Shrout 2003). When toddlers take their first steps, almost every movement they make contributes to their stability and balance. For example, each step is short with little hip and knee extension, and each step tends to be independent of the next. The toes point outward and the stance is widened, which maximizes the base of support. All other movements are minimized; children lock their arms in high guard position and do not rotate very much in their trunk.

As children continue to develop, they shed those movements that maximize stability at the expense of mobility in order to get more speed and greater ease of movement. They drop their arms to waist level ("middle guard"), and later to an extended position at the sides ("low guard"), and then eventually begin to swing them, although not in the regular pattern that older children and adults use (Roberton 1978; 1984). By about the age of 4, children walk similarly to adults (Sutherland 1997).

Running. Young children quickly learn that walking does not suffice when they want to go somewhere quickly; to get a toy, for example. Therefore, not surprisingly, running emerges soon after walking, within approximately 6–7 months (Clark & Whitall 1989; Whitall & Getchell 1995). In order to gain speed, children must modify movement characteristics that add stability at the expense of mobility. First, they add a "flight phase" to their walking pattern. This replaces the part of the movement in which both feet are on the ground between steps with a period of "flight" between steps during which neither foot is on the ground.

Adding a flight phase requires dynamic balance when landing on—then projecting again from—a single foot. Therefore, new runners often re-adopt the high guard position for their arms while they learn how to manage the balance requirements of running. As children become more proficient at running, they begin to eliminate some of the lateral movements in their legs, so that movements become more closely limited to the forward-backward plane.

To gain greater speed, children also tend to turn out their toes, so the base of support is narrower. They have more trunk rotation, as well as greater dynamic range of motion in the arms and legs. Finally, their arms swing forward and back, with the elbows approaching right angles, and the arms move in opposition to the legs. All of these changes produce a more forceful stride, which in turn allows young children to move faster.

Safety for running. When children begin to move quickly and efficiently around their environment, teachers can begin to arrange experiences that will allow safe exploration of the play space. Shoes are a safety concern, as many shoes for young children do not allow safe movement. Parents should be encouraged to provide footwear that protects and supports the foot and also provides safe footing on all surfaces within their child's environment, especially including surfaces available for locomotion and surfaces on climbing equipment.

Surfaces themselves can also be a safety concern. Running on thick or high

> Most children love to run and will engage freely in any activity that encourages and allows them to run in open spaces.

grass is difficult and will interfere with children's ability to run freely. Uneven surfaces that contain holes or rocks are unsafe for running activities. To help children avoid scraped knees and elbows, a firm, well-maintained surface that allows plenty of space is ideal. Areas can be covered with safety surfaces that are purposely soft to cushion falls, but some of these materials are too soft to allow children to push off and move effectively.

Teachers should ensure that the play space allows children to move safely around the obstacles of equipment and other moving children. Most children love to run and will engage freely in any activity that encourages and allows them to run in open spaces. Tasks can be easily designed to allow free running and exploration of the dimensions of space using different pathways (straight, diagonal, curved, circular), combined with directions (right, left, forward, back), levels (up, down, high, low), and orientations (beneath, behind, between, around, through). Having children run around a piece of playground equipment and crawl under another one before running back to the start combines several of these elements. Colored shapes spread around the play space can provide more combinations that enhance these explorations (e.g., "run to the black line and walk on the black line to the red circle"; Graham, Holt-Hale, & Parker 2004).

Since sequencing is a higher-level thought process, these tasks should begin simply, using one or two elements, and combine references already known to the children to encourage optimal movement. Older children can soon handle longer sequences and more difficult constructs.

Jumping. Soon after young children develop the ability to run, they will begin to jump, hop, gallop, and skip, which are the most commonly observed locomotor patterns. Jumping (taking off from and landing on two feet) emerges relatively early in childhood. Children's development advances through a series of progressively difficult jumping skills (Wickstrom 1983). At approximately 2 years old, children learn to step down off a higher surface from one foot to the other; then they can jump off the floor with both feet, and from progressively greater heights. By the time they are 4 years old, most have mastered forward jumps, jumps over objects, and hopping a few times on one foot.

When children begin to perform long jumps, at first they lean less than 30 degrees from the vertical, and at landing they pull their toes off the floor to "catch" their balance as their weight is shifting forward. Children use their arms ineffectively at takeoff and land with arms like a parachute (Wickstrom 1983). As children become more proficient jumpers, they begin to use a preparatory crouch, arms held backward; then at takeoff, they move their arms vigorously forward to increase force, maximally extend their body, and push off with both feet at the same time.

Jumping is also a skill that young children love. Early jumping tasks should not assume that all children are able to get both feet off the ground with equal effectiveness. Jumping over a line or crack on the floor or sidewalk is an appropriate early jumping task. The jumping can be facing in a variety of directions, allowing jumping forward, sideways (left and right), and backward over the crack.

Jumping on a flat surface should also include the advanced extensions of changing direction in the air (jumping and turning to the right or left). Older children can be guided with markings on the floor (footprints or tape marks) to jump through a series of patterns that have them turn-ing in the air in every direction (right, left, reverse).

Rope jumping. When a child can jump maturely enough to get both feet off the ground at the same time, a kind of long rope jumping can be initiated, in which teachers move the rope under children's feet while the jumpers are in the air. Children from about 3–4 years of age will quickly understand this idea; but jumping into a moving rope, timing their bounces, and jumping in a long series are more advanced skills. Children who are highly motivated to jump rope can do so at much earlier ages and can even learn to use self-turned, single ropes very effectively in the preschool years.

Hopping. Hopping on one foot is a more difficult skill for children to acquire, since they must balance on, project from, and land on the same foot. Young children's first hopping attempts often include a "fall and catch" movement with only a momentary flight phase (when both feet are off the ground). Their non-support leg is held stationary and in front of their body. Often, children do not use their arms, or else they hold them out like wings for balance; in either case, the arms do not produce force.

As children advance in hopping ability, they begin to use the non-support leg to produce force by swinging it prior to the hop. They begin to use their arms, as well, to produce force, swinging one or both arms, and eventually extend the leg at takeoff.

Ballistic skills

Ballistic skills involve using the body to apply force to an object in order to project the object. These include skills such as throwing, kicking, and striking with a second object (e.g., a bat or racket). Proficient movements produced using ballistic skills often have similar characteristics, primarily because they involve optimizing the movement pattern to create maximum force on the projectile.

Throwing. One of the most used—and most studied—ballistic skills is throwing, particularly the overarm form. As a fundamental motor skill, throwing is used in many sports, such as baseball, softball, and football. A throwing-like motion is used in a variety of other sports, including soccer and basketball.

Children attempt to throw early, typically before the age of 3. Early throws usually consist of only an arm movement (flexion/extension of the elbow, similar to a push; Marques-Bruna & Grimshaw 1997). Children usually do not move their feet or rotate their trunk, although they may flex their hips with the arm movement. As children progress in throwing proficiency, they change in their leg, trunk, and arm movements. When they first begin to move their legs, children often take a step forward with the leg on the same side from which the ball is thrown.

Eventually, they begin to step with the leg opposite to the throwing arm, too. Their trunk changes from making a flexion/extension action to a rotational action. The limb that changes the most is the arm. Early throws have no wind-up; as children's throws develop, they begin to bring their arm back and down in a circular wind-up. In a more proficient throw, the arm forms an L shape at a right angle to the trunk, and as the trunk rotates, the upper arm follows through (Haywood & Getchell 2005). Furthermore, the forearm begins to lag behind, waiting to come forward until the upper trunk and shoulders rotate into the direction of the throw. At the point of release, the arm is fully extended and follows through toward the intended target after the thrower releases the object.

These changes that occur in the overarm throwing form should allow the thrower to administer a more forceful throw that travels a greater distance (Bar-

rett & Burton 2002). For example, by taking a stride, the thrower actually increases the distance over which force is generated in the throw, which helps the throw go farther and faster. The same occurs when rotation replaces flexion/extension in the trunk: The distance over which force is generated increases, resulting in a faster, harder throw (Gagen & Getchell 2008). In fact, many of the developmental changes seen in the overarm throw can be seen in other ballistic skills such as kicking and striking.

Current research suggests that certain changes in the action of one limb lead to changes in other limbs. For example, Garcia and Garcia (2002) found that using a contralateral step (opposite side to the throwing arm) leads to trunk rotation in young throwers; and Langendorfer and Roberton (2002) determined that trunk rotation preceded more advanced arm action. Common to this research is the notion that children must begin to use trunk rotation in order to achieve a proficient arm action.

Research is somewhat contradictory on *when* children reach motor proficiency in throwing. Several studies have suggested that skillfulness can be reached by 6 years old (McClenaghan & Gallahue 1978; DeOreo & Keogh 1980; Zaichkowsky, Zaichkowsky, & Martinek 1980). Still other studies have indicated that age is not a good marker for throwing proficiency. In a study examining proficiency in kindergarten, first, second, and seventh grades, Halverson, Roberton, and Langendorfer (1982) found that almost twice as many boys as girls threw at an advanced level by the time they reached seventh grade.

Probably the most extensive study of throwing in young children was undertaken by Garcia and Garcia (2002), where they observed a total of 3,469 throws taken by six children ages 2–5 over a two-year period. The children did not progress linearly in throwing proficiency during that time.

Rather, their individual skill levels varied between different movement forms, with factors such as the learning context, the environment, and individual motivation influencing a child's performance on any given day. The results suggested that age alone does not correlate well with throwing proficiency. Although children generally progress over time, the timing and rate of their progression is highly variable and context dependent.

When devising throwing tasks for young children, one of the important considerations is the size and weight of the object thrown. Children should be encouraged to throw objects of different sizes and shapes to gain experience in how their bodies adapt to and accommodate different equipment constraints. The throwing objects can be beanbags, small balls, stuffed toys, or even a pair of socks rolled and turned inside out. The key consideration is whether the object fits into a child-size hand and is light enough for children to manipulate easily. Large balls should be eliminated from consideration, since children cannot balance them in their small hands and therefore cannot achieve an effective throwing movement. Using two hands to manipulate a large ball does not allow children to practice a correct throwing motion.

Tasks designed to practice throwing should also consider children's skill level. For initial throwing experiences, making the whole wall the target is most appropriate (Langendorfer & Roberton 2002). Children throwing at a wall without directional or space limitations are free to explore force generation and coordination in their throwing movement. As children gain skill, the target can be reduced— for example, smaller sections of the wall (the left half, the top half) or large objects such as a playground swing set or a large trashcan. Throwing at small targets or throwing to other children are advanced

> Young children may be able to kick a stationary ball but have great difficulty kicking a moving ball, even if it is rolling slowly.

skills, appropriate for children of a higher skill level. Providing children with tasks that have an appropriate target and with well-fitted throwing equipment, and then giving them many opportunities for repetition (practice), develops throwing skills most effectively.

Kicking. Kicking and striking activities are related, as kicking is a form of striking that uses the foot. Just as in their early attempts at throwing, children restrict their movements—of their leg in kicking and of their arm in striking. In their early kicking, children use a single movement where they lock their knee (often slightly bent) and flex and extend their leg at the hip to make contact with the ball or other object. As a result, children "push" the ball forward. They tend to hold their arms at their sides and don't rotate their trunk. Perceptual motor ability is essential, too, in kicking. Young children may be able to kick a stationary ball but have great difficulty kicking a moving ball, even if it is rolling slowly.

As children develop their kicking skill, changes occur similar to those in throwing. For example, children begin to take a contralateral step with their support leg prior to kicking. They start to use a wind-up, cocking their kicking leg behind them. They keep that leg flexed until just before the point of contact and then fully extend the leg quickly. Finally, they follow their kick through by extending the leg.

As with the other fundamental motor skills, kicking proficiency does not come naturally, as a function of maturation only. In fact, Haubenstricker, Seefeldt, and Branta (1983) found that only 10 percent of children ages 7½–9 they studied exhibited advanced kicking form.

In kicking tasks, choosing an appropriate ball is again a critical element. The ball should be large, but not too large, and lightweight enough to be kicked easily. In sizing the ball, teachers need to understand where a child's kicking foot should be at the time the ball is kicked to exert force in the correct place—that is, a spot both just below the middle of the ball and close to the ground. That spot on a very large ball, such as the 18" or 22" playground balls favored by many early childhood centers, would be almost knee high on a small child. Such a large ball would not allow a young child to develop an effective kicking movement. Balls that are 6"–9" in size or gallon-size plastic milk jugs are much better matched to the young children who are early kickers.

As with throwing, if children are kicking at a target, it should be a whole wall, in an area with few space and direction limitations. Those conditions can be refined as children's skill level increases. Kicking a moving ball, kicking at small targets, and kicking to another child are advanced skills.

Striking. In their early striking, children often use an overarm "chopping" motion, which later becomes a sidearm swing at about waist level (Langendorfer 1987). As with kicking, teachers initially should have children practice striking a stationary object rather than a moving one (such as a tossed ball). This removes the need for the highly developed perception required to judge where to swing in order to connect with an elevated object that is moving to a spot away from the body. The addition of a striking implement, such as a racket, paddle, or bat, makes this a more difficult task.

For earliest striking, teachers can design a task where children use their hand as their first striking implement. Lightweight objects to strike, such as balloons and beach balls, can be used to introduce and practice the skill. Self striking in a self space (striking a lightweight ball straight up in the air with one hand while standing in one spot, so that it comes back down to where it started) would be a good initial striking task. Children can explore the movement of the object as it is struck and experiment on their own with different force applications.

Later tasks can include striking a stationary ball placed on a batting tee or affixed to a hanging rope with hook and loop tape (Langendorfer 1987). The batting tee affords an opportunity for children to use thin bats but not rackets or paddles, and they must be very precise in connecting with the ball to avoid hitting the tee apparatus. A tennis ball similarly hung from a rope offers another stationary object that can react to the forcefulness of the strike but allows a more forgiving strike with a wider implement.

If rackets or paddles are used, they should be short-handled, with a lightweight but large striking area, and be easy for the child to manipulate. A good first paddle is a simple paper plate attached to children's hand; this simulates a paddle but eliminates the distance of a handle that moves the striking surface farther from the hand, a perceptual puzzle. Appropriate bats would be short, with a small hand grip and a large batting surface close to the hands. The long, thin, lightweight, plastic bats popular for yard games are too long and too narrow in striking surface for young strikers, and the short, fat, plastic bats with large striking surfaces often have grips too large for small hands to manage.

Manipulative skills

Manipulative skills involve children using their hands and fingers to handle, capture, or explore an object. These include gross motor skills such as catching and fine motor skills such as reaching, grasping, coloring, drawing, and writing.

Catching. From a young age, children attempt to catch objects rolled, thrown, or kicked towards them. As many parents and teachers of young children know, catching is harder to master than throwing. When young children first attempt to catch a ball or other object, they often stand with their arms rigidly outstretched. They often do not respond to the ball; that is, they allow it to hit their arms and bounce away, or they trap it against their chest and upper body (Seefeldt, Reuschlein, & Vogel 1972; Haubenstricker, Branta, & Seefeldt 1983). In fact, these initial catches involve little force absorption, which is a key component of effective catching.

Another common early error is that rather than tracking the trajectory of the ball, children often close their eyes and turn their head away as it reaches them. This is a typical reaction of a child who is fearful of getting hit by a throw, possibly motivated by a past negative experience. Finally, young children initially do not move or adjust their location to match the flight of the ball (Strohmeyer, Williams, & Schaub-George 1991).

As young children develop into more proficient catchers, they begin to catch the ball with their hands. Further, they begin to "give" with their hands once they grasp the ball, so its force is absorbed over the course of the catch. This giving action helps to prevent the ball from bouncing out of children's grip.

Children also begin to adjust their body to match the ball's trajectory, taking a step left or right to position themselves in front of the oncoming object. One final adjustment that generally comes later in childhood occurs in hand position: As they become more proficient catchers, children position their hands with fingers pointing up when making a catch above their waist, and with fingers pointing down for one below their waist.

There is relatively little research examining developmental progressions in catching. One study examined catching in children between ages 5 and 12 and determined that body adjustments preceded hand adjustments (Strohmeyer, Williams, & Schaub-George 1991). All of the children older than 8 made some adjustment in their body position relative to the oncoming ball; 11- and 12-year-olds successfully adjusted their body position about 80 percent of the time. However, even the oldest group had difficulty adjusting their hand position for throws above and below their waist, doing so only 40 percent of the time when the ball was thrown directly to them and just 10 percent of the time when the ball was thrown to one side or the other.

As with all other motor skills, the choice of equipment is critical in learning to catch. While many people think that throwing and catching are natural mates and should be learned together using the same equipment, this is not the case. Catching requires children to accommodate their body movements and position to a moving object; throwing does not, making catching the more difficult perceptual task.

The best ball for throwing is small and hand-sized, but the best ball for catching is larger, in the 7"–9" range, and very soft (Payne & Koslow 1981; Payne 1982). Beanbags work well for catching because they configure to children's hands and are easier to hold onto. Balloons and some beach balls do not work well because they are too light and do not travel in a uniform trajectory, so children cannot judge their movements well.

As in throwing, once children have some basic skill it is valuable to have them catch a variety of differently sized and shaped objects. But early catching should be about having fun and getting lots of practice with different types of objects (balls, bean bags, etc.). Throwing and catching with another child is a very advanced skill, and many kindergartners still cannot manage the demands of this task.

Reaching and grasping. These two are critical skills for young children to acquire so they can perform activities of daily living such as eating and dressing. Early researchers presumed that skill in reaching and grasping depended solely on neural maturation (Halverson 1931). However, it has been suggested that other factors, such as hand size relative to object size, can profoundly influence grasping ability (Butterworth, Verweij, & Hopkins 1997). That is, young children's ability to grasp is mediated by the relationship between hand size and the object they desire to grasp. Children functionally change their grasp to accommodate the size of the object—termed *body scaling*.

Body scaling occurs even in relatively young children. In two studies with children ages 3–5 and adults (Newell et al. 1989) and children ages 5, 7, and 9 (van der Kamp, Savelsbergh, & Davis 1998), researchers found that as object size increased, all of the study participants (regardless of age) used a relatively constant ratio of hand size to object size to determine when to switch from using one hand to using two hands to pick up the objects.

Fine motor control. Because control develops later in the most distal joints of the fingers, skills needed for manipulation that use the fine muscles in the fingers, such as writing, coloring, drawing, and tooth brushing, emerge later than gross motor skills such as catching. Practice with implements that are of appropriate size (in both length and grip) and weight for young children should be encouraged. Opportunities to use implements that provide a variety of different movements and grip configurations are also important.

Conclusion

The emergence of movement behavior and movement ability in the early years is a complex process involving the interaction between a growing and maturing child and the child's environment. Although children progress over time, the timing and rate of their progression is highly variable and context dependent. As they progress in motor development, at any age, children can be structurally and functionally very different from one another and certainly from adults. Thus, each child interacts differently with his or her own individual surroundings.

As children grow and change, they learn first to move and then to control their movement as opportunities to use their body arise within their environment. Teachers and parents should provide well-constructed opportunities for appropriate movement tasks so children can learn, explore, and control a wide range of movements as they are appropriate. These tasks should not be designed with adult or one-size-fits-all expectations for every child within any group. To be most effective, the tasks should rather be arranged to take into account each child's individual needs and abilities.

Arranging fun practice experiences that provide motor learning opportunities is a worthy classroom undertaking because children who become proficient movers are more likely to use those movement skills in activities that will enhance the state of their health and well-being over their entire lifespan.

This chapter was commissioned specifically for this volume and did not appear first as a *Young Children Research in Review* article.

Linda M. Gagen is an assistant professor at Old Dominion University. **Nancy Getchell** is an associate professor at the University of Delaware. **Greg Payne** is a professor at San Jose State University.

References

Adolph, K.E., B. Vereijken, & M.A. Denny. 1998. Learning to crawl. *Child Development* 69 (5): 1299–312.

Adolph, K.E., B. Vereijken, & P.E. Shrout. 2003. What changes in infant walking and why. *Child Development* 74 (2): 475–97.

Barrett, D.D., & A.W. Burton. 2002. Throwing patterns used by collegiate baseball players in actual games. *Research Quarterly for Exercise and Sport* 73 (1): 19–27.

Bayley, N. 1935. The development of motor abilities during the first 3 years: A study of sixty-one infants tested repeatedly. *Monographs of the Society for Research in Child Development* 1: 26–61.

Bower, T.G.R. 1977. *A primer of infant development.* San Francisco: Freeman.

Butterworth, G., E. Verweij, & B. Hopkins. 1997. The development of prehension in infants: Halverson revisited. *British Journal of Developmental Psychology* 15: 223–36.

Clark, J.E. 2007. On the problem of motor skill development. *Journal of Physical Education, Recreation, and Dance* 78: 39–44.

Clark, J.E., & J. Whitall. 1989. Changing patterns of locomotion: From walking to skipping. In *Development of posture and gait across the lifespan,* eds. M. Woollacott & A. Shumway-Cook, 128–51. Columbia, SC: University of South Carolina Press.

Clark, J.E., J. Whitall, & S.J. Phillips. 1988. Human interlimb coordination: The first 6 months of independent walking. *Developmental Psychobiology* 21 (5): 445–56.

de Onis, M., C. Garza, A.W. Onyango, & E. Borghi. 2007. Comparison of the WHO child growth standards and the CDC 2000 growth charts. *Journal of Nutrition* 137 (1): 144–48.

de Onis, M., C. Garza, C.G. Victora, A.W. Onyango, E.A. Frongillo, J. Martines. 2004. The WHO Multicentre Growth Reference Study: Planning, study design, and methodology. *Food and Nutrition Bulletin* 2004 (25): S15–26.

DeOreo, K., & J. Keogh. 1980. Performance of fundamental motor tasks. In *A textbook of motor development,* 2d ed., ed. C.B. Corbin, 174–91. Dubuque, IA: Brown.

Gagen, L.M., & N. Getchell. 2008. Applying Newton's apple to elementary physical education: An interdisciplinary approach. *Journal of Physical Education, Recreation, and Dance* 79 (8) 43–51.

Garcia, C., & L. Garcia. 2002. Examining developmental changes in throwing: A close up look. In *Motor development: Research and reviews, vol. 2,* eds. J.E. Clark & J.H. Humphrey. Reston, VA: NASPE Publications.

Graham, G., S.M. Holt-Hale, & M. Parker. 2004. *Children moving: A reflective approach to teaching physical education.* New York: McGraw-Hill.

Halverson, H.M. 1931. An experimental study of prehension in infants by means of systematic cinema records. *Genetic Psychology Monographs* 10: 107–286.

Halverson, L.E., M.A. Roberton, & S. Langendorfer. 1982. Development of the overarm throw: Movement and ball velocity changes by seventh grade. *Research Quarterly for Exercise and Sport* 53: 37–44.

Haubenstricker, J.L., C.F. Branta, & V.D. Seefeldt. 1983. *Standards of performance for throwing and catching.* Paper presented at the Annual Conference of the North American Society for Psychology of Sport and Physical Activity, Asilomar, CA.

Haubenstricker, J.L., V.D. Seefeldt, & C.F. Branta. 1983. *Preliminary validation of a developmental sequence for the standing long jump.* Paper presented at the American Alliance of Health, Physical Education, Recreation and Dance, Houston, TX.

Haywood, K.M., & N. Getchell. 2005. *Lifespan motor development.* Champaign, IL: Human Kinetics.

Herschkowitz, N. 2000. Neurological bases of behavioral development in infancy. *Brain Development* 22 (7): 411–16.

Langendorfer, S.J. 1987. Prelongitudinal screening of overarm striking development performed under two environmental conditions. In *Advances in motor development research 1,* eds. J.E. Clark & J.H. Humphrey, 17–47. New York: AMS Press.

Langendorfer, S.J., & M.A. Roberton. 2002. Individual pathways in the development of forceful throwing. *Research Quarterly in Exercise and Sport* 73 (3): 245–56.

Malina, R.M., C. Bouchard, & O. Bar-Or. 2004. *Growth, maturation, and physical activity.* 2d ed. Champaign, IL: Human Kinetics.

Marques-Bruna, P., & P.N. Grimshaw. 1997. 3-Dimensional kinematics of overarm throwing action of children age 15 to 30 months. *Perceptual and Motor Skills* 84: 1267–83.

McClenaghan, B.A., & D.L. Gallahue. 1978. *Fundamental movement: Observation an assessment.* Philadelphia: W.B. Saunders.

Newell, K.M., D.M. Scully, F. Tenenbaum, & S. Hardiman. 1989. Body scale and the development of prehension. *Developmental Psychobiology* 22 (1): 1–13.

Okamoto, T., K. Okamoto, & P.D. Andrew. 2001. Electromyographic study of newborn stepping in neonates and young infants. *Electromyographic and Clinical Neurophysiology* 41 (5): 289–96.

Okely, A.D., M.L. Booth, & J.W. Patterson. 2001. Relationship of physical activity to fundamental movement skills among adolescents. *Medicine and Science in Sport and Exercise* 33 (11): 1899–904.

Payne, V.G. 1982. Simultaneous investigation of effects of distance of projection and object size on object reception by children in grade 1. *Perceptual and Motor Development* 54: 1183–87.

Payne, V.G., & L.D. Isaacs. 2008. *Human motor development: A lifespan approach.* New York: McGraw-Hill.

Payne, V.G., & R. Koslow. 1981. Effects of varying ball diameters on catching ability of young children. *Perceptual and Motor Skills* 53: 739–44.

Piek, J.P. 2006. *Infant motor development.* Champaign, IL: Human Kinetics.

Roberton, M.A. 1978. Longitudinal evidence for developmental stages in the forceful overarm throw. *Journal of Human Movement Studies* 4: 161.

Roberton, M.A. 1984. Changing motor patterns during childhood. In *Motor development during childhood and adolescence,* ed. J.R. Thomas, 48–90. Minneapolis, MN: Burgess.

Rochat, P. 1992. Self-sitting and reaching in 5- to 8-month-old infants: The impact of posture and its development on early eye-hand coordination. *Journal of Motor Behavior* 24 (2): 21–220.

Seefeldt, V., S. Reuschlein, & P. Vogel. 1972. *Sequencing motor skills within the physical education curriculum.* Paper presented at the American Alliance of Health, Physical Education, Recreation and Dance, Houston, TX.

Shirley, M.M. 1931. *The first two years: A study of twenty-five babies. Postural and locomotor development, vol. 1.* Minneapolis, MN: University of Minnesota Press.

Strohmeyer, H.S., K. Williams, & D. Schaub-George. 1991. Developmental sequences for catching a small ball: A prelongitudinal screening. *Research Quarterly for Exercise and Sport* 62 (3): 257–66.

Sutherland, D. 1997. The development of mature gait. *Gait and Posture* 6: 162–70.

van der Kamp, J., G.E. Savelsbergh, & W.T. Davis. 1998. Body-scaled ratio as a control parameter for prehension in 5- to 9-year-old children. *Developmental Psychobiology* 33 (4): 351–61.

Whitall, J., & N. Getchell. 1995. From walking to running: Applying a dynamical systems approach to the development of locomotor skills. *Child Development* 66 (5): 1541–53.

WHO (World Health Organization), Multicentre Growth Reference Group. 2006. WHO Motor Development Study: Windows of achievement for six gross motor development milestones. *Acta Pædiatrica* 2006 (450): 86–95.

Wickstrom, R.L. 1983. *Fundamental motor patterns.* 3d ed. Philadelphia: Lea & Febiger.

Zaichkowsky, L.D., L.B. Zaichkowsky, & T.J. Martinek. 1980. *Growth and development: The child and physical activity.* St. Louis, MO: Mosby.

Zelazo, N.A., P. Zelazo, K.M. Cohen, & P.D. Zelazo. 1993. Specificity of practice effects on elementary neuromotor patterns. *Developmental Psychology* 29 (4): 686–91.

14 Growing Children: The Physical Side of Development

Rebecca A. Marcon

Early childhood educators work hard to ensure that children have the early literacy and numeracy skills they will need to succeed in school. It is important to remember that all domains of children's development are closely connected. What happens in one domain of development both affects and is affected by other domains. This article takes a closer look at research on physical development, what affects it, and how it is linked to children's cognitive and social development.

Malnourished or misnourished?

Children's development depends on a diet sufficient in nutrients and calories. Research in countries where malnutrition is widespread reports that growth retardation (due to poor nutrition and other social-environmental factors) often has a negative effect on children's cognitive and social development.

Although children in the United States do not experience the extent of malnutrition found in developing countries, there is a serious nutritional problem that can affect young children's development.

Many American children from all types of families are *mis*nourished, not because of a lack of food but because of what they *do* eat—that is, they underconsume important nutrients and overconsume calories and high-fat foods (Bhattacharya & Currie 2001).

In 1992, an estimated 12 million American children fell well below the recommended allowances of nutrients established by the National Academy of Sciences (Brown & Pollitt 1996). *America's Children 2008* (Federal Interagency Forum on Child and Family Statistics 2008), an annual report on children's well-being, found that most children's diets are poor or in need of improvement. As children get older, the quality of their diet drops—27 percent of children ages 2 through 6 have good diets, but only 9 percent of children ages 7 through 12 have a Healthy Eating Index score in the "good" range. Some children's diets may be poor because of food insecurity: when access to nutritionally adequate and safe foods is either limited or uncertain. In 2006, an estimated 12.6 million U.S. children (17 percent of all children, 44 percent of poor children) lived in food insecure homes (Federal Interagency Forum on Child and Family Statistics 2008). What happens to a young child's development when diet is insufficient?

Physical growth and cognitive development

Height-for-age and weight-for-height are two good indicators of physiological maturity. Children who are more physiologically mature have a cognitive advantage over same-age peers whose physical development lags (Tanner 1979). This relationship holds even after socioeconomic differences are considered. Research shows that optimal physical growth and cognitive growth go hand in hand.

When children are chronically undernourished, height-for-age is the better indicator of physiological maturity, as height is more likely to reflect their nutritional history rather than their genetic growth potential. In such populations, adequate nutrition would be a major social-environmental factor that maximizes children's physical growth, making height a good indicator of their physical maturity. Among well-nourished children, however, weight-for-height is better (Pollitt, Mueller, & Leibel 1982). In these populations, differences in children's heights at any particular age are more likely due to genetic rather than social-environmental factors. For example, Garn and Haskell (1960) found the amount of body fat between the ages of 8½ and 9½ was associated with girls' age of onset of menstruation (that is, more fat, earlier onset) and age at which both girls and boys reached skeletal maturity. In well-nourished populations, then, social-environmental factors play a role in children's weight-for-height.

The next sections look at how this relationship identified by Tanner (1979) between physiologically maturity and cognitive advantage plays out for the two indicators.

Height-for-age

Studies of infants, toddlers, preschoolers, and school-age children consistently show a small but statistically significant, positive relationship between height-for-age and a variety of cognitive competencies. Historical studies such as the Harvard Growth Study (Dearborn, Rothney, & Shuttleworth 1938) found somewhat higher mental test scores for children with greater physical growth (see, e.g., Rothney 1941), but these earlier studies were more descriptive and rarely tried to answer specific questions about physical growth and cognitive development (Bogin 1999).

When later researchers began to ask more specific questions about the relation between these two domains of development, they found some interesting links. In a classic study of severely malnourished Peruvian infants and toddlers, Brockman and Ricciuti (1971) observed how children sorted and categorized different objects during spontaneous play. Object categorization shows predictable cognitive changes with age in typically developing children. It involves an ability to discriminate similarities and differences between objects and then to group objects based on these discriminations (by size, color, sound, texture, form).

A comparison group of well-nourished but equally poor children (who had been individually matched with the malnourished children for age and sex) scored twice as high on object categorization as the malnourished infants and toddlers. Even after 12 weeks of nutritional intervention, there was virtually no improvement in scores of malnourished children. After hospital admission, however, physical growth indicators told a more promising story. There was a significant positive relationship between increases in percentage of children's expected height-for-age and more advanced sorting. Malnourished infants and toddlers whose height increased most rapidly also gained ground in cognitive development (Brockman & Ricciuti 1971).

Studies of preschoolers and kindergartners find positive relationships between children's height-for-age and developing cognitive competencies. For example, mothers of U.S. preschoolers rated taller boys as being more competent than average size or smaller boys of the same age, and these taller boys did, in fact, perform better on Piagetian conservation tasks measuring logical skills (Eisenberg et al. 1984). In this same study, mothers rated smaller girls as being less competent than average size or taller girls of the same age, but girls' height was not related to their understanding of conservation (i.e., two objects that are equal according to some measure remain equal when physical appearance is altered, so long as nothing has been added or taken away from either object).

In a study of kindergartners from families with low incomes, researchers in Philadelphia found children's physical growth significantly related to neurodevelopment and early school achievement (Karp et al. 1992). After taking into account age differences among kindergartners, it was found that those who were smaller than their classmates were more likely to do poorly in school and had less developed visual-motor perceptual skills. Kindergartners' height and weight were positively related to their early mathematical skills, phonemic awareness, oral comprehension, and general knowledge. Clearly, factors that affect young children's physical growth can also affect early school learning.

The connection between height and cognitive development continues in school-age children. After controlling for differences in children's socioeconomic backgrounds, Tanner (1979) found a small but significant positive correlation of height and IQ, height and school achievement, and physical maturity and mental development within this age group. Short-term memory appears to be especially sensitive to the factors affecting children's physical growth.

> **Factors that affect young children's physical growth can also affect early school learning.**

Data from the U.S. National Longitudinal Survey of Youth (NLSY) were used to look at the effect of growth retardation on other aspects of children's development. Based on National Center for Health Statistics standards (Kuczmarski et al. 2000), Korenman, Miller, and Sjaastad (1995) defined *stunting* to include children below the 10th percentile in height-for-age. They defined *wasting* to include children below the 10th percentile in weight-for-height. These researchers found stunting to be one of the greatest predictors of poorer cognitive development above and beyond control variables including income, age, race, sex, number of siblings, birth order, and maternal characteristics including education, age at first birth, and marital status (Korenman, Miller, & Sjaastad 1995). Stunting predicted especially negative outcomes for children growing up in long-term poverty. In fact, stunting and wasting were associated with notably lower test scores in six of eight cognitive and social outcomes. Of these outcomes, short-term memory were most strongly predicted by children's growth retardation.

Beginning at age 7, NLSY children were tested on a digit span task, in which they were asked to repeat in sequence numbers that the examiner spoke aloud. Digit span is a widely used measure of auditory short-term memory, and a good attention span is required in order to succeed on this task. Korenman, Miller, and Sjaastad (1995) found that children whose height-for-age was below the 10th percentile had great difficulty recalling numbers just heard.

Although children's physical size is affected by many factors other than nutrition (e.g., genetics, illness, poverty), growth retardation appears to have a negative effect on cognitive development throughout the early childhood period.

Weight-for-height

Research shows that weight-for-height can be linked to children's intellectual development, cognitive reasoning, and attention. In a study of well-nourished Massachusetts preschoolers (ages 3 through 6), weight-for-height was the only physical growth measure that could account for differences in IQ (Pollitt, Mueller, & Leibel 1982). Unlike findings for undernourished children, height-for-age and IQ were not significantly related in these well-nourished preschoolers.

A study of Brazilian school-age children (ages 7 through 10) contrasted cognitive development of upper-middle-class children with development in children of domestic servants who had lived in these middle-class homes for an average of three years and development of children who remained in the impoverished Brazilian communities called *favelas* (Paine et al. 1992). The live-in servants came also from *favelas* but were able to raise their children in an environment in which they ate a middle-class diet and attended middle-class schools.

The most interesting findings of this study involved the children of domestic servants. Although they were significantly taller and heavier than children who stayed in the *favela,* servants' children remained significantly shorter than middle-class children and their cognitive development was still notably lower than middle-class children's. Only among children of domestic servants were height-for-age and weight-for-height positively related to cognitive development. Servants' daughters (who were, on the average, notably heavier than sons) scored higher in cognitive reasoning, accuracy, and attention than *favela* girls. Sons of servants performed similarly to *favela* boys on all cognitive measures.

Researchers thought these differences could be due to a dual catch-up in both physical growth and cognitive development among some children of domestic servants. Those who recovered in height and weight after moving to a middle-class environment could also have been the ones who recovered cognitively, and children who did not have a growth spurt probably stayed at their previous level of cognitive development (Paine et al. 1992).

Complexities of the physical-cognitive relationship

It was once believed that malnutrition directly caused cognitive deficits through its negative effect on brain growth during critical periods of development. This view is no longer widely held because the relationship between childhood undernutrition, physical growth, and cognitive development is complex. Researchers now look at nutritional influences in the context of social-environmental factors that often coincide with undernutrition (see, e.g., Pollitt 1987; Ricciuti 1991; 1993; Pollitt et al. 1993; Sigman 1995; Sigman & Whaley 1998).

Children who vary notably from the norm in physical growth most likely also differ on other biological and psychosocial variables that affect cognitive development. For example, children who are less well fed are often less supervised, less stimulated, and less educated than children who are well nourished (Wachs 1995). However, well-fed children can "learn and perform better only if they have access to experiences that shape their development appropriately for the demands of their culture" (Sigman & Whaley 1998, 175). When other social-environmental risk factors are present, even mild undernutrition can have a negative impact on developmental outcomes.

Poverty is an especially strong social-environmental risk factor that interacts with children's nutritional status to affect physical growth and cognitive development. In the United States, the rate of growth retardation is especially high among children from families with low incomes; national data indicate stunting is twice as high for preschoolers from these families (Cook & Martin 1995). More than 14 percent of girls living in poverty and more than 11 percent of boys living in poverty (ages 2 through 5) are atypically short for their age.

In contrast, the rate of stunting is less than 6 percent for preschoolers not living in poverty in the United States. By first grade, children from high poverty areas are twice as likely to be short for their age compared with children living in areas of low poverty (Sherry et al. 1992). Additionally, national monitoring consistently finds 3 to 4 percent of children from families with low incomes have low weight-for-height ratios that indicate wasting (Cook & Martin 1995).

Likewise, the adverse effects of mild to moderate undernutrition on cognitive development are more prevalent when combined with the poverty factor. Undernutrition during any period of childhood can have detrimental effects on cognitive development (Center on Hunger and Poverty 1998). Poverty status is a strong correlate of children's cognitive development, with low family income during the early childhood years having the greatest negative impact on later academic achievement (Duncan et al. 1998). Children from families with low incomes have less access to resources that can buffer the negative effects of poverty.

One such buffer may be adequate nutrition. Nutritional supplementation has the greatest positive effect on cognitive development of children whose families are the poorest (Pollitt et al. 1993). Undernourished children who live in poverty experience significant developmental delays, whereas middle-class children whose malnutrition is secondary to medical illness show no such delays (Pollitt 1987). In each case, the context in which nutri-

tional deficits occur affects developmental outcomes.

For middle-class children, the environment acts as a buffer that neutralizes effects of nutritional deficits. For impoverished children, consequences of chronic nutritional deficits are accentuated by the social-environmental risk factors that accompany poverty. Even within low-income populations, there are differences in families with poorly nourished and well nourished children. Poorly nourished children often live in families that make poor use of medical resources, provide inadequate parental support, and have less educated mothers who do not regularly prepare meals for their children (Karp et al. 1984).

The relationship between nutritional status, physical growth, and early cognitive development is not direct. It is embedded in an environmental context in which a number of other biological and psychosocial factors operate. As Wachs (1995, 2247S) concluded, "Chronic mild-to-moderate postnatal malnutrition may be a necessary but insufficient influence explaining variability in [children's] cognitive performance."

Because the problem is multifaceted, a solution also must be. In summarizing results from a number of interventions that provided nutritional supplements to poor mothers and infants, Pollitt and Oh (1994) concluded that supplementation has the greatest effect on infant motor skills, and these motor skills are predictive of children's later cognitive development (Whaley et al. 1998). But nutritional supplementation alone will not solve the problem of higher rates of growth retardation among impoverished children nor reverse the negative effects of earlier undernutrition on cognitive development.

Intervention programs are needed to improve the overall health and developmental environment of children in poverty (Ricciuti 1991). In a two-year study of undernourished children in Jamaica, the combination of nutritional supplementation and family intervention increased overall development more than either one alone (Grantham-McGregor et al. 1991). Follow-up studies of these Jamaican children who showed growth stunting early in life had mixed results.

Although there were no long-term benefits of nutritional supplementation alone, some sustained benefits were found for the weekly one-hour, home-based intervention that sought to improve mother-child interactions through play. By ages 11 to 12, benefits of home-based stimulation were evident in children's higher cognitive functioning and IQ (Walker et al. 2000), but these benefits did not translate into better school achievement or a reduction in behavior difficulties at school (Chang et al. 2002).

By late adolescence (ages 17 to 18), however, stunted children who had received home-based stimulation in early childhood once again showed cognitive and educational benefits including higher IQ and a school dropout rate similar to that of non-stunted children from the same neighborhood (Walker et al. 2005). These benefits resulted from a two-year intervention in early childhood. Imagine the benefits that might have accrued if early intervention had been continued beyond age 4. Brown and Pollitt (1996) believed that sustained and comprehensive intervention (e.g., nutritional supplementation plus health care, tutoring, and guidance from concerned adults) would have the best chance of helping undernourished children who face persistent challenges because they live in environments that do not adequately support their development.

How social development enters into the physical-cognitive relationship

How might social development influence cognitive development in children whose physical growth is below average? First,

children whose physical growth is slowed by undernourishment may reduce their social and exploratory activity to conserve energy—they just don't have the energy to play. For example, malnourished Senegalese children (ages 3 through 6) who were short for their age, or both short and underweight, were less active, and had not developed motor skills to the same extent as their typical-size peers (Benefice 1990). On the playground, better-nourished Kenyan children (ages 6½ through 8) were more active, happier, and more likely to be leaders than undernourished peers, who were generally less active and appeared more anxious (Espinosa et al. 1992).

> Undernourished children, who are less likely to engage in vigorous physical activity, may be missing out on valuable opportunities to acquire new skills.

Through play, children explore their physical and social environments and acquire new cognitive and social skills. The lower cognitive development that often accompanies growth retardation could be the result of less active exploration of the environment (see, e.g., Barrett & Radke-Yarrow 1985; Grantham-McGregor, Stewart, & Powell 1991). Furthermore, vigorous physical activity itself has beneficial consequences for children's physical, cognitive, and social development (Pellegrini & Smith 1998). The running, chasing, jumping, pushing, and climbing that characterize "exercise play" of preschoolers all help build strength and endurance, develop a sense of mastery, and provide a playful break from cognitively demanding tasks. Undernourished children, who are less likely to engage in vigorous physical activity, may be missing out on valuable opportunities to acquire new skills across developmental domains.

Second, reduced activity may alter the way children interact with their caregivers and actually change the way caregivers behave with them (Pollitt 1987). Development is bidirectional—what a child does or does not do affects the caregiver's response, and what the caregiver does or does not do, in turn, has an effect on the child. If undernourished children with growth delays are less social (Whaley et al. 1998), more anxious (Espinosa et al. 1992), or apathetic (Grantham-McGregor 1995), then caregivers may not be as likely to engage these children. Reduced interactions with other people could negatively affect children's social and cognitive development.

Third, adults may treat children who grow more slowly as if they were younger, simply because they look younger than their peers. Smaller body size and delays in motor skills and physical development can trigger a protective response from caregivers at a time when other children are seeking autonomy and independence from adults. Some caregivers also may hold lower expectations for children who appear to be younger. Without the same challenges provided to other children of their age, smaller children face a larger risk of a lag (Pollitt et al. 1993; Brown & Pollitt 1996).

Implications for practice

Provide age-appropriate challenges for children. If educational experiences are appropriately matched to children's development, education can help buffer the negative effects of inadequate nutrition. It's very easy to assume that smaller children are less able than their average-size peers. The danger comes when teachers start to treat smaller children as though they actually *are* younger. Of course there are some things that smaller children have difficulty doing, but that's true of all children, and teachers adjust their care and teaching to meet these individual needs. Teachers can help all children grow by providing challenges that are age appropriate.

> Delays in physical development can trigger a protective response from caregivers at a time when other children are seeking autonomy from adults.

Make a point to notice children's physical growth patterns. Take a fresh look at the children in a classroom and notice all the different sizes and shapes they come in. What physical changes can be observed in each child since the year began? Are some children growing more rapidly than others? Why might that be the case? Are there any other areas in which these children have made great strides?

Think about the role that physical development may have played in their strides forward. Physical development is rarely continuous; there are spurts and plateaus throughout the childhood years. Look closely at the children who have remained pretty much the same since the year began. Have they plateaued, or is there reason to suspect that something may be holding back their physical growth? Here's where being good observers will help teachers figure out whether or how they might intervene.

Provide opportunities for vigorous physical play. It's easy to get caught up in classroom activities and the push to help children acquire early academic skills; after all, these are crucial skills in American culture. Success in this effort will be even greater if teachers remember that all domains of young children's development—cognitive, social, emotional, and physical—are interrelated. If the focus is primarily on a single domain to the exclusion of others, educators will paradoxically miss important opportunities to foster development in the very domain they seek to emphasize.

Physically active play is not just about getting in shape; there is growing evidence that performing motor acts actually alters brain development (Byers 1998). Growing children need lots of vigorous physical play. A classroom is probably too small for them to fully develop and practice gross motor skills, so look at time on the playground as time well spent. Running; hopping; starting, stopping, and changing direction; throwing; and catching are the prerequisite skills for the games of middle childhood that further advance children's cognitive and social development. And physically active play provides a great break from cognitively challenging classroom tasks.

Be a good model. Children watch adults to see what they are doing, and, not surprisingly, they often imitate what they see. If teachers share meal and snack times with the children in their care, they should model healthy eating. Healthy Eating Index (U.S. Dept. of Agriculture 1995; Guenther et al. 2007) scores go up substantially just by adding more fruit to the diet and reducing salt intake. On the playground, teachers should be more active participants. Children love it when their teachers join in on playground games, like kickball. Not all adults can play kickball, of course, but teachers can make it a point to vigorously interact (as best as possible) with children during outdoor time. Adults, too, need a refreshing break from the challenges of the classroom.

Programs that offer help

1. **Afterschool Snack Program** (www.fns. usda.gov/cnd/Afterschool/factsheet. htm) and other federally funded food programs. Part of the National School Lunch Program (NSLP), this program provides reimbursement for nutritious snacks served to children enrolled in afterschool programs sponsored or operated by schools.

2. **Child and Adult Care Food Program** (CACFP) (www.fns.usda.gov/cnd/ care/cacfp/cacfphome.htm). CACFP reimburses child care centers, family child care homes, homeless shelters, and after-school programs for meals and snacks served to income-eligible children. Meals and snacks must meet U.S. Department of Agriculture (USDA) requirements for nutrition and age-related serving sizes.

3. **Commodity Supplemental Food Program** (CSFP) (www.fns.usda.gov/fdd/ programs/csfp/). CSFP provides USDA commodity foods to state agencies and Indian Tribal Organizations for distribution to income-eligible pregnant and breastfeeding women, other new mothers (for up to one year after childbirth), infants, and children up to age 6.

4. **The Emergency Food Assistance Program** (TEFAP) (www.fns.usda.gov/ fdd/programs/tefap/). TEFAP provides commodity foods to states for distribution to local agencies such as food banks. These agencies distribute the food to soup kitchens, food pantries, homeless shelters, and other groups that serve the public.

5. **Food Stamp Program** (FSP) (http:// www.fns.usda.gov/fsp/). The FSP provides low-income households with coupons or electronic cards that can be used to purchase food at most grocery stores. Eligibility is based on income and countable resources such as a bank account. Monthly benefits are based on household size.

6. **National School Lunch Program** (NSLP) (www.fns.usda.gov/cnd/Lunch/default.htm). This program operates in public and nonprofit private schools and residential child care settings. Eligible children receive free or reduced-price lunches that meet USDA dietary requirements.

7. **School Breakfast Program** (SBP) (www. fns.usda.gov/cnd/Breakfast/Default. htm). States receive funds to serve free or reduced-price breakfasts to children whose families meet income eligibility requirements.

8. **Special Supplemental Nutrition Program for Women, Infants, and Children** (WIC) (www.fns.usda.gov/wic). WIC is targeted to income-eligible pregnant women and mothers and their children ages birth to 5 who are at risk for not meeting their basic nutritional needs. WIC's services include supplemental foods, access to health care, and breast-feeding and nutrition education.

9. **Summer Food Service Program** (SFSP) (www.fns.usda.gov/cnd/Summer/ default.htm). The SFSP serves nutritious meals and snacks during the summer months to children living in lower-income areas. Without SFSP, many children might not eat the nutritious foods they need for good health.

Other resources on nutrition and health

1. **Feeding America** (www.feedingamerica. org). Formerly known as Second Harvest, this organization fights childhood hunger through food banks and other innovative efforts.

2. **Food Research and Action Center** (FRAC) (www.frac.org). FRAC is a nonprofit and nonpartisan research and policy organization devoted to supporting and providing information on anti-hunger efforts. The website is an excellent source of information on the latest news and research on ending hunger.

3. **KidsHealth: Nutrition and Fitness Center** (www.kidshealth.org/parent/ nutrition_fit/center/nutrition_center. html). The Nemours Foundation's Center for Children's Health Media created the KidsHealth website on nutrition and fitness to provide jargon-free health information that parents and others can use. Physicians and other health experts review all content before its publication on KidsHealth.

4. **National Head Start Association** (NHSA) (www.nhsa.org). On the NHSA website, see the area titled Healthy Kids (listed under Programs heading for Child Health and Development) for information on the role of Head Start and Early Head Start in supporting children's health. There are separate sections on physical health, mental health, and nutrition.

5. **PE Central** (www.pecentral.org). This website on health and physical education offers information and activities for teachers, families, and children. Its goal is to provide up-to-date information on developmentally appropriate physical education programs. One section is dedicated to preschool physical education.

6. **President's Council on Physical Fitness and Sports** (www.fitness.gov). Since 1956, this federal program has encouraged Americans to lead healthy and physically active lives. The President's Challenge Youth Physical Fitness Awards Program assesses the fitness level of youth ages 6 to 17 and provides individual recognition for fitness.

Updated from the Research in Review article in the January 2003 issue of *Young Children*.

Rebecca A. Marcon is a professor at the University of North Florida.

References

Barrett, D., & M. Radke-Yarrow. 1985. Effects of nutritional supplementation on children's response to novel, frustrating, and competitive situations. *American Journal of Clinical Nutrition* 42: 102–20.

Benefice, E. 1990. Motor skills of mild-malnourished compared with normal preschool Senegalese children. *Early Child Development and Care* 61 (August): 81–91.

Bhattacharya, J., & J. Currie. 2001. Youths and nutrition risk: Malnourished or misnourished? In *Risky behavior among youths: An economic analysis*, ed. J. Gruber, 483–521. National Bureau of Economic Research. Chicago: University of Chicago Press.

Bogin, B. 1999. *Patterns of human growth*. 2d ed. Cambridge: Cambridge University Press.

Brockman, L.M., & H.R. Ricciuti. 1971. Severe protein-calorie malnutrition and cognitive development in infancy and early childhood. *Developmental Psychology* 4: 312–19.

Brown, J.L., & E. Pollitt. 1996. Malnutrition, poverty, and intellectual development. *Scientific American* 274 (February): 38–43.

Byers, J.A. 1998. The biology of human play. *Child Development* 69: 599–600.

Center on Hunger and Poverty. 1998. *Statement on the link between nutrition and cognitive development in children*. Waltham, MA: Center on Hunger and Poverty.

Chang, S.M., S.P. Walker, S.M. Grantham-McGregor, & C.A. Powell. 2002. Early childhood stunting and later behaviour and school achievement. *Journal of Child Psychology and Psychiatry* 43: 775–83.

Cook, J.T., & K.S. Martin. 1995. *Differences in nutrient adequacy among poor and non-poor children*. Boston: Tufts University, Center on Hunger, Poverty and Nutrition Policy.

Dearborn, W.F., J.W.M. Rothney, & F.K. Shuttleworth. 1938. Data on the growth of public school children. *Monographs of the Society for Research in Child Development* vol. 3, no. 1.

Duncan, G.J., W.J. Yeung, J. Brooks-Gunn, & J.R. Smith. 1998. How much does childhood poverty affect the life chances of children? *American Sociological Review* 63: 406–23.

Eisenberg, N., K. Roth, K.A. Bryniarski, & E. Murray. 1984. Sex differences in the relationship of height to children's actual and attributed social and cognitive competencies. *Sex Roles* 11: 719–34.

Espinosa, M.P., M.D. Sigman, C.G. Neumann, & N.O. Bwibo. 1992. Playground behaviors of school-age children in relation to nutrition, schooling, and family characteristics. *Developmental Psychology* 28: 1188–95.

Federal Interagency Forum on Child and Family Statistics. 2008. *America's children: Key national indicators of well-being, 2008*. Washington, DC: U.S. Government Printing Office, Federal Interagency Forum on Child and Family Statistics.

Garn, S., & J.A. Haskell. 1960. Fat thickness and developmental status in childhood and adolescence. *American Journal of Diseases in Children* 99: 746–51.

Grantham-McGregor, S.M. 1995. A review of studies of the effect of severe malnutrition on mental development. *Journal of Nutrition Supplement* 125: 2233s–38s.

Grantham-McGregor, S.M., C.A. Powell, S.P. Walker, & J.H. Himes. 1991. Nutritional supplementation, psychological stimulation, and mental development of stunted children: The Jamaican study. *Lancet* 338: 1–5.

Grantham-McGregor, S.M., M. Stewart, & C.A. Powell. 1991. Behavior of severely malnourished children in a Jamaican hospital. *Developmental Medicine and Child Neurology* 33: 706–14.

Guenther, P.M., J. Reedy, S.M. Krebs-Smith, B.B. Reeve, & P.P. Basiotis. 2007. *Development and evaluation of the Healthy Eating Index-2005: Technical report*. Alexandria, VA: Center for Nutrition Policy and Promotion. U.S. Department of Agriculture.

Karp, R., R. Martin, T. Sewell, J. Manni, & A. Heller. 1992. Growth and academic achievement in inner-city kindergarten children. *Clinical Pediatrics* 31: 336–40.

Karp, R., E. Snyder, J. Fairorth, M. Nelson, G. Solimano, W. Acker, G. Greene, & W.A. Krehl. 1984. Parental behavior and the availability of foods among undernourished inner-city children. *Journal of Family Practice* 18: 731–35.

Korenman, S., J.E. Miller, & J.E. Sjaastad. 1995. Long-term poverty and child development in the United States: Results from the NLSY. *Children and Youth Services Review* 17: 127–55.

Kuczmarski R.J., C.L. Ogden, L.M. Grummer-Strawn, et al. 2000. CDC growth charts: United States. *Advance data from vital and health statistics; No. 314*. Hyattsville, MD: National Center for Health Statistics.

Paine, P., J.G. Dorea, J. Pasquali, & A.M. Monterior. 1992. Growth and cognition in Brazilian school children: A spontaneously occurring intervention study. *International Journal of Behavioral Development* 15: 169–83.

Pellegrini, A.D., & P.K. Smith. 1998. Physical activity play: The nature and function of a neglected aspect of play. *Child Development* 69: 577–98.

Pollitt, E. 1987. A critical review of three decades of research on the effects of chronic energy malnutrition on behavioral development. In *Chronic energy deficiency: Consequences and related issues*, eds. B. Schürch & N.S. Scimshaw, 77–93. Lausanne, Switzerland: International Dietary Energy Consultative Group.

Pollitt, E., K.S. Gorman, P.L. Engle, R. Martorell, & J. Rivera. 1993. *Early supplementary feeding and cognition*. Monographs of the Society for Research in Child Development, vol. 58, no. 7, serial no. 235.

Pollitt, E., W. Mueller, & R.L. Leibel. 1982. The relation of growth to cognition in a well-nourished preschool population. *Child Development* 53: 1157–63.

Pollitt, E., & S. Oh. 1994. Early supplementary feeding, child development, and health policy. *Food and Nutrition Bulletin* 15: 208–14.

Ricciuti, H.N. 1991. Malnutrition and cognitive development: Research-policy linkages and current research directions. In *Directors of development: Influences on the development of children's thinking,* eds. L. Okagaki & R.J. Sternberg. Hillsdale, NJ: Lawrence Erlbaum.

Ricciuti, H.N. 1993. Nutrition and mental development. *Current Directions in Psychological Science* 2 (2): 43–46.

Rothney, J.W.M. 1941. Recent findings in the study of the physical growth of children. *Journal of Educational Research* 3: 161–82.

Sherry, B., D.A. Springer, F.A. Connell, & S.M. Garrett. 1992. Short, thin, or obese? Comparing growth indexes of children from high- and low-poverty areas. *Journal of the American Dietetic Association* 92: 1092–95.

Sigman, M. 1995. Nutrition and child development: More food for thought. *Current Directions in Psychological Science* 4 (2): 52–55.

Sigman, M., & S.E. Whaley. 1998. The role of nutrition in the development of intelligence. In *The rising curve: Long-term gains in IQ and related measures,* ed. U. Neisser, 155–82. Washington, DC: American Psychological Association.

Tanner, J.M. 1979. *Education and physical growth.* 2d ed. Madison, WI: International Universities Press.

U.S. Department of Agriculture. 1995. *The Healthy Eating Index* (CNPP-1). Alexandria, VA: Center for Nutrition Policy and Promotion.

Wachs, T.D. 1995. Relation of mild-to-moderate malnutrition to human development: Correlational studies. *Journal of Nutrition Supplement* 125: 2245S–54S.

Walker, S.P., S.M. Chang, C.A. Powell, & S.M. Grantham-McGregor. 2005. Effects of early childhood psychosocial stimulation and nutritional supplementation on cognition and education in growth-stunted Jamaican children: Prospective cohort study. *Lancet* 366: 1804–07.

Walker, S.P., S.M. Grantham-McGregor, C.A. Powell, & S.M. Chang. 2000. Effects of growth restriction in early childhood on growth, IQ, and cognition at age 11 to 12 years and the benefits of nutritional supplementation and psychosocial stimulation. *Journal of Pediatrics* 136: 36–41.

Whaley, S.E., M. Sigman, M.P. Espinosa, & C.G. Neuman. 1998. Infant predictors of cognitive development in an undernourished Kenyan population. *Journal of Developmental and Behavioral Pediatrics* 19: 169–77.

15 Children's Eating: The Development of Food-Acceptance Patterns

Alison K. Ventura, Susan L. Johnson, and Leann L. Birch

For caregivers and parents, young children's health and well-being are of primary concern. Because much research has elucidated the important links between nutrition and children's health and growth, young children's eating (or not eating) can generate a high degree of anxiety for caregivers.

For most of human history, parent and caregiver concern over children's eating was primarily focused on getting children to eat *enough*; threats of food scarcity and malnutrition motivated parents to adopt feeding practices that ensured children consumed a sufficient amount of food to meet caloric, growth, and nutritional needs.

Today, however, the environment has changed for parents. The culmination of many societal changes over the past century has created an "obesigenic" environment where physical activity levels are low, sedentary behaviors are the leisure time norm, and large portions of energy-dense foods are inexpensive and readily available. Thus, in many families, parents are now concerned with making sure

their children do not eat too much—or too much of the "wrong" foods.

A recent survey of infants and toddlers showed that young children are consuming between 10 and 31 percent more calories than they need (Devaney et al. 2004). These excess calories, however, do not appear to be related to better diet quality, as this survey also found that these same children were not consuming the recommended amounts of most nutrients. Additionally, in a given day, approximately 18 to 33 percent of infants and toddlers consumed no servings of vegetables, and 23 to 33 percent consumed no servings of fruit. French fries were the most commonly eaten "vegetable." Instead of fruits and vegetables, young children are consuming desserts, sweets, and sweetened beverages on a daily basis (Fox et al. 2004). These data illustrate that the diets of young children are in need of thoughtful attention and improvement.

The consequences of these trends are reflected in the fact that the percentage of young American children being classified as overweight has increased dramatically since the 1970s. Current estimates indicate that 13.9 percent of 2- to 5-year-olds and 18.8 percent of 6- to 11-year-olds are classified as overweight (Ogden et al. 2006). In light of these statistics, information about child eating patterns and about the effect of parents on the development of children's eating styles, preferences, and dietary intake take on new meaning and importance for preventing the continuation and worsening of this obesity epidemic.

The purpose of this chapter is to review what is known about the factors that influence children's developing food-acceptance patterns, including children's sensory responsiveness; their innate preferences, ability to learn about food, and understanding of the consequences of eating; and the effect of child-feeding practices on children's food-acceptance patterns. The term *food-acceptance patterns* encompasses what foods are selected and how much is consumed. The focus will be primarily on the evidence showing how early experience with food and eating contributes to the development of food-acceptance patterns and the control of food intake.

Innate preferences and predispositions

In the absence of adult coercion, young children eat what they like and leave the rest. In making their food choices, they are blissfully ignorant of the caloric content and nutrient value and do not hesitate to express their likes and dislikes. These food-acceptance patterns begin to be exhibited in infancy with the reflexive facial expressions elicited by the basic tastes.

The taste system is functional at birth. Newborns respond reflexively with a positive facial expression to sweet and a negative expression to sour and bitter (Desor, Maller, & Turner 1973; Steiner 1977; Steiner et al. 2001). By about 4 months, infants begin to show a preference for salt (Beauchamp et al. 1994). The infant's reflexive facial expressions in response to

sweet, sour, and bitter are unambiguous. Thus, adults who watch infants tasting sweet substances interpret the expression as "she likes it," and the opposite for bitter and sour.

Caregivers interpret the infant's facial and gestural responses to foods and make decisions about whether to continue feeding a food, to stop the feeding, or to try a different food. The fact that these early responses to the basic tastes are reflexive may lead some to believe that food-acceptance patterns may be "hardwired" or, in other words, fixed and difficult to change. However, research on the development of food-acceptance patterns reveals that this is not the case. The positive response to sweetness and the rejection of bitter and sour tastes are "built-in," but from very early in life, even before birth, responses to these basic tastes change with the child's experience with flavors, food, and eating.

One of the first aspects of this learning comes from the transmission of flavors through the amniotic fluid and breast milk. The work of Mennella and others showed that flavors, especially strong flavors such as garlic, carrot, and anise, are passed from the mother's diet to the child (Mennella & Beauchamp 1991; 1999; Mennella, Jagnow, & Beauchamp 2001). Formulas, although more homogenous than breast milk, also have distinct flavorings that may influence infant flavor recognition during the introduction of solid foods (Mennella & Beauchamp 2002; Mennella, Griffin, & Beauchamp 2004; Mennella, Kennedy, & Beauchamp 2006).

Early experience with flavors creates a "flavor bridge": The child appears to recognize and even prefer these flavors, as evidenced by increased consumption of these flavors when introduced as solid foods later during infancy (Mennella & Beauchamp 1999; Mennella, Jagnow, & Beauchamp 2001). Mennella and colleagues also showed that the effect and influence of maternal diet on child diet

Caregivers interpret the infant's facial responses to foods and make decisions about whether to continue feeding a food.

and food preferences is further augmented in that the foods eaten by mothers during pregnancy are often similar to the types of foods fed to infant when solids are introduced (Mennella et al. 2005). This consistency may help to solidify children's preferences for cultural and regional foods and food practices, because flavors and cultural preferences are both transmitted from mother to child during this early experience with food and eating.

The role of familiarity

If we look at diets across cultures, dramatic differences exist in what substances are considered to be food, what items tend to be valued and preferred, and what substances are seen as unappealing or disgusting (Fallon, Rozin, & Pliner 1984). Humans are omnivores, which means that humans need a variety of foods to obtain adequate nutrition, unlike specialized species that can survive on one or a few foods. Along with this need for variety comes the ability to adapt readily to consuming whatever edible substances happen to be available in our environment. This adaptability implies that learning and experience must play central roles in shaping our food-acceptance patterns. As noted above, children come into the world with predisposed likes and dislikes for flavors, but they are also primed and willing to learn from their environmental experience with food and eating (e.g., very sour candy, coffee drinks, yogurt).

Although there is striking cross-cultural diversity in adult diets, mammals all begin life consuming an exclusively milk diet. By the time children are 5 or 6 years old, they are consuming many of the foods that make up the adult diet of their culture, and within that cultural group, they will have developed individual patterns of food likes and dislikes; for example many South American 6-year-olds like the risk of trying chilies, but a young child from the midwestern United States would probably find the idea of eating a hot chili very noxious. From a developmental perspective, this implies that learning occurs relatively rapidly in the first few years of life.

Foods are complex stimuli; they provide input to several sensory systems in addition to taste. Foods have textural components (e.g., crunchiness, creaminess, greasiness), and the smell of food contributes greatly to what is commonly referred to as the taste of food. A food's appearance also can influence its attractiveness. Thus, food preferences result from a response to a complex combination of stimulation, involving the food's taste, smell, appearance, tactile, and energy characteristics. As will be discussed in more detail below, food and the act of eating also have significant social components: A large percentage of adult-child interactions, especially in the first few years of life, are focused on food as a way for the caregiver to nurture the child. The climate and nature of this social component is also an important contributor to food preferences. Ultimately, children's responses to the culmination of these physical and social characteristics of foods are strongly influenced by prior experience with the food.

In some initial research on children's food preferences, Birch (1979) investigated the question of which of the many dimensions of solid foods are central in forming children's food preferences. For example, one question asked by this research was how central textural characteristics are, relative to the food's flavor, in determining whether a food will be accepted or rejected? This initial work revealed that sweetness was a primary determinant of children's preferences for foods, which came as no surprise; however, a second factor—familiarity—was also important in determining preference. This is not a characteristic of the food but a function of the child's experience: Children tended to prefer foods that were familiar over those that were not, relatively independent of the foods' sensory characteristics.

Learned food preferences: How do they develop?

Here the effect of children's early experience with food and eating on development of preferences and food-acceptance patterns is investigated.

Repeated exposure and pickiness

Infancy and early childhood involve a dramatic dietary transition from consuming an exclusively milk diet to eating a variety of foods (Devaney et al. 2004). At one point, all foods are novel to the child. To obtain adequate nutrition, children must come to accept some of the new foods that parents offer. Although infants and young children are primed to learn from their experiences with flavors and foods, in general, they do not readily accept new foods (unless they happen to be sweet).

Birch and colleagues have investigated this rejection of the new, or *neophobia*, and how children's initial rejection of new foods can be altered. Fortunately, many of children's initial rejections of new foods can be changed to acceptance simply by providing children with a number of opportunities to sample the new food.

Experiments conducted by Birch and colleagues have shown that as exposure to a food increases so does the child's preference for the food (Birch & Marlin 1982; Birch, McPhee, Shoba, Pirok et al. 1987). For example, in one experiment, children were repeatedly offered samples of new foods during the course of their ongoing preschool program. Children were encouraged to take a small taste of the food, and the changes in their acceptance of these foods were compared with

children who did not taste but only looked at and smelled the food (Birch, McPhee, Shoba, Pirok et al. 1987). Repeated exposure enhanced acceptance only when children actually tasted the foods; looking at and smelling the food did not increase children's acceptance. These changes in acceptance of new foods occur relatively slowly, often requiring 10 or more exposures before clear changes in acceptance are achieved (Sullivan & Birch 1990).

Further, children appear to employ a sequence of exploratory behaviors in their acquisition of new food preferences. In a study conducted in Head Start, children's behaviors were observed when they were presented with a novel food (a daikon radish). At first, children touched, smelled, played with, and even tasted and spat out the food. Over time, these behaviors diminished, and more children began to taste and swallow the food (Johnson et al. 2007).

It appears that children use exploratory behaviors to learn about new foods as a path to become willing to ingest them. These same behaviors are often ones that adults discourage, as they are perceived to fall into the realm of "bad manners." It may be useful for those who feed children to reframe some of these behaviors as exploratory learning that helps children learn about food and eating.

Unfortunately, in many cases children do not have repeated opportunities to eat new foods because caregivers interpret the child's initial rejection as reflecting a fixed and persistent dislike of the food. If the caregiver views the child's initial rejection as reflecting a dislike that cannot be altered, she may not serve this food to the child again. Alternatively, the caregiver may view the child's food refusal as a rejection of the caregiver, not just a rejection of the food, and may be unwilling to persist in offering the food in the face of such perceived rejection (Blissett et al. 2005). As a result, caregivers may become frustrated and anxious about feeding the child, and the child may not learn to accept new foods and thus may be labeled as "finicky" or as a "picky eater."

When children's pickiness persists, it appears to have negative consequences for their diet quality. Although children who are labeled by their parents to be picky eaters tend to have lower weight status than children not labeled as picky eaters (Carruth et al. 2004), this does not seem to be due to consumption of a healthier diet. Children who are picky consume a lower variety of foods, fewer fruits and vegetables, and lower amounts of nutrients such as fiber, vitamins, and minerals compared with children who are not picky (Galloway, Lee, & Birch 2003; Galloway et al. 2005). Parents report higher levels of coercive or pressuring feeding practices with picky children (Carruth et al. 1998), which may have undesirable influences on the development of children's eating patterns and food preferences.

Parents who report that their children are picky eaters also report that they typically only present new foods a few times before they decide the child does not like it (Carruth et al. 2004); this may be in response to the child's picky behaviors, but it may also be a cause of pickiness. Results of several studies indicate that if caregivers are willing to persist in offering a new food *multiple* times (i.e., 10 to 15), repeated exposure can be a slow but effective means of expanding the variety of foods that children will accept (Birch, McPhee, Shoba, Pirok et al. 1987; Wardle, Cook et al. 2003; Wardle, Herrera et al. 2003).

The effect of repeated exposure on food acceptance is not restricted to young children; it is also effective with infants (Sullivan & Birch 1994) and adults (Pliner, Pelchat, & Grabski 1993). In fact, there is evidence that infants who are breastfed are less neophobic during the introduction of solid foods (Sullivan & Birch 1994) and less picky later in life (Galloway, Lee, &

Birch 2003); this observation most likely stems from the aforementioned "flavor bridge," where early, repeated exposure to a diverse array of flavors through the amniotic fluid and breast milk may reduce the strength and duration of neophobic responses during infancy and early childhood by reducing the novelty of flavors in new foods (Mennella, Jagnow, & Beauchamp 2001). Thus, breastfeeding may be an important first step for parents to help their children be familiar with and accepting of a wide variety of flavors and foods.

> Repeated exposure can be a slow but effective means of expanding the variety of foods that children will accept.

As children begin eating solid foods, parents and caregivers should be patient when introducing foods that are initially rejected and should remember that children are naturally neophobic. Most children need to become familiar with a food before they will readily accept it. Given the evidence for the poorer dietary quality of picky children, circumventing the development of pickiness should be an important and attainable goal for parents.

Learned preferences for high-energy foods

Children's preferences for foods are shaped by their reactions to the basic tastes in foods, like their innate enjoyment of sweet. Through associative learning, children's early experiences with foods have a major impact on their developing food-acceptance patterns. Research has shown that the physiological consequences of ingesting food can also modify children's preferences and can influence how much of those foods is consumed.

Research has demonstrated that children can form associations between the sensory cues of energy dense foods (e.g., creaminess) and the positive physiological consequences (e.g., feeling pleasantly full) that normally follow eating those energy-dense foods (Birch et al. 1990; Johnson, McPhee, & Birch 1991; Kern et al. 1993). In this research, children were given repeated opportunities to consume fixed amounts of high- and low-energy density versions of the same distinctively flavored food. The foods used included yogurt and puddings, which can be made either high or low in energy density, depending on the fat or carbohydrate content. When adults were asked to taste the different preparations, they could not tell with reliability whether the preparations were high or low energy, nor did they consistently prefer one over the other.

After repeated opportunities to eat these foods as snacks, children showed clear preferences for the high-energy version, which was made with added fat or carbohydrates (Birch et al. 1990; Johnson, McPhee, & Birch 1991). The children's preferences for the high-energy foods were particularly clear when they were hungry, providing additional support for the fact that preferences were mediated by the physiological consequences of the food's energy density (Kern et al. 1993).

These findings indicate that, in addition to the child's natural preference for sweet taste, the child is biased to learn to prefer foods that are high in energy. This ability to learn to associate a food's flavor cues with the physiological consequences of eating that food can be viewed as serving an adaptive function, especially in contexts of food scarcity. Forming associations between the food's sensory cues and the food's energy content would lead to learning to prefer foods with high-energy contents.

This natural tendency for children to learn to prefer energy-dense foods is no longer an adaptive advantage, given that, in America, we do not live in a context of food scarcity. The availability of energy-dense foods combined with the ease of children's learning to prefer these foods can easily lead to over-consumption and excess weight gain.

Additionally, because the energy-dense foods most readily available in our current food environment are often also nutrient poor (and often sweet and very palatable), children whose diets are mainly comprised of these energy-dense foods run the risk of not meeting recommendations for fiber, vitamins, and minerals, despite consuming more than the recommended values for calories and fat. Unfortunately, another challenge for parents arises from the finding that children's tendency to learn to prefer energy-dense foods is augmented by specific social influences such as modeling, use of food as a reward, and use of pressure or coercion.

Associative learning in social contexts

The emotional tone of the social interactions surrounding feeding can shape children's food-acceptance patterns when associations are formed between food and the child's emotional response to the feeding interaction. Meals are an important context for family or child care staff interactions, and meals also have a meaningful temporal structure. Children learn very early that certain foods are served in particular order at meals and that particular social occasions require special foods. Even 2-year-olds can explain what foods should be served at birthday parties and that dessert comes after the vegetables.

In Western cultures, sweet desserts come at the end of the meal, probably because we still find them palatable, even when we are relatively full after consuming other courses (Hetherington et al. 2006). The sequencing of courses in Western cuisines fosters the use of sweet, palatable foods as effective rewards for finishing the previous course ("Finish your vegetables and you may have dessert"). Investigations into the impact of the use of food in these social contexts on children's formation of food preferences reveal that some common feeding practices may have unintended and untoward effects on children's food-acceptance patterns.

Modeling. Food likes and dislikes are influenced by learning, most of which occurs during children's routine experiences at mealtimes and in the absence of explicit teaching. For young children, eating is a social occasion because they need help; they cannot yet prepare and serve their own food, and they may also need help in feeding themselves. Siblings, peers, and adults can serve as models when they are present at meals and snacks. This influence may be diminishing, however, as the frequency of family meals where parents and children eat together and share the same food is reported to be declining (Gallup Organization 1995; Princeton Survey Research Associates 1997).

Related issues for child care settings include whether staff sit with children during mealtimes and whether staff eat the same food as children. In a recent survey of licensed child care centers in the western United States, most child care staff reported sitting with children during the meal but described having to "get up and down" frequently during meals (Sigman-Grant et al. 2008). Further, 36 percent of centers reported that children brought their own food, and therefore opportunities for adults to model healthful eating or try new foods were strongly diminished.

Birch (1980) noted that one way to increase children's acceptance of disliked vegetables is to expose children to peers who happen to enjoy the disliked food. Additionally, children eat more of both novel and familiar foods when a parent or older child models consumption of that food (Hendy & Raudenbush 2000; Cullen et al. 2001; Hendy 2002; Young, Fors, & Hayes 2004; Addessi et al. 2005).

Positive associations between the dietary patterns of parents and children suggest that parents' own intake encourages similar intake patterns in children (Fisher et al. 2002) and that observation of parent dietary behaviors indicates to children what combinations of foods and flavors are normal to eat and in what contexts, amounts, and frequencies.

Food as reward. When foods are given to children in positive social contexts (as rewards, or paired with positive social interaction with an adult), children's preferences for those foods are enhanced (Birch, Marlin, & Rotter 1984; Wardle, Herrera et al. 2003). The opposite effect on food acceptance can occur when caregivers force children to eat "nutritious" foods to obtain rewards ("Eat your vegetables and you can watch TV"). The strategy of having a child eat a food in order to obtain a reward tends to reduce the child's liking for the food she is rewarded for eating (Birch, Marlin, & Rotter 1984; Newman & Taylor 1992).

Pressure to eat. The use of pressure in child feeding (i.e., verbal or physical coercion to eat certain foods), even in the absence of a reward or contingency, has been linked to lower intakes of "healthy" foods, such as vegetables, fruits, and milk (Carper, Fisher, & Birch 2000; Fisher et al. 2002; Keller et al. 2006). In fact, retrospective reports reveal that many common food dislikes can be traced back to children's experiences of being pressured to eat specific foods (Batsell et al. 2002), suggesting that pressuring children to eat may be causally linked to the development of food dislikes and rejections.

In summary, social contexts of feeding that are perceived as positive by the child enhance liking; those that are perceived as negative by the child reduce liking. It may not be immediately obvious how this associative learning can contribute to the

> Many common food dislikes can be traced back to children's experiences of being pressured to eat specific foods.

formation of food-acceptance patterns inconsistent with good nutrition and healthy weight status. However, this occurs because particular foods are consistently paired with particular social contexts. For example, foods presented in positive social contexts and as rewards tend to be palatable foods high in fat, sugar, and salt. These foods are preferred by children without much prior experience and with minimal learning, but are also the same foods that current dietary guidelines tell us to consume in moderation.

Caregivers can increase the chances that children will come to accept a wide variety of foods by providing repeated opportunities to try new foods in positive, or relatively neutral, social contexts and by avoiding coercive feeding tactics. Parents should be aware that while coercive feeding tactics (e.g., rewarding children for eating foods they do not spontaneously consume) may have the immediate effect of increasing intake, these tactics might also have negative long-term effects on children's food-acceptance patterns.

Children's ability to regulate energy intake

Do young children "know" how much to eat? Davis (1939) observed that when presented with a variety of nutritious foods, children self-selected a diet sufficient to maintain adequate health. This path-breaking research suggested that young children possess an innate ability to regulate food intake, independent of adult supervision. Davis pointed out, however, that the "trick" of her experiment was that the foods she presented to children, and from which children could choose, were a set of simply prepared, healthful foods (Davis 1928).

Davis' work has prompted studies aimed at examining the ability of infants and young children to regulate energy intake. With respect to infants, Fomon and

> Children may possess the ability to regulate how much they eat based on the caloric content of the foods.

colleagues (1975) examined infants' ability to adjust their formula intake in response to changes in the formula's energy density. Infants older than 6 weeks adjusted their formula intake in response to alterations to the energy density of a given formula, consuming more of the energy-dilute formula and less of the energy-dense version. Later work by Dewey and Lonnderdal showed some breastfed infants had similar ability to adjust intake in response to alterations in milk supply. When supplemental pumping after every feed was used to increase maternal milk supply, infants initially consumed more milk but half of the sample then adjusted their intake back to baseline levels of intake (Dewey & Lonnerdal 1986). Thus, it appears that some young children have an ability to self-regulate intake in response to the composition or supply of formula or milk available, and, under optimal circumstances, do not consume more calories than needed in response to alterations in the amount or energy density of foods offered.

To determine whether the responsiveness to energy density seen in infants persisted into childhood, investigators first looked at the effect that varying the caloric density of a meal's first course had on children's food intake in subsequent meals (Birch & Deysher 1985; 1986; Birch et al. 1993). In these experiments, children were observed during a pair of meals, which were eaten on different days. The meals, consisting of a first and second course, differed only in the caloric content of the first course. The children first consumed a fixed amount of a first course (e.g., half a cup of yogurt) that was either low or high in calories. A few minutes later, the children were offered a variety of foods from which they could self-select a meal, consuming as much of the foods as they wished.

The hypothesis was that if children were responsive to the caloric density of foods in controlling their food intake, they would eat less in the self-selected portion of the meal following the high-calorie first course. In fact, this is what many children did; they adjusted their intake in the second course almost calorie for calorie with the energy in the first course, so that their total caloric intake for the first and second meals were the same whether or not they consumed the high-calorie or low-calorie first course. These findings are consistent with the idea that children may possess the ability to regulate how much they eat based on the caloric content of the foods eaten.

Children's knowledge of how much to eat may be based on a sensitivity to the caloric content of foods not only within a given meal but also over a number of meals. This may seem quite contrary to what parents and practitioners believe about children's meal-to-meal eating behavior. For instance, children are often inconsistent in what and how much they eat, consuming large portions of food at lunch one day and very little of the food offered at lunch on other days. It is, therefore, not surprising that caregivers and practitioners often approach child feeding with concern and frustration, with the misconception that children are incapable of meeting their energy needs without adult supervision or intervention.

However, research has found that although children's meal-to-meal energy intake is somewhat erratic, children are consistent in the total amount of calories they consume during 24-hour periods. Children's caloric intake over the course of a 24-hour period varied, on the average, by only about 10 percent (Birch et al. 1991; Birch 1993). Although these measurements were made in a relatively controlled laboratory school setting, similar patterns of

children's food intake have been observed in other less-controlled contexts (Shea et al. 1992).

More recent feeding studies have attempted to look at children's sensitivity to energy density within a meal and over the course of several meals. Instead of giving children a high- or low-energy density preload and assessing their later caloric compensation, these studies serve children with more and less energy-dense entrées within two separate lunch settings and assess whether caloric intakes during these lunches differ (Fisher, Liu et al. 2007; Leahy et al. 2008; Leahy, Birch, & Rolls 2008a; 2008b).

These studies have found that children *do* eat more calories when more energy dense foods are served, which contradicts earlier findings showing children are able to detect and adjust subsequent intake in response to more energy-dense foods. This discrepancy may be due to differences in study design, in that the later studies do not provide a delay between the consumption of a high- or low-energy density food and the subsequent meal; this delay may be important for allowing a child to register and detect energy density and satiety cues. But the energy density of foods served is only one component of a meal; more recent research has revealed that children also respond to other food characteristics, such as portion size.

Parents may serve children large portions of foods to ensure children have plenty to eat, or because they do not know what constitutes an age-appropriate portion for their child. Several studies have shown that when children are served larger portions of foods, they eat more food overall, despite not having differences in hunger before the meal or particular preference for the food.

In these studies, children were served different sized portions of a lunch entrée on different days; these entrées were typically amorphous foods such as macaroni and cheese, where increases in portion sizes are not obvious. When children were served larger portions, they consumed, on average, more of the entrée (in terms of both volume and calories) and did not eat less of other foods served at the meal (beverages and side dishes) to compensate for the increased entrée intake (Rolls, Engell, & Birch 2000; Fisher, Rolls, & Birch 2003; Fisher, Arreola et al. 2007). When these same children who ate more in response to larger portions were allowed to serve themselves, they took less food, as well as consumed significantly fewer calories, from both the entrée and the total meal (Fisher, Rolls, & Birch 2003).

It is quite plausible, and very likely given our current "obesigenic" food environment, that children may be presented with large portions of energy-dense foods. What happens when the effects of energy density and portion size are combined? A recent study found that these effects are independent but additive, in that children consume 76 percent more energy from the manipulated entrée and 34 percent more energy from the entire meal when a larger portion of a more energy-dense entrée was served (Fisher, Liu et al. 2007).

This mounting evidence that the ability to self-regulate energy intake during infancy may fade as soon as early childhood is likely due to an increasing number of environmental and psychological factors that influence—and even override—sensitivity to internal cues that tell us how much to eat. In today's food environment, where large portions of energy-dense foods are cheap and readily available, this observation (i.e., that people can lose sensitivity to internal satiety cues early in childhood) explains, at least in part, why rates of childhood obesity are on the rise.

Individual differences in the regulation of energy intake

Although a fair portion of children can be classified as overweight, there are also many children who are able to maintain a healthy weight. What distinguishes children who are not able to meet appropriate growth and weight standards from those who do?

An attempt has been made to characterize individual differences in children's ability to regulate energy intake and identify influences that result in these differences. Experimental work has focused on the individual child to determine the kinds of relationships that exist between a child's eating behaviors and his body fatness (Johnson & Birch 1994). Building on their previous work, Johnson and Birch investigated differences among children in their ability to respond to energy density cues. Using the same experimental procedure described above (i.e., children self-selected meals after either a high-calorie or a low-calorie preload) to investigate children's individual differences in self-regulation ability, these researchers also obtained information on the children's body fat stores by measuring height, weight, and skinfolds. Findings indicated that children's ability to regulate intake was related to their body fat stores: The children who showed less ability to regulate their energy intake had the greatest body fat stores (Johnson & Birch 1994). This indicates that a systematic relationship exists between children's ability to regulate energy intake, their eating styles, and their weight outcomes.

In a recent study of 5- to 11-year-old children's self-regulation of energy intake, Hispanic and non-Hispanic white children were found to have similar patterns of self-regulation as those found in the previous study; that is, children incompletely compensated for changes in energy density of the diet, and individual children varied greatly in the degree to which they self-regulated (Johnson & Taylor-Holloway 2006). Children's self-regulation of energy intake declined modestly with age; however, no differences were noted that related either to ethnicity or to gender. Therefore, it seems that many children maintain the capacity to self-regulate energy intake when the mealtime circumstances provide adequate opportunity to do so.

Individual differences in the accuracy of energy-intake regulation are probably due, at least to some extent, to genetic variability—that is, some genetic predisposition or familial similarity exists in patterns of body fatness and food-intake regulation, and these biological characteristics account for some portion of individual differences in body type (Keller et al. 2002). These predispositions can be shaped or altered by various environmental factors, including food availability; type and variety of foods consumed; and the more social aspects of feeding, such as parents' or caretakers' attitudes and behaviors related to food and eating.

How parents influence their children's eating behaviors

Research on parenting style and child development outcomes has revealed that authoritarian or rigid control over children's behavior is associated with unfavorable developmental outcomes (Baumrind 1973). When feeding-specific parenting styles are identified, similar observations are found. Specifically, an authoritarian style of feeding, in which eating demands placed on children are high and responsiveness to children's needs are low, is associated with child overeating and overweight (Hughes et al. 2005). Conversely, an authoritative style of feeding, characterized by high demands on eating behavior and also high responsiveness to eating cues, is associated with healthier child eating behaviors (Rhee et al. 2006).

Costanzo and Woody (1985) developed a model of domain-specific parenting, whereby they associated problematic outcomes in children with over-restrictiveness of the parent in a certain domain.

> **Restriction of children's access to foods can promote over-consumption of those foods when available in the absence of parental controls.**

They suggested that parents, motivated by concern for their children, are likely to impose more control over their children in areas of development that (1) they value highly, or (2) they believe their child may be especially at risk. Costanzo and Woody further suggested that parents' attempts to impose control inhibit the child's likelihood of developing *self*-regulation in that particular area of development.

Costanzo and Woody's model can be applied to the eating domain by considering the relationship between parents' child-feeding strategies and children's regulation of energy intake. Many parents impose rules and regulations related to eating that are both implicit and explicit. These rules include such practices as using foods to bribe and reward or making access to highly desirable foods contingent upon the consumption of less desirable ones ("If you finish your Brussels sprouts, I will give you a cookie"). They may also include restricting children's access to certain foods, such as highly palatable, energy-dense snack foods or desserts.

Evidence shows that use of rewards can systematically alter children's food preferences in directions incompatible with healthy diets. Excessive restriction of children's dietary intake tends to backfire: Restriction of children's access to and intake of foods can promote increased preference for those same foods as well as over-consumption of those foods when available in the absence of parental controls (Fisher & Birch 1999a; 1999b; Birch, Fisher, & Davison 2003; Faith et al. 2004).

Both encouragement and restriction of children's intakes as control strategies can also negatively affect children's food-acceptance patterns by decreasing children's ability to self-regulate energy intake.

When researchers instructed one group of children to focus on "cleaning their plates," or eating the amount of food remaining on the plate, these children were much less responsive to energy density cues than children who had been taught to focus on internal cues, such as feelings of hunger or fullness (Birch, McPhee, Shoba, Steinberg et al. 1987). A follow-up study conducted in the child care setting revealed similar findings: When children received information about hunger and satiety cues, their self-regulation of energy intake at mealtime improved. This improvement was noted both for children who were heavier and initially overate and for children who were thin and ate very little (Johnson 2000). Thus, in as much as caregiver feeding practices may sometimes derail children's acquisition of healthy eating behaviors, so, too, can positive feeding practices help to facilitate healthy eating.

Children of parents who report using more control over children's food intake, specifically more restriction of children's food intake, show greater tendencies to eat when not hungry if presented with highly palatable snack foods in the absence of external controls on intake (i.e., when left alone with the food) (Fisher & Birch 1999a). Eating in the absence of hunger is associated with higher energy intakes and higher weight status in children (Birch, Fisher, & Davison 2003), as well as greater weight gain across childhood (Francis et al. 2007). Together, these findings suggest that parental control exerted to regulate the quantity of food that children consume results in a decrease in development of the children's self-control of energy intake and ultimately, perhaps, in increases in children's amount of body fat.

Conclusions for child care providers

The current food environment in the United States is such that foods are readily available for most Americans, overcon-sumption is the most prevalent nutritional problem, and rates of overweight children have more than tripled in the last 20 years (Ogden et al. 2006). The ready availability of high-fat foods, their association with positive social contexts, and children's predisposition to learn to like high-fat and other high-energy foods may significantly contribute to this increased incidence of childhood obesity. The interaction between parents and children over food and feeding can either diminish or exacerbate children's responsiveness to hunger and satiety cues, as well as their food preferences and eating styles.

A primary responsibility of parents and caregivers is to ensure that children are healthy. Part of providing an optimal environment for growth and health is to make sure children get enough to eat and consume a wide variety of foods. Parents and caregivers establish standards or rules about food and eating, in part because they are concerned for children's welfare; these rules provide children with the tools and information necessary to gain an understanding of the importance of healthy eating.

Cuisine rules and rules of etiquette are necessary and positive when they provide the opportunity for children's learning and allow for the development of proper eating behaviors (Birch 1993). But when these strategies are overpowering—when they control but do not empower the child—they become problematic. Here are some specific child-feeding recommendations for parents and caregivers:

- Eat a varied diet during pregnancy and breastfeeding to ensure that the child experiences and becomes familiar with a wide variety of flavors.
- During the introduction of complementary foods, do not interpret children's initial rejection of a new food as a permanent dislike.
- When children first begin to try new foods, set clear and consistent expecta-

tions that foods will be explored and tasted when they are offered.

- Present a new food 10–15 times over the course of a couple of months to provide the child an opportunity to become familiar with it. Let the child be the one who then decides how much he or she would like to eat of a food.
- Do not coerce or pressure children into trying or consuming foods.
- Do not use food as a reward or offer children rewards for finishing foods.
- Model appropriate eating behaviors and food-acceptance patterns for children by sitting with them at mealtimes and by eating the same foods they eat.
- Make a wide variety of developmentally appropriate, nutrient-dense foods available to children at meals and snacks.
- Early on, trust children's ability to self-regulate their own energy intake. Adults should select the foods, and children should select the amounts consumed.
- Do not completely restrict foods; rather adopt an "everything in moderation" attitude and teach children to learn to make healthy food choices.
- Serve meals and snacks in appropriate eating environments. For example, avoid feeding children in cars (where choking becomes a hazard) or in strollers.
- Make sure children have appropriate child-sized utensils and serving dishes that facilitate their ability to feed themselves.
- Structure meals and snacks so that eating starts and stops. Continuous eating or stimulus to eat (offering food throughout the day or having food available at all times of the day) does not facilitate children's self-regulation

of eating. Children need to eat every 2–3 hours.

- Mealtime is a time of learning and part of the child care curriculum. Facilitate children's learning at mealtime by engaging children in conversation (e.g., language acquisition) and in social development (e.g., learning to share).

Research supports what informed parents and caregivers have been doing for the past 50 years: Assume responsibility for providing children with a variety of healthful foods in a positive social environment and then allow children the freedom to eat what they wish.

Updated from the Research in Review article in the January 1995 issue of *Young Children*.

Alison K. Ventura is a postdoctoral fellow at the Monell Chemical Senses Center. **Susan L. Johnson** is an early childhood nutritionist at the University of Colorado at Denver. **Leann L. Birch** is a professor at the Pennsylvania State University.

References

Addessi, E., A.T. Galloway, E. Visalberghi, & L. Birch. 2005. Specific social influences on the acceptance of novel foods in 2–5-year-old children. *Appetite* 45 (3): 264–71.

Batsell, W.R., Jr., A.S. Brown, M.E. Ansfield, & G.Y. Paschall. 2002. "You will eat all of that!": A retrospective analysis of forced consumption episodes, *Appetite* 38 (3): 211–19.

Baumrind, D. 1973. The development of instrumental competence through socialization. In *Minnesota symposia on child psychology*, vol. 7, Ed. A. Pick, 3–46. Minneapolis, MN: University of Minnesota Press.

Beauchamp, G.K., B.J. Cowart, J.A. Mennella, & R.R. Marsh. 1994. Infant salt taste: Developmental, methodological, and contextual factors. *Developmental Psychobiology* 27 (6): 353–65.

Birch, L.L. 1979. Dimensions of preschool children's food preferences. *Journal of Nutrition* 11 (2): 77–80.

Birch, L.L. 1980. Effects of peer models' food choices and eating behaviors on preschoolers' food preference. *Child Development* 51: 489–96.

Birch, L.L. 1993. Children's eating: Are manners enough? *The Journal of Gastronomy* 7 (1): 18–25.

Birch, L. L., & M. Deysher. 1985. Conditioned and unconditioned caloric compensation: Evidence for self-regulation of food intake by young children. *Learning and Motivation* 16: 341–55.

Birch, L.L., & M. Deysher. 1986. Caloric compensation and sensory specific satiety: Evidence for self regulation of food intake by young children. *Appetite* 7 (4): 323–31.

Birch, L.L., J.O. Fisher, & K.K. Davison. 2003. Learning to overeat: Maternal use of restrictive feeding practices promotes girls' eating in the absence of hunger. *American Journal of Clinical Nutrition* 78 (2): 215–20.

Birch, L.L., S.L. Johnson, G. Andresen, J.C. Peters, & M.C. Schulte. 1991. The variability of young children's energy intake. *New England Journal of Medicine* 324 (4): 232–35.

Birch, L.L., & D.W. Marlin. 1982. I don't like it; I never tried it: Effects of exposure on two-year-old children's food preferences. *Appetite* 3 (4): 353–60.

Birch, L.L., D.W. Marlin, & J. Rotter. 1984. Eating as the "means" activity in a contingency: Effects on young children's food preferences. *Child Development* 55: 432–39.

Birch, L.L., L. McPhee, B.C. Shoba, E. Pirok., & L. Sternberg. 1987. What kind of exposure reduces children's food neophobia? Looking vs. tasting. *Appetite* 9 (3): 171–78.

Birch, L.L., L. McPhee, B.C. Shoba, L. Sternberg, & R. Krehbiel. 1987. "Clean up your plate": Effects of child feeding practices on the conditioning of meal size. *Learning and Motivation* 18: 301–17.

Birch, L.L., L. McPhee, L. Sternberg, & S. Sullivan. 1990. Conditioned flavor preferences in young children. *Physiology & Behavior* 47 (3): 501–05.

Birch, L.L., L. McPhee, J.L. Bryant, & S.L. Johnson. 1993. Children's lunch intake: Effects of mid-morning snacks varying in energy density and fat content. *Appetite* 20 (2): 83–94.

Blissett, J., C. Meyer, C. Farrow, R. Bryant-Waugh, & D. Nicholls. 2005. Maternal core beliefs and children's feeding problems. *International Journal of Eating Disorders* 37 (2): 127–134.

Carper, J.L., J.O. Fisher, & L.L. Birch. 2000. Young girls' emerging dietary restraint and disinhibition are related to parental control in child feeding. *Appetite* 35 (2): 121–29.

Carruth, B.R., J. Skinner, K. Houck, J. Moran III, F. Coletta, & D. Ott. 1998. The phenomenon of "picky eater": A behavioral marker in eating patterns of toddlers. *Journal of the American College of Nutrition* 17 (2): 180–86.

Carruth, B.R., P.J. Ziegler, A. Gordon, & S.I. Barr. 2004. Prevalence of picky eaters among infants and toddlers and their caregivers' decisions about offering a new good. *Journal of the American Dietetic Association* 104 (1, Supplement 1): s57–64.

Constanzo, P., & E. Woody. 1985. Domain specific parenting styles and their impact on the child's development of particular deviance: The example of obesity proneness. *Journal of Social & Clinical Psychology* 3 (4): 425–45.

Cullen, K.W., T. Baranowski, L. Rittenberry, C. Cosart, D. Hebert, & C. de Moor. 2001. Child-reported family and peer influences on fruit, juice and vegetable consumption: Reliability and validity of measures. *Health Education Research* 16 (2): 187–200.

Davis, C.M. 1928. Self selection of diet by newly weaned infants: An experimental study. *American Journal of Diseases of Children* 36 (4): 651–79.

Davis, C.M. 1939. Results of self-selection of diets by young children. *Canadian Medical Association Journal* 41: 257–61.

Desor, J.A., O. Maller, & R.E. Turner. 1973. Taste in acceptance of sugars by human infants. *Journal of Comparative Physiology & Psychology* 84: 496–501.

Devaney, B., P. Ziegler, S. Pac, V. Karwe, & S.I. Barr. 2004. Nutrient intakes of infants and toddlers. *Journal of the American Dietetic Association* 104 (1, Supplement 1): s14–21.

Dewey, K.G., & B. Lonnerdal. 1986. Infant self-regulation of breast milk intake. *Acta Paediatrica Scandinavica* 75 (6): 893–98.

Faith, M.S., K.S. Scanlon, L.L. Birch, L.A. Francis, & B. Sherry. 2004. Parent-child feeding strategies and their relationships to child eating and weight status. *Obesity Research* 12 (11): 1711–22.

Fallon, A.E., P. Rozin, & P. Pliner. 1984. The child's conception of food: The development of food rejections with special reference to disgust and contamination sensitivity. *Child Development* 55 (2): 566–75.

Fisher, J.O., A. Arreola, L.L. Birch, & B.J. Rolls. 2007. Portion size effects on daily energy intake in low-income Hispanic and African American children and their mothers. *American Journal of Clinical Nutrition* 86 (6): 1709.

Fisher, J.O., & L.L. Birch. 1999a. Restricting access to foods and children's eating. *Appetite* 32 (3): 405–19.

Fisher, J.O., & L.L. Birch. 1999b. Restricting access to palatable foods affects children's behavioral response, food selection, and intake. *American Journal of Clinical Nutrition* 69 (6): 1264–72.

Fisher, J.O., Y. Liu, L.L. Birch, & B.J. Rolls. 2007. Effects of portion size and energy density on young children's intake at a meal. *American Journal of Clinical Nutrition* 86 (1): 174–79.

Fisher, J.O., D.C. Mitchell, H. Smiciklas-Wright, & L.L. Birch. 2002. Parental influences on young girls' fruit and vegetable, micronutrient, and fat intakes. *Journal of the American Dietetic Association* 102 (1): 58–64.

Fisher, J.O., B.J. Rolls, & L.L. Birch. 2003. Children's bite size and intake of an entree are greater with large portions than with age-appropriate or self-selected portions. *American Journal of Clinical Nutrition* 77 (5): 1164–70.

Fomon, S.J., L.J. Filer, Jr., L.N. Thomas, T.A. Anderson, & S.E. Nelson. 1975. Influence of formula concentration on caloric intake and growth of normal infants. *Acta Pediatrica Scandinavica* 64 (2): 172–81.

Fox, M.K., S. Pac, B. Devaney, & L. Jankowski. 2004. Feeding infants and toddlers study: What foods are infants and toddlers eating? *Journal of the American Dietetic Association* 104 (1, Supplement 1): s22–30.

Francis, L.A., A.K. Ventura, M. Marini, & L.L. Birch. 2007. Parent overweight predicts daughters' increase in BMI and disinhibited overeating from 5 to 13 years. *Obesity (Silver Spring)* 15 (6): 1544–53.

Galloway, A.T., L. Fiorito, Y. Lee, & L.L. Birch. 2005. Parental pressure, dietary patterns, and weight status among girls who are "picky eaters." *Journal of the American Dietetic Association* 105 (4): 541–48.

Galloway, A.T., Y. Lee, & L.L. Birch. 2003. Predictors and consequences of food neophobia and pickiness in young girls. *Journal of the American Dietetic Association* 103 (6): 692–98.

Gallup Organization, The. 1995. *Food, physical activity and fun: What kids think.* Chicago: American Dietetic Association, National Center for Nutrition and Dietetics.

Hendy, H.M. 2002. Effectiveness of trained peer models to encourage food acceptance in preschool children. *Appetite* 39 (3): 217–25.

Hendy, H.M., & B. Raudenbush. 2000. Effectiveness of teacher modeling to encourage food acceptance in preschool children. *Appetite* 34 (1): 61–76.

Hetherington, M.M., R. Foster, T. Newman, A.S. Anderson, & G. Norton. 2006. Understanding variety: Tasting different foods delays satiation. *Physiology & Behavior* 87 (2): 263–71.

Hughes, S.O., T.G. Power, J.O. Fisher, S. Mueller, & T.A. Nicklas. 2005. Revisiting a neglected construct: Parenting styles in a child-feeding context. *Appetite* 44 (1): 83–92.

Johnson, S.L. 2000. Improving preschoolers' self-regulation of energy intake. *Pediatrics* 106 (6): 1429–35.

Johnson, S.L., L. Bellows, L. Beckstrom, & J. Anderson. 2007. Evaluation of a social marketing campaign targeting preschool children. *American Journal of Health Behavior* 31 (1): 44–55.

Johnson, S.L., & L.L. Birch. 1994. Parents' and children's adiposity and eating style. *Pediatrics* 94 (5): 653–61.

Johnson, S.L., L. McPhee, & L.L. Birch. 1991. Conditioned preferences: Young children prefer flavors associated with high dietary fat. *Physiology & Behavior* 50 (6): 1245–51.

Johnson, S.L., & L.A. Taylor-Holloway. 2006. Non-Hispanic white and Hispanic elementary school children's self-regulation of energy intake. *American Journal of Clinical Nutrition* 83 (6): 1276–82.

Keller, K.L., A. Pietrobelli, S.L. Johnson, & M.S. Faith. 2006. Maternal restriction of children's eating and encouragements to eat as the "non-shared environment": A pilot study using the child feeding questionnaire. *International Journal of Obesity (London)* 30 (11): 1670–75.

Keller, K.L., A. Pietrobelli, S. Must, & S.M. Faith. 2002. Genetics of eating and its relation to obesity. *Curr Atheroscler Rep* 4 (3): 176–82.

Kern, D.L., L. McPhee, J.O. Fisher, S.L. Johnson, & L.L. Birch. 1993. The postingestive consequences of fat condition preferences for flavors associated with high dietary fat. *Physiology & Behavior* 54 (1): 71–76.

Leahy, K.E., L.L. Birch, J.O. Fisher & B.J. Rolls. 2008. Reductions in entree energy density increase children's vegetable intake and reduce energy intake. *Obesity (Silver Spring)* 16 (7): 1559–65.

Leahy, K.E., L.L. Birch, & B.J. Rolls. 2008a. Reducing the energy density of an entree decreases children's energy intake at lunch. *Journal of the American Diet Association* 108 (1): 41–48.

Leahy, K.E., L.L. Birch, & B.J. Rolls. 2008b. Reducing the energy density of multiple meals decreases the energy intake of preschool-age children. *American Journal of Clinical Nutrition* 88 (9): 1459–69.

Mennella, J.A., & G.K. Beauchamp. 1991. Maternal diet alters the sensory qualities of human milk and the nursling's behavior. *Pediatrics* 88 (4): 737–44.

Mennella, J.A., & G.K. Beauchamp. 1999. Experience with a flavor in mother's milk modifies the infant's acceptance of flavored cereal. *Developmental Psychobiology* 35 (3): 197–203.

Mennella, J.A., & G.K. Beauchamp. 2002. Flavor experiences during formula feeding are related to preferences during childhood. *Early Human Development* 68 (2): 71–82.

Mennella, J.A., C.E. Griffin, & G.K. Beauchamp. 2004. Flavor programming during infancy. *Pediatrics* 113 (4): 840–45.

Mennella, J.A., C.P. Jagnow, & G.K. Beauchamp. 2001. Prenatal and postnatal flavor learning by human infants. *Pediatrics* 107 (6): E88.

Mennella, J.A., J.M. Kennedy, & G.K. Beauchamp. 2006. Vegetable acceptance by infants: Effects of formula flavors. *Early Human Development* 82 (7): 463–68.

Mennella, J.A., B. Turnbull, P.J. Ziegler, & H. Martinez. 2005. Infant feeding practices and early flavor experiences in Mexican infants: An intracultural study. *Journal of the American Dietetic Association* 105 (6): 908–15.

Newman, J., & A. Taylor. 1992. Effect of a means-end contingency on young children's food preferences. *Journal of Experimental Child Psychology* 53 (2): 200–16.

Ogden, C.L., M.D. Carroll, L.R. Curtin, M.A. McDowell, C.J. Tabak, & K.M. Flegal. 2006. Prevalence of overweight and obesity in the United States, 1999–2004. *Journal of the American Medical Association* 295 (13): 1549–55.

Pliner, P., M. Pelchat, & M. Grabski. 1993. Reduction of neophobia in humans by exposure to novel foods. *Appetite* 20 (2): 111–23.

Princeton Survey Research Associates. 1997. *State of the union mother's day poll*. Dayton, OH: Roper Center, University of Connecticut.

Rhee, K.E., J.C. Lumeng, D.P. Appugliese, N. Kaciroti, & R.H. Bradley. 2006. Parenting styles and overweight status in first grade. *Pediatrics* 117 (6): 2047–54.

Rolls, B.J., D. Engell, & L.L. Birch. 2000. Serving portion size influences 5-year-old but not 3-year-old children's food intakes. *Journal of the American Dietetic Association* 100 (2): 232–34.

Shea, S., A.D. Stein, C.E. Basch, I.R. Contento, & P. Zybert. 1992. Variability and self-regulation of energy intake in young children in their everyday environment. *Pediatrics* 90 (4): 542–46.

Sigman-Grant, M., E. Christiansen, L. Branen, J. Fletcher, & S.L. Johnson. 2008. About feeding children: Mealtimes in childcare centers in four western states. *Journal of the American Dietetic Association* 108: 340–46.

Steiner, J.E. 1977. Facial expressions of the neonate infant indicating the hedonics of food related chemical stimuli. In *Taste and development: The genesis of sweet preference*, ed. J.M. Weiffenbach. Washington, DC: U.S. Government Printing Office.

Steiner, J.E., D. Glaser, M.E. Hawilo, & K.C. Berridge. 2001. Comparative expression of hedonic impact: Affective reactions to taste by human infants and other primates. *Neuroscience and Biobehavioral Reviews* 25 (1): 53–74.

Sullivan, S.A., & L.L. Birch. 1990. Pass the sugar, pass the salt: Experience dictates preference. *Developmental Psychology* 26: 546–51.

Sullivan, S.A., & L.L. Birch. 1994. Infant dietary experience and acceptance of solid foods. *Pediatrics* 93: 271–277.

Wardle, J., L.J. Cooke, E.L. Gibson, M. Sapochnik, A. Sheiham, & M. Lawson. 2003. Increasing children's acceptance of vegetables: A randomized trial of parent-led exposure. *Appetite* 40 (2): 155–62.

Wardle, J., M.L. Herrera, L. Cooke, & E.L. Gibson. 2003. Modifying children's food preferences: The effects of exposure and reward on acceptance of an unfamiliar vegetable. *European Journal of Clinical Nutrition* 57 (2): 341–48.

Young, E.M., S.W. Fors., & D.M. Hayes. 2004. Associations between perceived parent behaviors and middle school student fruit and vegetable consumption. *Journal of Nutrition Education & Behavior* 36 (1): 2–8.

Part V

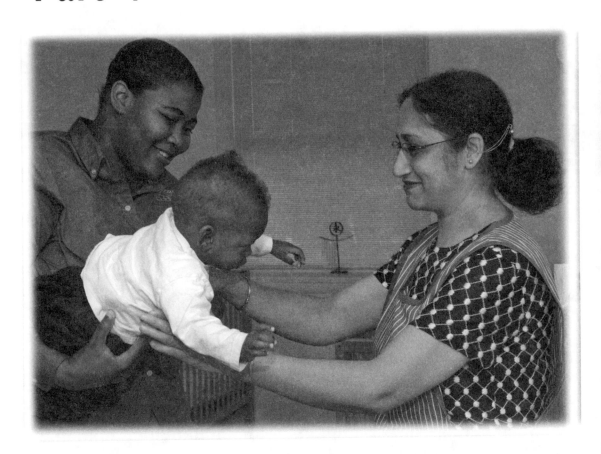

Influences on Development

Introduction

The previous sections of this book have dealt with young children's development by isolating the social, emotional, cognitive and linguistic, and physical domains. But development does not occur in isolation; children's development in one domain influences and is influenced by what takes place in the other domains. Moreover, research provides ample evidence that the trajectory of development is as much the product of external factors as of inborn, genetic forces. This section considers some of these other influences on children's development, including family, socioeconomic status, culture and ethnicity, and disability. These chapters provide an overview of the importance of various outside factors both on young children's development and on programs that serve young children in order to increase awareness and understanding that development does not occur in a vacuum, free from cultural context.

Douglas Powell provides an updated version of his 1998 research review, "Reweaving Parents into the Fabric of Early Childhood Programs." In collaboration with Patrick O'Leary, Dr. Powell's new chapter, **"Strengthening Relations Between Parents and Early Childhood Programs,"** offers new insights from recent research into the importance and potential impact of strong parent-teacher ties, as well as practical ideas

for how early childhood programs can strengthen their relationships with families. The authors define modes of parent involvement by citing and referring to the standards set by the National Parent Teacher Association (PTA). There is not much research on the extent of parent involvement in early childhood programs or on the effects on children's development; however, existing research has confirmed the existence of concurrent and long-term, positive effects on children's language, motor, and daily living skills, as well as school achievement when parents are involved. This chapter provides an important reminder for early childhood professionals that family involvement plays a significant role in young children's development and underscores the importance of efforts to improve parent involvement in early childhood settings.

Frances Campbell and Karen Taylor provide an update of their 1996 article, **"Early Childhood Programs That Work for Economically Disadvantaged Children."** In particular, the authors offer reviews of the latest information from several longitudinal studies that have followed young children from low-income families enrolled in model early childhood programs into their adult years. The chapter provides updates from several research projects that have continued to follow their subjects, including the Perry

Preschool Program, the Chicago Child-Parent Center and Expansion Program, the Abecedarian and CARE studies, and the Infant Health and Development Program. In addition, the authors review new analyses of Head Start findings that consider longitudinal benefits from early intervention programs in adulthood. A public understanding of the value of early intervention initiatives is essential if advocacy efforts are going to maintain support for such programs. The updated research in this chapter provides early childhood professionals with data-based support for arguments to reinforce the importance of early intervention for at-risk children.

Two chapters in this volume consider the role of culture, ethnicity, and home language in young children's development. Lynn Okagaki and Karen Diamond provide an updated chapter, titled **"Cultural and Linguistic Differences in Families with Young Children: Implications for Early Childhood Teachers,"** which expands on their 2000 research review. The authors begin their chapter with the most recent statistics about the growing number of children from diverse ethnic, cultural, and linguistic backgrounds who enter early childhood programs in the United States. They focus on how cultural values and beliefs are reflected in parents' expectations for their children, noting that such expectations may be different from those of the teachers, and they caution teachers not to assume that everyone shares the same ideas about good behavior and performance. The chapter provides updated research and strategies for early childhood professionals working with diverse populations of children.

The refreshed version of Eugene García's 1997 research review, **"The Education of Hispanics in Early Childhood: Of Roots and Wings,"** examines the cultural and linguistic contexts of Hispanic children, who have become the largest single cultural subgroup in America. In the last decade, the number of Hispanic children in early education programs has increased by nearly 300 percent. This substantive increase has been coupled with continued advance-

ments in research, policy, and practice with regard to the education of this group of children. García makes a strong case for high-quality, universal early childhood programs as a way of improving academic outcomes for young Hispanic children, since research shows a correlation between early academic achievement and success in later schooling. The chapter provides early childhood professionals with a number of recommendations for working with Hispanic children and their families, as well as recommendations for larger policy changes that would help Hispanic children have successful experiences in early childhood and beyond.

The final chapter in this section is a new version of Karen Diamond, Linda Hestenes, and Caryn O'Connor's 1994 article, "Integrating Young Children with Disabilities in Preschool: Problems and Promise." The current chapter, retitled **"Including Young Children with Disabilities in Preschool: Moving Forward from 1994,"** was authored by Karen Diamond, Linda Hestenes, Swetha Chakravarthi, and Linlin Li. The authors note that questions raised in the earlier article about the appropriateness of inclusion are no longer as relevant as they were in the 1990s; a substantial body of research shows that inclusion is effective for both children with disabilities and their non-disabled peers. The chapter provides early childhood professionals with suggestions for effective instructional strategies, particularly activity-based intervention, which is intended to help children develop skills that are functional and that can be generalized to other situations.

All the chapters in this section provide an overview of topics relevant to the development of young children in early childhood settings. They underscore the importance of recognizing outside influences on children's development. Considering children's development in the contexts within which it occurs, and understanding the importance of outside factors that influence development will help early childhood professionals to understand children better as individuals.

16 Strengthening Relations Between Parents and Early Childhood Programs

Douglas R. Powell and Patrick M. O'Leary

Imagine an early childhood program as a woven fabric made of three different colors of threads representing children, parents, and staff. A common pattern weaves the child and staff threads together, but most or all of the parent threads are woven into a separate section as a parent involvement component.

A pattern in which parent threads are interwoven throughout the fabric, representing a more inclusive program approach to working with parents, is increasingly viewed as a better design. Or in a refinement of this pattern, the separate child and parent threads are replaced by a *family* thread that is interwoven with staff threads; in this pattern, programs are meant to work with children *and* parents within their family contexts.

The latter designs reflect current recommended practices in early childhood programs by major professional organizations. The National Association for the Education of Young Children (NAEYC) calls for programs to support close ties between child and family and to view children in the context of family, culture, and society. Program goals are to be developed in collaboration with families, and program staff are to learn about each child through relationships with the child's family (Copple & Bredekamp 2009).

Similarly, the NAEYC position paper on responding to linguistic and cultural diversity recommends that teachers become familiar with the child's community (NAEYC 1996). The NAEYC Code of Ethical Conduct and Statement of Commitment emphasizes ideals and principles that focus on mutual trust as well as respect for family child-rearing values and decision-making rights (NAEYC 2005). Further, the Division for Early Childhood of the Council for Exceptional Children specifies that families are to be equal to professionals in formulating decisions about a child's program of care and education (Sandall, McLean, & Smith 2000).

The basic themes of these recommendations—collaborating with parents and working within family contexts—are major modifications of the professionally driven parent education tradition that has dominated the field's approach to parent-teacher relations for most of the 20th century, and of the "child saver" view that early childhood programs are a compensation for deficient home environments (Powell & Diamond 1995). The image of early childhood programs as family support systems that function as modern-day versions of the traditional extended family has been evolving over the past three decades (e.g., Galinsky & Hooks 1977). The reconfiguration of parental roles in early childhood programs has also been part of an international trend toward increased parent involvement in early childhood programs (Cochran 1993; Olmsted & Weikart 1994).

Many factors are driving recent recommendations for closer ties between families and early childhood programs. Collaborative parent-staff relations have been advocated from the perspective of parental rights, parent empowerment, and program responsiveness to family values and cultural traditions. Ecological views of children and families—well captured by the proverb, "It takes a whole village to raise a child"—have been influential. Attention to differences across families and communities in parent and child experiences has increased understanding of how poverty, race, ethnicity, family structure and transitions, parental age, and other contexts interact with children's development. A challenging yet achievable task for early childhood programs is accommodating and supporting a wide range of parenting circumstances. Research spanning some 35 years on what parents gain from Head Start, for example, points to more positive parent-child interactions in teaching interactions and more parental involvement in children's later schooling (Pizzo & Tufankjian 2004).

In addition to the developments just discussed, sweeping social changes in the United States have shaped current ideas about relationships between families and early childhood programs. The growing ethnic, racial, and cultural diversity of the population increases the chances that children will be cared for by adults whose expectations and practices differ from those of the child's family members. Further, profound demographic and economic changes have led to concerns about the adequacy of support systems for families (Bronfenbrenner & Morris 2006).

This chapter reviews recent research that offers guidance on how early childhood programs might strengthen ties with parents. It examines dimensions of parent-teacher partnerships, identifies parent characteristics and circumstances that contribute to parent participation in programs, and recommends provisions that would enable programs to work closely with parents.

Dimensions of parent-teacher partnerships

Parent-teacher partnerships are multidimensional. They include different modes of parent involvement in the life of an early childhood program, parent-teacher communication, and agreement on goals for and practices with a child.

Modes of parent involvement

The standards developed by the National Parent Teacher Association (1997) for parent involvement in schools are applicable to early childhood programs. Based on a widely used typology of family-school relationships (Epstein & Sanders 2002), the PTA standards include the following:

- communication between home and school is regular, two-way, and meaningful;
- parenting skills are promoting and supported;
- parents play an integral role in assisting student learning;
- parents are welcome in schools, and their support and assistance are sought;
- parents are full partners in school decisions that affect children and families; and

• outreach is done in the community for resources to strengthen schools.

The extent to which early childhood programs provide and parents pursue these opportunities is mostly unknown. Some information is available on parent involvement in the federal Head Start program, which has long embraced parent involvement as a program cornerstone (Zigler & Muenchow 1992). Studies consistently indicate there is considerable variability across parents in levels of program participation. For example, Head Start's Family and Child Experiences Survey (FACES), which is based on a sample of 40 randomly selected U.S. programs, shows that in 2001, 70 percent of parents participated in parent-teacher conferences, 75 percent observed in their children's classrooms for at least 30 minutes, 69 percent met with a Head Start staff member in their homes, 60 percent volunteered in their child's classroom, and 58 percent prepared food or materials for special events. However, less than half helped with field trips (42 percent), attended social events (42 percent) and workshops (42 percent), or participated in policy councils (22 percent) (Tarullo & O'Brien 2002).

Whether the modes of parent involvement included in the PTA standards individually or collectively contribute to improved outcomes for children has received minimal research attention in preschool programs (Henrich & Blackman-Jones 2006). A study of 708 preschoolers and their parents found that more parent involvement (i.e., attending conferences, class participation) in public preschool programs and Head Start was positively linked to children's achievement. Children of parents with higher levels of involvement in their child's education made significantly greater gains in receptive vocabulary, personal and community daily living skills, coping skills, and fine motor skills (Marcon 1999).

Research evidence also points to long-term effects of parent involvement on children's school achievement. The Chicago Longitudinal Study found parent participation in preschool and kindergarten to be positively related to their children's reading achievement at age 14. Parent participation in the early years of school was also associated with lower rates of grade retention and special education placement through the eighth grade (Meidel & Reynolds 1999).

Communication

Communication is at the core of supportive connections between families and early childhood programs. Studies point to benefits of frequent parent-teacher communication for children. Positive teacher-child interactions are more likely when there is open communication between teachers and parents. Owen and colleagues found that when teachers and parents reported higher levels of seeking and sharing information about the child (i.e., teachers asking about home, parents asking about school), interactions between teachers and children were observed to be more sensitive, supportive, and stimulating (Owen, Ware, & Barfoot 2000). This supports the notion that high-quality caregiving is based in part on the teacher's knowledge of the child's behaviors in settings other than schools.

Parent-staff communication is an obvious challenge when there are language barriers. For example, more than one half of directors and one third of the teaching staff in a study of 92 California child care centers reported difficulty communicating with parents due to language barriers. Relatively few of these centers employed teachers who spoke the same language as minority children enrolled in the center (Whitebook, Sakai, & Howes 1997). In these situations, translators are necessary for an equitable relationship between families and their early childhood pro-

Studies found that how satisfied mothers were with their child care arrangement was unrelated to the actual quality.

grams. Ideally, programs should provide translators, but often such resources are spread thin. Okagaki and Diamond (2009, elsewhere in this volume) suggested asking the families to provide translators (i.e., family members or friends who speak English) if the school can not consistently provide one.

More generally, it is the teacher's responsibility to know her students, their families, and their various backgrounds and histories. Teachers should share their own values and experiences and should encourage parents to do the same. At the same time, teachers should remember that even when linguistic minority families speak English, the amount of speech heard in the home, how it is employed, and what is linguistically expected of the child may differ from the classroom's communication style. In these cases, language can also reveal cultural differences between families and classrooms (Okagaki & Diamond 2009).

Agreement on goals and practices

An important goal of communication between parents and early childhood program staff is to move toward agreement on teaching and caregiving practices for the child. Many early childhood educators approach this topic with concerns about how well parents really understand what makes up a high-quality environment for young children. Do parents adequately understand, for example, the value of learning through play and other child-initiated activities, as encompassed in developmentally appropriate practice?

Research findings lend support to these concerns at a general level. Many parents believe a good early childhood setting uses didactic methods such as

rote memorization, drill, and practice (for reviews, see Dunn & Kontos 1997; Powell 2001). Preference for didactic program experiences can be found among parents of all economic strata, but it is more widespread among lower-income and minority populations (Hyson et al. 1991; Stipek et al. 1992; Sonnenschein et al. 2000).

Research on a national sample also indicates that parents give greater emphasis than kindergarten teachers do to kindergarten readiness skills, such as being able to count to 20 or above and knowing the letters of the alphabet (West, Hausken, & Collins 1993). In a study of mostly Hispanic and African-American parents of preschool children in an urban school district, a higher percentage of parents than preschool teachers indicated that basic knowledge (e.g., knows ABCs) and advanced knowledge (e.g., knows own address/telephone) were "absolutely necessary" for kindergarten (Piotrowski, Botsko, & Matthews 2000).

Another set of studies indicates that parents often are satisfied with the quality of an early childhood setting that experts judge to be low or mediocre (for a review, see Powell 1997). One study found that even though parents said they placed high importance on many of the program quality criteria recommended by experts, in reality they placed their children in centers that generally did not fare well on these criteria, and parents overestimated the quality of the care their children received (Cryer & Burchinal 1997). Other studies found that how satisfied mothers were with their child care arrangement was unrelated to the actual quality of that arrangement as assessed by independent experts using common professional criteria, whether it was family child care (Kontos et al. 1995) or center care (Clarke-Stewart, Gruber, & Fitzgerald 1994).

It is unlikely that parents' preferences for didactic (or nondidactic) program experiences or their limited understandings of child care quality as measured by experts are widespread sources of serious difficulty for individual parent-staff relationships. Studies indicate that parents tend to select providers and programs that conform to their images of appropriate experiences for young children.

For example, Stipek and colleagues (1992) found that parents who enrolled their children in preschool and kindergarten programs that emphasized academics rated basic skills acquisition as more important than did parents who enrolled their children in programs that emphasized play and other nondidactic activities. Parents' beliefs about how children learn basic skills were also strongly associated with their choice of program. Further, parents who believed in didactic instruction also reported engaging in more formal than informal learning activities at home (Stipek et al. 1992; see also Hyson et al. 1991; Clarke-Stewart, Gruber, & Fitzgerald 1994). These findings do not mean there are no problems in congruence between parents' and providers' preferred program approaches to working with young children. It is common for one or more parents to have fundamental disagreements with the general pedagogical practices of a program or provider.

Probably of greater importance in parent-staff agreement about program practices is whether parent and staff share similar goals for a particular child. Theoretical arguments indicate that children's development is enhanced when parents and other primary caregivers such as teachers agree on the types of experiences and outcomes to promote for a child (Bronfenbrenner 1979). Although few studies have been conducted on this topic, research on an economically and ethnically diverse school-age population suggests there is value in parents and teachers holding similar views of the child's competence and classroom experiences.

At a dyadic level of analysis, mother-teacher congruence in perceptions of the child's developmental competence and classroom engagement at school were significant correlates of children's academic achievement in the early elementary school grades (Peet, Powell, & O'Donnel 1997). It is unclear from this study whether a child's positive outcomes stemmed from the parent and teacher sharing similar perceptions of the child and/or from the adults creating appropriately responsive and complementary environments for the child in both settings. An alternative explanation for the association is that the child's behaviors may have provided similar cues to parents and teachers about overall competence, thereby leading mothers and teachers to independently form congruent views of the same child (Peet, Powell, & O'Donnel 1997).

Responsive engagement

Across all populations and programs, a major challenge is to develop ways of engaging parents that respond to a family's interests and life circumstances. There is potential benefit in marshaling resources that speak to parents as people and also to a broad range of family topics, recognizing the role of parent beliefs in participation decisions and maximizing opportunities to interact with parents on an individual basis.

Accommodating family differences

Responsive engagement of parents begins with an understanding of family contexts that influence relations with early childhood programs. Major factors here include family characteristics, including stressors, and parents' beliefs about contributions to their child's education.

Studies show that parents' employment and marital status are associated with participation in early childhood programs. A study of four Head Start programs in a southeastern state found that employed parents were less likely to volunteer in program activities than parents who were not employed (Castro et al. 2004). Parents' education level also was positively related to higher levels of participation in school activities (Fantuzzo, Tighe, & Childs 2000). Another study in a large urban school district found higher rates of communication with the teacher (e.g., talk with teacher about child's accomplishments) but not higher participation in program involvement activities (e.g., volunteer in child's classroom) among married parents. In addition, married parents and parents who are not employed have been found to be more satisfied with their teacher contact than single parents and parents who are employed full time (Fantuzzo, Perry, & Childs 2006).

Not surprisingly, family stress factors serve as significant barriers to family-program partnerships. A study of mostly African-American parents in two Head Start programs found that economic stress and neighborhood social disorder were negatively related to parent involvement (Waanders, Mendez, & Downer 2007). In a study of Head Start families in New York City, the two most frequently reported barriers to Head Start participation were having a schedule that conflicted with Head Start activities and having a baby or toddler at home. Other barriers included housing difficulties (e.g., lack of heat, hot water) and having children with a disability or behavioral problem. Mothers reporting a higher number of possible barriers to program participation had less involvement in the Head Start program than mothers reporting fewer barriers (Lamb-Parker et al. 2001).

In addition to family characteristics and circumstances, it is useful for programs to consider parental beliefs about involvement in their child's education. Well designed school opportunities and in-

centives for parent involvement may have only limited success if they do not also address parents' ideas about their role in children's education and parents' sense of efficacy for helping their children succeed in school.

Hoover-Dempsey and Sandler (1997) reached this conclusion in a review of research literature on parent involvement. They proposed three factors as central to parents' decisions to become involved in their children's formal education: (1) parents' construction of the parental role ("What am I supposed to do in relation to my child's education and educational progress?"); (2) parents' sense of efficacy for helping their child succeed in school ("Can I exert a positive influence on my child's educational outcomes?"); and (3) invitations, demands, and opportunities for parent involvement ("Do both my child and the school want me to be involved?"). A recent study found these parental motivations for involvement in their child's education to be associated with actual involvement during elementary and middle school years (Green et al. 2007). One recent study conducted in two Head Start programs found that parents' sense of efficacy was predictive of parent involvement (Waanders, Mendez, & Downer 2007). But more research is needed at the early childhood level.

Initiatives to support families

Locally developed responses to the family characteristics and circumstances cited above offer the best promise of maximizing opportunities for fostering meaningful connections between parents and early childhood programs. Finding times to meet with parents that accommodate work and family schedules, for example, is most appropriately determined in collaboration with parents. And it may be useful for program staff to reflect on whether biases about single parents are implicitly communicated to families (Kontos & Dunn 1989).

It is useful for programs to consider parental beliefs about involvement in their child's education.

Responses to family stressors also may warrant additional programming. One model of how early childhood programs can provide supportive services to families is the Parent Services Project (Link, Beggs, & Seiderman 1997). The project began in the San Francisco Bay area and has been adopted by many programs nationally. A longitudinal study of the project found that program parents had lower levels of stress than parents in a nonequivalent comparison group (Stein & Haggard 1990).

The project views early childhood programs as a natural means of serving entire families through activities that seek to ease family stress (Link, Beggs, & Seiderman 1997). The model calls for a local parent committee to set policies, plan activities, and allocate funds; some programs employ a parent time coordinator. There is not a predetermined curriculum: Each program generates activities tailored to the interests of the parents in the program. Activities might include practical skills workshops (e.g., car repair, stress reduction), family outings with children, adult social events without children, or peer support groups.

Enabling provisions

The task of "reweaving" parents into the life of an early childhood program requires conceptual and structural provisions that enable all staff to maintain meaningful connections with families.

Early childhood programs serve families, not children alone. All policies and practices, no matter how large or small, should undergo a two-part family impact test: How does this policy or practice impact families? How does this policy or practice genuinely incorporate information from or direct involvement of family members?

Program practices for relating to parents must be in tune with widespread demographic changes, especially the characteristics and circumstances of families being served by the program. Methods of working with parents should be "locally grown" and shaped by the expressed preferences and needs of families. One size does not fit all. Programs need to work toward employing staff who speak the languages of the families served, and all staff need a respectful understanding of the values and traditions represented among families.

Parent and teacher confidence in each other is the foundation of healthy relationships. Parents want firm assurances that child care providers and teachers are skilled, knowledgeable, and caring individuals. Are there varied and frequent opportunities for parents to get to know staff? Conversely, staff confidence in parents seems to focus heavily on judgments about parenting competence, including attitudes toward mothers who work outside the home. Staff confidence in parents' perceived child-rearing abilities is an element of the parent-teacher relationship (Elicker et al. 1997). Staff training should help strengthen skills in taking family perspectives and identifying parent strengths.

Relations with parents should be individualized in a way that informs staff understandings of and work with each child. Communication must be frequent, personal, and consistent with a child's primary teacher or caregiver. What is the availability of staff when parents are most likely to be present, especially at drop-off and pickup times? Is there assignment of a primary teacher who knows the child well and takes responsibility for daily communication with parents? Are there informal or formal procedures in place to facilitate the development of shared goals for a child? There is great potential in developing or using tools that systematically lead to shared parent-staff goals for a child (see, e.g., Murphy 1997). The development of shared goals helps staff understand and respect each child's family and contributes to staff confidence in the parents because there is agreement on program practices.

Programs should actively acknowledge parents as people. Many roles and aspects of daily life influence parenting. Model programs described in this article offer innovative ways for early childhood programs to address a range of adult interests, especially when parents define their own needs. More generally, what might happen to staff views of parents if staff were encouraged to find alternatives to referring to a particular parent as someone's mother or father?

Parent beliefs about *whether* to participate may be as important as basic supports that facilitate participation in meetings and other activities. Basic supports, such as providing onsite child care while parents are attending meetings, are essential. But research suggests that also central to parents' decisions about participation are their beliefs about their parenting role, the chances of having a positive impact on their child's education, and perceptions of whether a program is interested in their involvement. What sincere and clear messages do programs give to parents about the role they play in their child's life and in the life of their child's early childhood program?

Definitions and assessments of the quality of an early childhood program need to give greater attention to parent perspectives and to program practices with parents and families. Existing definitions of quality have been developed with little regard for parent perspectives (Larner 1996), and widely used tools for assessing program quality give scant attention to relations with parents (Raab & Dunst 1997). Parents consider how an early childhood program arrangement will mesh with family life and resources; their concerns encompass a broader set of considerations than typically included in quality criteria focused on the program setting.

Professional education and credentials should promote skills in relating to parents. The currently weak attention to teachers' demonstrated skills in relating to parents must be strengthened in professional education and state certification requirements. It appears that, among the many competencies required for effective work the parents, special emphasis should be given to skills in learning and appreciating the perspectives of families.

This review suggests that teachers' collaborative relations with parents and work within a family context do not come about naturally or easily. There are numerous challenges at multiple levels. Fortunately, research findings and lessons from model programs offer promising directions for widespread implementation of recommended practices that, in essence, call for a new era in the early childhood field's approaches to families.

Updated from the Research in Review article in the September 1998 issue of *Young Children*.

Douglas R. Powell is a professor at Purdue University. **Patrick M. O'Leary** is a doctoral candidate at Purdue University.

References

Bronfenbrenner, U. 1979. *The ecology of human development: Experiments by nature and design.* Cambridge, MA: Harvard University Press.

Bronfenbrenner, U., & P.A. Morris. 2006. The bioecological model of human development. In *Handbook of child psychology, vol. 1: Theoretical models of human development*, 6th ed., ed. R.M. Lerner, 793–828. Hoboken, NJ: John Wiley & Sons.

Castro, D.C., D.M. Bryant, E.S. Peisner-Feinberg, & M.L. Skinner. 2004. Parent involvement in Head Start programs: The role of parent, teacher and classroom characteristics. *Early Childhood Research Quarterly* 19: 413–30.

Clarke-Stewart, K.A., C.P. Gruber, & L.M. Fitzgerald. 1994. *Children at home and in day care.* Hillsdale, NJ: Lawrence Erlbaum.

Cochran, M. 1993. Public child care, culture, and society: Crosscutting themes. In *International handbook of child care policies and programs*, ed. M. Cochran, 627–58. Westport, CT: Greenwood.

Copple, C., & S. Bredekamp, eds. 2009. *Developmentally appropriate practice in early childhood programs serving children from birth through age 8*. 3d ed. Washington, DC: NAEYC.

Cryer, D., & M. Burchinal. 1997. Parents as child care consumers. *Early Childhood Research Quarterly* 12: 35–58.

Dunn, L., & S. Kontos. 1997. What have we learned about developmentally appropriate practice? *Young Children* 52 (5): 4–13.

Elicker, J., I.C. Noppe, L.D. Noppe, & C. Fortner-Wood. 1997. The parent-caregiver relationship scale: Rounding out the relationship system in infant child care. *Early Education and Development* 8: 83–100.

Epstein, J., & M.G. Sanders. 2002. Family, school, and community partnerships. In *Handbook of parenting*, 2d ed., ed. M. Bornstein, 407–37.

Fantuzzo, J., M.A. Perry, & S. Childs. 2006. Parent satisfaction with educational experiences scale: A multivariate examination of parent satisfaction with early childhood programs. *Early Childhood Research Quarterly* 21: 142–52.

Fantuzzo, J., E. Tighe, & S. Childs. 2000. Family involvement questionnaire: Amultivariate assessment of family participation in early childhood education. *Journal of Educational Psychology* 92: 367–76.

Galinsky, E., & W.H. Hooks. 1977. *The new extended family: Day care that works*. Boston: Houghton Mifflin.

Green, C.L., M.J.T. Walker, K.V. Hoover-Dempsey, & H.M. Sandler. 2007. Parents' motivations for involvement in children's education: An empirical test of a theoretical model of parent involvement. *Journal of Educational Psychology* 99: 532–44.

Henrich, C.C., & R. Blackman-Jones. 2006. Parent involvement in preschool. In *A vision for universal preschool education*, eds. E. Zigler, W.S. Gilliam, & S.M. Jones, 149–68. New York: Cambridge University Press.

Hoover-Dempsey, K.B., & H.M. Sandler. 1997. Why do parents become involved in their children's education? *Review of Educational Research* 67: 3–42.

Hyson, M.C., K. Hirsh-Pasek, L. Rescorla, J. Cone, & L. Martell-Boinske. 1991. Ingredients of parental pressure in early childhood. *Journal of Applied Developmental Psychology* 12: 347–65.

Kontos, S., & L. Dunn. 1989. Attitudes of caregivers, maternal experiences with day care, and children's development. *Journal of Applied Developmental Psychology* 10: 37–51.

Kontos, S., C. Howes, M. Shinn, & E. Galinsky. 1995. *Quality in family child care and relative care*. New York: Teachers College Press.

Lamb-Parker, F., C.S. Piotrkowski, A.J.L. Baker, S. Kessler-Sklar, B. Clark, & L. Peay. 2001. Understanding barriers to parent involvement in Head Start: a research-community partnership. *Early Childhood Research Quarterly* 16: 35–51.

Larner, M. 1996. Parents' perspectives on quality in early care and education. In *Reinventing early care and education: A vision for a quality system*, eds. S. Kagan & N. Cohen, 21–42. San Francisco: Jossey-Bass.

Link, G., M. Beggs, & E. Seiderman. 1997. *Serving families*. San Rafael, CA: Parent Services Project.

Marcon, R. 1999. Positive relationships between parent school involvement and public school inner-city preschoolers' development and academic performance. *School Psychology Review* 28: 395–412.

Meidel, W.T., & A.J. Reynolds. 1999. Parent involvement in early intervention for disadvantaged children: Does it matter? *Journal of School Psychology* 37: 379–402.

Murphy, D.M. 1997. Parent and teacher plan for the child. *Young Children* 52 (4): 32–36.

NAEYC. 1996. NAEYC position statement: Responding to linguistic and cultural diversity—Recommendations for effective early childhood education. *Young Children* 51: 4–12.

NAEYC. 2005. *Code of ethical conduct and statement of commitment*. Rev. ed. A position statement. Washington, DC: NAEYC.

National Parent Teacher Association. 1997. *National standards for parent/family involvement programs*. Chicago: Author.

Okagaki, L. & K. Diamond. 2009. Cultural and linguistic differences in families with young children: Implications for early childhood teachers. *Informing our practice: Useful research on young children's development*, eds. E.L. Essa & M.M. Burnham. Washington, DC: NAEYC.

Olmsted, P.P., & D.P. Weikart. 1994. *Families speak: Early childhood care and education in 11 countries*. Ypsilanti, MI: HighScope Press.

Owen, M.T., A.M. Ware, & B. Barfoot. 2000. Caregiver-mother partnership behavior and the quality of caregiver-child and mother-child interactions. *Early Childhood Research Quarterly* 15: 413–28.

Peet, S.H., D.R. Powell, & B.K. O'Donnel. 1997. Mother-teacher congruence in perceptions of the child's competence and school engagement: Links to academic achievement. *Journal of Applied Developmental Psychology* 18: 373–93.

Piotrowski, C.S., M. Botsko, & E. Matthews. 2000. Parents' and teachers' beliefs about children's school readiness in a high-need community. *Early Childhood Research Quarterly* 15: 537–58.

Pizzo, P.D., & E.E. Tufankjian. 2004. A persistent pattern of progress: Parent outcomes in longitudinal studies of Head Start children and families. In *The Head Start debates*, eds. E. Zigler & S.J. Styfco, 193–214. Baltimore: Paul H. Brookes.

Powell, D.R. 1997. Parents' contributions to the quality of child care arrangements. In *Advances in early education and day care, vol. 8: Family policy and practices in early education and child care programs*, eds. C.J. Dunst & M. Wolery, 133–55. Greenwich, CT: JAI.

Powell, D. R. 2001. Visions and realities of achieving partnership: Parent-teacher relationships at the turn of the century. In *Children in play, story and school*, eds. A. Göncü & E. Klein, 333–57. New York: Guilford.

Powell, D.R., & K.E. Diamond. 1995. Approaches to parent-teacher relationships in U.S. early childhood programs during the twentieth century. *Journal of Education* 177: 71–94.

Raab, M., & C.J. Dunst. 1997. Early childhood program assessment scales and family support practices. In *Advances in early education and day care, vol. 8: Family policy and practice in early education and child care programs*, C.J. Dunst & M. Wolery, 105–31. Greenwich, CT: JAI.

Sandall, S., M.E. McLean, & B.J. Smith. 2000. *DEC recommended practices in early intervention/early childhood special education*. Longmont, CO: Sopris West.

Sonnenschein, S., L. Baker, R. Serpell, & D. Schmidt. 2000. Reading is a source of entertainment: The importance of the home perspective for children's literacy development. In *Play and literacy in early childhood: Research from multiple perspectives*, eds. K.S. Roskos & J.R. Christie, 107–24. Mahwah, NJ: Lawrence Erlbaum.

Stein, A.R., & M. Haggard. 1990. *Parent Services Project evaluation: Final report findings*. San Rafael, CA: Parent Services Project.

Stipek, D., S. Milburn, D. Clements, & D.H. Daniels. 1992. Parents' beliefs about appropriate education for young children. *Journal of Applied Developmental Psychology* 13: 293–310.

Tarullo, L.B., & R.W. O'Brien. 2002. *A descriptive study of Head Start families: FACES technical report I*. Washington, DC: U.S. Department of Health and Human Services.

Waanders, C., J.L. Mendez, & J.T. Downer. 2007. Parent characteristics, economic stress and neighborhood context as predictors of parent involvement in preschool children's education. *Journal of School Psychology* 45: 619–36.

West, J., E.G. Hausken, & M. Collins. 1993. *Profile of preschool children's child care and early education program participation*, NCES 93-133. National Household Education Survey. Washington, DC: National Center for Education Statistics, Office of Educational Research and Improvement.

Whitebook, M., L. Sakai, & C. Howes. 1997. *NAEYC accreditation as a strategy for improving child care quality: An assessment*. Washington, DC: National Center for the Early Childhood Work Force.

Zigler, E., & S. Muenchow. 1992. *Head Start: The inside story of America's most successful educational experiment*. New York: Basic.

17 Early Childhood Programs That Work for Economically Disadvantaged Children

Frances A. Campbell and Karen B. Taylor

In 1996, we surveyed early childhood pro-grams for children from low-income families to learn what child and family benefits had been reported from these programs and how long the benefits appeared to last. We would have hoped that by now, some 15 years later, the status of children and families in our county would have improved significantly. Although many aspects of life have showed progress, sadly the major challenge of millions of children and families living in poverty remains.

* * *

In a recent review of the literature, Karoly, Kilburn, and Cannon (2005) noted that in a cohort of children enter-ing kindergarten in 1998–99 (ECLS-K) at least one in four was facing a condition posing a risk to school success, such as living in poverty, having a single parent, or having a mother with less than a high school education (Moore 1999). Almost one in six of the children faced more than one risk factor. Moreover, the ECLS-K data show that children who come from disadvantaged homes enter school with lower levels of knowledge and social skills than their more advantaged peers, and these gaps persist and widen as children

move through school. In turn, academic difficulties are associated with undesired outcomes in later life, such as higher un-employment, use of welfare, and criminal activity (Karoly, Kilburn, & Cannon 2005).

Do early childhood intervention programs for low-income children and families improve such outcomes?

Intervention programs and outcome data

The 1996 version of this research review surveyed early childhood intervention programs whose intent was to provide education, guidance, and support to enhance the early childhood development of children from low-income families in ways that would lead to greater success in school. Only studies that permitted strong scientific comparison of outcomes between children and families who did and did not receive services were included in that review. The programs differed in their tim-ing, intensity, and goals.

- The Mobile Unit for Child Health (Gutelius et al. 1972); the Nurse Home Visiting Program (Olds 1988; Goodman 2006); and the Yale Child Welfare Research Program (Provence & Naylor 1983) began working with mothers before target children were born.

- The Milwaukee Project (Garber 1988), the Syracuse University Family Development Research Program (Lally, Mangione, & Honig 1988), the Carolina Abecedarian Project (Ramey & Campbell 1991), Project CARE (Wasik et al. 1990), the Brookline Early Education Project (Pierson 1988), and the Infant Health and Development Program (IHDP 1990) began intervention during infancy.
- The Houston Parent-Child Development Center (PCDC; Johnson & Walker 1991) began working with families when target infants were 1 year old.
- The Harlem Study (Palmer 1983) contrasted outcomes in children who experienced short-term treatment either as 2-year-olds or 3-year-olds.
- The Verbal Interaction Project (Levenstein, O'Hara, & Madden 1983) provided a home-based language stimulation program for 2- or 3-year-olds.
- Other programs, such as the Perry Preschool Program (Beruetta-Clement et al. 1984), the Early Training Project (Gray, Ramsey, & Klaus 1982), the Chicago Child-Parent Center and Expansion Program (Reynolds 1994), and Head Start (McKey et al. 1985) began working with children in preschool, beginning at age 3 or 4. The Chicago program continued to offer family supports and school-based intervention through the primary grades.

Four early childhood programs stood out as being more extensive than the rest, in terms of the duration of intervention they provided. These were the Syracuse University Family Development Research Program, which provided intervention for

five years; the Milwaukee Project, in which children were served from infancy through kindergarten (age 6); and Project CARE and the Abecedarian study, whose maximal treatment was provided for children from infancy through age 8 (some Abecedarian groups had either five or three years of intervention).

Parent components were included in many programs because of the belief that early intervention would succeed only if parents became heavily involved and themselves made major changes (Bronfenbrenner 1974). Several programs combined home visits with center-based child care; some provided parents with personal development opportunities such as job training; others used a home visit model alone. A few programs had maternal and child health as their primary objective and used nurses as their visitors, while others had social workers to provide emotional support to parents.

A major outcome for almost all the early childhood programs surveyed concerned children's cognitive or intellectual development. Because children reared in low-income families are more likely to have academic and behavior problems in school (Patterson, Kupersmidt, & Vaden 1990; Connell 1994; Karoly, Kilburn, & Cannon 2005), and because preschool intellectual levels and early language development are so strongly associated with school success, almost all early childhood programs emphasized activities to enhance such development. Some interventionists attempted to do this through direct teaching of children in child care centers or preschools. Others modeled interactive and teaching behaviors for parents with the expectation that parents would then teach their children.

All programs had endpoint evaluations when their intervention was terminated, but not all had longer-term data on their participants. To the extent possible, the original version of this review included the most long-term information available from each program. Child outcomes were examined in terms of three domains: cognitive/academic benefits, socioemotional benefits, and health benefits.

Cognitive/academic benefits

Almost all programs, at their intervention endpoints, could show cognitive benefits for treated children. The positive reports of such gains from early programs, such as the Early Training Project (Gray, Ramsey, & Klaus 1982), led to the inception of America's most massive nationwide early childhood program for children from low-income families: Project Head Start. However, early enthusiasm for this kind of effort was dampened considerably when the first large-scale evaluation of Head Start showed that after only three years in school, mean IQs of Head Start children were not significantly different from those of children who had not attended Head Start (Cicirelli 1967).

The study that delivered this bad news was attacked on methodological grounds, with many arguing that it did not fairly assess the benefits of Head Start. To provide a definitive investigation of the effects of preschool interventions for low-income children, a Consortium for Longitudinal Studies was formed, in which 11 investigators followed intervention participants to learn how long early benefits persisted (Lazar et al. 1982). Results pooled across all 11 programs showed that statistically significant IQ differences between intervention and control subjects were largely gone after three to four years in public school, and significant differences on academic tests of reading and mathematics were gone after five to six years. On the other hand, an important discovery by the Consortium was a lasting benefit in terms of fewer grade retentions and fewer placements into special education for treated children, which results in a significant saving of public funds.

> The most enduring IQ benefits were associated with child-centered programs that began early.

The Consortium results have been widely cited by both critics and proponents of early intervention as being supportive of their own positions. Focusing on the erosion of significant IQ and academic benefits, the critics concluded that lasting, positive effects of early childhood programs have not been demonstrated. Some policy makers have labeled these programs ill-advised and wasteful. Proponents, however, argue that not all Consortium programs failed to find lasting IQ or academic benefits, and, in aggregate, they definitely showed benefits for treated children in terms of fewer placements into special education and fewer grade retentions. Moreover, a number of early childhood studies carried out since those in the Consortium have subsequently reported significant IQ or academic gains that persisted beyond the elementary school years (e.g., the Abecedarian study, IHDP).

In general, the most enduring IQ benefits were associated with child-centered programs that began very early in the life span and provided many hours of treatment, as did the Milwaukee and Abecedarian studies. On the other hand, participants in the Consortium's Harlem Study also showed long-term performance IQ gains with a much shorter period of intervention that began no earlier than age 2. Other preschool experiences that started at age 3 or 4, such as the Early Training Project, Head Start, and the Perry Preschool study, reported significant IQ differences when their programs ended. Like Head Start gains, however, these gains eroded within a few years. The Nurse Home Visiting Program reported mixed results for children's cognitive and academic gains, finding none in the original New York site, but researchers found higher cognitive and language scores for children of visited mothers at the Memphis site for up to four years after the program ended (Olds et al. 2004).

Long-term (fifth grade or higher) academic test results or indices of school progress (retentions, placements, or graduation rates) are available for the Early Training Project, the Harlem Study, the Perry Preschool Program, the Houston PCDC program, the Syracuse Family Development Research Program, the Milwaukee Project, the Chicago Child-Parent program, and the Abecedarian study. Girls who participated in the Syracuse study had higher grades than girls in the control group in grades seven and eight. Participants in the Early Training Project had fewer retentions or placements into special education, and girls in this program were more likely to graduate from high school and to return to school if they became teen mothers.

Children participating in the Carolina Abecedarian Project in preschool had significantly higher scores on tests of reading and math through age 15 and fewer retentions and placements into special education than those who did not receive the intervention. The Chicago program found that participating children showed cognitive gains when they began formal schooling, and they had higher achievement scores during elementary school (Reynolds et al. 2001). The Milwaukee Project found no academic test score differences after 10 years in school, but significant IQ differences persisted through age 14. All of these programs contained child-centered components. The evidence thus shows that children from low-income families can derive significant and long-lasting cognitive and academic benefits from child-oriented preschool programs.

There are also reports of long-term positive effects on child IQ and academic performance from some of the more parent-oriented programs, but the evidence

for long-term benefits is more mixed. Programs that emphasized parents as the mediators of treatment, such as the Mobile Unit for Child Health and the Brookline Early Education Project, found significant child IQ or "language" benefits just after their programs ended. The Verbal Interaction Project had mixed results: Some, but not all, of the treatment variations resulted in significant and relatively long-lasting IQ gains for participating children.

In contrast, the Family Education group from Project CARE and the Yale, Syracuse, and Houston programs did not find significant treatment/control child IQ differences at their endpoints, although as noted, Syracuse and Houston later found evidence of academic benefits, as did some variations of the Verbal Interaction Project. Child IQ and academic benefits appear to have eroded quickly in the case of the Mobile Unit for Child Health (Gutelius et al. 1977).

> Enduring cognitive or educational gains attributable to early educational programs have now been demonstrated convincingly.

The evidence is also mixed on the value of continuing to provide intervention for graduates of preschool programs into public school. In their summary of findings from a Follow-Through project in a northern urban area, Seitz and colleagues (1983) found that Follow-Through children had higher IQs at the intervention endpoint than did children in the control group, and they had higher scores on academic tests of math and general knowledge at the end of third grade.

The findings through eighth grade showed that Follow-Through graduates continued to demonstrate modest positive effects. Their academic test scores declined less over the years than those of the control group, although there were some wave (i.e., year of entry) and gender differences in this regard, and positive effects were not found in all areas tested. There were none in reading, for example. At age 15, participants in the Chicago Child-Parent program demonstrated positive outcomes over their peers who had not participated—including greater social competence, higher achievement scores, more consumer skills, less grade retention, and fewer placements into special education programs (Reynolds 2000). This program had provided both a parent component and follow-through into the early primary school years.

For children in the Abecedarian study, the effects of the school-age program were weaker than those of the preschool program. There was no evidence that having the three years of follow-up in the primary grades helped to maintain IQ gains even through age 8. The mean reading scores through age 15 favor the group that had both preschool and school-age follow-through, but the difference between preschool graduates with and without the follow-through program was not significant by age 15. The preschool effect is stronger for mathematics; by age 15, there was no longer an advantage associated with having had the school-age program in addition to preschool (Campbell & Ramey 1995).

A final note about school-age programs concerns the outcome from the nationwide randomized controlled study extending Head Start benefits into the elementary grades. The Head Start Transition Demonstration Program provided extra learning supports for children, as well as family supports. The results showed that having the transition services was not associated with differential gains for children. However, the children in that study did not show the kind of fade out seen in earlier studies of Head Start graduates. Results showed that during the first three years of elementary school, Head Start graduates moved closer and closer to the national average in language and math scores (Ramey et al. 2000).

Enduring cognitive or educational gains that are attributable to early educational programs have now been demonstrated convincingly. For the Abecedarian study, positive effects of the early childhood center-based educational intervention were seen at age 21. Children who had preschool intervention continued to show a positive effect on intellectual and academic test performance, with moderate to large effect sizes (Campbell et al. 2001). Those in the early childhood program were more likely to attend a four-year college and to have skilled employment in young adulthood (Campbell et al. 2002).

Young adult data collected from participants in Project CARE replicated these findings (Campbell et al. 2008). Noting that IHDP's intervention for children with low birth weight was modeled on the Abecedarian/CARE programs, its investigators reported that their late adolescent data somewhat replicated the Abecedarian young adult outcomes, in that the heavier premature infants with early childhood intervention had higher IQ scores and higher math achievement scores at age 18 as compared with those in the control group (McCormick et al. 2006). These benefits were not seen for premature infants in the low-low birth weight category, leading McCormick and colleagues to speculate on the increased difficulty of intervening to overcome the risk posed by serious biological impairments in early infancy.

Participants in the Perry Preschool study have been followed through age 40. At that age, treated females were significantly more likely to have completed high school, but no treatment/control differences were found for scores earned on a brief test of reading and math skills (Schweinhart et al. 2005).

Socioemotional benefits

Socioemotional outcomes for children can be roughly grouped into three categories: behavioral adjustment, attitudes and attributions, and self-concept. Socioemotional outcomes for parents largely consisted of measures of maternal behaviors, such as affection and punitiveness.

Parents who participated in the Houston project were observed to be more affectionate and less punitive with their children, and mothers participating in the Verbal Interaction Project were observed to behave more positively toward their children than did mothers in the control group. The Nurse Home Visiting Program participants showed a lower incidence of child neglect and abuse during the early programs years (Olds et al. 1995).

Where follow-up data are available, it appears that treatment/control differences in socioemotional development have generally been short term. Head Start researchers found strong positive effects on immediate behavioral adjustment in school, but this difference dropped sharply during the first year (McKey et al. 1985). Mothers of children in the Infant Health and Development Program rated their 3-year-olds lower on problem behaviors than did mothers of nonparticipating children. This difference was not found when the children were 5 (Brooks-Gunn et al. 1994). Kindergarten observers rated children who participated in the Brookline program significantly higher on "social adjustment" and "use of time" as compared with children in the control group, but this effect was not seen by the time children reached second grade. Children in the Syracuse Family Development Research Program were rated as superior in socioemotional functioning in kindergarten, but by first grade, they sought teacher attention in negative ways.

A few long-term follow-up studies have reported on aspects of behavioral adjustment associated with early childhood programs. A follow-up of the Syracuse sample showed that girls who had received the intervention were more positive toward peers in adolescence. When participants in the Yale Child Welfare Research Program were followed up after 10 years, boys who participated in the program had better behavioral adjustment than boys in the control group (Seitz & Provence 1990). Treated mothers in the Nurse Home Visiting Program reported fewer behavior problems when their children were 15 years old, and the adolescents had fewer instances of running away, law breaking, smoking, drinking alcohol, and drug use (Olds et al. 1998; Goodman 2006).

The Syracuse study found that program participants had fewer court records for delinquent acts, and the Perry Preschool Program found that program graduates had fewer arrests (Schweinhart & Weikart 1980). This reduction in criminal involvement has persisted for the Perry Preschool study. At age 40, program participants were found to have had fewer arrests and less time incarcerated. In addition, those who had the preschool experience showed economic gains in terms of higher earnings and home and car ownership (Schweinhart et al. 2005).

Long-term follow-up studies have revealed significant benefits in terms of mental health for two of the early childhood programs. Both the Chicago study (Smokowski et al. 2004) and the Abecedarian investigators (McLaughlin et al. 2007) found a reduction in self-reported depressive symptoms among young adults who had early childhood treatment compared with those in the control group.

Not all socioemotional differences associated with intervention were positive. The primary grade teachers of the Milwaukee Project children described program graduates as less cooperative and less compliant than children from the control group. As noted, Syracuse program graduates displayed some negative behaviors

> Where follow-up data are available, treatment/ control differences in socioemotional development have generally been short term.

toward teachers in first grade. Haskins (1985) found that primary grade teachers rated children who had the Abecedarian preschool intervention higher on verbal and physical aggression than they rated children in the control group.

As for attitudes, some investigators reported positive effects of early childhood programs on children's academic motivation and self-concept. The Early Training Project, the Perry Preschool Program, and the Verbal Interaction Project found a significant difference in the proportion of program graduates who reported being proud of themselves for academic achievement compared with control subjects, but this finding was mainly true of younger program graduates; it was not true for groups aged 15–19 (Lazar et al. 1982).

Schweinhart and Weikart (1980) found that their program graduates placed a higher value on education at age 15. Meta-analyses of Head Start outcomes suggest immediate, small, positive effects on both self-esteem and academic motivation, but both dropped sharply after one year in school. Academic motivation, however, appeared to make a modest recovery during the third year. Abecedarian program graduates scored more like middle-class peers on achievement attributions in the primary years (Walden & Ramey 1983), but this effect did not persist into adolescence.

By age 15, early childhood treatment was not significantly associated with differences in student ratings of intellectual achievement responsibility (Campbell 1995). Self-ratings of perceived scholastic competence showed a complex relationship between preschool and school-age treatment. The higher academic scores earned by those who had intervention in both the preschool and school-age phase were not associated with academic self-esteem scores as high as those self ascribed by students who had only the school-age intervention, whose actual academic scores were lower (Campbell, Pungello, & Miller-Johnson 2002).

Health, dental, and nutrition benefits

The importance of providing young children with safer environments, better nutrition, and better dental and health care is obvious. The investigators of the Nurse Home Visiting Program found a reduction in accidents and poison ingestions within homes of treated children. The better nutrition associated with Head Start resulted in both higher growth rates and higher serum levels of iron and other beneficial trace elements in participating children. There is not clear evidence of a lasting reduction in rates of illness for Head Start versus non–Head Start children, even though Head Start children had better rates of immunization. Head Start children had better dental care and more dental treatment than did non–Head Start children (McKey et al. 1985). These important outcomes are based on site-specific studies; the long-term consequences of these benefits are not known, but they are clearly important in their own right, even if not sustained.

Large-scale programs

Only two of the studies originally reviewed had large numbers of participants: the Chicago Child-Parent Centers and Head Start. Only the latter was a nationwide effort. To date, other large-scale efforts to improve the academic performance of low-income children have been implemented across the country. Of note are (1) the Title 1 programs that funnel into schools Federal dollars targeted toward educational supplements and extra supports for children from low-income families, and (2) Even Start, a program that has been focused on pre-literacy and early literacy skills. In both of these, evaluators have attempted to assess the efficacy of various program components such as follow-through assistance in elementary school and programs for parents as well as students.

In a follow-up study of the Chicago Child-Parent Center and Expansion Program at age 20, the individuals who had early childhood intervention had a lower incidence of crime at age 18 and higher rates of high school graduation by age 20 (Reynolds et al. 2001).

The fact that Head Start programs differed so widely in implementation and that none of them had prospective randomized designs that permitted outcomes to be attributed to the program itself has made it difficult to demonstrate convincingly the extent to which Head Start is associated with lasting benefits for participants. However, research is now emerging that suggests that Head Start does have benefits—long-lasting ones.

For example, economists have examined adult outcomes for children who self-reported having gone to Head Start in comparison with others who reported not having done so. The benefits found in that study varied according to ethnicity of the respondents. White children who attended Head Start were more likely to go to college than white children who did not attend, a benefit not seen for African Americans. However, African-American males were more likely to graduate from high school if they had attended Head Start, and they reported less involvement in crime than African-American males who did not attend Head Start (Garces, Thomas, & Currie 2002). Using a slightly different basis of comparison (Head Start attendees against their siblings who did not attend Head Start), another study found educational gains for both African-American and white attendees (Ludwig & Phillips 2007).

Title 1 programs are difficult to evaluate. As summarized by Zigler and Styfco (2003), little apparent benefit has been demonstrated for individual children as a result of having Title 1 programs in schools. These authors point out that Title 1 funds were provided to schools without firm requirements as to how they should be utilized, making it difficult to assess the overall value of the effort.

The same difficulty exists with respect to Even Start. Based on research linking early language and "pre-emergent literacy" skills to later reading success (e.g., Hart & Risley 1995; Whitehurst & Lonigan 1998), a number of researchers have launched "family literacy" programs. The goal of Even Start was to support the development of emergent literacy skills in young children and also the encouragement of educational and vocational gains in parents. Even Start programs, however, can vary from site to site according to local plans.

Even Start funds have been used to embed literacy programs within homes, preschools, or the primary grades. Evaluations of these programs have generally failed to demonstrate clear benefits on children's literacy skills. As described by Fuligni and Brooks-Gunn (2004), the most recent of these studies, which involved a rigorous, scientific comparison both to children in a control group and also to children who had other early childhood programs such as Head Start, showed that the control group and the children in the other programs gained at the same rate as those exposed to Even Start. Thus, Even Start seemed to provide little benefit over and above what children would have "experienced in Head Start or even in other community early childhood services" (129). To date, these family literacy efforts have not demonstrated a degree of benefit comparable with those seen for more intensive programs. In fairness, however, such programs have not yet been evaluated over a very long period of time.

Conclusion

Providing appropriate and stimulating learning environments for young children of low-income families and supporting their parents benefits both parents and children. Although some programs found only transitory effects on intellectual test scores, the more intensive intervention programs have now demonstrated modest but long-lasting IQ gains. Participants in many programs had higher academic test scores and made better progress through school as reflected in fewer retentions, fewer placements into special education, and higher rates of high school graduation. Parents in some programs made positive changes in their own educational and employment levels or showed reductions in child abuse and neglect. Early childhood programs clearly can help to overcome the barriers imposed by impoverishment.

Newer research gives encouraging evidence that benefits of early childhood programs can be long lasting. This is true even for massive efforts such as Head Start, whose initial value was questioned by many researchers. The long-term reports for Head Start, as well as for smaller experimental studies of intensive early childhood education such as the Abecedarian and CARE studies, IHDP, the Perry Preschool Program, and the Chicago Child-Parent program, have all demonstrated that benefits from early childhood programs can persist for many years. Across programs, late adolescent or young adult gains have been seen in terms of more years of education, increased likelihood of going to college, higher levels of employment, greater economic power, and reductions in crime.

The program delivery models varied, and not all programs could show the same pattern of benefits, but all can be said to be cost effective in terms of savings in schooling costs, increased education leading to a better chance to achieve self-sufficiency, or reductions in costly societal problems such as criminal behaviors. Thus, while some of the model early childhood programs have been criticized as unrealistic in terms of their cost, some economists now argue that if the programs were to be applied on a massive scale, money spent on early childhood programs ultimately pays off to a greater extent than money invested in later childhood or adolescent programs (Clemant 2005).

> The more intensive intervention programs have now demonstrated modest but long-lasting IQ gains.

Cost-benefit analyses have been conducted for some of the programs included in this review. Because largest dollar benefits come later in life, programs that end their evaluations before adulthood may not be discovering all of their effects. The Perry Preschool Program recipients have participated in the longest follow-up study. Results at age 40 showed a benefit-cost ratio of $17 saved for each dollar spent (Karoly, Kilburn, & Cannon 2005). Those programs that helped prevent grade retentions and special services saved local school systems significant additional funds soon after the early childhood program ended. It is logical that savings would increase over time if program participants were less involved with expensive, long-term public costs such as prison, unemployment, and use of welfare funds.

No one model can be said to be clearly superior to another in terms of optimizing children's outcomes, especially children's early cognitive development. In the past 10 years, research has greatly expanded using new techniques for directly studying the development and functioning of the brain in the first five years of life. While a direct link between brain development and particular child care practices has yet to be demonstrated, all of the evidence suggests that early childhood experiences are critical in providing the basis for optimal development.

In *Success in Early Intervention: The Chicago Child-Parent Centers*, Reynolds (2000) described three hypotheses as to why early childhood programs might produce long-term outcomes for their participants. First, programs that offer a curriculum based on language and learning concepts provide children with knowledge and skills that are necessary for school success. Second, programs that include a component of parent involvement can improve family functioning, particularly associated with school success, which continues into later school years. Third, if children are prepared when they enter kindergarten, then the school system will more effectively support these initially successful students as they progress on to graduation. In addition to these factors, Reynolds goes on to note that success in school is also influenced by a child's motivation and social skills, which are often shown to have increased due to involvement in early educational experiences.

Typical gains from even the best early education programs are not likely to completely eliminate the readiness and achievement gaps experienced by children from low-income families, but they might make the situation better than it would have been without the child and family participation in the program. Beginning early with a high-quality child care or preschool setting that provides academic content, including a parent component to emphasize the need for parents' continued role in school involvement, and then moving on to a good elementary school is the formula for the most success for young children.

Those who are quick to discount the importance of early childhood programs have not suggested constructive alternatives. Early childhood programs ultimately save taxpayer dollars in terms of reductions in the costs of education, welfare, and crime (Berrueta-Clement et al. 1984; Schweinhart et al. 2005). These benefits were associated with child and family interventions provided in the preschool years. The message for lawmakers is plain. If economically disadvantaged parents are to improve their situation through joining the work force, high-quality child care must be provided from the earliest years.

Schools and businesses should be given all possible incentives for providing child care and family supports. Tax incentives could be given to corporations who have family-enhancing benefit plans. Leaders in education, business, and industry will have to make a strong commitment to young children and their families for this to happen on a broad scale.

Karoly, Kilburn, and Cannon (2005) found three common characteristics of the most effective early childhood programs: better trained caregivers, smaller child:staff ratios, and more intensive programs—that is, more hours in good care. All three are expensive program components. Pressing needs exist for every tax dollar that legislators allocate. It is up to the early childhood professionals to make sure that the importance of putting resources into early childhood programs is clearly understood by our policy makers.

Updated from the Research in Review article in the May 1996 issue of *Young Children*.

Frances A. Campbell is a scientist at the Frank Porter Graham Child Development Institute. **Karen B. Taylor** is a research associate at the Frank Porter Graham Child Development Institute.

References

Berrueta-Clement, J.R., L.J. Schweinhart, W.S. Barnett, A.S. Epstein, & D.P. Weikart. 1984. Changed lives: The effects of the Perry Preschool Program on youths through age 19. *Monographs of the High/Scope Educational Research Foundation* 8. Ypsilanti, MI: HighScope Press.

Bronfenbrenner, U. 1974. Is early intervention effective? *Day Care and Early Education* 44: 12–18.

Brooks-Gunn, J., C.M. McCarton, P.H. Casey, M.C. McCormick, C.R. Bauer, J.C. Bernbaum, J. Tyson, M. Swanson, F.C. Bennett, D.T. Scott, J. Tonascia, & C.L. Meinert. 1994. Early intervention in low-birth-weight premature infants: Results through age 5 years in the Infant Health and Development Program. *Journal of the American Medical Association* 272 (16): 1257–62.

Campbell, F.A. 1995. *The development of academic self-concept and its relationship to academic performance and self-esteem: A longitudinal study of African American students.* Poster presented at the Biennial Meeting of the Society for Research in Child Development, March, Indianapolis, IN.

Campbell, F.A., E.P. Pungello, & S. Miller-Johnson. 2002. The development of perceived scholastic competence and global self-worth in African American adolescents from low-income families: The roles of family factors, early educational intervention, and academic experience. *Journal of Adolescent Research* 17: 277–302.

Campbell, F.A., E.P. Pungello, S. Miller-Johnson, M. Burchinal, & C.T. Ramey. 2001. The development of cognitive and academic abilities: Growth curves from an early childhood educational experiment. *Developmental Psychology* 37: 231–42.

Campbell, F.A., & C.T. Ramey. 1995. Cognitive and school outcomes for high-risk African American students at middle adolescence: Positive effects of early intervention. *American Educational Research Journal* 32 (4): 743–72.

Campbell, F.A., C.T. Ramey, E.P. Pungello, J. Sparling, & S. Miller-Johnson. 2002. Early childhood education: Young adult outcomes from the Abecedarian Project. *Applied Developmental Science* 6: 42–57.

Campbell, F.A., & K.T. Taylor. 1996. Early childhood programs that work for children from economically disadvantaged families. *Young Children* 51 (4): 74–80.

Campbell, F.A., B.H. Wasik, E.P. Pungello, M.R. Burchinal, O. Barbarin, J.J. Sparling, & C.T. Ramey. 2008. Young adult outcomes from the Abecedarian and CARE early childhood educational interventions. *Early Childhood Research Quarterly* 23: 452–66.

Cicirelli, V.G. 1967. *The impact of Head Start: An evaluation of the effects of Head Start on children's cognitive and affective development* (Report no. PB 184 328, presented to the Office of Economic Opportunity). Washington, DC: Westinghouse Learning Corporation.

Clement, D. 2005. Interview with James J. Heckman. *The Region*, a publication of the Federal Reserve Bank of Mineapolis. Online: minneapolisfed.org/pubs/region/05-06/heckman.cfm.

Connell, R.W. 1994. Poverty and education. *Harvard Educational Review* 64 (2):125–49.

Fuligni, A.S., & A. Brooks-Gunn. 2004. Early childhood intervention in family literacy programs. In *Handbook of family literacy*, ed. B. Wasik, 117–36. Mahwah, NJ: Lawrence Erlbaum.

Garber, H.L. 1988. *The Milwaukee Project: Prevention of mental retardation in children at risk.* Washington, DC: American Association on Mental Retardation.

Garces, E., D. Thomas, & J. Currie. 2002. Longer-term effects of Head Start. *American Economic Review* 92: 999–1012.

Goodman, A. 2006. *The story of David Olds and the Nurse Home Visiting Program.* Robert Wood Johnson Foundation. Online: www.rwjf.org/files/publications/other/DavidOldsSpecialReport0606.pdf.

Gray, S.W., B.K. Ramsey, & R.A. Klaus. 1982. *From 3 to 20: The Early Training Project.* Baltimore: University Park Press.

Gutelius, M.F, A.D. Kirsch, S. MacDonald, M.R. Brooks, & T. McErlean. 1977. Controlled study of child health supervision: Behavioral results. *Pediatrics* 60: 294–304.

Gutelius, M.F., A.D. Kirsch, S. MacDonald, M.R. Brooks, T. McErlean, & C. Newcomb. 1972. Promising results from a cognitive stimulation program in infancy: A preliminary report. *Clinical Pediatrics* 11: 585–93.

Hart, B., & T.R. Risley. 1995 *Meaningful differences in the everyday experience of young American children.* Baltimore: Paul H. Brookes.

Haskins, R. 1985. Public school aggression among children with varying daycare experience. *Child Development* 56: 689–703.

IHDP (Infant Health and Development Program). 1990. Enhancing the outcomes of low-birth-weight, premature infants: A multisite, randomized trial. *Pediatrics* 263: 3035–42.

Johnson, D.L., & T. Walker. 1991. A follow-up evaluation of the Houston Parent-Child Development Center: School performance. *Journal of Early Intervention* 15: 226–36.

Karoly, L.A., M.R. Kilburn, & J.S. Cannon. 2005. *Early childhood interventions proven results, future promise.* Santa Monica, CA: Rand.

Lally, J.R., P.L. Mangione, & A.S. Honig. 1988. The Syracuse University Family Development Research Program: Long-range impact on an early intervention with low-income children and their families. In *Annual advances in applied developmental psychology, vol. 3: Parent education as early childhood intervention: Emerging directions in theory, research, and practice*, ed. D.R. Powell, 79–104. Norwood, NJ: Ablex.

Lazar, I., R. Darlington, H. Murray, J. Royce, & A. Snipper. 1982. Lasting effects of early education: A report from the Consortium for Longitudinal Studies. *Monographs of the Society for Research in Child Development* 47, nos. 2-3, serial no. 195.

Levinstein, P., J. O'Hara, & J. Madden. 1983. The mother-child home program of the Verbal Interaction Project. In *As the twig is bent: Lasting effects of preschool programs*, ed. the Consortium for Longitudinal Studies, 237–64. Hillsdale, NJ: Lawrence Erlbaum.

Ludwig, J., & D. Phillips. 2007. The benefits and costs of Head Start. *Social Policy Report of the Society for Research in Child Development* 21 (3).

McCormick, M.C., J. Brooks-Gunn, S.L. Buka, J. Goldman, J. Yu, M. Salganik, D.T. Scott, F.C. Bennett, L.K. Libby, J.C. Bernbaum, C.R. Bauer, C. Martin, E.R. Woods, A. Martin, & P.H. Casey. 2006. Early intervention in low birth weight premature infants: Results at 18 years of age for the Infant Health and Development Program. *Pediatrics* 117 (3): 771–80.

McKey, R.H., L. Condelli, H. Ganson, B.J. Barrett, C. McConkey, & M.C. Plantz. 1985. *The impact of Head Start on children, families, and communities*. Publication No. (OHDS) 90-31193. Washington, DC: U.S. Department of Health and Human Services.

McLaughlin, A.E., F.A. Campbell, E.P. Pungello, & M. Skinner. 2007. Depressive symptoms in young adults: The influences of the early home environment and early educational child care. *Child Development* 78: 746–56.

Moore, K. 1999. *A birth cohort study: Conceptual and design considerations and rationale* (NCES 999-001). Washington, DC: National Center for Education Statistics.

Olds, D. 1988. The Prenatal/Early Infancy Project. In *14 Ounces of Prevention: A Casebook for Practitioners*, eds. R.H. Price, E.L. Cowen, R.P. Lorion, & J. Ramon-McKay, 9–23. Washington, DC: American Psychological Association.

Olds, D., C.R. Henderson, H. Kitzman, & R. Cole. 1995. Effects of prenatal and infancy nurse home visitation on surveillance of child maltreatment. *Pediatrics* 95 (3): 365–72.

Olds, D., C.R. Henderson, R. Cole, J. Eckenrode, H. Kitzman, D.W. Luckey, L. Pettitt, K. Sidora, P. Morris, & J. Powers. 1998. Long-term effects of nurse home visitation on children's criminal and antisocial behavior: 15-year follow-up of a randomized controlled trial. *Journal of the American Medical Association* 280 (14): 1238–44.

Olds, D., H. Kitzman, R. Cole, J. Robinson, K. Sidora, D.W. Luckey, C.R. Henderson, C. Hanks, J. Bondy, & J. Holmberg. 2004. Effects of Nurse Home-Visiting on maternal life course and child development: Age 6 follow-up results of a randomized trial. *Pediatrics* 114: 1550–59.

Palmer, F.H. 1983. The Harlem Study: Effects by type of training, age of training, and social class. In *As the twig is bent: Lasting effects of preschool programs*, ed. the Consortium for Longitudinal Studies, 201–36. Hillsdale, NJ: Lawrence Erlbaum.

Patterson, C.J., J.B. Kupersmidt, & N.A. Vaden. 1990. Income level, gender, ethnicity, and household composition as predictors of children's school-based competence. *Child Development* 61: 485–94.

Pierson, D.E. 1988. The Brookline Early Education Project. In *14 ounces of prevention: A casebook for practitioners*, eds. R.H. Price, E.L. Cowen, R.P. Lorion, & J. Ramon-McKay, 24–31. Washington, DC: American Psychological Association.

Provence, S., & A. Naylor. 1983. *Working with disadvantaged parents and their children*. New Haven, CT: Yale University Press.

Ramey, C.T., & F.A. Campbell. 1991. Poverty, early childhood education, and academic competence: The Abecedarian experiment. In *Children in poverty*, ed. A. Huston, 190–221. New York: Cambridge University Press.

Ramey, S.L., C.T. Ramey, M.M. Phillips, R.G. Lanzi, C. Brezausek, C.R. Katholi, & S. Snyder. 2000. *Head Start children's entry into public school: A report on the National Head Start/Public School Early Childhood Transition Demonstration Study*. Birmingham, AL: Civitan International Research Center, University of Alabama at Birmingham.

Reynolds, A.J. 1994. Effects of a preschool plus follow-on intervention for children at risk. *Developmental Psychology* 30: 787–804.

Reynolds, A.J. 2000. *Success in early intervention: The Chicago Child-Parent Centers*. Lincoln, NB: University of Nebraska Press.

Reynolds, A.J., J.A. Temple, D.L. Robertson, & E.A. Mann. 2001. Long-term effects of an early childhood intervention on educational achievement and juvenile arrest. *Journal of the American Medical Association* 285: 2339–46.

Schweinhart, L.J., J. Montie, Z. Xiang, W.S. Barnett, C.R. Belfield, & M. Nores. 2005. Lifetime effects: The High/Scope Perry Preschool study through age 40. *Monographs of the High/Scope Educational Research Foundation* 14. Ypsilanti, MI: HighScope.

Schweinhart, L.J., & D.P. Weikart. 1980. Young children grow up: The effects of the Perry Preschool Program on youth through age 15. *Monographs of the High Scope Educational Research Foundation* 7. Ypsilanti, MI: HighScope.

Seitz, V., N.H. Apfel, L.K. Rosenbaum, & E. Zigler. 1983. Long-term effects of projects Head Start and Follow-Through: The New Haven Project. In *As the twig is bent: Lasting effects of preschool programs*, ed. the Consortium for Longitudinal Studies, 299–332. Hillsdale, NJ: Lawrence Erlbaum.

Seitz, V., & S. Provence. 1990. Caregiver-focused models of early intervention. In *Handbook of early childhood intervention*, eds. S. Meisels & J. Shonkoff, 400–27. New York: Cambridge University Press.

Smokowski, P.R., E.A. Mann, A.J. Reynolds, & M.W. Fraser. 2004. Childhood risk and protective factors and late adolescent adjustment in inner city minority youth. *Children and Youth Services Review* 26: 63–91.

Walden, T., & C.T. Ramey. 1983. Locus of control and academic achievement: Results of a preschool intervention program. *Journal of Educational Psychology* 75: 865–76.

Wasik, B.H., C.T. Ramey, D.M. Bryant, & J.J. Sparling. 1990. A longitudinal study of two early intervention strategies: Project CARE. *Child Development* 61: 1682–96.

Whitehurt, G.J., & C.J. Lonigan. 1998. Child development and emergent literacy. *Child Development* 69: 848–72.

Zigler, E., & S.J. Styfco. 2003. The Federal commitment to preschool education: Lessons from and for Head Start. In *Early childhood programs for a new century*, eds. A. Reynolds, M. Wang, & H. Walberg, 3–33. Washington, DC: Child Welfare League of America Press.

Cultural and Linguistic Differences in Families with Young Children: Implications for Early Childhood Teachers

18

Lynn Okagaki and Karen E. Diamond

Sophanara stands in the doorway holding her mother's hand. They are next in line to enter the Head Start classroom. She has watched other 4-year-olds enter the room with their mothers or fathers. But Sophanara hesitates. Miss Miller, the teacher, smiles and says hello to her. Sophanara looks down at her shoes. She doesn't understand what Miss Miller is saying.

Sophanara's parents are from Cambodia. Although her father has learned a little English where he works, no one speaks English at home. Miss Miller invites Sophanara's mother to come into the classroom with her and gestures her welcome with her hands. Her mother has had very little experience with people outside of their Cambodian community. Although she had only two years of formal schooling in Cambodia, she believes that education is important for her daughter. She expects the school to do what is best for her daughter and believes that the school is responsible for making sure that her daughter does well.

Sophanara's mother listens to Miss Miller but doesn't understand what the teacher is saying. After a moment's hesitation, she nods and brings Sophanara into this new world with her.

In 2005, one in every five children in the United States lived in a family in which at least one parent was born outside the United States. The proportion of young children who are non-Hispanic white is declining, and by 2030, projections indicate that the population of children (birth to 18) will be 26 percent Hispanic; 16 percent Black; 5 percent Asian; and 4 percent Native American, Hawai'ian, or Pacific Islander (Hernandez, Denton, & Macartney 2007).

These young children reflect the great racial, ethnic, and cultural diversity of American society: There are young children whose families speak languages other than English, whose families have social customs that differ from those of the mainstream culture, and whose families have different beliefs about child development and different expectations for their children. What are the implications of this diversity for teachers in early childhood classrooms? It is impossible to know all of the variations in beliefs and the sometimes subtle nuances that distinguish beliefs and practices across cultural groups in the United States.

This review provides illustrations of the ways in which cultural differences in parents' beliefs and practices may affect children's adjustment to early childhood settings as well as suggestions for working with young children who may be bridging two cultures as they transition between home and early childhood classroom.

Cultural values, beliefs, and socialization goals

All parents have goals and expectations for their children. Differences in parental goals and expectations arise, in part, because parents have children for different reasons (Hoffman 1988) and because societies have different expectations for the members of their communities (LeVine 1988). For example, in many Western societies, including European-American traditions in the United States, there is a general emphasis on people being independent, self-reliant, and self-assertive, and a focus on individual achievement (Spence 1985; Triandis et al. 1988). In contrast, in many Asian and Latin American cultures, interdependence, cooperation, and collaboration represent values that are widely esteemed (Harrison et al. 1990).

Differences in these general cultural values or expectations for members of communities can lead to differences in the socialization goals and strategies which parents adopt for their children (Ogbu 1981; Garcia Coll 1990). Families' values, beliefs, and behaviors vary by their country of origin, their reasons for immigrating to the United States, residence in an ethnic or integrated neighborhood, family structure (e.g., extended or nuclear family unit), and income (Halgunseth, Ispa, & Rudy 2006).

This section begins by discussing examples of the ways in which cultural values are translated into parents' expectations for their children and then highlights cultural variation in parents' beliefs about development.

Goals and expectations

First, consider parents' ideas about the characteristics which are most desirable in children. In a series of studies, Harwood and others have compared the socialization goals of mothers in different Latino populations to those of European-American mothers (e.g., Harwood 1992; Miller & Harwood 2001; Leyendecker et al. 2002). Mothers of infants (typically, 8 months to 24 months old) described the qualities and behaviors they would like and not like their child to develop. Compared to European-American mothers, Latino mothers identified more goals related to being respectful, obedient, and getting along well with others and fewer goals related to the child maximizing his or her own potential, becoming independent, and becoming self-assertive.

This finding has been replicated in several Latino populations, including immigrant Central American mothers (Leyendecker et al. 2002), middle-class Puerto Rican mothers (Miller & Harwood 2001), and lower-class Puerto Rican mothers (Harwood 1992), and by other researchers (e.g., Gonzalez-Ramos, Zayas, & Cohen 1998). Parents consider different characteristics to be most important to their children's development, and these differences appear to reflect general cultural orientations toward individuals and relationships.

Another example of cultural variation in parents' goals for their children can be seen in a study of a diverse sample of immigrant and U.S.-born parents of kindergarten, first, and second grade youngsters (Okagaki & Sternberg 1993). In this study, the parents from the four immigrant groups (i.e., Cambodian, Filipino, Mexican, and Vietnamese) rated developing obedience and conformity to external standards as more important for children's development than developing their independent thinking and problem-solving skills. In contrast, the parents who were born in the United States (i.e., European-American and Mexican-American) rated developing independent behaviors as more important than developing conforming behaviors. In particular, the parents who were born in the United States believed that creative thinking skills were the most important skills.

Finally, how do cultural values and socialization goals shape parents' interpretations of their child's behaviors? Like the previous examples, an individualistic cultural orientation is contrasted with a collectivist or mutual interdependent orientation. In this example, the attitudes of Canadian parents of European origin who have held a more individualistic orientation and Chinese parents who have traditionally valued mutual interdependence are considered.

In any group of infants or toddlers, there is variation in children's responses to novel objects and unfamiliar situations. Some children are relatively relaxed when confronted with an unfamiliar situation and show little indication of distress. Other children react to novel objects and situations with high anxiety. They want to stay close to their mother or other primary caregiver. They do not readily explore novel objects or easily interact with unfamiliar people. These actions are indicators of "behavioral inhibition." Researchers have found that the meaning parents place on these behaviors varies across cultural groups (Chen et al. 1998).

In Chinese families, behavioral inhibition in toddlers was *positively* associated with maternal acceptance of the child and with maternal belief in encouraging children's achievement. In contrast, in Canadian families, behavioral inhibition was *negatively* associated with maternal acceptance and encouragement. Chinese mothers of children who displayed *higher* levels of behavioral inhibition were *less* likely to believe that physical punishment is the best way to discipline the child and *less* likely to feel angry toward the child. But Canadian mothers of such children were *more* likely to believe in physical punishment. In

short, behavioral inhibition was associated with exactly opposite attitudes in Chinese mothers versus Canadian mothers. Each perspective, however, is consistent with the broader values of their culture.

Beliefs about development

In addition to the general orientation toward individualism or collectivism influencing parenting, other culturally-based beliefs undergird parents' beliefs about child development. For example, in their study of immigrant and non-immigrant families, Okagaki and Sternberg (1993) found that parents have different ideas about what constitutes intelligent behavior.

The Latino and Asian parents held implicit theories of intelligence in which non-cognitive aspects were as important as or more important to the meaning of intelligence than cognitive skills were. That is, they seemed to have a broader conception of intelligence—a view of intelligence that did not rely as heavily on cognitive skills, such as creativity and verbal expression, but rather incorporated and emphasized other attributes, such as motivation and social skills.

For the Latino parents, social skills constituted a relatively important aspect of intelligence. For the Filipino and Vietnamese parents, motivation was a very important characteristic of intelligent first-graders: To be intelligent is to work hard at achieving one's goals. This is different from the Western psychological model of intelligence that focuses on innate cognitive abilities.

Implications for teachers and caregivers

These examples of distinctions in cultural groups' beliefs about children's behavior and development suggest that teachers cannot assume that everyone holds the same template for what constitutes an ideal child. There is substantial diversity in beliefs and practices within a single cultural group, as well (Tudge et al. 2006). For the child whose parents' expectations for behavior and development are congruent with the teacher's expectations, the transition to the early childhood setting may be relatively easy. When there is a lack of congruence between parents' and teachers' expectations, then children may have the additional burden of determining the implicit rules and expectations that govern the early childhood classroom.

How might teachers help children make a successful transition from their families' expectations for their behavior at home to the rules and expectations in their classrooms? An important first step for teachers is understanding parents' perspectives and goals for their children; this requires that parents and teachers get to know and trust each other.

Establishing an understanding between school and home involves more than traditional strategies in which teachers educate parents about the "best" strategies for encouraging children's development (cf. Powell & Diamond 1995). It requires that teachers talk with parents about their own experiences, beliefs and values, and listen to parents when they talk about their perspectives. Understanding parents' perspectives, and the ways in which they are similar to and different from teachers' own, provides the basis for working together to support the development of each child. Ramsey (1998) offers a variety of strategies that teachers can use to develop collaborations with the parents of children in their classes.

Parental roles

What does it mean to be a "good" parent? What are the attributes of a good parent? Cultural groups vary in the ways in which they understand the role and responsibilities of parents. In research comparing immigrant Chinese mothers and European-American mothers, Chao (1994; 2000)

observed differences in the ways in which mothers defined their roles. For example, in contrast to European-American mothers, the Chinese immigrant mothers believed that young children should only be cared for by their mothers or by some other family member.

> Establishing an understanding between school and home involves more than traditional strategies in which teachers educate parents about the "best" strategies.

Also in contrast to European-American mothers, the Chinese immigrant mothers placed a strong emphasis on training and teaching children. Being a good mother meant that one started training the child as soon as the child was ready to learn. The Chinese immigrant mothers endorsed the belief that the primary way in which mothers express their love to their child is by helping the child succeed, especially in school. From this perspective, early childhood programs that emphasize play and a constructivist approach might be viewed with suspicion if the parent could not see a clear academic focus in the curriculum.

Among Native American nations, the role of the parent is defined in ways that are distinct from Western models of parenting. For example, in some Native American nations, responsibility for the care and nurturing of the child is extended beyond the parents. Grandparents, aunts, or uncles, for example, may have primary responsibility for the discipline of the child (Machamer & Gruber 1998). Tribal elders may need to be consulted on matters regarding the care of the child (Joe & Malach 1992). The parent does not take sole authority for making decisions about the child. An implication of shared parenting responsibilities is that the parents may want to include other people in meetings in which decisions regarding the child will be made, or they may want to delay giving a response to the teacher until they can consult with others.

In addition, cultural orientations affect how individuals view themselves in their parenting role. In a cross-national study of mothers of 20-month-old infants from Argentina, Belgium, France, Israel, Italy, Japan, and the United States, researchers found, for example, that Japanese mothers were more likely than other mothers to attribute parenting successes to their child's behavior and parenting failures to their own lack of effort (Bornstein et al. 1998). Although the Japanese mothers rated themselves as high in their investment in parenting, they rated themselves as low in terms of their satisfaction with their parenting and their competence as parents.

This pattern of beliefs fits with the emphasis Japanese culture places on being modest and on the importance of working hard. When parenting is going well, the Japanese mother attributes the success to her child and not to her own ability. When something is wrong, it is because she has not put enough effort into her parenting. Mothers from the United States, however, rate themselves as relatively competent and satisfied with their parenting skills. When U.S. mothers feel that something is wrong in their parenting, they are much less likely than Japanese mothers to attribute the problem to something that they have (or have not) done.

Implications for teachers and caregivers

Why should these differences matter to early childhood teachers? As Ramsey (1998) noted, teachers often expect that parents and schools share common philosophies and practices about young children. Yet, teaching practices reflect each teacher's own—and his or her culture's—goals for children's development and education. Understanding the ways in which parents (mothers *and* fathers) and extended family members view their parenting roles and

> Even though teachers and parents may disagree about how to handle situations, understanding the different ways in which adults think enhances the family-teacher collaboration.

responsibility for the child's behavior provides another way to understand parents' behaviors and interactions with teachers.

For example, most parents and teachers want children to learn to get along with each other and to solve disputes without fighting. The Western understanding of typical development suggests that a 2- or 3-year-old can be expected to resort to hitting and pushing to get what he or she wants. Western teachers and parents intervene in these disputes but see the source of the behavior as growing from a child's individual characteristics and they act accordingly (e.g., by teaching the child more appropriate behaviors).

But in non-Western cultures that consider *parents* to bear primary responsibility for their child's behavior, the response might be different. Parents and teachers holding these cultural beliefs would also intervene in disputes, but their natural response would be to inform the parents of the children involved in the fight of their (mis)behavior and to suggest that parents need to do a better job of teaching their child. Even though teachers and parents may disagree about how to handle situations such as this, understanding the different ways in which adults think about parenting and children's behaviors enhances the family-teacher collaboration.

Language

Language is one of the most salient sources of diversity in early childhood classrooms. Although type of language—actual language (e.g., English, Spanish, Korean), amount, complexity, and manner—spoken in the home is not a parenting practice, per se, language usage in the home can have a profound effect on children's adjustment to early childhood programs. A report on Head Start enrollment for the 2003–2004 school year revealed that almost 30 percent of children spoke a language other than English. Of those children who did not speak English, 83 percent spoke Spanish, 5 percent spoke East Asian or Pacific Island languages, and 3 percent spoke native Central/South American languages other than Spanish. An additional 6 percent of children spoke one of more than 130 other languages (Administration for Children and Families 2005). Spanish-speaking preschool children who are learning English are more likely than any other group of children to live in poverty and to have mothers without a high school education (Espinosa 2007).

There has been increasing attention on the best ways to respond to such diversity in children's language in preschool classrooms, and researchers have particularly sought to answer questions about the best ways to teach young children whose home language is not English. Research has highlighted the apparent cognitive benefits for young children of learning two different languages (Hakuta & Garcia 1989). Children who have better oral language skills in their home language do better in school, even when English is the language of the classroom (Tabors 2008). There is evidence that preschool programs that provide instruction in the child's home language and in English can promote children's academic and language development in both languages (Barnett et al. 2007). While bilingual and two-way language immersion classrooms appear to have important advantages for young children, researchers are only beginning to identify the teaching strategies most effective for supporting academic and social competence of young children who are learning English in addition to a different home language (Barnett et al. 2007).

If bilingual programs are effective, how should teachers and programs respond when classrooms include children who come from a variety of home language backgrounds? In these classrooms, it would be much more difficult to provide instruction to each child in his or her home language, and teachers typically use English as the classroom language. Teachers must provide instruction that is appropriate for each child in their classroom, and children must learn how to decode an unfamiliar language. The organization of the classroom (e.g., the use of consistent daily routines, small-group activities that allow teachers to group children by similar or different language ability) and the supports that teachers provide (e.g., the use of gestures and pictures or signs that illustrate the words or concepts) when speaking English are strategies that are especially useful in multilingual classrooms (Administration for Children and Families 2005; Tabors 2008).

Not only do many children enter early childhood programs speaking (or having primarily heard) a language other than English, but they have been exposed to varying amounts of language and have been socialized to use language in different ways. For example, in a longitudinal study focusing on the ways in which parents in 42 midwestern families interacted with their young children, Hart and Risley (1995) observed a vast range in the amount the parents talked to the child, from a low of about 50 utterances per hour to a high of approximately 800 utterances per hour when the children were 11–18 months of age. Because the amount the parent talked to the child when the child was an infant was highly correlated with the amount the parent talked to the child at age 3, the consistency in parenting behavior results in an important cumulative difference in children's environments.

If a child hears 50 utterances an hour for an average of 14 waking hours per day, that child will be exposed to about 700 utterances each day. On the other hand, if parents address their child 800 times per hour, the child will hear more than 11,000 utterances each day. Thus, children entering early childhood programs at age 3 or 4 already may have experienced great differences in their exposure to language. Hart and Risley (1995) found that greater diversity in parents' language was associated with more rapid growth in children's vocabulary. Consequently, some children in early childhood education and care programs may have a greater need for language exposure than other children do. Some young children may function at a lower level, not because of any inherent cognitive limitations but because they have heard less language.

Cross-cultural studies have identified numerous ways in which language socialization varies across cultures. For example, Fernald and Morikawa (1993) observed mother-infant interaction in white, middle-class American families and in Japanese families temporarily residing in the United States. Although the American and Japanese mothers adapted their language to the abilities of their infants in similar ways (e.g., simplifying their speech, adding interesting sounds to attract their infant's attention), several differences emerged in the ways the mothers spoke to their infants.

American mothers labeled the target objects more often and were more likely to use the adult form of the target label (e.g., "dog" instead of names such as "doggie," "woof-woof," or "Mr. Doggy"). Japanese mothers were less likely to identify the object with a name. Whereas American mothers were more likely to talk about the object, Japanese mothers used the object to involve their infant in social interactions:

> "*Hai buubuu*. (Here! It's a vroom vroom [car].) *Hai doozo*. (I give it to you.) *Hai kore choodai*. (Now give this to me.) *Choo-dai*. (Give me.) *Hai arigatoo*. (Yes! Thank you.)" (Fernald & Morikawa 1993, 653)

The Japanese mothers also encouraged their infant to be warm and empathetic toward the toy. For example, as the mother helped the infant gently pat the dog, she would say,

> "*Hai wan-chan*. (Here! It's a doggy.) *Kawaii kawaii shi-te age-te*. (Give it a love.) *Kawaii kawaii kawaii*. (Love, love, love.)" (Fernald & Morikawa 1993, 653)

While the American mothers emphasized teaching their child about the objects in the world around them, the Japanese mothers focused on socializing their child's interpersonal skills.

Implications for teachers and caregivers

One implication of learning to use language in different ways is that some children may be less familiar with standard classroom uses of language. For example, Heath (1983) observed young children in a community in the Piedmont Carolinas in which children did not often take the role of information givers. In particular, young children were not asked questions to which the adult already knew the answer (e.g., "What color is this?"). When teachers asked children these types of questions, the children were confused. They did not understand that the purpose of this type of question-asking was for the children to demonstrate what they knew and not for the teacher to learn something.

Similarly, children in this community did not understand that teachers were giving them directions when they made indirect statements or questions about something (e.g., "Someone else is talking now; we'll all have to wait," "Is this where the scissors belong?" Heath 1983, 280). Language reveals cultural differences. It is not simply that the child and the teacher may speak different languages—they may both use English, but they may be accustomed to using the language in different ways.

How can teachers respond to such diversity in language among the children and families in their classrooms? First, teachers need to develop strategies to communicate with parents when these parents are not fluent English speakers and the teachers are not fluent speakers of parents' home language. This may mean locating a translator for meetings with the entire class as well as with individual families. Translators may be people whom teachers know in the community, or they may be friends (or family members) of parents. Although speaking through a translator makes the conversation more stilted, it provides a beginning way to bridge the gap between home and school.

When the teacher and a child speak different languages—whether in a classroom in which there are several children who speak the same language, several children speak several different languages, or only one child's home language is not English—there are many things the teacher can do to help a child adjust to the classroom. The first of these, of course, is that teachers need to learn how to pronounce children's names. In addition, Tabors (2008) suggested that teachers learn a few useful words in the child's language (e.g., *bathroom, eat, stop, listen, look, sit, here, boys, girls*). Using sheltered English strategies—gesturing, using objects and pictures to help convey ideas—gives children additional cues to help decode the message.

Providing some activity choices (e.g., manipulatives) that the child can enter without having to negotiate interactions with other children offers the child who is learning English a "safe haven" (Tabors 2008) or respite from having to constantly work hard to try and understand other people and be understood. Talking about immediate events, objects, and activities that are ongoing and that children can see also helps children who are learning English. For example, when a teacher talks about the colors a child is using to paint,

that teacher is teaching English vocabulary and grammar in a way that respects the child as an individual and supports language and cognitive development. Encouraging children to respond in English and responding positively to children's early attempts at speaking English are additional strategies for supporting children's development of English (Tabors 2008).

> It is not simply that the child and the teacher may speak different languages—they may both use English, but they may be accustomed to using the language in different ways.

From the child's perspective, observing and following what other children are doing is one of the most useful strategies for coping in the classroom. If teachers include the child in a small group of children so that there are models to follow, the child who is learning English will have a better chance of understanding the teacher's instructions (Okagaki & Sternberg 1994). Similarly, if the teacher establishes consistent routines for the class, the child who is learning English can more easily participate in classroom activities.

Teachers can bring children's home language into the classroom by, for example, encouraging children to speak their home language to classmates who share that language, introducing new vocabulary words in English and in children's home language(s), and including books in children's home languages (Administration for Children and Families 2005). Teachers can also have storybooks that they read to children in English translated on tape for children to listen to in their home language. Asking parents to teach the class their child's favorite songs (in the child's home language) is another way to share the linguistic diversity of the classroom with all children. This also provides the child an opportunity to be an "expert," teaching classmates something that is familiar to him or her.

Developing sensitivity to parents' beliefs and practices

Given the great diversity in the United States, it is virtually impossible to know what parents from each cultural group believe about child development and parenting practices. Even if it were possible to learn what each cultural group believes, there is always great variation within each group in terms of what individuals value and practice. What can early childhood teachers do to enhance their ability to work with all families of children in their classrooms?

First, don't make assumptions about a family's practices. Within any cultural group, be it ethnic, racial, socioeconomic, or religious, individuals and families within the group vary in their beliefs and adherence to the social conventions of their community. Listening to parents and sharing perspectives with them is one way that teachers can begin to understand individual families' goals for their child and the ways in which they try to help their child achieve these goals. Asking parents about how to complement their efforts, rather than telling parents what they ought to be doing, supports this type of communication. This requires, as well, that teachers understand that some families' beliefs will be quite different from their own and that teachers learn to appreciate these differences.

For example, in one family, many of the parents' (culturally-based) values reflected goals of interdependence, rather than independence, for their young children. One way that this was expressed was in mealtime activities; in this family, the mother fed her 12-month-old, who had not yet been given any opportunity to feed himself. Imagine this child's surprise when he entered an infant-toddler classroom in which children had the opportunity to finger-feed themselves Cheerios and to drink from sippy-cups! First, he sat quietly watching other children eat, and then whimpered for a teacher to feed him. How might the teacher respond? Is it important that this little boy learn to become more independent (a goal of many parents)? To what extent should the teacher (and the school) accept the family's goals and alter their ways of offering children snack?

Even in a classroom in which all children share a similar cultural, ethnic, and linguistic background, family experiences will be different for each child. Providing children and families opportunities to share their own "family cultures" with other children is another way to bring a child's experiences from home into school. There are variety of ways that this might be accomplished: in small- and large-group activities where children (and teachers) have the opportunity to share something special about their family and their life at home, by using photographs of children's and teacher's families for a bulletin board or classroom book, by asking parents to provide copies of their children's favorite music or stories for use during free-choice and group activities, and by inviting parents into the classroom to share a family activity with the other children.

There are many more strategies that teachers can use to understand and reflect the beliefs and values of families and children (see, e.g., Derman-Sparks & the A.B.C. Task Force 1989; Lynch & Hanson 1992; Ramsey 1998; Tabors 2008). Reviewing teaching practices and thinking about ways to change classrooms into more accommodating and empowering environments for a wider range of children and families is an important task. As teachers experience more success in this, they begin to reflect and appreciate community diversity.

Updated from the Research in Review article in the May 2000 issue of *Young Children*.

Lynn Okagaki is professor emerita at Purdue University. **Karen E. Diamond** is a professor at Purdue University.

References

Administration for Children and Families. 2005. How can teachers and parents help young children become (and stay) bilingual? *Head Start Bulletin* 78. Online: www.headstartinfo.org/publications/hsbulletin78/hsb78_10fix.htm

Barnett, W.S., D.J. Yarosz, J. Thomas, K. Jung, & D. Blanco. 2007. Two-way and monolingual English immersion in preschool education: An experimental comparison. *Early Childhood Research Quarterly* 22: 277–93.

Bornstein, M.H., O.M. Haynes, H. Azuma, C. Galperin, S. Maital, M. Ogino, M. Painter, L. Pascual, M.G. Pêcheux, C. Rahn, S. Toda, P. Venuti, A. Vyt, & B. Wright. 1998. A cross-national study of self-evaluations and attributions in parenting: Argentina, Belgium, France, Israel, Italy, Japan, and the United States. *Developmental Psychology* 34 (4): 662–76.

Chao, R.K. 1994. Beyond parental control and authoritarian parenting style: Understanding Chinese parenting through the cultural notion of training. *Child Development* 65: 1111–19.

Chao, R.K. 2000. The parenting of immigrant Chinese and European American mothers: Relations between parenting styles, socialization goals, and parental practices. *Journal of Applied Developmental Psychology* 21 (2): 233–48.

Chen, X., K.H. Rubin, G. Cen, P.D. Hastings, H. Chen, & S.L. Stewart. 1998. Child-rearing attitudes and behavioral inhibition in Chinese and Canadian toddlers: A cross-cultural study. *Developmental Psychology* 34 (4): 677–86.

Derman-Sparks, L., & the A.B.C. Task Force. 1989. *Anti-bias curriculum: Tools for empowering young children*. Washington, DC: NAEYC.

Espinosa, L.M. 2007. English-language learners as they enter school. In *School readiness and the transition to kindergarten in the era of accountability*, eds. R.C. Pianta, M.J. Cox, & K.L. Snow, 175–95. Baltimore: Paul H. Brookes.

Fernald, A., & H. Morikawa. 1993. Common themes and cultural variations in Japanese and American mothers' speech to infants. *Child Development* 64: 637–56.

Garcia Coll, C.T. 1990. Developmental outcome of minority infants: A process-oriented look into our beginnings. *Child Development* 61: 270–89.

Gonzalez-Ramos, G., L.H. Zayas, & E.V. Cohen. 1998. Child-rearing values of low-income, urban Puerto Rican mothers of preschool children. *Professional Psychology: Research and Practice* 29 (4): 377–82.

Hakuta, K., & E. Garcia. 1989. Bilingualism and education. *American Psychologist* 44: 374–79.

Halgunseth, L.C., J.M. Ispa, & D. Rudy. 2006. Parental control in Latino families: An integrated review of the literature. *Child Development* 77: 1282–97.

Harrison, A.O., M.N. Wilson, C.J. Pine, S.Q. Chan, & R. Buriel. 1990. Family ecologies of ethnic minority children. *Child Development* 61: 347–62.

Hart, B., & T.R. Risley. 1995. *Meaningful differences in the everyday experiences of young American children*. Baltimore: Paul H. Brookes.

Harwood, R.L. 1992. The influence of culturally derived values on Anglo and Puerto Rican mothers' perceptions of attachment behavior. *Child Development* 63: 822–39.

Heath, S.B. 1983. *Ways with words: Language, life, and work in communities and classrooms*. New York: Cambridge University Press.

Hernandez, D.J., N.A. Denton, & S.E. Macartney. 2007. Demographic trends and the transition years. In *School readiness and the transition to kindergarten in the era of accountability*, eds. R.C. Pianta, M.J. Cox, & K.L. Snow, 217–82. Baltimore: Paul H. Brookes.

Hoffman, L.W. 1988. Cross-cultural differences in childrearing goals. In *Parental behavior in diverse societies*, eds. R.A. LeVine, P.M. Miller, & M.M. West, 99–122. San Francisco: Jossey-Bass.

Joe, J.R., & R.S. Malach. 1997. Families with Native American roots. In *Developing cross-cultural competence: A guide for working with young children and their families*, eds. E.W. Lynch & M.J. Hanson, 89–119. Baltimore: Paul H. Brookes.

LeVine, R.A. 1988. Human parental care: Universal goals, cultural strategies, individual behavior. In *Parental behavior in diverse societies*, eds. R.A. LeVine, P.M. Miller, & M.M. West, 3–11. San Francisco: Jossey-Bass.

Leyendecker, B., R.L. Harwood, M.E. Lamb, & A. Schölmerich. 2002. Mothers' socialisation goals and evaluations of desirable and undesirable everyday situations in two diverse cultural groups. *International Journal of Behavioural Development* 26 (3): 248–58.

Lynch, E.W., & M.J. Hanson, eds. 1992. *Developing cross-cultural competence: A guide for working with young children and their families*. Baltimore: Paul H. Brookes.

Machamer, A.M., & E. Gruber. 1998. Secondary school, family, and educational risk: Comparing American Indian adolescents and their peers. *The Journal of Educational Research* 91 (6): 357–69.

Miller, A.M., & R.L. Harwood. 2001. Long-term socialisation goals and the construction of infants' social networks among middle class Anglo and Puerto Rican mothers. *International Journal of Behavioral Development* 25 (5): 450–57.

Ogbu, J.U. 1981. Origins of human competence: A cultural-ecological perspective. *Child Development* 52: 413–29.

Okagaki, L., & R.J. Sternberg. 1993. Parental beliefs and children's school performance. *Child Development* 64: 36–56.

Okagaki, L., & R.J. Sternberg. 1994. Perspectives on kindergarten: Rafael, Vanessa, and Jamlien go to school. *Childhood Education* 71 (1): 14–19.

Powell, D.R., & K. Diamond. 1995. Approaches to parent-teacher relationships in U.S. early childhood programs during the twentieth century. *Journal of Education* 177 (3): 71–94.

Ramsey, P. 1998. *Teaching and learning in a diverse world: Multicultural education for young children.* 2d ed. New York: Teachers College Press.

Spence, J.T. 1985. Achievement American style: The rewards and costs of individualism. *American Psychologist* 40: 1285–95.

Tabors, P.O. 2008. *One child, two languages: A guide for early childhood educators of children learning English as a second language.* 2d ed. Baltimore: Paul H. Brookes.

Triandis, H.C., R. Bontempo, M.J. Villareal, M. Asai, & N. Lucca. 1988. Individualism and collectivism: Cross-cultural perspectives on self-ingroup relationships. *Journal of Personality and Social Psychology* 54: 323–38.

Tudge, J.R.H., F. Doucet, D. Odero, T.M. Sperb, C.A. Piccinini, & R.S. Lopes. 2006. A window into different cultural worlds: Young children's everyday activities in the U.S., Brazil, and Kenya. *Child Development* 77: 1446–69.

19 The Education of Hispanics in Early Childhood: Of Roots and Wings

Eugene E. García

As a researcher who has often been asked to speak in a language other than that solely the purview of research, I have sought to engage my *professional* research, experience, and expertise with my *personal* cultural and linguistic experience to address national education policy. The professional in me has been nurtured at some of the best educational institutions in the United States, while the nonprofessional has been nurtured in a large, rural, Mexican-American family. I was born in the United States, as were my great-grandparents, grandparents, mother, father, and my nine brothers and sisters. We spoke Spanish as our primary language of communication, while our schooling language was English. In my immediate family of 10 children, only 4 of us graduated from high school.

Bringing these *personas* (Spanish for "persons") together was not as difficult as I had expected and the mixture was quite helpful to the wide variety of people I interacted with in my national role. Bringing together these personas, I communicated with individuals in ways not possible had I spoken only with one voice or separate voices. Similarly, to help further our understanding of life in a diverse society—particularly of Hispanics growing up in the United States during their early childhood years—this chapter presents my intersecting but distinct voices: *Eugene*, who represents my academic life; *Gene*, representing my social and cultural roles; and *Gino*, my linguistic and cultural "Hispanic-ness."

The three voices here address issues of the past, present, and future. They recognize the multiple selves that make up not only my own persona but those that are a reality for all of us. It is useful to recognize that we all walk in varied and diverse cultures. There is great diversity within each individual, just as there is diversity among individuals and the many cultures they belong to or represent. We all live with diversity, some of us more than others. No one escapes this challenge or its advantages and disadvantages.

The research

The historical pattern of the education of Hispanics in the United States is a continuous story of underachievement. It need not continue to be that way.

The following research discusses vulnerability factors for Hispanics both within and outside the education arena, along with data related to the "effective" treatment of this growing population of young children and families. The discussion addresses the following:

1. an overall demographic assessment of factors related to the schooling of culturally diverse populations, including issues of poverty, family stability, and immigrant status;

2. a particular analysis of the challenges associated with the growing number of language-minority students who are Hispanic—children who come to school with limited or no proficiency in English; and

3. a presentation of conceptual and empirical perspectives that sets the stage for a more informed approach to the education of Hispanics in early childhood.

Demographic attributes

Children of Hispanic (or Latino) heritage in the United States are not a homogenous group but embody diverse social, cultural, and linguistic backgrounds (Ramirez & de la Cruz 2003; Montemayor & Mendoza 2004). Hispanic children represent, for

example, long-term U.S.-born populations along with those from various other countries-of-origin, each of which is associated with a unique combination of histories, cultural practices, perspectives, and traditions.

Recent growth in the young Hispanic population in the United States has largely been driven by immigration patterns from Latin America (Ramirez & de la Cruz 2003). In 2000, one in five children ages 0–8 in the United States was Hispanic (Hernandez 2006). Of these children, more than 64 percent were born into *immigrant families*, which means that at least one parent was born outside the United States. A large majority of young Hispanic children are of Mexican origin (68 percent), but substantial proportions have origins in Puerto Rico (9 percent), Central America (7 percent), South America (6 percent), or Cuba or the Dominican Republic (3 percent each) (Hernandez 2006).

Two thirds of Mexican-origin and Cuban-origin young children live in immigrant families, rising to about 90 percent for those with origins in the Dominican Republic and Central or South America. Especially important is that the vast majority of young Hispanic children are, themselves, U.S. citizens: 85 percent of those

Roots and wings: Three voices

While English First, an organization committed to establishing English as the official U.S. language, is passionately concerned that multilingualism will produce divisiveness, indigenous people whose roots in the Americas outdistance the "white man's" presence mourn just as passionately the loss of their languages and cultures. As this country and the world shrink communicatively, economically, socially, and intellectually, diversity is becoming harder to hide—but it has always been there. In the following pages, I address issues related to the education

of Hispanics in early childhood with the varied voices within me.

My three voices

This article presents my intersecting but distinct voices to help further our understanding of life in a diverse society—particularly of Hispanics growing up in the United States during their early childhood years.

Eugene. This voice often represents my intellectual upbringing. It is recognized primarily by my academic credentials: degrees received (and where and when), my success in those environments, academic positions I have held and their status in the academic with South American origins, 88 percent of those with Mexican origins, and 91–92 percent of those with origins in the Dominican Republic and Central America (Capps et al. 2004; Hernandez 2006).

Compared with white populations and other racial/ethnic groups, Hispanic children and families demonstrate a number of favorable demographic attributes. In an analysis of 2000 Census data, Hernandez (2006) found that a large proportion of Hispanic children live in two-parent households. Indeed, 77 percent of young Hispanic children (ages 0–8) overall lived with two parents in 2000. Among them, the proportion rises to 81–86 percent for young children in immigrant families from Mexico, Central and South America, and Cuba. These proportions decrease, however, in families with U.S.-born parents with roots in these regions, as well as from the Dominican Republic and Puerto Rico.

Young Hispanic children, on average, live in families with a strong work ethic and desire to succeed (Hernandez 2006). Ninety-three (93) percent of these children have fathers who worked during the year previous to the 2000 Census survey. The proportion is the same in both U.S.-born and immigrant families. Moreover, Hispanic children are approximately three times more likely to have one or more adult in the home in *addition* to father and mother also in the workforce.

Despite low socioeconomic circumstances, Hispanic families demonstrate various positive physical health outcomes. Studies have consistently found that Hispanics have lower infant morality rates, better birth outcomes, healthier diets, and lower rates of obesity compared with white populations (Escarce, Morales, & Rumbaut 2006). These domains have been found to vary between national origin groups and by immigrant generation status. Hispanics of Puerto Rican descent, for example, tend to have worse health status indicators than other national origin groups, while Hispanics of Mexican and Central American origin often exhibit the most favorable health outcomes despite their poverty status.

Survey data have also highlighted that Hispanic parents demonstrate a positive attitude toward education and the schooling of their children. Although parents of young Hispanic children do not have high levels of formal education attainment on average, they express interest in enrolling their children in early education programs and supporting them through postsecondary schooling. They have high educational

world, my empirical research, my teaching, and of course, the articles and books I have written.

I have used my set of experiences and accomplishments to attempt to broaden in critical and strategic ways an understanding of language acquisition, teaching, learning, and schooling, and the specific relevance of these to language-minority populations—that is, to learners who come to the educational enterprise not knowing the language of that formal enterprise, and particularly to students like me, who are classified as Hispanic in the present jargon of educators and demographers.

I did not begin my academic pursuits with this specific population in mind but have naturally gravitated toward using my professional skills to address issues of relevance to it, but not only to it…

Gene. Other parts of me are more rooted in the non-academic world, in my social and cultural realities. I am a son, brother, husband, father, and so on. In such social and cultural roles, I have experienced a wonderful family environment, learning much from my father and mother—neither of whom ever had the opportunity to attend school. They taught me to respect them, my elders, my brothers and sisters, and others

Hispanic Demographics

Demographic character

• Of the approximately 6.8 million young Hispanic children in the continental United States, the following information characterizes the population's ethnic diversity.

Country/Area of Origin	Number (in thousands)	Percentage
Mexico	4,400	65
Puerto Rico	630	9
Central America	490	7
South America	370	6
Cuba	160	2
Other Hispanic countries	700	10

• In 2000, 64 percent of young Hispanic children were born into immigrant families in which at least one parent was born outside the United States.

• Although most young Hispanic children are from immigrant families, close to 90 percent of Hispanic children are U.S. citizens.

• Almost 60 percent of young Hispanic children in the United States are concentrated in three states: California (31.2 percent), Texas (18.3 percent), and New York (7.3 percent).

• Young Hispanic children are a rapidly growing population in states with no previous history of housing Hispanics. For example, in both Georgia and North Carolina, the share of births by Hispanic mothers grew from 2 percent in 1990 to 14 percent in 2004.

Indices of "vulnerability"

• In 2006, the median income for Hispanics was $37,781, compared with $52,423 for non-Hispanics.

• Most Hispanics (78 percent) live in areas with populations exceeding 500,000 people; almost 50 percent live in one of ten traditional major metropolitan areas.

• In 1998, about 30 percent of Hispanic children who started kindergarten were not proficient enough in oral English to be given a reading readiness assessment in English at the beginning of the school year.

Education

• Young Hispanic children are significantly below national norms on academic achievement tests of reading and math skills.

• In 2000, about 44 percent of the Hispanic children had mothers who had not graduated high school.

• In 2000, about 20 percent of Hispanic children had mothers who had not gone beyond the eighth grade.

Sources: Hernandez 2006; National Task Force on Early Childhood Education 2007; Neut 2006; U.S. Bureau of the Census 2006.

aspirations for their children (Nuñez, Cuccaro-Alamin, & Carroll 1998). A survey conducted by the Tomás Rivera Policy Institute found that more than 90 percent of Hispanic parents felt that it is very important or somewhat important for children to attend preschool (Perez & Zarate 2006).

Using data from a national sample of children born between December 2001 and January 2002, López, Barrueco, and Miles (2006) described the home language environments of Hispanic infants. The largest group (34 percent) of Hispanic infants lived in homes in which Spanish was the primary language, with some English spoken. Twenty-two (22) percent lived in homes in which primarily English was spoken, with some Spanish; 21 percent in English-only homes; and 19 percent in Spanish-only homes. In sum, it was found that approximately three in four Hispanic infants were exposed to Spanish in the home.

The positive attributes that Hispanic children and families demonstrate—two-parent households, strong work ethic, physical health, positive attitude toward school/education, and so on—tend to decrease the negative effects of poverty and low parent education (Shields & Behrman 2004). However, these attributes are not generally sufficient to sustain Hispanic students on a trajectory of educational success over time. Robust early interventions are necessary, and have proven successful, to increase school readiness and decrease pervasive achievement gaps.

Early education

Currently, Hispanics lag behind their white and Asian-American peers at all proficiency levels for reading and mathematics (by five to six months) at the beginning and throughout K–12 schooling (Braswell, Daane, & Grigg 2003; NCES 2003; García et al. 2005; Reardon & Galindo 2006). Educational achievement patterns of virtually all racial/ethnic groups are established during the early years of school and change little thereafter (García et al. 2005). Although some of the difference between racial/ethnic groups is accounted for by socioeconomic differences between groups (on average Hispanics have lower socioeconomic status (SES) than white and Asian-American populations), much of it is not (Reardon & Galindo 2006).

Using data from the Early Childhood Longitudinal Study, Kindergarten Cohort (ECLS-K), Reardon and Galindo (2006) found that Hispanic children scored four to six months lower in mathematics and

as my teachers—and most of all, to respect myself. They never gave me a formal lesson about these things, they just lived them in the harsh realities of poverty and the hard work any migrant or sharecropping family understands. This teaching and learning included experiences of outright racism in which our language, color, and heritage were not always met with either individual or group respect. From these experiences and teachers emerged the voice of Gene (a name used most often by my family and friends).

As Gene, I agreed as an undergraduate to work in the migrant camps, tutoring adults in English and related subjects so they could earn a GED. The Gene persona realized early that he was different. I spoke primarily Spanish; my peers only English. My family and I worked in the fields; my peers and their families hired us to work in their fields. My peers enjoyed a much higher standard of living; I recall being embarrassed that my family did not take summer vacations or have running water and inside toilets. Quite honestly, most of the time, these differences did not weigh heavily on my mind or affect my behavior—I had lots of friends, some like me and others quite different from me.

reading than their white peers within all five SES quintiles (SES in ECLS-K is a composite of household income and parent occupation/level of education) from kindergarten through fifth grade. Hence, race/ethnicity had a substantial effect on early achievement over and above SES. In a separate analysis of ECLS-K data, Reardon (2003) noted that these achievement differences by SES and by race/ethnicity from kindergarten through first grade were attributable to processes within, between, and out of schools. That is, home and school practices have been shown to have important relationships, both positive and negative, on racial/ethnic achievement gaps in early education (García, Jensen, & Cuéllar 2006).

Because academic achievement during the early elementary grades is strongly associated with sustained success throughout secondary and postsecondary schooling (Gilliam & Zigler 2004; Magnuson & Waldfogel 2005), Hispanic children are especially positioned to benefit from involvement in a high-quality universal prekindergarten (UPK) program. No extensive study exists regarding the longitudinal impacts of Hispanic participation in prekindergarten across the country, but current evidence suggests that Hispanics—and children generally—who attend prekindergarten programs learn language, social skills, and practical skills that are related to enhanced achievement in the future.

Indeed, an evaluation of the UPK program in Tulsa, Oklahoma, revealed several benefits for young Hispanics (Gormley et al. 2005). In this study, authors estimated the impact of prekindergarten on achievement for letter-word identification, spelling, and applied problems. The sample consisted of 1,567 children enrolled in prekindergarten and 1,461 kindergarten children who had just completed prekindergarten. Gains for Hispanic children in the UPK program were especially impressive. They experienced a 79 percent gain in letter-word identification, a 39 percent gain in spelling, and a 54 percent gain in applied problem solving. These outpaced gains that would have occurred naturally during one year of children's development.

Momentum is currently building in the United States at all levels of government to make substantial investments and commitments to UPK programs. The provision of high-quality educational access for young children in the country is motivated by research not only in child development but also in economics. In

Later, it was likely more Gene than Eugene who ran for and was elected to the local school board and accepted the invitation to join the Clinton administration and Secretary of Education Richard Riley in the U.S. Department of Education. In political/policy roles like this one, I realized that policymakers and practitioners of education do not always act based on the best theory, proven educational practices, or even promising educational innovations. They act mostly out of political motives.

Gino. Another voice within me is identified best by the endearing name that my mother used for me: Gino. In my large, quite Catholic family, baptizing a child is a distinct honor and, in recognition of that honor, *los padrinos* ("the godparents") are given the authority to name the child. At my birth, my parents selected my eldest sister and her husband to serve as my *padrinos*, and my sister was enchanted with the name Eugene. That is how I came to have a Greek name in a cohort of brothers and sisters named Antonio, Emelio, Cecelia, Ciprianita, Abel, Federico, Tiburcio, Ernesto, and Christina, born of parents named Lorenzo and Juanita. My mother could not pronounce Eugene, so to her and my immediate family, I became Gino.

terms of development, neuropsychological research shows that the brains of very young children are extremely malleable during the early years of life (Ramey & Ramey 1998; Shonkoff & Phillips 2000).

Indeed, a key characteristic of early childhood (0–3 years old) is the remarkably rapid brain development that occurs during this period. In many ways, these early years provide the foundation for the brain's lifelong capacity for growth and change. A strong neurological groundwork is established in early childhood through rich experiences, which allows the brain to develop to the point of being able to process, encode, and interact with the environment (Kagan & Kauerz 2005). High-quality early education programs are able to provide the necessary scaffolding and facilitate this development. Given the size, rapid growth, and comparatively low achievement levels of young Hispanic children in the United States, these children are particularly situated to benefit from high-quality prekindergarten programs (García & Gonzáles 2006). However, although enrollments among Hispanics are on the rise, these children are less likely than their white, Asian-American, and African-American peers to attend any sort of prekindergarten program (García

et al. 2005). Currently, only 40 percent of 3- to 5-year-old Hispanics attend a prekindergarten program, compared with about 60 percent of white and African-American children (NCES 2002).

The low enrollment of Hispanic children in these programs is often misinterpreted as a function of the reluctance of Hispanic families to place their children in a center-based program. However, availability of high-quality and publicly funded programs is frequently limited in Hispanic communities, which reduces access and, therefore, enrollment (Fuller, Bridges, & Livas 2006).

Addressing quality

When they are enrolled in prekindergarten, Hispanic children are more likely than their peers to attend low-quality programs: those with less-prepared teachers, fewer resources, higher teacher:child ratios, and larger class sizes. Moreover, even when high-quality programs exist within communities, many parents are unaware that services are available because of a lack of community outreach. Language can also be a barrier to enrollment. Parents need to be able to communicate with the center, understand the enrollment paperwork, and engage meaningfully with their child's teacher.

Gino carries a distinct sense of cultural "Hispanic-ness," "Chicanismo," "Latino-ness," or "Raza-ness." These concepts reflect a deep regard for the linguistic and cultural roots that foster identity, best exemplified by this lesson from my father:

> For farmworkers and sharecroppers, winter was a time to prepare for work because there was not much work during this period. One winter on the high plain of Colorado, where I was born and raised, my father pointed to an *árbol*—a cottonwood tree. He asked, *"Por qué puede vivir ese árbol en el frío del invierno y en el calor del verano?"* ("How can that tree survive the bitter cold of winter and the harsh heat of summer?") My

> father was a man of few words—relatives often characterized him as quiet and shy—but when he spoke, we all listened very carefully. I rambled on about how big and strong the tree was and how its limbs and trunk were like the strong arms and bodies of my elder brothers. Then he kindly provided a different perspective by referring to a common Spanish proverb (a dicho/consejo): *"El árbol fuerte tiene raíces maduras"* ("A strong tree has mature roots").

In articulating this significant piece of the analysis that was absent from my youthful thoughts, my father made clear that without strong roots, strong trees are impossible—and we don't even see

Targeted preschool programs are often associated with low quality and do not always reach eligible children. Head Start, for example, reaches only about 35 percent of eligible children (Currie 2001), and targeted prekindergarten programs in Arizona, California, and Texas meet only four of the 10 quality benchmarks identified by the National Institute of Early Education Research (Barnett et al. 2005). Thus, because Hispanic children from all socioeconomic levels have been shown to benefit cognitively from enrollment in high-quality preschool, best evidence suggests that providing state-funded UPK programs constitutes a viable approach to early education delivery.

Research evidence also suggests that the success of UPK programs for Hispanics depends on the extent to which language and culture are incorporated into the center, classroom, and instruction. Because approximately three in four young Hispanics are exposed to Spanish in the home (Lopez, Barrueco, & Miles 2006), the integration of Spanish and culturally relevant content is essential. A trademark of high-quality prekindergarten programs for young Hispanic children is the provision of dual-language (English and Spanish) content and instruction by school staff who

are bilingual and culturally competent (Barnett et al. 2006; Borman et al. 2006). This approach validates the child's cognitive and linguistic abilities while bridging home-school cultural differences—establishing an environment in which parents feel comfortable and are able to express themselves to teachers.

In their study, Barnett and colleagues (2006) compared the effects of a dual-language program with a monolingual English program within the same school district. Children in the study were from both Spanish- and English-speaking backgrounds. Programs were compared on measures of children's growth in language, emergent literacy, and mathematics skills. Among the native Spanish-speaking children, those enrolled in the dual-language program demonstrated greater gains in phonological awareness in both English and Spanish, as well as gains in Spanish vocabulary. Authors of this study concluded, therefore, that programs built around valuing and teaching relevant culture and traditions and directly addressing language differences and needs were among the most effective. This is consistent with research by Borman and colleagues (2006), who conducted a meta-analysis of the research on the achievement effects of the

the roots! The roots of many Hispanics in this country have been either ignored or stripped away in the name of growing strong. Many have been directed to stop speaking Spanish, to perceive their culture as "less than" the dominant one, and to assimilate as quickly as possible so they can succeed in American society (Chavez 1991). Unfortunately, many have suffered the fate of the rootless tree—they have fallen socially, economically, academically, and culturally.

However, to Gino, my mother made it very clear: Roots and their concomitant integrity and self-respect were not enough.

She wanted the very best for all her children, certainly not the long and painful fieldwork that she had endured for a lifetime. She wanted us *bien educados*, having a set of formal and marketable skills. She made very clear that children needed wings, like the wings she insisted we children grew every night upon falling asleep, so as to fly to heaven to be with God. "All children," she said, "are angels."

In recent stories by Hispanic author Victor Villaseñor (1991), his mother elaborates further on this notion, saying that the children fly to God each night and station themselves as stars in His heaven. Both our mothers expressed a special regard for nationally disseminated school improvement programs (known as "comprehensive" school reforms) implemented in predominantly Hispanic elementary school contexts.

Recommendations

The following recommendations are offered to improve educational opportunities for young Hispanics in United States. They emphasize the need for policy and practice in early education to directly address language and for curriculum and instruction to reflect relevant culture and traditions. Findings from the available research literature on schooling, language, and policy highlight the need for expanded UPK access *and* for these programs to have rich language environments, dual-language programs, and high-quality teachers and staff. These recommendations are directed to those who influence early education policy and practice at the federal, state, and local levels, including governments, private foundations, nonprofit organizations, and parents.

Universal prekindergarten. Young Hispanic children ages 3 and 4 years old should be given access to free, state-funded preschools where enrollment is open and voluntary—that is, universal prekin-

dergarten. Evidence suggests that high-quality prekindergarten programs improve school readiness for young Hispanic children and decrease achievement gaps between racial/ethnic groups at kindergarten entry. These programs should have bilingual and culturally competent staff to effectively engage children and to develop sustainable relationships with family members.

Moreover, states would be wise to adopt prekindergarten curricula in both Spanish and English. States and local communities should work together to offer high-quality educational experiences with a variety of schedule options. In states where access to state-funded prekindergarten is not yet universal—that is, not available to all children—policymakers and program administrators should expand definitions of eligibility to include children with limited English proficiency. This should be an intermediate step, intended to increase Hispanic enrollments and serve more at-risk children, until the larger goal of universal access is attained.

Rich language environments. UPK environments of young Hispanic children should be rich in language. Richness is defined through frequency and quality of language use. In terms of frequency,

the sanctity of childhood and required children to have wings to perform their related roles. My mother emphasized the she could not provide the kind of wings that God and a good education could provide. She knew that the teachers and schools would have to take me further than she could personally. Education would need to provide the strong and elaborate wings for me to succeed where she often felt she had failed: "Go to school—strong wings like those of an eagle are also what you need in this world to raise your family and provide for them all that we have been unable to provide for you."

The "Hispanic" debate

Eugene, Gene, and Gino realize that their voices are not alone, nor are their views held by all Hispanics in the United States. Most critical of the views of an interactive relationship of "roots and wings" for Hispanics are two well regarded and influential Hispanic authors, each in her or his own way refuting the importance of roots and the relationship of those roots to the educational development of Hispanics.

Linda Chavez, an adviser in the Reagan White House, commentator, and author of *Out of the Barrio: Toward a New Politics of Hispanic Assimilation* (1991), suggests that research on cognitive development, language, and early experiences shows that the amount of talk and conversational exchange between adults and young children is strongly associated with school readiness and academic success in formal schooling. Teachers, aides, and other school personnel should engage young Hispanic children in casual talk as much as possible and, where feasible, encourage parents to do the same.

Quality refers to language systems and culture. Young Hispanics should be exposed to English and Spanish in the classroom and provided with many opportunities to speak and express themselves in either language—allowing for linguistic exploration and mixtures. For young children managing more than one language, academic skills are much more likely to develop and transfer between languages when environments allow access to knowledge through all language systems, in culturally relevant ways (August & Shanahan 2006). Otherwise, cognitive development is stifled.

Rich language environments that integrate Spanish and English on an ongoing basis will also facilitate important parent-school associations. Spanish-speaking parents are more likely to involve themselves in schools and classrooms in which Spanish is regularly used.

Dual-language programs. Young Hispanic children should have access to high-quality dual-language programs (i.e., two-way immersion) that teach English and Spanish language skills through content. Integrating native English and Spanish speakers in the same classroom, thereby fostering linguistic and ethnic equity among peers, dual-language programs have been shown to support literacy development in English for Hispanic children without compromising Spanish skills. Moreover, research shows that academic achievement levels of young Spanish-speaking Hispanics as well as their native English-speaking peers enrolled in dual-language programs are equivalent or, in many cases, superior to outcomes of children in English-only classrooms.

Dual-language programs should be strategically structured to promote and sustain the development of children enrolled. Researchers at the Center for Applied Linguistics (CAL 2005) have provided a set of principles to help school personnel establish and maintain high-quality programs. These suggest that the program:

Every previous group—Germans, Irish, Italians, Greeks, Jews, Poles—struggled to be accepted fully into the social, political and economic mainstream, sometimes against the opposition of a hostile majority. They learned the language, acquired education and skills, and adapted their own customs and traditions to fit an American context. (2)

The key for Hispanic success in America, Chavez argues, is minimizing the public/governmental recognition of Hispanic roots and the individual and governmental promotion of assimilation. She chides the federal government, particularly federal bilingual education programs, and Hispanic leaders for promoting permanent victim status and vying with African Americans for the distinction of being the poorest, most segregated, and least educated minority, thereby entitling them to government handouts. She concludes that these actions in turn encourage Hispanics to maintain their language and culture and their specific identity in return for rewards handed out through affirmative action and federal, state, and local educational policies that thwart assimilation.

This does not sound like my father's concern for the importance of roots or my mothers' emphasis on wings.

- create and maintain an infrastructure that supports an accountability process;
- use curriculum that promotes and maintains the development of bilingual, biliterate, and multicultural competencies for all students;
- use student-centered instructional strategies derived from research-based principles of dual-language education;
- recruit and retain high-quality dual-language staff;
- have knowledgeable leaders who promote equity among groups and support the goals of additive bilingualism, biliteracy, and cross-cultural competence;
- have a responsive infrastructure for positive, ongoing relations with students' families and the community; and
- be adequately funded and supported by school staff, families, and the community.

High-quality teachers in dual-language programs. The provision of rich language environments and high-quality UPK programs necessitates high-quality teachers. This means teachers are bilingual (proficient in both English and Spanish) and knowledgeable regarding the cultural and linguistic circumstances of Hispanic families, particularly the educational strengths and needs of their children. Indeed, research shows that the transfer of academic skills between languages is heightened and early achievement outcomes improved for young bilingual and emergent bilingual students when teachers use Spanish in the classroom.

The most successful teachers are fluent in both languages, understand learning patterns associated with second-language acquisition, have a mastery of appropriate instructional strategies (i.e., cooperative learning, sheltered instruction, differentiated instruction, and strategic teaching), and have strong organizational and communication skills. With these skills, teachers will be able to interact with Hispanic parents appropriately, encouraging them to engage in literacy activities with their children at home; to find out as much detail as possible about the linguistic backgrounds of their students; and to develop creative and accurate assessments of each child's linguistic ability and development.

The optimal situation is for lead teachers and school staff in general to be

Another Hispanic author, Richard Rodriguez, is very eloquent in his description of his upbringing in a Mexican home and a Catholic school where the English-speaking nuns literally beat the Spanish language and the "Hispanic-ness" out of him. His book *Hunger of Memory* (1982) describes this forced assimilation, painful as it was, that propelled him to new heights of education achievement. Although he himself never articulates the conclusion, he leaves open the suggestion that such treatment of Hispanics is exactly what they need to get over their "problems."

Eugene, Gene and Gino reach a very different conclusion in this discussion. Gino feels that Hispanics, such as those he and his family represent, have been educationally shortchanged.

For Hispanics in the United States, the emphasis on building wings in school has strategically focused on teaching English language skills: "Teach them English well, and then they will succeed." Yet all educators realize that in today's information age, education must provide broad and strong intellectual wings related to fundamental linguistic, mathematical, scientific, and technological literacies. English literacy is important, but it is not enough.

proficient in both languages and familiar with students' cultures. However, when this is not possible, it is recommended that a "language specialist" be provided. Language specialists are bilingual professionals who serve as consultants to teachers and aides in the classroom to help English language learners to learn and achieve, recognizing and leveraging their existing strengths. Having a language specialist in the classroom will also help English-speaking teachers make essential links with Spanish-speaking parents.

Conclusion

It remains so important to understand the specific linguistic and cultural *raíces* ("roots") and how early education can assist in developing the academic *alas* ("wings") that these children need. Success of the above-mentioned recommendations is contingent upon the development of educational policies that target the needs of young Hispanic children. Specific policies at all levels of government should strive to provide and support rich language environments and high-quality dual-language prekindergarten programs, and to support efforts to recruit and prepare highly qualified teachers. In addition, it is recommended that educational policies support the expansion of state-funded prekindergartens, increase Hispanic enrollments in these programs, develop parent outreach initiatives, and improve assessment procedures and accountability measures.

Regarding teacher quality, state governments need to fund programs to increase the number of prekindergarten teachers in their states who are proficient in Spanish, and the federal government needs to develop strategic programs designed to achieve this end. As a part of their training, teachers should be taught about second-language acquisition and about how content learning intersects with the process of managing two language

systems. States may consider aggressively recruiting teachers from Hispanic communities as a way to increase the body of linguistically and culturally competent teachers. Colleges and universities should be engaged as partners to ensure that bilingual teachers are recruited to the field of early education and that teachers receive appropriate training.

State governments should continue to expand their state-funded prekindergarten initiatives with the objective of creating voluntary universal prekindergarten systems within the next 10–20 years. For Hispanic children, that expansion should be accompanied by curriculum development and instructional approaches that integrate both Spanish and English. In addition, educational policymakers should seek to increase enrollment rates of Hispanics in such programs by funding extensive local efforts to provide information to Hispanic parents on the availability of prekindergarten programs in their communities.

Local education agencies should be allotted the necessary supports to develop dual-language programs. These programs should be developed based on empirical evidence and strategies shown to be successful (CAL 2005). Such programs should constantly be assessed and, where/when necessary, modified to optimize learning, language development, and general academic performance of Hispanic children.

Finally, assessment practices geared to evaluating the academic progress of young Hispanic students must be improved to better measure progress and evaluate program effectiveness. The fundamental purpose of assessment should be to improve learning outcomes and service provision for these children. To accurately determine language and cognitive competency of young Hispanic students, appropriate tests and testing procedures are necessary.

For several decades many of these specific reform initiatives have been aimed at linguistically and culturally diverse students. As implemented, the "reforms" have generated some movement at the policy, practice, and achievement levels. But they have not produced the robust changes in early educational performance that are needed, ignoring what counts for the academic success of young Hispanic students. However, new educational practices that have the following characteristics are beginning to demonstrate significant promise for young Hispanic learners:

- strategies that begin with the linguistic and cultural attributes of the children and build from there—they respect and engage previous knowledge bases regarding the child and cultural conceptualizations of academic content areas;

- strategies that are directly responsive to the linguistic background of the child that bridge to high levels of vocabulary, concept, and repertoires in English;

- strategies that assess in various ways the development and learning and are used to effect changes in instructional architectures and delivery;

- strategies that make use of multiple resources—human, fiscal, physical, temporal, technological—to address instruction; and

- strategies that invest in early development of linguistic and cognitive development, building on the child's existing competencies.

Thinking differently about Hispanic children involves viewing them and our education system in new ways that may contradict conventional notions. This change in thinking allows early childhood professionals to come to a new set of realizations about the value and importance of schooling experiences, and it leads in the direction of innovation in education versus reform.

Updated from the Research in Review article in the March 1997 issue of *Young Children*.

Eugene E. García is a professor at Arizona State University.

References

August, D., & T. Shanahan, eds. 2006. *Report of the national literacy panel on language minority youth and children*. Mahwah, NJ: Lawrence Erlbaum.

Barnett, S., J.T. Hustedt, K.B. Robin, & K.L. Schulman. 2005. *The state of preschool: 2005 state preschool yearbook*. New Brunswick, NJ: National Institute of Early Education Research.

Barnett, W.S., D.J. Yarosz, J. Thomas, & D. Blanco. 2006. *Two-way and monolingual English immersion in preschool education: An experimental comparison*. New Brunswick, NJ: National Institute for Early Education.

Borman, G.D., G.H. Hewes, M. Reilly, & S. Alvarado. 2006. *Comprehensive school reform for Latino elementary-school students: A meta-analysis.* A report to the National Task Force on Early Childhood Education for Hispanics. Online: www.ecehispanic.org/work/csr_Borman.pdf.

Braswell, J., M. Daane, & W. Grigg. 2003. *The Nation's Report Card: Mathematics highlights 2003.* NCES 2004451. Washington, DC: U.S. Department of Education, National Center for Education Statistics.

CAL (Center for Applied Linguistics). 2005. *Guiding principles for dual language education*. Washington, DC: Author.

Capps, R., M. Fix, J. Ost, J. Reardon-Anderson, & J. Passel. 2004. *The health and well-being of young children of immigrants*. Washington, DC: The Urban Institute.

Chavez, L. 1991. *Out of the barrio: Toward a new politics of Hispanic assimilation*. New York: Basic Books.

Currie, J. 2001. *A fresh start for Head Start?* Washington, DC: Brookings Institution.

Escarce, J., L. Morales, & R. Rumbaut. 2006. Health status and health behaviors of Hispanics. In *Multiple origins, common destinies: Hispanics and the American future*, eds. M. Tienda & F. Mitchell. Washington, DC: National Research Council.

Fuller, B., M. Bridges, & A. Livas. 2006. *The supply of child care centers across Latino communities*. Paper presented at the Annual AERA Conference, San Francisco, CA, April 11.

García, E.E., & D. Gonzáles. 2006. *Pre-K and Latinos: The foundation for America's future*. Washington, DC: Pre-K Now.

García, E.E., B.T. Jensen, & D. Cuéllar. 2006. Early academic achievement of Hispanics in the United States: Implications for teacher preparation. *The New Educator* 2: 123–47.

García, E.E., B.T. Jensen, L.S. Miller, & T. Huerta. 2005. *Early childhood education of Hispanics in the United States*. Tempe, AZ: The National Task Force on Early Childhood Education for Hispanics. Online: www.ecehispanic.org/work/white_paper_Oct2005.pdf.

Gilliam, W., & E. Zigler. 2004. *State efforts to evaluate the effects of prekindergarten: 1977 to 2003*. New Haven, CT: Yale University Child Study Center.

Gormley, W.T., T. Gayer, D. Phillips, & B. Dawson. 2005. The effects of universal pre-k on cognitive development. *Developmental Psychology* 41: 872–84.

Hernandez, D. 2006. *Young Hispanic children in the U.S.: A demographic portrait based on Census 2000*. A report to the National Task Force on Early Childhood Education for Hispanics. Albany, NY: University at Albany–SUNY.

Kagan, S., & K. Kauerz. 2005. Preschool programs: Effective curricula. In *Encyclopedia on early childhood development*, eds. R.E. Tremblay, R.G. Barr, & R. Peters. Montreal, Quebec: Centre of Excellence for Early Childhood Development.

López, M., S. Barrueco, & J. Miles. 2006. *Latino infants and their families: A national perspective of protective and risk factors for development*. A report to the National Task Force on Early Childhood Education for Hispanics. Online: www.ecehispanic.org/work/Latino_Infants.pdf.

Magnuson, K., & J. Waldfogel. 2005. Early childhood care and education: Effects of ethnic and racial gaps in school readiness. *The Future of Children* 15 (1) 84–97.

Montemayor, R., & H. Mendoza. 2004. *Right before our eyes: Latinos past, present, and future*. Tempe, AZ: Scholarly Publishing.

National Task Force on Early Childhood Education. 2007. *Expanding and improving early education for Hispanics executive report*. Tempe, AZ: Arizona State University

NCES (National Center for Education Statistics). 2002. *The condition of education 2002*. NCES 2002-025, Table 1-1. Washington, DC: U.S. Government Printing Office.

NCES (National Center for Education Statistics). 2003. *Status and trends in the education of Hispanics*. NCES 2003-007. Washington, DC: U.S. Government Printing Office.

Neut, A. 2006. *Monitor Hispano*. Online: mediaserver.fxstreet.com/Reports/9c1b6d93-dd98-4fa6-b31a-4e881a171ed3/fab08094-62cb-4cb2-9fac-6028b70ac984.pdf.

Nuñez, A., S. Cuccaro-Alamin, & C.D. Carroll. 1998. *First-generation students: Undergraduates whose parents never enrolled in postsecondary education*. Washington, DC: U.S. Department of Education, Office Of Education Research and Improvement.

Perez, P., & M.E. Zarate. 2006. *Latino public opinion survey of pre-kindergarten programs: Knowledge, preferences, and public support*. Los Angeles: Tomas Rivera Policy Institute.

Ramey, C., & S. Ramey. 1998. Early intervention and early experience. *American Psychologist* 53 (2): 109–20.

Ramirez, R.R., & P.G. de la Cruz. 2003. *The Hispanic population in the United States: March 2002*. Washington, DC: U.S. Census Bureau and U.S. Department of Commerce, Economic and Statistics Administration.

Reardon, S. 2003. *Sources of educational inequality: The growth of racial/ethnic and socioeconomic test score gaps in kindergarten and first grade*. University Park, PA: Pennsylvania State University, Population Research Institute.

Reardon, S., & C. Galindo. 2006. *K-3 academic achievement patterns and trajectories of Hispanics and other racial/ethnic groups*. Paper presented at the Annual AERA Conference, San Francisco, CA, April 11.

Rodriguez, R. 1982. *Hunger of memory: The education of Richard Rodriguez*. Boston: D.R. Godine.

Shields, M., & R. Behrman. 2004. Children of immigrant families: Analysis and recommendations. *The Future of Children* 14 (2): 4–16.

Shonkoff, J.P., & D.A. Phillips. 2000. *From neurons to neighborhoods: The science of early childhood development*. Washington, DC: National Academies Press.

U.S. Bureau of the Census. 2006. Income, Poverty, and Health Insurance Coverage in the United States: 2006. Online: www.census.gov.

Villaseñor, V. 1991. *Rain of gold*. New York: Harcourt.

20 Including Young Children with Disabilities in Preschool: Moving Forward from 1994

Karen E. Diamond, Linda L. Hestenes,
Swetha Chakravarthi, and Linlin Li

Three-year-old Amy and her next door neighbor, Kate, attend a preschool program at their neighborhood community center. Making new friends at school has been fun for both of them. They enjoy art and circle time, especially the new songs and finger plays that their teacher sings with them. Kate always looks forward to running on the playground and climbing the monkey bars. Amy spends her time outdoors sitting in the sandbox or on the swing.

They are like a lot of other girls their age, with one important difference: Amy has cerebral palsy. She cannot walk or crawl, and only her mother understands what she is trying to say. She uses a wheelchair, or is carried by an adult, to move from place to place. She understands what people say to her, and she is beginning to use a computer to help her communicate with others.

In her community in 1994, children with disabilities similar to Amy's received special intervention services in special classes and outpatient clinics at the hospital. This remains the case in many places in the U.S. Yet, in Amy's community, parents, teachers, and school administrators worked together to develop inclusive preschool programs. Although she receives some extra help from therapists at the local clinic, Amy is offered the stimulation and the challenges of attending school with her neighborhood friends.

Early childhood professionals know from many research studies that early intervention makes a positive difference in the development of young children with disabilities (Cole, Dale, & Mills 1991; Guralnick 1997). The passage of Public Law 99-457 in 1986 ensured that all preschool children (3–5 years old) with identified disabilities could receive free, appropriate public education. Subsequent reauthorizations have strengthened the requirement that intervention services for preschool children be provided in the least restrictive environment, with services provided in "natural environments" for infants and toddlers (e.g., the Individuals with Disabilities Education Improvement Act 2004 [U.S. Dept. of Education 2004]). Not surprisingly, the numbers of young children with disabilities who receive early intervention grew to more than 230,000 infants and toddlers and more than 660,000 preschool children in the 2003–2004 school year (U.S. Dept. of Education 2006).

The ways in which early intervention is provided continue to change. It is increasingly likely that community preschool programs include at least one child with disabilities, like Amy. Although model preschool programs that include children with and without disabilities in the same classroom have been in existence since the mid-70s (Bricker 1978), it is only in recent years that inclusive programs have become more common in many communities. Head Start programs are a frequent setting for inclusion, corresponding to the mandate that at least 10 percent of enrolled children have an identified disability (Buscemi et al. 1995). Particularly given the ongoing participation of parents in the work force, community child care programs increasingly provide inclusive placements for many children (Knoche et al. 2006).

While providing early intervention in an inclusive environment designed to meet the diverse needs of all children is regarded as best practice, concerns remain about the best approach to meeting the learning needs of individual children. The use of efficient instructional strategies and making revisions based on ongoing evaluations of individual children's progress are important components of education for children with disabilities (Carta et al. 1991). The developmentally appropriate practice (DAP) guidelines were revised in 1997 and 2009 and now include attention to both child-guided and teacher-guided learning (Bredekamp & Copple 1997; Copple & Bredekamp 2009). These guidelines provide an explicit framework for individualized instruction in early childhood classrooms and have addressed many of the earlier concerns about their appropriateness for children with identified disabilities.

The two major professional organizations serving young children (National Association for the Education of Young Children [NAEYC]) and young children with disabilities (Division for Early Childhood [DEC]) have worked together in recent years to develop licensing standards for the professional development of teachers to insure that "all early childhood teachers are well-prepared to teach young children with and without developmental delays or disabilities" (NAEYC 2001, 1).

What is known about inclusion?

Inclusion is described in policy statements of DEC and NAEYC as reflecting "the right of all children, regardless of their diverse abilities, to participate actively in natural settings within their communities. A natural setting is one in which a child would spend time had he or she not had a disability" (DEC 1993). High-quality early childhood classrooms provide a necessary foundation for high-quality inclusion (Odom, Schwartz, & ECRII Investigators 2002).

High-quality programs are also ones that provide adaptations and supports to meet children's individual needs, rather than requiring children to meet specified entrance criteria (e.g., being toilet-trained). These programs provide specialized instruction, ranging from adaptations and modifications in the classroom environment to individualized teaching, which addresses children's individual educational objectives while they are full and active participants in classroom activities (Horn et al. 2002).

Questions about whether inclusive settings provide learning opportunities for young children with disabilities are no longer as relevant as they were in 1994, when the earlier version of this chapter was written. There is substantial research evidence that children with disabilities enrolled in inclusive classes make gains in language, cognitive, and motor skill development that are comparable to gains made by peers with disabilities in self-contained special education classrooms (Holahan & Costenbader 2000). In addition to such foundational skills for academic competence, developmental tasks for preschoolers include "the ability to get along with other children, to make friends, and become engaged in a social group" (Shonkoff & Phillips 2000, 386). Preschool children with positive social skills are more likely to be included in activities with their peers and also to have higher levels of academic achievement (Doctoroff, Greer, & Arnold 2006).

Children with mild or moderate disabilities (e.g., communication disorders, Down syndrome) are more likely to be enrolled in inclusive classrooms than are children with more significant disabilities such as autism. Decisions about inclusive placements appear to be motivated by special education teachers' and early childhood teachers' concerns about including children with significant disabilities in preschool classrooms, feelings of competence at providing appropriate services, and the perception that children with significant disabilities might not benefit developmentally (Gemmel-Crosby & Hanzlik 1994; Buysse et al. 1996).

Yet, research on the benefits of inclusive settings for children with significant disabilities provides equivocal evidence in support of such concerns. For example, Hundert and colleagues (1998) found that children with significant disabilities made more progress in inclusive than in self-contained special education classrooms. Hauser-Cram, Bronson, and Upshur (1993) found that children with disabilities engaged in more interactions with peers when they were enrolled in inclusive classrooms that included more, rather than fewer, children who were typically developing. Thus, the research literature provides evidence that preschool children with significant disabilities make substantial developmental progress when they attend school with their typically developing peers.

Research in inclusive settings that has examined interactions between young children with disabilities and their typically developing peers presents a somewhat more complicated picture. Children with disabilities engage in more frequent and more sophisticated play with peers in inclusive settings (Guralnick et al. 1996; Odom & Diamond 1998). Teachers in inclusive classrooms report that, overall, young children with disabilities have friends who are typically developing, and the number of friends does not differ between children with disabilities and their peers (Buysse, Goldman, & Skinner 2002). However, even in inclusive classrooms, young children with disabilities are more likely to engage in isolated and non-interactive play, less likely to participate in play groups with their peers, and are chosen as a desired playmate significantly less frequently than are their peers without disabilities (Odom & Brown 1993).

Many preschool children with disabilities are at risk for exclusion from play activities (Wolfberg et al. 1999; Odom et al. 2006), although about an equal proportion appear to be well accepted by their peers. Odom and colleagues (2006) found that preschool children with disabilities who were accepted by their classmates were those who were interested in their peers and had good communication and social skills. They found that the path to social rejection appeared to include persistent interactions reflecting either (or both) aggressive (i.e., externalizing) and withdrawn (i.e., internalizing) behaviors.

Similarly, Harper and McCluskey (2002) found that children who used little or no productive language and children without the ability to move independently were more likely to spend time alone. Although sometimes requiring more teacher support, children who could move independently and use language to make their wants and needs known engaged in peer-related social interactions as frequently as did their peers without disabilities.

> Many preschool children with disabilities are at risk for exclusion from play activities.

Results such as these suggest that teachers must continue to focus on early identification of children with behaviors that put them at risk for social rejection and on the development of effective interventions that promote children's social skills and peer acceptance. The findings of Harper and McCluskey (2002) highlight the importance of attending to the opportunities for social interaction for children with significant mobility issues. For example, some teachers have organized their classrooms by positioning a child in a wheelchair at a popular activity, making it more likely that other children will join that activity, and, thus, increasing opportunities for interaction (Diamond & Stacey 2000).

It is important to remember that children's experience of inclusion may be much different from that of their teachers and families (Peck 1993). Schnorr (1990) found that, while teachers and parents perceived a part-time inclusion experience in a first grade classroom as quite successful for a child with Down syndrome, the elementary students involved interpreted many of the instructional practices, such as taking the child from the classroom for specialized services, as indicating that the child did not belong in their room.

Similarly, Janko and colleagues (1997) identified other ways children with disabilities are separated from their classmates. They described one school district in which children with disabilities were transported to school by a district school bus, while children without disabilities were transported by their families (a common practice in many programs). Children asked about "the difference between the 'car kids' and the 'bus kids,'" (293) who not only rode a bus but also stayed at school for lunch. Whether or not they rode a bus appeared to be a salient social characteristic that divided children: Bus kids were children with disabilities, car kids were typically developing.

In contrast, practices such as collaboration between a special education teacher and an early childhood teacher (Horn & Sandall 2000) or including children who are typically developing in interventions with their peers with physical or communication disabilities provide opportunities for children to cooperate in play. Although there is strong support for the developmental benefits of inclusive classrooms, there is still evidence that not all children with disabilities are viewed as "full" members of the class nor engage in social interactions and activities at the same rate as their peers (Diamond & Stacey 2000).

Recent research suggests that inclusive classrooms are of equal or higher quality than are those that include only typically developing children, even after accounting for higher teacher education levels and lower teacher:child ratios in inclusive classrooms (LaParo, Sexton, & Synder 1998; Buysse et al. 1999; Knoche et al. 2006; Hestenes et al. in press). It is not known if parents of children with disabilities actually enroll their children in higher-quality programs, if programs improve in quality once they become inclusive (perhaps either due to increased attention to individual needs or improved funding), or if some combination of these two factors is behind the higher quality of inclusive programs.

What are the experiences of children who are typically developing and enrolled in inclusive programs?

There is ample evidence that children can acquire attitudes toward others through direct personal experiences, and there is every reason to expect that children's attitudes toward individuals with disabilities are shaped by their experiences in inclusive classrooms (Nikolaraizi et al. 2005). Parents and teachers believe that inclusive programs offer important benefits for children who are typically developing,

> Children who had social contact with at least one classmate with a disability were more accepting of individuals with disabilities.

including promoting acceptance of human differences, awareness of others' needs, and feelings of comfort in interactions with people with disabilities.

Parents whose typically developing children attended inclusive programs reported that their children displayed less prejudice and fewer stereotypes and were more responsive and helpful to others than were children without experiences in inclusive settings (Peck, Carlson, & Helmstetter 1992). Similar findings are revealed in several recent studies (Seery, Davis, & Johnson 2000; Rafferty, Boettcher, & Griffin 2001; Rafferty & Griffin 2005). Buysse and colleagues (1996) found that typically developing children benefited from the opportunity to learn about individual differences. Teachers' interviews also revealed that the opportunity to learn about and accept differences and to learn empathy, tolerance, and compassion for others were benefits for typically developing children in inclusive settings (Lieber et al. 1998).

There is evidence from a number of studies that preschool children have some understanding of physical and sensory disabilities, but limited understanding of disabilities that affect cognition or behavior, such as autism spectrum disorder (Conant & Budoff 1983). The research literature is relatively weak in identifying specific connections between children's experiences in inclusive programs, interactions with classmates with disabilities, and their attitudes toward individuals with disabilities (Diamond & Huang 2005).

In one study, Diamond and colleagues (1997) interviewed preschool children enrolled in either inclusive classes or classes including only typically developing peers about their understanding of physical and sensory disabilities and their acceptance of individuals with disabilities. Compared to children in classes that included only typically developing peers, children in inclusive settings gave higher acceptance ratings to hypothetical children with and without disabilities. This study highlights potential benefits of inclusive classrooms for promoting acceptance of individuals with disabilities.

Hestenes and Carroll (2000) found that children's stated preference to play with hypothetical peers with disabilities predicted their understanding of disability, yet neither stated preference nor understanding predicted children's actual interactions with peers with disabilities. Rather, younger children were more likely to interact with peers with disabilities than were older children, and these interactions occurred more often when the teacher was present.

Recently, Diamond (2001) found that children who had social contact with at least one classmate with a disability were more accepting of individuals with disabilities than were children who were observed playing only with their typically developing classmates. While results such as these support the suggestion that specific experiences in inclusive settings support children's positive attitudes and, perhaps, prosocial behaviors, it is not known whether a child's initial dispositions made interacting with classmates with disabilities more or less likely, or whether children's interactions promoted increased understanding and sensitivity.

What are critical issues for parents and teachers?

Parents are generally supportive of the concept of inclusion, but they also express concerns about whether or not teachers and classroom staff will be able to fully address the instructional needs of all children (Green & Stoneman 1989). Not surprisingly, families' perceptions of inclusion are

> Collaborations among teachers and interventionists in support of children's inclusion are a critical feature in the success of inclusive programs.

related to their overall perceptions of the quality of the preschool program (Beckman, Hanson, & Horn 2002). Families tend to report positive experiences when the services that a program provides match their child's needs.

All families want their children to do well, make progress, have friends and be happy in school; when this happens, parents are likely to express satisfaction with the program. Children's participation in inclusive programs may also influence parents' attitudes toward inclusion. A study by Green and Stoneman (1989) found that parents with previous experiences with inclusive programs held significantly more positive attitudes toward inclusion than did other parents. There is evidence, as well, that parents may become more confident over the course of the school year in an inclusive program's ability to teach all children (Seery, Davis, & Johnson 2000).

Collaborations among teachers and interventionists in support of children's inclusion are a critical feature in the success of inclusive programs (Lieber et al. 2002). Lieber and colleagues from the Early Childhood Research Institute on Inclusion found a number of factors that support positive professional relationships among adults in inclusion programs. These include joint planning and shared responsibility for the program, a shared teaching philosophy, shared responsibility for all children, formal and informal communication among team members, a willingness to be flexible in professional roles, stability in program staff, and administrative support.

Clearly, it is critical for all of the adults who provide services for children in a single program to develop positive, collaborative working relationships. In addition, ongoing administrative support in the form of training, planning time, allocation of resources, and encouragement is critical for the success of inclusive programs (Odom, Schwartz, & ECRII Investigators 2002).

What is known about inclusive programs that "work"?

Successful inclusive programs must meet the educational needs of children while addressing the concerns of parents, teachers, and administrators that the program be high quality and developmentally appropriate for all. Two important issues in developing an inclusive program are (1) the administrative structure, and (2) approaches to instruction.

Administrative structure

Several investigators have described characteristics of inclusive programs that "work" for teachers and that are associated with a program's survival. Peck, Furman, and Helmstetter (1993) found that critical factors in the continued success of inclusive early childhood programs were (1) an articulated philosophy that emphasized the importance of acceptance of diversity, and (2) recognition of the value of belonging to and participating as a member of a community.

Remediation of deficits for children with disabilities was not perceived as the only important objective to be met in an inclusive early childhood program. In long-term inclusion programs, inclusion and community membership become important goals in themselves. Similarly, Lieber and colleagues (2002) found that cooperation, collaboration, and mutual respect between teachers, other interventionists, and administrators were important components of successful inclusion programs (see also Purcell, Horn, & Palmer 2007).

Implementation of specialized interventions that provide access to the curriculum for all children is also an important factor in insuring the success of an inclusive program.

Peck, Furman, and Helmstetter (1993) found that struggles between professionals were the major issue in programs that became re-segregated into "special" and "regular" early childhood classrooms. Dissention over management of time during the school day, types of classroom activities, and intervention strategies often led to a decision to re-segregate children. These issues have been identified by Rose and Smith (1993) as being among the major barriers to the development of inclusive programs in local communities.

Giangreco and colleagues (1993) reported similar results in a study with elementary teachers. Teachers reported that special education and support personnel provided a valuable contribution when they shared a common framework and goals with the classroom teacher. Such cooperation served to validate the classroom teacher's contribution to the child's development.

However, "help" that disturbed the classroom routine (such as pull-out therapy) and was overly technical was often more disruptive than helpful. When interventionists, teachers, administrators and families work toward a common, agreed-upon goal, programs are more likely to grow and flourish. Conversely, frequently changing policies and regulations pose problems in continuation of inclusive programs (Purcell, Horn, & Palmer 2007).

Teaching strategies

Among the challenges facing teachers in inclusive programs is how to implement a child's individual IEP or IFSP goals in ways that "neither supplant the classroom curriculum nor restrict the child's participation in classroom activities" (Horn et al. 2000, 208). In the earlier version of this chapter, considerable attention was devoted to research on the development and effectiveness of naturalistic teaching strategies. These are approaches such as activity-based intervention (Bricker, Pretti-Frontczak, & McComas 1998) and milieu language teaching (Kaiser, Hancock, & Nietfeld 2000), in which individualized intervention is provided within the context of naturally occurring activities in the child's environment.

These naturalistic intervention strategies reflect practices grounded in the theories of Piaget, Vygotsky, and Dewey. They complement the developmentally appropriate practice framework (Copple & Bredekamp 2009) and emphasize the importance of responding to each child's individual developmental capabilities, interests, and needs in a variety of classroom activities.

Activity-based intervention illustrates the principal of non-intrusive individual instruction as it may be applied in an inclusive preschool classroom. The goal of activity-based intervention is "to develop functional and generalizable skills" (Bricker, Pretti-Frontczak, & McComas 1998, 11) while the child participates in activities that are enjoyable and interesting. Functional skills are those that allow children to negotiate their social and physical environments in ways that are satisfying and encourage independence. For example, a functional skill would be learning to ask for juice and crackers at snack time, rather than to label pictures of food items during speech therapy. Generalizable skills, such as requesting items, are those which can be practiced and used by the child in many different settings (e.g., at home, in school, at a friend's house) (Bricker, Pretti-Frontczak, & McComas 1998).

A critical element of activity-based intervention involves embedding instruction related to children's individual goals and objectives in classroom activities. Principal responsibilities of the teacher include identifying a child's target learning objectives, teaching these objectives within ongoing activities, assessing the child's progress in meeting objectives, and modifying teaching approaches to enhance each child's learning.

Activity-based intervention highlights the importance of using child-initiated, planned, and routine activities as contexts for teaching and learning for children from infancy through school age and beyond. For example, a child's language goals could be incorporated into planned classroom activities such as circle time, routine activities such as mealtime, and child-initiated activities during free-choice or center time. Teaching of the objectives within ongoing classroom activities helps to ensure that the child is learning a functional skill that will be useful in meeting current and future environmental demands.

Since each child's objectives are addressed within the context of classroom activities, teachers are responsible for teaching children in the context of a stimulating, interesting classroom environment. Consultation from a special education teacher or therapist is often helpful in planning activities and targeting goals and objectives for individual children. Regular and ongoing evaluation of the child's progress toward meeting individual goals and objectives is a critical component of all naturalistic teaching approaches.

The effective use of strategies for embedding individual learning objectives within the general classroom curriculum is critical (Pretti-Frontczak & Bricker 2004). Horn and Sandall and their colleagues (Horn et al. 2000; Horn et al. 2002; Sandall et al. 2002) have identified a range of strategies for modifying the classroom curriculum and embedding objectives that support individual children's learning. These include curriculum modifications that involve "changing or adding materials or events within the classroom" (Horn et al. 2000, 49) in order to increase a child's participation and opportunities for learning as well as individualized teacher-supported instruction. Many curriculum modifications, such as the use of picture symbols for communication, are used frequently by early childhood teachers to make it easier for a child with disabilities to participate in the classroom curriculum.

Because curriculum modifications such as these may not be sufficient to ensure that the child has sufficient opportunities to learn and to practice important goals and objectives, additional recommendations have focused on embedding instruction related to a particular goal within meaningful, naturally occurring classroom activities (Horn et al. 2000; Sandall et al. 2002). Embedding strategies can be used effectively in inclusive early childhood classrooms, although they are more difficult to implement in whole- or large-group than in small-group activities (Horn et al. 2000).

Knowledge about the ways that inclusive programs can meet the needs of children and families for quality early childhood education and intervention has grown significantly since the original article was published in 1994. Early childhood professionals know that the active, ongoing involvement of families, teachers, interventionists, and administrators is critical in developing and maintaining inclusive programs in individual communities. Teachers and directors know that participation in a high-quality inclusive program can have positive effects on the academic and social development of all children. New, effective teaching strategies are being developed that offer effective ways to meet the individualized needs of young children with disabilities in inclusive preschool classrooms. The remaining task is that of building upon these findings to identify the best ways to provide effective, inclusive education that continues to be respectful of the talents and needs of individual children, families, and teachers.

Updated from the Research in Review article in the January 1994 issue of *Young Children*.

Karen E. Diamond is a professor at Purdue University. **Linda L. Hestenes** is an associate professor at the University of North Carolina at Greensboro. **Swetha Chakravarthi** is a doctoral student at the University of North Carolina at Greensboro. **Linlin Li** is an evaluator and researcher for Hatchuel Tabernik & Associates.

References

Beckman, P.J., M.J. Hanson, & E. Horn. 2002. Family perceptions of inclusion. In *Widening the circle: Including children with disabilities in preschool programs*, ed. S.L. Odom, 98–108. Baltimore: Paul H. Brookes.

Bredekamp, S., & C. Copple, eds. 1997. *Developmentally appropriate practice in early childhood programs*. Rev. ed. Washington, DC: NAEYC.

Bricker, D. 1978. A rationale for integration of handicapped and non-handicapped preschool children. In *Early intervention and the integration of handicapped and non-handicapped children*, ed. M. Guralnick, 3–26. Baltimore: University Park Press.

Bricker, D.D., K.L. Pretti-Frontczak, & N.R. McComas. 1998. *An activity-based approach to early intervention*. 2d ed. Baltimore: Paul H. Brookes.

Buscemi, L., T. Bennett, D. Thomas, & D.A. Deluca. 1995. Head Start: Challenges and training needs. *Journal of Early Intervention* 20 (1): 1–13.

Buysse, V., B.D. Goldman, & M. Skinner. 2002. Setting effects on friendship formation among young children with and without disabilities. *Exceptional Children* 68 (4): 503–17.

Buysse, V., P.W. Wesley, D. Bryant, & D. Gardner. 1999. Quality of early childhood programs in inclusive and noninclusive settings. *Exceptional Children* 65 (3): 301–14.

Buysse, V., P. Wesley, L. Keyes, & D.B. Bailey. 1996. Assessing the comfort zone of child care teachers in serving young children with disabilities. *Journal of Early Intervention* 20: 209–10.

Carta, J.J., I.S. Schwartz, J.B. Atwater, & S.R. McConnell. 1991. Developmentally appropriate practice: Appraising its usefulness for young children with disabilities. *Topics in Early Childhood Special Education* 11: 1–20.

Cole, K.N., P.S. Dale, & P.E. Mills. 1991. Individual differences in language delayed children's responses to direct and interactive preschool instruction. *Topics in Early Childhood Special Education* 11: 99–124.

Conant, S., & M. Budoff. 1983. Patterns of awareness in children's understanding of disabilities. *Mental Retardation* 21: 119–25.

Copple, C., & S. Bredekamp, eds. 2009. *Developmentally appropriate practice in early childhood programs serving children from birth through age 8*. 3d ed. Washington, DC: NAEYC.

DEC (Division for Early Childhood). 1993. *Inclusion*. A position statement of the Division for Early Childhood (DEC) of the Council for Exceptional Children, endorsed by the National Association for the Education of Young Children. Missoula, MT: Author.

Diamond, K.E. 2001. Relationships among young children's ideas, emotional understanding, and social contact with classmates with disabilities. *Topics in Early Childhood Special Education* 21: 104–13.

Diamond, K.E., L. Hestenes, E. Carpenter, & F. Innes. 1997. Relationships between enrollment in an inclusive class and preschool children's ideas about people with disabilities. *Topics in Early Childhood Special Education* 17: 520–36.

Diamond, K.E., & HH. Huang. 2005. Preschoolers' ideas about disabilities. *Infants and Young Children* 18 (1): 37–46.

Diamond, K.E., & S. Stacey. 2000. The other children at preschool: Experiences of typically developing children in inclusive programs. *Young exceptional children monograph series, no. 2: Natural environments and inclusion*, eds. S. Sandall & M. Ostrosky, 59–68. Longmont, CO: Sopris West.

Doctoroff, G.L., J.A. Greer, & D. Arnold. 2006. The relationship between social behavior and emergent literacy among preschool boys and girls. *Journal of Applied Developmental Psychology* 27: 1–13.

Gemmel-Crosby, S., & J.R. Hanzlik. 1994. Preschool teachers' perceptions of including pupils with disabilities. *Education and Training in Mentally Retarded and Developmental Disabilities* 29: 279–90.

Giangreco, M., R. Dennis, C. Coninger, S. Edelman, & R. Schattman. 1993. "I've counted Jon": Transformational experiences of teachers educating students with disabilities. *Exceptional Children* 59 (4): 359–72.

Green, A.L., & Z. Stoneman. 1989. Attitudes of mothers and fathers of nonhandicapped children. *Journal of Early Intervention* 13: 292–304.

Guralnick, M.J., ed. 1997. *The effectiveness of early intervention*. Baltimore: Paul H. Brookes.

Guralnick, M.J., R. Connor, M. Hammond, J.M. Gottman, & K. Kinnish. 1996. The peer relations of preschool children with communication disorders. *Child Development* 67: 471–89.

Harper, L.V., & K.S. McCluskey. 2002. Caregiver and peer responses to children with language and motor disabilities in inclusive preschool programs. *Early Childhood Research Quarterly* 17: 148–66.

Hauser-Cram, P., M. Bronson, & C. Upshur. 1993. The effects of the classroom environment on the social and mastery behaviors of preschool children with disabilities. *Early Childhood Research Quarterly* 8: 479–97.

Hestenes, L.L., & D.E. Carroll. 2000. The play interactions of young children with and without disabilities: Individual and environmental influences. *Early Childhood Research Quarterly* 15: 229–46.

Hestenes, L., D. Cassidy, J. Shim, & A. Hegde. In press. The quality of inclusive preschool classrooms. *Early Education and Development*.

Holahan, A., & V. Costenbader. 2000. A comparison of development gains for preschool children with disabilities in inclusive and self-contained classrooms. *Topics in Early Childhood Special Education* 20: 224–35.

Horn, E., J. Lieber, S. Li, S. Sandall, & I. Schwartz. 2000. Supporting young children's IEP goals in inclusive settings through embedded learning opportunities. *Topics in Early Childhood Special Education* 20, 208–23.

Horn, E., J. Lieber, S.R. Sandall, I.S. Schwartz, & R.A. Wolery. 2002. Classroom models of individualized instruction. In *Widening the circle: Including children with disabilities in preschool programs*, ed. S.L. Odom, 46–60. Baltimore: Paul H. Brookes.

Horn, E., & S. Sandall. 2000. The visiting teacher: A model of inclusive ECSE service delivery. In *Young exceptional children monograph series, no. 2: Natural environments and inclusion*, eds. S. Sandall & M. Ostrosky, 49–58. Longmont, CO: Sopris West.

Hundert, J., B. Mahoney, F. Mundy, & M.L. Vernon. 1998. A descriptive analysis of developmentally appropriate and social gains of children with severe disabilities in segregated and inclusive preschools in southern Ontario. *Early Childhood Research Quarterly* 13: 49–65.

Janko, S., I. Schwartz, S. Sandall, K. Anderson, & C. Cottam. 1997. Beyond microsystems: Unanticipated lessons about the meaning of inclusion. *Topics in Early Childhood Special Education* 17: 286–306.

Kaiser, A.P., T.B. Hancock, & J.P. Nietfeld. 2000. The effects of parent-implemented enhanced milieu teaching on the social communication of children who have autism. *Early Education and Development* 11: 423–46.

Knoche, L., C.A. Peterson, C.P. Edwards, & H.J. Jeon. 2006. Child care for children with and without disabilities: The provider, observer and parent perspectives. *Early Childhood Research Quarterly* 21: 93–109.

La Paro, K., D. Sexton, & P. Snyder. 1998. Program quality characteristics in segregated and inclusive early childhood settings. *Early Childhood Research Quarterly* 13 (1): 151–67.

Lieber, J., K. Capell, S.R. Sandall, P. Wolfberg, E. Horn, & P. Beckman. 1998. Inclusive preschool programs: Teachers' beliefs and practices. *Early Childhood Research Quarterly* 13: 87–105.

Lieber, J., R.A. Wolery, E. Horn, J. Tschantz, P.J. Beckman, & M.J. Hanson. 2002. Collaborative relationships among adults in inclusive preschool programs. In *Widening the circle: Including children with disabilities in preschool programs*, ed. S.L. Odom, 46–60, 81–97. Baltimore: Paul H. Brookes.

NAEYC. 2001. *2001 Standards at the initial licensure level*. Online: www.naeyc.org/faculty/pdf/2001.pdf.

Nikolaraizi, M., P. Kumar, P. Favazza, G. Sideridis, D. Koulousiou, & A. Riall. 2005. A cross-cultural examination of typically developing children's attitudes toward individuals with special needs. *International Journal of Disability, Development and Education* 52 (2): 101–19.

Odom, S.L., & W.H. Brown. 1993. Social interaction skill training for young children with disabilities in integrated settings. In *Integrating young children with disabilities into community-based programs: From research to implementation*, eds. C. Peck, S. Odom, & D. Bricker, 39–64. Baltimore: Paul H. Brookes.

Odom, S.L., & K.E. Diamond. 1998. Inclusion of young children with special needs in early childhood education: The research base. *Early Childhood Research Quarterly* 13: 3–25.

Odom, S.L., I.S. Schwartz, & ECRII Investigators. 2002. So what do we know from all this? Synthesis points of research on preschool inclusion. In *Widening the circle: Including children with disabilities in preschool programs*, ed. S.L. Odom, 154–74. Baltimore: Paul H. Brookes.

Odom, S.L., C. Zercher, S. Li, J.M. Marquart, S. Sandall, & W.H. Brown. 2006. Social acceptance and rejection of preschool children with disabilities: A mixed-method analysis. *Journal of Educational Psychology* 98: 807–23.

Peck, C.A. 1993. Ecological perspectives on implementation of integrated early childhood programs. In *Integrating young children with disabilities into community programs: Ecological perspectives on research and implementation*, eds. C. Peck, S. Odom, & D. Bricker, 3–15. Baltimore: Paul H. Brookes.

Peck, C.A., P. Carlson, & E. Helmstetter. 1992. Parent and teacher perception of outcomes for typically developing children enrolled in integrated early childhood programs: A statewide survey. *Journal of Early Intervention* 16: 53–63.

Peck, C., G. Furman, & E. Helmstetter. 1993. Integrated early childhood programs: Research on the implementation of change in organizational contexts. In *Integrating young children with disabilities into community programs: Ecological perspectives on research and implementation*, eds. C. Peck, S. Odom, & D. Bricker, 187–206. Baltimore: Paul H. Brookes.

Pretti-Frontczak, K., & D. Bricker. 2004. *An activity-based approach to early intervention.* 3d ed. Baltimore: Paul H. Brookes.

Purcell, M.L., E. Horn, & S. Palmer. 2007. A qualitative study of the initiation and continuation of preschool inclusion programs. *Exceptional Children* 74: 85–99.

Rafferty, Y., C. Boettcher, & K.W. Griffin. 2001. Benefits and risks of reverse inclusion for preschoolers with and without disabilities: Parents' perspectives. *Journal of Early Intervention* 24: 266–86.

Rafferty, Y., & K.W. Griffin. 2005. Benefits and risks of reverse inclusion for preschoolers with and without disabilities: Perspectives of parents and providers. *Journal of Early Intervention* 27: 173–92.

Rose, D.F., & B.J. Smith. 1993. Preschool mainstreaming: Attitude barriers and strategies for addressing them. *Young Children* 48 (4): 59–62.

Sandall, S., I. Schwartz, G. Joseph, H. Chou, E.M. Horn, J. Lieber, et al. 2002. *Building blocks for teaching preschoolers with special needs.* Baltimore: Paul H. Brookes.

Schnorr, R.F. 1990. "Peter? He comes and goes...": First graders' perspectives on a part-time mainstream student. *Journal of the Association for Persons with Severe Handicaps* 15: 231–240.

Seery, M.E., P.M. Davis, & L.J. Johnson. 2000. Seeing eye-to-eye: Are parents and professionals in agreement about the benefits of preschool inclusion? *Remedial and Special Education* 21: 268–78.

Shonkoff, J., & D.A. Phillips, eds. 2000. *From neurons to neighborhoods.* Washington, DC: National Academies Press.

U.S. Department of Education. 2004. *Individuals with Disabilities Education Improvement Act of 2004.* Pub. L. No. 108-446, 118 Stat. 2647, § 632 (2004).

U.S. Department of Education. 2006. *National Center for Education Statistics: Digest of Education Statistics.* Online: nces.ed.gov/programs/digest/d04/tables/dt04_052.asp.

Wolfberg, P., C. Zercger, J. Capel, K. Capel, S. Matias, M.J. Hanson, & S. Odom. 1999. "Can I play with you?" Peer culture in inclusive preschool programs. *Journal of the Association for Persons with Severe Handicaps* 24 (2): 69–84.

Index

join us

to build better futures for all young children...

naeyc®

National Association for the Education of Young Children

NAEYC delivers **VALUE** to our members through

PROFESSIONAL DEVELOPMENT. Attend the NAEYC Annual Conference & Expo, the largest gathering of early childhood educators in the world, and the National Institute for Early Childhood Professional Development. Receive NAEYC's research-based publications with the latest information about early childhood education.

ADVOCACY. NAEYC is the voice of the early childhood profession in Washington, D.C., and state and local Affiliates advocate for early childhood education issues in your community.

NETWORKING. NAEYC's members have access to great networking opportunities to make friends and build professional relationships through the many NAEYC Interest Forums and Web-based NAEYC Online Communities.

SERVICE. Join today to receive discounts with your membership. Members are our top priority, and the NAEYC staff are ready to serve you. Call the NAEYC Customer Service Center at 800-424-2460 or e-mail membership@naeyc.org.

Two easy ways to join!

Visit **www.naeyc.org** • Call **800-424-2460**